POOR SPLENDID WINGS

JOHN EVERETT MILLAIS

A PORTRAIT BY CHARLES LESLIE

Poor Splendid Wings

The ROSSETTIS and their CIRCLE

by

FRANCES WINWAR, 1900-

Poor splendid wings, so frayed and soiled and torn!
— SWINBURNE

BOSTON
LITTLE, BROWN, and COMPANY
1933

THE ATLANTIC MONTHLY PRESS BOOKS
ARE PUBLISHED BY
LITTLE, BROWN, AND COMPANY
IN ASSOCIATION WITH
THE ATLANTIC MONTHLY COMPANY

In Memoriam

JOHN MACY

"They told me, Heraclitus, they told me you were dead"

AUTHOR'S NOTE

THIS is not fictionized history or biography, though it read like a novel; nor is it a Freudian study of the men and women who played their part in the Pre-Raphaelite drama, though the student will detect the methods of modern psychology without those barbarisms that should have no place outside of clinical reports. No statement is made, no scene depicted, that is not warranted by authoritative sources, nor thought process extended that is not implicit in some phase of the subject's work.

If the figure of Dante Gabriel Rossetti looms large amid the original Pre-Raphaelites, it is because both by achievement and by personality he towered above them. With him, as with Ruskin, Swinburne, Christina, and the rest, the written word, whether in the subtle transmutation of art or in cursory jottings, has first been consulted for revelatory indications and then brought into correlation with trustworthy biographical matter. Gossip holds no place here. Out of the dust of the dead letter the author has sought to reanimate the living spirit.

For the first time Rossetti's two great loves are drawn from the pious mists of innuendoes and brought to the light in an attempt to interpret his otherwise irreconcilable actions. Here, as elsewhere in the book, the author with no false modesty may claim the pioneer delving that struck the buried gold.

. . . We are such stuff
As dreams are made on, and our little life
Is rounded with a sleep.
                    —*The Tempest*

CONTENTS

PART FOUR

". . . Is rounded with a sleep"

ILLUSTRATIONS

PART ONE

"We are such stuff . . ."

I

YOUTH AND IDEALS

JOHN MILLAIS and his wife Emily were proud of their son, the genius who had been born into their family. Since the age of ten, when Johnny had been admitted to the Academy drawing school, he had ridden from one distinction to another; and a collection of prizes was steadily growing in the maternal keeping. Still other honors, less tangible but of infinitely more worldly value, filled Emily's dreams of this wonder child, the fruit of her second marriage. He was so like her — the same eyes, the same determined, tight-lipped mouth; unlike his brother William, who had also been touched with talent, but not with the will to ride it. She had an almost religious faith in Johnny. Long hours, while he was at school, she would look up historical data at the British Museum for his pictures; and at home she helped him with studies of ancient armor, or read to him as he painted. The elder Millais kept himself trim, knowing that any moment he might be called upon to don fancy dress and sit, as a knight or a monk or a burgher, to his son. Often, when Johnny painted and had no wish for reading, Emily took in her netting to keep him company, while her husband strummed softly on his guitar or entertained them with airs on the flute — for, like Pepys, he delighted in any audience. Johnny worked and laughed, retailed the little gossips of the school, discussed his pictures, and encouraged criticism. The door of his aspirations, as of his painting room, was always open to them; and so, to the rhythm of clicking needles and thrumming guitar, they watched, as it were, the young nautilus building richer chambers for his genius.

What was their astonishment, one memorable day, to find the studio door closed to their music and unyielding to repeated knocking. The voices of young men came confusedly to their ears, and above them Johnny's, a little harshly, bidding the knockers, "Please go away."

It was a grave moment. For the first time in his nineteen years, Johnny had made his mother feel she was unwanted. Yet when Emily heard him sending her away, she was not sure but that she had expected something of the sort — especially since that foreign-looking boy had taken to visiting Johnny with William Holman Hunt. She had always liked Hunt. He was a serious young man, full of ambition and promise, though not half so gifted as her Johnny. Moreover, he was poor, and had no encouragement from his folk, who looked upon a painting career as the surest way to the debtors' prison. And so it was, to most young men with only a little talent. Not so with her Johnny. At fifteen he had begun receiving commissions. Now, in 1848, he was an artist with an income that kept the household in comfort, if not yet in luxury. But that would come; that would come. Meanwhile the Millaises pitied Hunt, who had no such understanding parents, and encouraged his visits as steadying to their Johnny, what with the advantage of his seniority, and the example of his actual experience in an inclement world — a world which, thanks to them, Johnny had been spared.

But Emily had felt uneasy from the moment when that dark, slouching Italian youth, another Academy student, had set foot in the Gower Street home. He was not altogether Italian — only on his father's side, and partly on his mother's; he himself had been born in London. But it was known that the elder Rossetti had been a revolutionist in Italy, and that he had been smuggled away from certain death by a kind Englishwoman and her husband. He was

now a respectable professor of Italian at King's College, and
the father of four English children. Still, one can never
tell how the traits of the parents may be visited upon the
sons; and Gabriel, Johnny's friend, disturbed her peace of
mind. To begin with, he wore his hair long instead of in
a becoming crest like Johnny. His eyes were always far-
off and dreaming, and only when one spoke to him did
they brighten to a direct look. His pouted mouth sulked
when he did not smile. His wide nostrils betrayed an
unruly spirit—and then, his clothes were shabby; not to
mention the pockets bulging with papers. They said he
was also a poet.

Somehow, with the stepping of Charles Dante Gabriel
Rossetti into John Everett Millais's life the old domestic
order came to an end. The studio was now full of other
Academy students, and young men with untidy hair, and
shirts open at the collar, who spoke with words and voices
that echoed Gabriel's. He seldom came alone. When
he did, the others were sure to follow, as at the wake of
another Pied Piper. And they always brought good appe-
tites. There would be long confabulations behind the bolted
door, and voices raised in heated speech; then whispered
discussions; and now and again peals of laughter and the
commotion of chairs. Emily listened anxiously, and pleaded
to be let in. "I appeal to you, Hunt," she whimpered.
"Is that the way for Johnny to treat his mother?" But
Johnny was obdurate, and Hunt could only say something
vaguely conciliatory. Only after the mysterious business
was over would Johnny bring his friends into the parlor,
where Emily gave them tea and Mr. Millais entertained
them with melancholy tunes.

One day Lasinio's book of engravings from the Campo
Santo of Pisa was taken from the shelf and carried into the
studio. Monckton Milnes's *Life, Letters and Literary Remains of John Keats* followed. The two Keats volumes,
in their grained, purple-brown cloth binding blocked with

·a floral scroll design,—the same that had adorned Tennyson's *Princess* and Landor's *Hellenics* the year before,—
were never out of Gabriel's hands. Hours long he read
aloud to his rapt companions, interrupting himself to cry
out, "A glorious fellow! Glorious!" The young men's
delight reached its highest when Keats in one of the letters
said that, after having examined a folio of the first and
second schools of Italian painting, he had come to the conclusion that some of the early men surpassed Raphael himself. "A glorious fellow," they chorused.

Discussions grew louder and more heated, and preposterous views on art and life filtered through the door to the
shocked ears of Emily. Artists whom she was used to
hearing mentioned with reverence resounded with anathema
in Gabriel's voice, while applause greeted foreign names
she had never met in the British Museum. Something *was*
happening; and Johnny was in it.

At last Johnny broke the news to her. "And please
don't call me Johnny any more before my friends." It was
startling news. Johnny, the wonder of the Academy school,
was a member of a revolutionary society! She had feared
it from the first, with the advent of that Rossetti boy and
his following of wild youths. One thing alone consoled
her: the thoughtful Holman Hunt was with him. That
the revolutionary society busied itself with art and was not
directed against the Queen comforted her not at all. It
was as much as she could do to understand what the foolish
boys were aiming at.

They called themselves the "Pre-Raphaelite Brotherhood." Why "Pre-Raphaelite"? Because only before
Raphael had there been sincerity and truth in painting; because after him all painters tried to be little Raphaels,
slavishly copying him instead of drawing from nature and
their own invention; because—ah, this was heresy indeed!
—they had nothing but contempt for the pictures appearing on the Royal Academy walls, with their mawkishness

DANTE GABRIEL ROSSETTI

A SELF-PORTRAIT PAINTED IN 1847

and "sloshy" treatment. That was a common adjective with the crew. "Sloshy," from Sir Joshua Reynolds, or "Sir Sloshua"—Gabriel's invention.

There was a great deal of talk now about the brotherhood, not only behind the studio door, but in the sitting room, over the tea; highly pitched, heated talk, much of which neither Emily nor her husband grasped—nonsense about the artist's duty to depict what he sees as he sees it, to obey his natural impulses in his work, and not to follow rules made by incapable dotards. His parents knew only that the stability of Johnny's career was threatened; and so, whenever into the torrent of Gabriel's talk they could throw a word of protest, they did it bravely. Bravely, but vainly; for it had no more power against his force than a twig against the flood.

"We must protest against the intellectual emptiness of our so-called painters. We must protest in deed as well as in thought. Look at the stunners in the Campo Santo of Pisa. Have we anything like them now? No! It is for us to bring dignity and sincerity back to art; for us to strip art of conventionality—"

"But how can you—?"

"—and to go to Nature, not to what others have done before us! We must be sincere in our invention, truthful in our representation. We must be Early Christian—Pre-Raphaelite!"

"Yea, Pre-Raphaelite," came the stirring chorus.

Emily could only shake her head. The meetings at the Millais home became rarer and rarer; then they ceased altogether. The Pre-Raphaelite Brotherhood was preparing to astonish the world at the next opening of the Royal Academy.

Had Emily been present at the gatherings that now took place at the studio shared by Holman Hunt and Rossetti, she would have been more anxious still for her son. The brotherhood, not counting the hangers-on, had now grown from three members to seven. Besides aiming at a revolution in painting, they grew bold and planned to storm the bulwarks of the Philistines.

As a beginning they formulated their creed by drawing up a list of people they deemed immortal — no mere immortality of the soul, but the nobler immortality conferred upon them by their works. "We declare that the following list of Immortals constitutes the whole of our creed, and that there exists no other Immortality than what is centred in their names and in the names of their contemporaries, in whom this list is reflected." Followed some sixty names, marked with stars by order of importance. Christ received four, the highest number; while the author of Job followed, and Shakespeare — each with three. Keats, Shelley, and Byron were among the names; and Washington, and Kosciusko, and one Cavalier Pugliesi, perhaps out of regard to the sympathies of Professor Rossetti. Bellini loomed big in solitude to represent the musicians. None of the brethren much cared for music. Only two women were found worthy of Immortality: Joan of Arc and Mrs. Browning, one star marking the poet's superiority over the warrior maiden, though the light of her orb was dimmed by the double effulgence beside her husband's name.

So much of their creed laid down, Millais, Hunt, and Rossetti painted, posed for one another, and made plans for the future. Thomas Woolner, a sculptor and a brother, modeled and cursed society in turn, enriching invective with an inflammable temper. He was also an Academy student. His exhibited works — a curious medley of classical groups and realistic portraits — had gained him the salt of publicity and the friendship of Tennyson, Browning, and Carlyle; assets to which Gabriel had not been blind when he invited him to join the brotherhood.

Frederic Stephens, another member, had not yet found himself. Lured by two loves, writing and painting, in his fidelity to the one he neglected the other. William Michael Rossetti, Gabriel's brother, painted not at all, though he

struggled bravely under Gabriel's teaching. To compensate
for his lack, however, he kept the books of the brotherhood,
in a fair hand and resounding polysyllables. James Collinson alone gave the brothers concern, though Gabriel called
the slight, small, thick-necked youth a "stunner" and would
hear nothing against him. Had n't Collinson astounded the
Academy school with the fine finish of his "Charity Boy,"
so that for months everyone had talked of nothing but
Collinson's finish? Still, at the meetings Collinson was
oftener asleep than awake, neither discussion nor merriment
rousing him to life. When he did laugh, it was with a shy,
deprecating cackle. Only when Christina, Gabriel's young
sister, was visiting, would he shake himself out of his somno-
lence to stare at her—and also whenever talk turned to
religion. William Michael would look from him to Christina, and then, with lifted brows, to Gabriel. But Gabriel
affirmed more loudly that Collinson was a stunner; and,
with the authority of elder brother, gave him permission to
paint a portrait of Christina.

Sometimes the meetings were richer by the presence of
Ford Madox Brown, a versatile though unpopular artist
introduced by Gabriel to the brotherhood. In March of
that year he had seen some work of Brown's at an exhibition.
Struck by its earnestness and lack of affectation, he had
written the painter a letter extravagant with praise, ending
with an offer to become his pupil. Now Brown, though
not yet thirty, had found life more cruel than kind, and art
like a woman who, when not decked with wanton beguilements, has the attention of few. At competitions the works
of less capable men were preferred above his; again and
again, he had seen flashy prettiness extolled above beauty.
Tragedy and disappointment had been known visitors at
his bedstead. In his depression, Gabriel's letter came like
an insult. Brown, in whom sensitiveness had frozen, more
brittle than an icicle, felt it snap. Taking a stout stick, he
set out toward the house of the wag. Become his pupil,

would he? He would learn what a drubbing of his bones could teach! To his astonishment, he discovered that the letter had been written in genuine, if overstated, enthusiasm; instead of the insolent jester he had expected there stood a youth — embarrassed, yet bold enough to repeat his prayer. Brown invited him to his studio; and their friendship began.

Gabriel was a trying scholar. At the Academy school, impatient of drudgery, he would fret and fidget and fall into dreaming. Sometimes he failed to appear in his classes and, when asked what had kept him away, answered nonchalantly that he had had a fit of laziness. Then unaffectedly he read, to those who cared to listen, the poems he had produced during his lazy fit.

At Brown's studio he proved no better as a student. Brown sensed immediately in his young friend a power capable of greatness, but dangerously in need of discipline. The flights of Gabriel's fancy bore him bodily from the painting room to dream halls filled with maidens in splendid raiment and faces such as no poet, or perhaps only poets, had seen before him. Brown caught the shadow of those visions in the rapt look in Gabriel's eyes, guessed at the spell in the immobility of the paintbrush in mid-air. With a laugh he would clatter the pickle bottles on the model stand. And Gabriel, starting, would move the brush toward the easel. One day he kicked over the pickle bottles and the canvas on which he had been reproducing their homely forms, thanked Brown, and assured him they were better friends than ever. His freedom declared, he determined to face the world, perhaps as a poet.

Making a bundle of his writings, he sent them with a letter to Leigh Hunt, then a broken old Priam, living with the memory of his great dead. For twenty-seven years the violets of a Roman spring had bloomed and faded over the grave of the youngest singer of them all. "Ah, I can almost feel them growing over me!" Noble Keats, who had ranked him with them that had borne the chain for Freedom's sake—him, the sunset cloud of that glorious day! Gone, all of them; the impetuous rebel, whose dreams transcended the universe, gone; his imperishable heart alone there, in the Roman burial-ground. Gone, that other, the earthly Lucifer, as deathless in his works as in the heavens the red gleaming of the planet. Gone, all gone; and he alone—the least god-favored—yet lingered of the poetic line. Now, as long ago, he was asked to read the first fruits of a young mind, and give his counsel. Leigh Hunt read. He wrote with no small praise of the poems, but advised the poet—how genuinely, his penurious years knew—not to look to poetry for his bread, but to follow painting, no matter how slight the prospect of success.

Gabriel went back to his canvas, as zealous now as he had been negligent. When in the mood, he worked in spells of feverish concentration during which he became oblivious of the world—eating nothing but what was within reach, sleeping in his chair, and plunging again into his painting the moment his eyes were open. In vain, then, the brethren came knocking at his door with invitations to midnight walks by the glow of the full moon; he neither heard nor saw.

At the next exhibition of the Royal Academy, Millais showed "Lorenzo at the House of Isabella," inspired by Keats, posed for by his friends, painted in the new method, and with the mystic P.R.B. carved in the base of Isabella's chair. Hunt, too, had had a canvas accepted, his "Rienzi," each detail wrought with minute—too minute—precision. Weary months he had worked on it, dreamed of it, lived for nothing but the painting. He had not the prodigious facility of Millais. Whatever he accomplished came as the result of labor, the cost of which, in sleepless nights and haunted days, he alone knew. But his picture was well hung, as well hung as that of Johnny Millais.

Gabriel's "Girlhood of Mary, Virgin" was not seen anywhere on the Academy walls. Yet it had already been reviewed, and very favorably. He was, moreover, being spoken of as the leader of a new school.

Emily murmured, and in the murmuring was the word "treason." "I told you, Johnny, I never trusted that boy. First you and William get him into your brotherhood, and in the end he plays you false. Why did n't he show his picture at the Royal Academy? You think it may have been rejected? Still, it was treason for him to show it at the Hyde Park Gallery, which opens a week earlier. No, I never trusted him."

At this, the first exhibition of the Pre-Raphaelite Brotherhood, no great stir was made. Perhaps the mystic letters were not seen. At any rate, they passed unnoticed, and no one outside of the little circle was aware that a league of youth had been formed to revolutionize British art. Royal Academicians and popular painters slept soundly in their beds. "P.R.B."? They knew nothing of it.

Within a few weeks two of the three paintings found purchasers. Gabriel's, thanks to the reviews and the offices of Aunt Charlotte Polidori, was sold for eighty guineas to the Marchioness of Bath, at whose home she was employed as companion. It was not the first time Aunt Charlotte had been of pecuniary assistance to her artist nephew, so chronically out of pocket. As for "Isabella," three Bond Street tailors starting out as art dealers pooled their resources and bought the many-figured canvas for one hundred and fifty pounds "with a suit thrown in," to ease their consciences for a successful bargaining. "Rienzi" was carried home unsold by the unhappy Hunt, whose circumstances were sadly straitened: he had staked his last halfpenny on the painting. The landlord refused to wait longer for his rent. One morning he seized all the artist's marketable sketches, books, and possessions, and left him on the street. Fortunately, through the interest of Augustus Egg in the work of a younger artist, the "Rienzi" was brought at his suggestion to his own home where a friend of his might have the opportunity to examine it. What was Hunt's delight when the friend turned out to be none other than Gibbons, the collector, who sent him a check for one hundred and five pounds—as payment for the picture *and* the frame!

II

P.R.B.

THE founding of the Pre-Raphaelite Brotherhood was no isolated phenomenon in the story of art. Like all vital movements, art manifests itself in successive curves of action and reaction, the rise and fall making for progress. Surely, when Elohim in sublime unrest took up a handful of mud and fashioned the being called Adam, some whisper must have stirred the quiet, saying, "I should have fashioned Adam otherwise." And that dissenting artist, filled, too, with the unrest of his vision, planned and strove until, with beguilements breathed into a receptive ear, he made Adam's son, flesh of flesh.

Toward the middle of the nineteenth century, little of divine discontent animated the brushes and, with rare exceptions, the pens of artists and poets in the comfortable island of Victoria Regina. There had been Blake,—it seemed so long ago,—and Keats, and Shelley; and Byron, who had lived a demon and died an angel. But Blake, wrapped in his own luminous obscurity, had been well-nigh forgotten; Keats was still the pathetic boy whom the critics had slain; Shelley, a madcap dangerous youth who flung his life away as recklessly as he had lived it; and Byron— the less said of him the better. Even now virgins read him in the privacy of intimate chambers, ready to thrust him between the covers of the family Bible at the danger of interruption. The Bible received him, but closed unwillingly.

In art there was Turner, now an old man. Born in the last quarter of the past century, he seemed the survivor of a vanishing race. For the last time he showed his paintings in 1850. They were the works of a noble wreck, and the critics spared neither ink nor sarcasm in taunting the failing master — they, the "vultures to the conqueror's banner true." For years now, the colors on Turner's canvases had been blossoming in terrible glory, in mingled media that betrayed the unsure mind. No more were his "mists and exhalations" painted by the sun of his genius with "fleecy skirts of gold," but with the aching ruddiness of a tropical conflagration. Color, which he had mastered in all the subtle enchantments of its beauty, at last conquered him. The lonely old monarch, deafened by the discord of the critics, — which yet was not so loud as to drown another, a quieter, call, — lost himself in the generous bigness of London, alone with the figments of his mind, to wait for death. More fortunate than many an artist before him, he left one to act as his prophet to the future. For years John Ruskin had been a voice for Turner in a wilderness of indifference. The voice sounded on — throbbing, if monotonous.

With the exception, then, of Turner, and perhaps Mulready, Maclise, and Landseer, British art was generally represented by miles of wall space covered with canvases easy to look at, easier to forget. Convention had set a stamp on each as proprietary as the label on more stomachic commodities: *John Bull Pinxit*. One pretty picture followed the other, with simpering damsels in landscapes never visited by sun or moon. Comfortable still-lifes repeated the theme of fish in platters surrounded by the ingredients that would convert them to palatable dishes, or a brace of defunct partridges guarded by the master's dog — dog and master (shown in a near-by portrait) sharing features with touching democracy. Then came pictures with architectural backgrounds that afforded the critics the stones to break their heads on when they could not use them for sharpening their hatchets. The flesh of the maidens for whom the artists built the gorgeous architectural shell was of porcelain-doll smoothness, of the rosy hue tradition had sanctified. On canvas, flesh must have this tone and texture. If it was good enough for the great men before us, it is good enough for us. Now and then some incautious soul dared to paint things as he saw them — even after a course of rigid school-ing to purge him of originality. Alas, his work was doomed to blush and fade unseen of the gallery-visiting public.

Perhaps the clear eyes of youth, still unfalsified by con-vention, perhaps the happy accident that threw Lasinio's book of engravings in their way, perhaps the fact that they had been born at an intersection of the curves of progress — perhaps all these together fired the handful of bold idealists to break free from tyranny to the view that the world of beauty was theirs to regenerate. That the moment was ripe for the creation of the Pre-Raphaelite Brotherhood in that eventful year of social and political revolutions is certain. Years before them, Cornelius and Overbeck, feeling that art was dying through its own excesses, founded in Rome a movement known as the German Pre-Raphaelite. Their society was mystic and ascetic. Starting out with the con-viction that only the pure can produce spiritual works, they mortified the flesh for the soul's sake. Strange stories were told of hair shirts, of long fasts, and daily flagellations that the devil might be driven out of them before they set them-selves to the task of creating sublime art. But because the flesh was tortured the spirit weakened.

Madox Brown in his early youth had gone to see the German brethren in Rome. He found Overbeck in a black velvet dressing gown sweeping to his feet, a furred cap on his head, explaining the virtues of his paintings to a group of visitors. All the subjects were sacred; he never painted flesh from nature, to keep the spirit clean of sensual promptings. "So wherever naked flesh was shown," said Brown, "it looked like a wooden doll's or a lay figure's."

Millais, Rossetti, and Hunt, ranging in years from nine-

teen to twenty-one at the time they founded their brotherhood, also set out with ideals of chastity. But their ideals
differed in kind from those of the German mystics. No
mortification of the flesh for them. They loved life, for
it was new; a cup still to drain, a garment to don. Mortification is for the life-weary. Chastity to them meant no
curb to restrain their natural inclinations, but that quality
which appeared in their work as sincerity, truth, and simplicity. Far from sallow-faced ascetics, they were robust
youths, vibrant with the powers they had not yet discovered,
and attracting men and women to them as beautiful young
animals attract. It was said of Walter Deverell, one of
the group, that ladies would hurry round by side-streets to
get another glimpse of his face. What was true of him was
true of the others, and their faces did reciprocal service in
their paintings.

Apart from their art they did not differ from other young
men of their class who went on pedestrian excursions and
imbibed culture at very literary *conversazioni*. One night
they swam breast-high through a sea of mist on the out-
skirts of London, ranged for hours over the countryside,
and at last arrived at a hamlet close-shuttered in profoundest
sleep. In an access of animal spirits, and also to wake up
Collinson who was dozing on his feet, they gave a concerted
cheer. Windows until then black brightened with light;
a hundred nightcapped heads peered into the darkness for
the disturbers of the peace. It was long before the village
returned to its slumber and the startled dogs ceased howling.
The friends listened in a hush, mightily pleased with their
schoolboy prank. For a moment even the serious business
of the brotherhood was forgotten.

Gabriel was undeniably the magnet to which the youths
were attracted. An ardent proselytizer, it needed but the
persuasion of his rich voice to get members by the score for
the society. But it was to be exclusive, and candidates had
to be of proved ability in their special field before they could

be admitted. The first year it consisted of seven members, all painters but for the sculptor Woolner and William Michael Rossetti.

Hunt, self-contained, fervent, and hard-working, set the example for patient industry and well-defined aims. No hardship was too great for him to endure for his art's sake. Imbued with strong religious feeling, he seemed, like the mediæval artist, to approach his work kneeling. His vision, however, was always keen to the actuality of things; and if, even in his early youth, he aimed to inculcate a moral lesson, that lesson was one which the simplest could understand. Symbols strewed his work, sometimes obvious, sometimes only for such eyes as Ruskin's to perceive and interpret. Never would he descend to the trivial. For some inexplicable reason, he had earned for himself among the brothers the name of "Maniac."

Though Hunt's painting cost him agony of body and mind, Millais's was accomplished with a facility short of miraculous. Gabriel, to whom the mechanics of painting were drudgery, marveled — perhaps secretly envied. Millais had drawn from the time his fingers could hold a pencil. He was a child in long curls when his parents came to London to show his sketches to Sir Martin Shee, President of the Royal Academy. Sir Martin, unaware that he was looking at the work of an infant, advised them to send the lad to Sass's drawing school. There Johnny made such rapid progress that he soon entered the Royal Academy classes. He was so small that he had to sit on a high stool to see the model, and many a heartache did Emily have when he was dragged feet-first by the rough boys and made to sweep the floor with the curls she took such pains to arrange. He was thirteen when he was awarded a medal; two years later he began to paint, and found his first purchaser. Then came Gabriel with his tempter's voice.

Thomas Woolner had already established himself as a

full-fledged sculptor, and boasted a vast studio shared with his friend and fellow artist, Bernhard Smith. No greater contrast could have existed between the two: Woolner short and squat, with fair hair and flashing eyes, attacking a clay figure towering to the ceiling, while Smith, a very giant, fondled delicately bas-reliefs that his great hands nearly covered. "I was cut out to be a sculptor . . ." Woolner would say, with the tentative bait of the raconteur. At the least flicker of interest, he would retail of how, when he had been a boy at Behne's studio, the famous Haydon came in to see his master. As he was about to leave, Tommy held the door open for him; whereupon Haydon, not content with thanking him for his courtesy, felt his cranium for indicative bumps under the fair thatch — and pronounced prophecy. Some things had verified themselves, Woolner assured his friends. But woe, woe! A sculptor's lot is a hard lot, lest you have any illusions about it!

The exhibition of 1849 over, with results more encouraging than not, both from patrons and from the press, Gabriel was seized with unrest. It was well for them, the Pre-Raphaelites, to go their way, resting silent in their paintings. Meanwhile, their gospel was not spreading; and the usual inanities were sure to be thrust upon the public by the "sloshy" ones the following year. Again, they might go on signing their work with the mystic P.R.B.; but if the meaning was to continue secret, what good would result? Praise and blame are equally efficient for the dispersal of intellectual seed. They had received not too much blame, and not enough praise; they would be at a standstill unless something were done.

The more cautious remained for secrecy. They were working hard, were they not? They were following the lead of the stunners who came before Raphael in accepting no teachers but Nature and their individual abilities. Academy rules had been thrown overboard. Let them keep on following their own light.

Gabriel was not content. More was to be done, and it was for them all to do it.

In the meantime he and Hunt had given up their joint studio: Gabriel was too difficult to live with. Hunt wanted quiet and solitude, while Gabriel always brought with him havoc and a string of hungry followers to whom he regularly dispensed the contents of the common larder. In those impecunious days the generosity of the night before meant the fast of the morning after.

Gabriel's new studio over a dancing academy, the "hop-shop," offered a grateful, if noisy, freedom. It was the first place he had occupied independently, and the novelty was half its charm. The brethren now held their monthly meetings as his guests at Newman Street, discussed the business on hand, and then listened through half the night to Gabriel's declamations. "Sordello" and "Paracelsus" he gave by heart, leaping over obscurities like a Pegasus over cloud racks. Not for him to question Browning, spirit of modernity and rebellion! Then came Taylor's *Philip van Artevelde*, with its burning simplicity and social message — not that any of the brethren were very much concerned with social messages. But the poetry they loved. And then William Bell Scott's popular odyssey of the fallen Rosabel, whose lot roused the chaste youths against man's injustice to woman and yet made sin attractive by a sorrowfully sweet redemption. Other singers were included in his repertory — the highly moral Coventry Patmore, newly arisen, for whom Monckton Milnes had procured a librarianship at the British Museum; and, from across the sea, Poe, whose slow, tolling, dolorous measures filled the room with mystery. He was a special favorite of Gabriel, who leaned strongly toward the macabre and the exotic.

Woolner listened, his head enhaloed in the reflective puffs of his Paris student's pipe. Soon, aided and abetted by the two Rossettis, he produced lyrical outbursts of his own. Of Gabriel's recitations, he enjoyed particularly the "Woodman's Daughter," and, feeling that a study of it in the privacy of his studio might be productive of excellence in himself, he went to secure it at the publisher's. It was out of print. "Why don't you write to Patmore?" suggested the practical Gabriel. Woolner wrote, and a new friend was made for the P.R.B.

One night in July Gabriel presented the plan he had been maturing for some time. The brethren should issue a magazine containing etchings, poems, and literary criticism. At first, they themselves should contribute all the material and bear the expense; later . . .

The project was variously received, and all night long pacings up and down kept the dancing master awake. The following night the meeting was resumed, and many nights thereafter. Gabriel had a considerable sheaf of writings. William wrote, too; and so did Stephens and Hunt and Woolner. Collinson could be made to,—he was so easily led,—and Millais, if he could be got away long enough from his paints.

By October, William Michael had been elected editor of the projected magazine. That accomplished, Gabriel took a trip with Hunt across the Channel to see what the world had to offer. They came back a few weeks later, elated with the discovery of a grand old stunner, Memmeling, who had painted in their own spirit, centuries ago. Among their treasures they brought a "self-concocting coffeepot," for state occasions of the P.R.B., and a book containing instructions for raising the devil—which, doubtless, they did with success.

In December the self-concocting coffeepot did service for a large gathering at the naming of the magazine. More than a hundred titles were considered and rejected: the *Accelerator*, the *Precursor*, the *Harbinger*, the *Adventurer*, the *Scholar*, the *Chalice*, the *Sower*, the *Acorn*, the *Seed*, the *Scroll*, and so on, through the kingdoms vegetable and philosophical.

It was named the *Germ*, at the suggestion of Cave Thomas, one of the brothers of the outer rim.

III

CHRISTINA

When the four Rossetti children were still young, on the evenings when the paternal sitting room had been too noisy with the polyglot oratory of the Professor's visitors they would go to the boys' garret and spend together the hours before bedtime. Sometimes Maria, the eldest, read aloud, while Gabriel and William colored stage prints, and Christina, the youngest, listened, her grave eyes fixed on her sister's lips. Sometimes they would peep into some formidable tome, always whispered of as *sommamente mistico*, over which their father, with his long-peaked cap shading his face, pored for hours at a time. They would shut it with a gasp of awe at the mountains of black-letter and furrows of small type covering the bottom of the page. Their favorite pastime was working out sonnets from end-rhymes, at which Christina excelled. There were nights, however, when the thunderous company overstayed, and serious amusements palled. On those occasions the children played cards. Through some quirk of fancy they had come to identify themselves with the four suits: Maria with the clubs, Gabriel the hearts, William the spades, and Christina with the diamonds. In three cases, at least, the choice was prophetic.

Christina at eighteen showed nothing of the hard, glittering quality of the diamond. James Collinson, tame and shrinking, had not been awed by her, though she did so much resemble Gabriel's Mary, Virgin, for which she had sat, —

As it were
An angel-watered lily, that near God
Grows and is quiet.

Outwardly Christina was soft and womanly, her rare gayety
lighting briefly the meek gravity of her face. But within,
where Collinson had not the sight nor the understanding
to see, there was a keen, white sharpness, protecting, like a
coat of armor, something she held above the treasures of
the world. Not that she did not yearn for the gifts of life.
Her lips were arched and full for the luscious fruit, though
ready to tighten at a whisper from within. The wide-
winged nostrils, like Gabriel's, sensitive to the fragrance of
living, quivering with the breath of her being, betrayed a
struggle the set face would not reveal. To Collinson, as
to those who saw her with her brothers, she was a good girl
ripe for marriage, who would make a virtuous wife and
a dutiful mother. That, her household duties over, she
would steal away to her room and write verses, such as had
already appeared in print, need not have frightened an
eligible groom.

Indeed, any fond grandfather with a printing press in
the shed of his garden would have done as much for a pretty
niece with a penchant for versifying. In 1842 old Polidori
had printed a translation of Maria's; two years later the
press in the Regent's Canal garden had produced Gabriel's
Sir Hugh the Heron, which he would not now hear mentioned. Then had come Christina's turn. But Grandpa
Polidori had had nothing to do with the publishing of Christina's poems in the reverend pages of the *Athenæum* in 1848.

From the day Gabriel had introduced Collinson to his family there had been a tacit understanding that Christina's
affections were engaged. James came of a solid family,
Christian and respectable. He attended the same church
as the Rossetti women, and in behavior was devout and
mild. Nothing could be said against him except, perhaps,

that he had none of Gabriel's dash or William's good sense. He seemed too easily led—but then, that was not always a fault.

By the time the *Germ* was talked of, Christina and Collinson were looked upon as betrothed. William had even visited at the Collinsons' for a number of weeks, during which he had indited much informative correspondence to Christina. Nothing stood in the way of the future marriage.

Collinson, meanwhile, roused by his love out of congenital torpor, did what he could to please Christina. He worked long at his portrait of her, in emulation of Gabriel's, but the two paintings were as unlike as if two different women had posed for them. Gabriel's, lit with spiritual beauty, gazed out "strong in grave peace" — the soul itself painted. Collinson's was a simple English girl, gentle, but not burdened with intellect. He saw her, he wanted her, that way —and as Leonardo painted himself in Mona Lisa, Collinson drew a self-portrait in Christina.

Perhaps in those hours when he saw her clearly he may have felt a sense of want in himself; perhaps the activity of his companions stung him to rival them. At any rate, when the brethren were all enthusiasm in the preparation of their magazine, he wrote a long, blank-verse poem, and illustrated it. Gabriel acclaimed both poem and etching. The stunner had at last done himself justice. Christina would be proud of him.

Christina was proud; but also saddened. For some months her love had given her little happiness. James had changed, and she knew what caused the change. It was not that he loved another; that Christina would have understood, and in herself the image of him would have been treasured as an unalterable relic. It was the image itself that had altered, superseded by the reality of the man. He was a weakling. Though she had long hidden the truth from herself, averting her eyes to fill them with the pleas-

CHRISTINA ROSSETTI AND HER MOTHER

PAINTED BY D. G. ROSSETTI

anter aspects of his talent and manhood, she could do so
no more.

Again and again she read over the script of his poem, the
"Child Jesus": —

> Joseph, a carpenter of Nazareth,
> And his wife Mary had an only child,
> Jesus. . . .

She had loved it because James had written it, and because
it was beautiful; but the reading of it gave her pain.
Brought up as she had been in the Church of England, —
though with Puseyite leanings, — she had no sympathy,
however, with anything that hinted of Rome. Collinson
had strong tendencies in the direction of ritual and mysticism. Lately he had forsaken her church. Again, he had
confessed to her that before their meeting he had been converted to Catholicism, but that upon learning that the difference of their worship would have stood in the way of
their understanding, he had returned to his former faith.
Christina was a devout member of her church. Religion
was the one thing in which she would neither make, nor
accept, compromise. Scrupulous to bigotry in her morality,
she had already given up the theatre and the opera, arguing
that since actors and singers were of easy virtue, it was one's
Christian duty to discourage their performances. How
much more was one to discourage laxity in faith!

She read James's description of what had been their
dream of home — an English home, though he laid it in
far-off Nazareth: —

> A honeysuckle and a moss-rose grew
> With many blossoms on their cottage front. . . .

Blossoms like those at her maiden aunts' at Holmer Green,
where she had spent heavenly weeks in her childhood. She
could see with James

> The orange belted wild bees when they stilled
> Their hum, to press with honey-searching trunk
> The juicy grape; or drag their waxèd legs
> Half buried in some leafy cool recess
> Found in a rose. . . .

He must have watched those bees in the garden of his home. Yet at the very time Collinson had been writing of flowers and bees she had been describing another dream land, in a dirge for an imaginary girl she had wept for in her heart.

> Where sunless rivers weep
> Their waves into the deep,
> She sleeps a charmèd sleep:
>   Awake her not.
> Led by a single star,
> She came from very far
> To seek where shadows are
>   Her pleasant lot.

Again and again, then when she had loved most and seemed most happy, she had written of that one who died in sorrow. In the abundance of a brooding imagination, she decked bier and funeral chamber with the flowers of her art. Sometimes she recognized herself in that corpse.

> The curtains were half-drawn, the floor was swept
> And strewn with rushes, rosemary and may
> Lay thick upon the bed on which I lay.

And once, in suffering for which she would confess no reason, she had written with trembling hand, pressing her breast against the washstand in her room,—

> Have patience with me, friends, a little while:
> For soon, where you shall dance and sing and smile,
> My quickened dust may blossom at your feet.

Why that gloom at the height of her happiness? Why the incessant mourning for that unhappy maiden of her imagination? Sometimes when her mother had tried to look too searchingly into her thoughts, she had turned away. To *her* she could not have lied as she was lying to herself. Had she borne that gaze longer, she would have had to avow that all those dead girls were dead selves, selves that she had wished dead, rather than in love unworthily. Yet she did want to love. She had given James love that was neither for mother nor brother. What had come to threaten it? Inquire as she would, she did not know. Not with her mind. But there were many things she felt, and in her feeling she had glimpses of clues to which she hastily shut her eyes.

She was attached to her mother. In that household, the head of which the children never remembered as other than elderly, Mrs. Rossetti was the teacher, the guardian, and, in all mildness, the playmate. When Professor Rossetti came home, his chair would be waiting for him by the fireplace, the Dante tomes open where he had left his abstruse researches. There he remained for hours unmolested. Occasionally a volume in Italian would appear, bearing his name on the title page. Profound, and of recondite learning, the Professor's studies on Dante were as far removed from Victoria's England as the works of some obscure monk in the thirteenth century. Only Maria would read them, admiration in her eyes. However, when not bent over his books or entertaining his nondescript revolutionists, the Professor was a doting and tender father, whom his children treated with the same respect his pupils had for him at King's College.

Gabriel and William had been sent to school, like other boys. Maria and Christina were taught entirely by their mother. By a tacit understanding the girls followed their mother's faith; and, since the Professor was in no sense religious,—leaning rather dangerously toward freethinking, —the male members of the family were left to make their choice. Nevertheless Mrs. Rossetti watched zealously over them all, and, if one of the boys seemed in danger of straying, — as when Gabriel stood accused of reading such immoral books as Shelley's, — she pulled him back firmly to wholesome pastures. It had never been necessary to play tithingman over Christina. Her mother's word was law; her look, command — not that Mrs. Rossetti had ever had to command her younger daughter, the most devoted of her devoted children. It was enough for Christina to give her pleasure. She was eleven years old when she wrote her first poem — to her mother, on her birthday.

Except for rare absences, when the girls took places as governesses to sustain the family budget, mother and daughters were never parted. Separation was torture to Christina. She worshiped her brothers, Gabriel especially, though she felt more comfortable with William, nearer her age. Gabriel had always been looked upon as the hope of the family whom the others might approach but never overshadow. In Christina's mind standards were set by Gabriel's accomplishments and by William's virtues. She had had few opportunities for measuring other youths against her brothers — or, indeed, other men, outside the odd friends who came to see the Professor. Her life was bounded between home and her family, the church and her mother.

It was like the discovery of a new realm for her when her brothers began going out into the world. At first she glimpsed it in reflection, through the mirror of their reports; little by little she set a timid foot in their domain, though with her eyes turning backward for maternal guidance. Sometimes that world was brought to the decent drabness of Charlotte Street, and the drabness colored through its magic. But it was not for long. Instead, the world claimed Gabriel, who from then on came home, in the young girl's eyes, as a voyager bearing strange and wonderful tales of places that were not hers to behold. She lived vicariously through his adventures, and if at times her cheeks flushed before her mother's gently lifted brows, her lips were quickly humbled to silent apology.

Then had come Collinson and the other young men.

They trooped to Charlotte Street — a jolly, well-mannered crew, converting the bare living room into a gay agora alive with youth and ideals. That happened seldom, and then it ceased altogether. Gabriel, however, took to inviting Christina to his studio, where she sat for his paintings. She loved it there; for, even when he drew away to the apartness of his work, life filtered in as persistently as light through his windows. At times she had been at the studio scarcely ten minutes before it was ringing with the voices of as many friends. James came oftenest.

In the beginning she had not been drawn to him. He was retiring in his ways, dull in his speech. Beside Gabriel with his bluff manliness, James seemed weak and pale. But then, few of Gabriel's friends could measure up to him. Millais might be handsomer, in a conventional sense, but he did not possess that fire from within that lighted her brother's face as he spoke and lent warmth to his actions. Woolner was uncouth in his speech: she was a little afraid of him. Hunt she found difficult of approach. Obsessed by his mission, he had little thought for anything else. Collinson was always at hand, with touching, if awkward, attentions. He was hopelessly plain. She had to admit that, whenever she looked from his to Gabriel's sensitive face with its spacious brow and fine, speaking eyes. Yet she took kindly to him, and whenever Gabriel spoke well of him and his work, her lids were moist with gratitude. She was content when she did not make comparisons, and it was then she allowed the joy of love to come into her life.

Unused to the precious gift, at first she had contemplated it in secret, dandled it, treasured it jealously, sharing it with none.

> My Mother said: "The child is changed
>   That used to be so still;
> All the day long she sings and sings
>   And seems to think no ill;
> She laughs as if some inward joy
>   Her heart would overfill."

But as the months wore on, an inexplicable melancholy possessed her, and she had no more pleasure at the thought of her love. That something, perhaps in James, perhaps in herself, robbed it of bloom. Oddly, when she was definitely promised to him, she wept for love as dead, made it a grave among the flowers and laid a stone at its feet. Setting the scene for herself and James, she wrote even the words they might say of the present, become past.

> To few chords sad and low
> Sing we so:
> Be our eyes fixed on the grass
> Shadow-veiled as the years pass,
> While we think of all that was
> In the long ago.

"When I am dead, my dearest, sing no sad songs for me," she could say, envisioning the ultimate sundering.

She had to confess disillusionment; but she could not blame James wholly. It was no fault of his if he was timorous and weak; no fault of his if he could not ever approach Gabriel. His home was not the home that could be hers. His mother—what angel could ever take the place of her own? The fledgling dove she had brought out to see the sun shrank back and was afraid. The tremulous wings folded closer to the nest.

Yet her heart mourned for James and for herself. She loved him as much as she could ever love any man not her brother; but that love was not sufficient. She dreamed of a hearth and children of her own; still, the maternal breast was sweet, the home nest safe. Passion stung her, wakening her virgin senses; the curb of devotion to her mother and her faith pulled her away. The months were eternities of struggle that left her weary and with her problem unsolved. Only in the haunting vision of death, with rest at last in the lap of earth, she found appeasement.

IV

DISCORD

CHARLES DICKENS was indignant; not only indignant, but breathing vengeance, for he, the Englishman, had been attacked in a thing which, next to home, is the holiest: his love of art. It was no personal affront, but in so far as it affected the whole British nation, it affected him, too. The indignity? Picture No. 518 in the current Academy exhibition, a monstrosity, on the text, "And one shall say unto him, What are these wounds in thine hands?"

Now Charles Dickens knew as much about art as any subject of Her Majesty. More fortunate than most Englishmen, he had a vehicle in which to make known his displeasure and take up the cudgels in defense of the suffering public of which he was a member. Hot with righteous wrath, he wielded a spluttering pen for his article in *Household Words*.

On reading his Dickens, John Bull, who seldom visited art galleries, put on his top hat and took his wife and growing daughter to Trafalgar Square, where stood the edifice that held the sacrilegious painting. Of course it was by a Pre-Raphaelite, one of those stiff-necked young men of whom London had been hearing so much lately. "Christ in the House of His Parents" it was called, painted by John Everett Millais. It showed the interior of a carpenter's shop, the floor littered with shavings, and all sorts of tools and boards about the room. Now, to be honest, John Bull and his family did not see anything objectionable in a scene that was as real as their daily living. But there were Dickens's words in clear type, and Dickens was a famous author.

"In the foreground of the carpenter's shop is a hideous, wry-necked, blubbering, red-haired boy in a nightgown, who appears to have received a poke in the hand from the stick of another boy . . . and to be holding it up for the contemplation of a kneeling woman, so horrible in her ugliness that (supposing it were possible for any human creature to exist for a moment with that dislocated throat) she would stand out . . . as a monster of the vilest cabaret in France, or the lowest gin-shop in England."

Dickens was not the only true Englishman to attack the painting, which became known derisively as "The Carpenter's Shop." The critic of *Blackwood's* could not conceive of anything "more ugly, graceless and unpleasant. . . . Such a collection of splay feet, puffed joints and misshapen limbs was surely never before made within so small a compass." But that was not all. "Another specimen from the same brush inspires rather laughter than disgust."

Reputable papers bristled with barbs against other paintings of the Pre-Raphaelites, most of which were to be seen at the Royal Academy; and one, a papist piece of mysticism by a certain Rossetti, at the National Institution.

The protest was directed not alone against the paintings, but more bitterly against the principles the rebel artists upheld. For the first time since the founding of the brotherhood, the British public was able to discover the meaning of the three initials, a meaning that was worse than a slap in the face of art. How the secret was divulged, nobody knew. The brothers, however, had strong suspicions of Gabriel's expansiveness. At any rate the mischief was done, and now, where they had been bound together by common enthusiasm, they were more closely linked by general opprobrium.

The attacks that periodically found their place in the art journals were systematic in their virulence. An apoplectic

CHRIST IN THE HOUSE OF HIS PARENTS

PAINTED BY J. E. MILLAIS, P.R.B.

unanimity made them chorus loud against the impudence
of youngsters who swept into the dustbin all art since
Raphael's. Critics decried a morbid infatuation which sacrificed truth and beauty; they spat venom against a "senile
imitation of the cramped style." One exhorted the other
to a concerted attitude of thumbs down. The movement
must be scotched for British art to survive. They, the up-
holders of all that was good and holy, must warn their
contemporaries against yielding to the enervating influence
of such effeminate art. Why effeminate, they could not
have said.

So loud was the tumult that Victoria, recovering from the
seventh blessing she had bestowed upon Prince Albert in the
person of a new little prince, commanded the Academy to
take Millais's picture off the walls and bring it to the royal
confinement chamber. The Academy officials transported
the painting with the utmost care, partly that it might reach
their sovereign unimpaired, partly because it had already
been sold for the sum of three hundred and fifty pounds.

The Queen's apartment in Buckingham Palace was thoroughly searched by the royal domestics after Her Majesty's
confinement. Beds were looked under, dark recesses prod-
ded with staves, cupboards and closets minutely explored;
for, after Her Majesty's experience with the boy Jones,
who had Satan's own power of invisibility, nobody knew
what next to expect. Of course, Jones's had been an unusual
mania for hide-and-seek. Nothing availed to keep him out
of the royal precincts. The first time, he had been pulled
out from under a bed in the nursery. Once again, he had
been haled by the scruff of the neck from another hiding
place, when he confessed that he had been prowling about
the place many days, and that he had heard Her Majesty
and Prince Albert talk of very important matters while he
was crouching under their sofa. His discovery, however,
had come none too soon so far as concerned the cooks,
who for three days had been accusing one another of de-

predations on Her Majesty's larders. Now, fortunately, the boy Jones was safely away as a seaman; and neither the Queen nor the cooks had anything to fear from his incursions. Still, he might have left behind a brother with the same proclivities, and with a valuable painting in the palace . . .

There is no record of what Her Majesty said of the picture, if she did voice her sentiments. She may have liked it and said, "We are pleased," or she may not, and turned to her own newest-born. Neither is it recorded whether Prince Albert expressed an opinion of the work. It may be the Prince admired this specimen of Pre-Raphaelite art and was moved to foster more artists in the realm; or perhaps he disapproved and would have set up a more orthodox movement under his royal patronage; the fact remains that he was busy from then on founding art schools all over the kingdom.

In due time Millais's canvas was returned without mishap to the Royal Academy, whither the curious flocked daily about the Pre-Raphaelite works, for already the movement was gaining adherents.

Gabriel's "Annunciation," the companion piece to the "Girlhood," shone, a white lily, in the small gallery. Many a month had he labored to get the desired expression in Christina, the Virgin, and William, the angel, and the right tones of white in the harmony of color. The season for lilies had come and gone before he achieved the painted flower, and he resorted at last — whisper it not among the enemy! — to an artificial stalk from Foster's shop on Wigmore Street.

Most of the visitors turned away shocked at the figure of the young girl in a nightdress, sitting up in her white bed as if awakened by the flame-borne presence in her chamber. Her face, large-eyed, full of spiritual expectancy and yet frightened with a human fear, turns toward the angel bearing in his hand the lily that announces to her, in her perfect purity, that "the fullness of the time was come," and

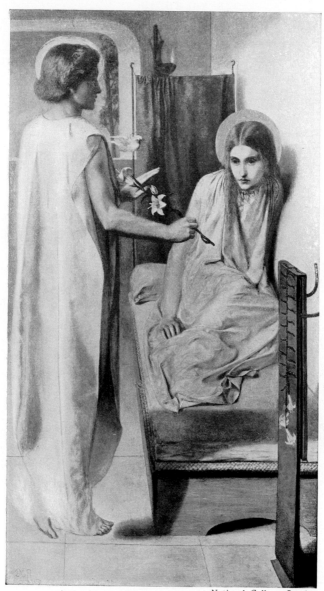

THE ANNUNCIATION

BY D. G. ROSSETTI, P.R.B.

(Posed by Christina and William Rossetti)

God the Lord
Shall soon vouchsafe His Son to be Her Son.

The sampler on which she had been embroidering the lily of
her innocence is now laid by, the flower itself broken from
its stalk and in the hand of the annunciatory angel. It was
a moving scene, simple in its rendering, awful in its implication of the sublime mystery.

Christina had gone to see how it was hung, and gazed on
the face of Mary, her own transformed with the light of
divinity, and thought of the fullness of her own time that
would never, never come.

A stay at the Collinsons' had brought her back humbled
and melancholy. Soon after, William, who was at that
time away from home, received a letter which told him more
than lay behind the words. "My correspondence with Mary
Collinson has come to an end by her desire. Do not imagine
we have been quarrelling: not at all: but she seems to
think her brother's affairs so unpromising as to render our
continuing to write to each other unpleasant. Does not
this sound extraordinary?"

It was not extraordinary to William, who watched Christina gradually changing from a light-hearted girl to a
brooding woman. Mrs. Rossetti often turned to him a
look of perplexity and concern, as Christina's head, in the
midst of family cheer, would sink upon her breast and her
fingers twine listlessly upon her lap. But to a leaf tucked
away she had confided the grief she could not tell her
mother, or him, or any living soul.

> How should I share my pain, who kept
>   My pleasure all my own?
> My spring will never come again;
>   My pretty flowers have blown
> For the last time; I can but sit
>   And think and weep alone.

A parcel of her heart lay on that paper; but nobody must
know.

Then Gabriel had a communication from Collinson which at first he could not make out. It was addressed to him as a Pre-Raphaelite brother, and in sanctimonious terms informed him that therewith he, Collinson, was tendering his resignation from the brotherhood. It was against his conscience to continue a member, for he "revered God's faith and loved His holy saints, and could not bear the accusation of dishonoring them to satisfy a little vanity." He had sold his easel, lay figure, and painting materials, and given up his lodgings.

At home Christina had more to impart. Collinson had again left his church to re-embrace Catholicism, this time not as a simple convert but with the intention of studying for the priesthood at Stonyhurst. She had given him back his freedom.

The weeks and months of anguish that followed Christina bore alone. Mrs. Rossetti knew only that her daughter was ill of disappointed love, as many girls had been before her, that she slept badly, and that if a salutary régime of common sense—blessed common sense!—were followed, Christina would be herself again. Collinson therefore was never mentioned. At first Christina had sought, a little ashamed, to relieve her overladen heart. But Mrs. Rossetti, seeing the pain it caused her, insisted with the firmness of her practical nature that he was never to be spoken of in her presence. Christina had released him, had she not? She had known what she was doing. No child of hers must be a weakling for love.

Maria, obedient to her mother as well as scrupulous of her own salvation, said never a word about him, either to comfort or to reprove her sister. Her thoughts were set on heaven, and, with her devotion to churchgoing, oblations, confession, and continued fasts and prayers, she had little leisure to be concerned with the troubles of this world. Christina watched her go her sainted way and tried bravely to follow.

Sometimes the loneliness and the craving for a word of James, even the least word about his doings, were stronger than her fear of displeasing her mother. Because she had promised not to speak of him, she wrote little heartbreaking notes that William received in his office. "Have you seen the 'Saint Elizabeth' lately? . . . Whilst I am here, if you can manage without too much trouble, I wish you would find out whether Mr. Collinson is as delicate as he used to be: you and Gabriel are my only resources, and you are by far the more agreeable. . . ." Gabriel had grown such a bear since he had met that new model. "I direct this to the Excise that Mamma may not know of it. Do not be shocked at the concealment. . . . Do have patience both with the trouble I occasion you and with myself. I am ashamed of this note, and yet want courage to throw it away."

A crushing sense of her unworthiness, freighted with the double charge of desire and renunciation in her heart, humbled her to the earth. And yet she could not say there was no sweetness in the weight that bowed her, nor peace in the knowledge that at last all was over. Security was hers in her mother's affection, — her strong, firm, practical mother, — and a sweet compensation in the sympathy of her brothers. But life held more, and sometimes, too often, her whole being cried out for it — only that she might push it from her with both hands and her face set as a flint.

William with his clerkship at the Excise office helped to fill up the gap in the family income caused by the Professor's declining health. He had many responsibilities preying on his mind. The editorship of the *Germ*, — it was known in fun as the *Gurm* among them, — the first number of which, alas, in spite of Woolner's opening rhapsody on his beautiful lady, had made no more impression upon the British mind than a summer shower in an ocean, occupied his spare hours, and worrisome hours they were. No wonder his fine crop of hair thinned visibly, until with shame and heartbreak he had it cropped close to give it strength, and appeared, to the delight of the heartless brethren, in a hirsute glory not his own. Whether the cares of home and office weighed too heavily upon his brain, or the wig mortified the natural growth, in a few months William's pate was as naked as a fledgling's, and no coaxing availed to raise the lightest down. In despair the wig was discarded and a skullcap worn in its place. That, too, was at last thrown away, and William, not without pangs at the ludicrous tragedy, resigned himself to the brow of middle age over his face of twenty.

The Pre-Raphaelite brothers had placed their all in the first issue of their magazine and launched it like a ship of hope on the dawn of the new year. They had made it beautiful with the adornments of their hands and minds; they had even obtained for it a poetic contribution from Coventry Patmore. Nevertheless, of the seven hundred copies printed only two hundred were sold. The second number sold even less, though it contained "The Blessed Damozel" by Gabriel and some lyrics of Christina's. Gabriel knew why she had refused to put her name to them and signed them Ellen Alleyn. She would have laid her heart too bare. Collinson's poem, with his own etching illustrating it, appeared in the same issue.

The *Germ*, despite the obvious immaturity of some of the contents, was no empty gesture of adolescents. It had a moral purpose, implicit in the essays, explicit in William's Malvolian sonnet that graced the cover of each issue. Besides, there was Gabriel's prose allegory, "Hand and Soul," which, in subtly veiled didacticism, showed what the aim of the artist should be. He had sat up all of a December night to write it while the revelation was upon him. Chiaro dell' Erma, — a projection of an ideal self, — early proved the futility of making art the handmaid of fame and henceforth strove for moral faith. Here, too, he failed; for in a moment of soul clearness he saw that "what he had mis-

taken for faith had been no more than the worship of beauty."
Tormented with doubt he cried, "May one be a devil and
not know it?" Feverish, he sat with his head bowed, without stirring, — "the warmth of the air was not shaken," —
and the vision came, clad to the hands and feet with a green
and gray raiment; and he "knew her hair to be the golden
veil through which he beheld his dreams." "I am an
image, Chiaro, of thine own soul within thee." She speaks,
and her words lift the doubt from his spirit. "Give thou
to God no more than He asketh of thee, but to man also
that which is man's. . . . Set thine hand and thy soul to
serve man with God."

Serve man with God. It might have been the motto of
the brotherhood; it was certainly Gabriel's.

If the public would have none of the *Germ*, the reviewers
accepted the complimentary copies. Two or three recognized therein the seed of something significant. The second number particularly delighted Lord Landsdowne's private secretary for the sincerely admiring review it contained
of *"The Strayed Reveller*, by A." It was his first poetic
volume, and Matthew Arnold was justifiably pleased.

The last two issues, though rechristened *Art and Poetry*
and advertised with posters paraded in Trafalgar Square,
had no better success. The magazine died, leaving its
editors with a common debt but with faith unshaken. Millais was left with something else besides, a story that was
to have adorned a fifth number which never appeared.
How zealously had he taken up the pen for the woeful history of two lovers, who eloped from a castle in winter only
to fall through the treacherous ice of the moat! With true
Pre-Raphaelite thoroughness, he had even tracked their
fate beyond death, showing them as skeletons, years later,
in the drained moat, the fabric of the lady's dress still clinging to the knight's armor. *Requiem aeternam dona eis!*

The young men still hoped. The renaissance, the first
glow of which had been vouchsafed to the hungering vision

of Keats, would one day, soon, burst to full glory before their light-filled eyes. Tennyson was the lark, Browning the clarion voice, to hail it. They, too, would be choristers of the new day.

V

RUSKIN TO THE RESCUE

IN 1823 a little boy of four was posing for his portrait to
James Northcote, R.A., a venerable gentleman of seventy-
seven. The boy's mother, a ruddy, plain, richly dressed
elderly lady, occupied a post of vantage whence she could
observe artist, model, and canvas, and, with her hands
folded, nodded approval or knitted stern brows according
to what struck her at the moment. Northcote was a solid
artist. He had been a pupil of Reynolds's, and had almost two thousand paintings to his credit — the right man
to paint the heir of John James Ruskin, of Ruskin, Telford,
and Domecq, wine merchants.

The little lad stood patiently, only now and then letting
his glance wander from the carefully attenuated light of
the room to the sunshine outside. A look from his mother
brought him quickly back to the pose. Northcote was adding the finishing touches to the figure, a quaint little chap
in a décolleté frock and a blue sash, looking out with bright-
eyed gravity on a bewildering world. The painted child
poised birdlike on his left foot and, with the other in mid-
air, was scarcely the good little fellow sedately studying
the holes in Northcote's rug, wondering why they were
there and who had made them. No more was the interior
of the actual room the grassy knoll with a misty valley in
the middle distance, nor the stiff-backed chair the tree of
the decorative background. Neither was the shaggy doggie
of the canvas, forepaws ready for a leap and tail awag at
the lifted finger of his master, the same subdued beastie
crouched at the skirts of the taffetaed lady. Against that

maroon setting even young doggies, fun-loving though they be, had to behave.

"Well, John Ruskin, what will you have off there in the background?" asked Northcote, pointing beyond the misty vale.

The little boy looked at him and at his mother, and then out of the window. "Blue hills," he said, gravely. Margaret Ruskin nodded.

The sitting over, the child was taken home to the study. Margaret Ruskin swished in soon after, holding up her trailing taffetas. For one long hour, leaning over the fair, faunlike head, she read the day's books of the Bible, pointed out the verses to him with a monitory finger and listened to him repeating them after her. If the pronunciation or the inflection did not suit her ear, John was made to say the word or phrase over and over, until he got it to perfection. There was no kiss to reward him for success, no word of praise for his valiant lispings, though the rod was spared when he stumbled on a name no less than when he tripped on a stair. She was as impersonal toward the child as if she were an embodied abstraction, devoid of everything but what pertained to the duty of the moment. Nevertheless, the cold eyes sparkled above the sandy head at each difficulty conquered and her heart leapt with the confidence that her son would justify the Calvinistic rigors of her teachings.

And rigors they were, with no mitigations for frail health and tender years. No gaudy toys had ever been given him — baubles of the Tempter who would too early have awakened the baby mind to vanity. A bunch of keys instead of a rattle for the infant hand; a rough cart, later; and bricks. A two-arched toy bridge signalized his coming to the years of discretion. Nor was there any dainty food for the child John; only the plainest fare, so that when once the stern Margaret gave him a bit of the custard his father had left, it was an experience to be remembered.

John accepted his mother as he accepted the sun and moon and the ticking of the clock, giving her no more of human affection than he gave them. Margaret Ruskin expected no more. If her son was dutiful, truth-telling, just, a good Christian and upright, that was all she could hope from the human creature. However, she was certain John would reward her care, for, besides a good man, he would be a great one. Her whole life and her husband's were bound up in the knowledge. Ruskin's family and hers had had nothing that could have been kept from the ears of their posterity. On his side, as on that of the related Coxes, hers, a Scots rectitude had been observed for generations, the strait path sown on either hand with Christian deeds. The flowers and fruits had been their children's harvest in sturdy bodies and healthy minds. Certainly the union of two such branches would be fraught with extraordinary good for the child Ruskin, son of first cousins.

The pastimes of the boy were of his own devising and chiefly imitative, thanks to that blessed faculty of make-believe that peoples the only-child's solitude and holds up a brighter mirror of the world. When Margaret Ruskin was not rehearsing him on Holy Writ, and Ruskin the elder had finished reading him Shakespeare and Milton, the child would withdraw to write his own poetry, taking care to be accurate in form and rhythm. He liked best, however, to deliver sermons before the household. At the first request, he would climb upon a chair, lean over the back of the sofa with a command of the red cushions, and, raising his right hand as he had seen the minister do, exhort the congregation: "People, be good" — words that were to be on the white banner of his crusades all the rest of his life.

The people were few to whom he could grow attached: Anne, the Scotch nursemaid, the servants, the grave guests who sometimes visited at Herne Hill and for whose coming the covers were taken off the pictures, and his mother and father, standing beside him like the embodied doctrines of Goodness and Rectitude in the frontispiece of his book of life. He had no playmates of his own age. Lacking human companionship, he threw himself with the passion of loneliness into things. The garden at Herne Hill, of which he knew every leaf on hedge and tree, the mosses, the pebbles of the correct walks, the flowers in their trim beds, the birds, the passing clouds, grew dearer to him than the taskmasters of his real living. And, too, he knew them better.

Mr. Ruskin's sherry business carried him all over the realm, and Margaret Ruskin, devoted wife and curious traveler, accompanied him. From the time their child could stand on his own feet, he went with them everywhere, in the care of the rigorous Anne; so that before he had been graduated from his blue-sashed petticoats to breeches, museums and castles were as familiar to him as his nursery. The mountains became his earliest and most lasting love. The ever-changing yet perdurable masses, snow-wreathed and cloud-haloed, mantled in glory and skirted in mists, awakened his precocious mind to a wonder for which even then he strove to find words. "Eudosia, a Poem of the Universe." He began it at an age when other children found most pleasure in their toys.

> When first the wrath of heaven o'erwhelmed the world,
> And o'er the rocks, and hills, and mountains hurl'd
> The waters' gathering mass; and sea o'er shore, —
> Then mountains fell, and vales, unknown before,
> Lay where they were. Far different from the earth
> When first the flood came down, than at its second birth . . .

Mountains, hills, vales? They shadowed him since that first blue background he begged for to make vivid a remembered beauty. The Scottish mountains, and later, the Alps, were blue—and gold and purple. They were more glorious than visions seen in sleep—a fairyland, yet earthly;

a magic, yet real. He brought home bits of rock crumbled from their ageless sides. To him they were as precious as the relics which in earlier days the faithful had gone over land and sea to seek. Lichens and mosses he added to his treasures; leaves, and the feathers fallen from birds in flight. Back home he would sit with the devotion of a worshiper and reproduce on paper the minute asperities of the rock, the branched intricacies of Alpine moss, the patterned perfection of leaf and flower.

John James Ruskin and his wife were convinced their son was one of the elect of the Lord. That His talent might not be lodged with them useless, they obtained for the boy the foremost scholars to tutor him in Latin and Greek, the best masters to train him with pencil and brush. Throughout he justified their care with erudite productions, illustrated minutely by himself. Margaret Ruskin had vowed him to the service of God. The Bishopric of Winchester? It would be attainable. With his powers, he could be Primate of England at fifty. Therefore when the time came for his maturer studies, he was entered as gentleman-commoner at Christ Church; and, to the astonishment of Oxford, Margaret, devoted and tyrannical, came with him bag and baggage, and Anne, to settle in the town. John James Ruskin visited only during week-ends, to bask in the society of his son's patrician friends.

Margaret knew what she was doing, and nothing could shake her from her resolve. With her watching over his diet and his hours, he might gain back the health he had lost pining for M. Domecq's heartless little chit. It was an ill day that had brought the Domecq girls to England, though at the time neither she nor her husband had thought anything would have come out of the visit. Of course she had never really countenanced any intimacy between John and the blonde, Spanish Adèle with her French education and popish faith. She trusted implicitly in her boy, and it was with no little satisfaction that she caught snatches of his conversations with the lass — about the Spanish Armada, the battle of Waterloo, even the doctrine of transubstantiation, expounded for Adèle from his Evangelical point of view. She never could understand why the girl always laughed. Then once Adèle had laughed too loud, when John told her he loved her; and the laugh had been as the cracking of a whip on his bared heart. Fortunately, Domecq had sent the girls back to France and John was well rid of Adèle, though not without pain. But she and her husband would see to it that his recovery be whole and for his soul's good. His convalescence took longer than she had expected, in spite of the trip abroad among his beloved hills. She knew nothing of an old glove he kept in a drawer among his treasures of rock and leaf, nor was she ever shown the dithyrambs and elegiacs in which he celebrated his love and loss. "Adèle is not the only girl in the world," she could only repeat to deaf ears. To her relief, the cruel one promptly married; now John could no longer honorably think of her.

Meanwhile he was writing searching articles on geology, æsthetics, Turner, and the poetry of architecture. Learned periodicals published them, and "Kata Phusin"[1] was acclaimed a brilliant mind. At twenty, on his third attempt, for he had in him much of his mother's tenacity, he carried off the Newdigate prize for his "Salsette and Elephanta," read at the Sheldonian Theatre — "before an audience of more than two thousand ladies and gentlemen," his father loved to say, as he enlarged upon their enthusiasm. In the pride of John's triumph he quite overlooked the slight incident of an award bestowed, that same evening, to William Wordsworth, a seedy-looking old gentleman, for *his* verses.

Unexpectedly John, to his parents' consternation, gave up all thought of adorning a bishopric and plunged himself into the study of art. The museums of Italy were now his ship, wafting him through space and time. He came home

[1] Ruskin's pseudonym.

burning with prophecy, his lips touched with the divine coal.
He was bearing the message of a rebirth, the rebirth of
wonder for the creations of man's mind and hands: he would
be the voice in the wilderness of the modern age, for the
true, the pure, and the beautiful.

His first thought was to turn his eyes upon the art of
England and on the great masses from whom it sprang like
a plant from the soil. Wherever he looked, nothing met his
wakened sight but sordidness and indifference. The flowering plant was there, but the people, like the clod, were
inert. Spurred on by his vision, he saw himself the sower,
scattering the seed of beauty with both hands, till not an
antheap but would grow green.

His parents, moved with the voice of his prophecy, accepted his new apostolate and were soothed of their earlier
disappointment. Now John's study became the sanctum
where, in solemn withdrawal, he performed his mysteries.
A few years before, he had found one who incorporated
his æsthetic doctrine, though the populace had never
recognized him and of late the priests of opinion had condemned him — Turner. The Ruskins bought his works
for their son's sake and hung them on their walls, though
on the Sabbath, out of respect to the Lord, there was not a
picture in the whole house that was not shrouded. At the
advent of a prized visitor, John talked vividly of Turner's
color as he glided softly about the rooms, taking down a
painting to illustrate a point, hanging up another where the
light might fall on it to advantage. The guests admired
politely, and secretly marveled at such worship. Not the
least surprised was the object of Ruskin's cult.

Turner, at bottom, was a simple, if crotchety, man. To
these, the declining years of his life, he had painted as the
birds had sung — because nature had given him the power
and it had been his delight to use it. He so loved his works
that he would put fabulous prices on them to discourage the
buyer. Trials and disappointments had been his; he knew

them as the hurts that proved one to be alive. Besides, he had had his share of honors. What man could hope for more? He was therefore taken aback, pleased, and puzzled all in one when he saw his name figuring prominently in the press of 1843, in connection with a volume, *Modern Painters*, by "A Graduate of Oxford" — the son of his wealthy patrons, as he knew.

The young author won fame at once. Another Pico della Mirandola come to light! All the literati who could afford it bought his book. Tennyson, temporarily impecunious, borrowed it by strategy. Poets, old and young, honest merchants, lords — everyone read it, discussed it, and wondered who this Graduate of Oxford could be who hid so modestly his extraordinary gift.

Margaret Ruskin was proud and thankful at her son's success; her husband, even prouder. Though John had not become a minister of the Lord, he was still His servant, as he had promised from earliest childhood. If this, his first long sermon, was filled with learning, wit, and flowers of style, the text was still that of the infant lips: "People, be good! Behold the glory of the blue hills!"

Turner became conscious of the true beauty of his work — conscious, and vain; and in his will he left two of his paintings to the National Gallery provided they were hung next to the two Claudes, that even such gold might be dimmed by the shine of his rarer metal.

Meantime John Ruskin's adolescent love had not left him heart-whole, as his parents fondly supposed. What in a less sensitive boy would have been the spark for the later flame became the devouring conflagration out of which he issued not reborn but scarred. For the first time in his life he had given himself completely to a human creature, only to be rejected. His experiences with things had wholly unfitted him for dealing with people, least of all with women — and with one, the vivacious Adèle, in particular. Things are studied, treasured, loved; they admit of everything, with the passiveness of the inanimate. Ideas, too, malleable as nothing else, can be shaped to the forms desired of the creating mind. They give pleasure above that afforded by material loves, and pain, but the hurt is of the mind of which they spring. Such pleasures, such hurts, the young boy had had. When Adèle had entered his life, he had treated her, too, as a laughing, brilliant abstraction, wooing her with the gifts of his intellect and with no music less noble than verse. He had met human eyes, widened with amused surprise, human ears, already accustomed to the flatteries of men. And because she was so young, she had shown more cruel frankness than a woman would have had.

Ruskin was little more than respectfully acquiescent, therefore, when his parents arranged a match in his twenty-ninth year between him and his cousin Euphemia Chalmers Gray of Perth. He had known Euphemia as a pretty child for whom he had written a fairy tale, *The King of the Golden River*. When she was older he had taken her to the galleries to improve her mind; but she had never fired him as the heartless little Domecq girl had done. Euphemia — vivacious, elegant, as fond of society as Ruskin of his geological specimens — found but dull living with a man who had wedded her in obedience to his parents. Margaret Ruskin alone seemed pleased, for now that he was a married man he would not go from home for months at a time on his endless researches. He would remain with his wife, and with her, his mother.

The joyless marriage, however, threw Ruskin more and more into his work. He was now recognized as the apostle of moral art, the critic of lucid judgment who spoke with the tongue of a poet. But the recognition of the public did not come without its gall. The people listened to him, applauded, willingly hailed him prophet. Nevertheless they went their way, indifferent to the beauty he would have had them wear as a seal upon their breasts. In their eyes he was a good man, but impossibly utopian.

He wrote on, nothing daunted; and preached, pointing out what was to be reverenced in art and life, and what to be scorned as evil and let die. Yet in spite of his passionate championship Turner had been suffered by the world to hide in loneliness and despair. Ruskin had foreknown the approaching end. The summer of 1851 he added a postscript to the first volume of *Modern Painters*, roused by the remark of the *Times* when on the walls of the Academy no longer shone the splendor of the master's paintings: "We miss those works of inspiration." "We miss! Who misses?" the prophet wrote in flame. "The populace of England rolls by to weary itself in the great bazaar of Kensington, little thinking that a day will come when those veiled vestals and prancing amazons, and goodly merchandise of precious stones and gold, will all be forgotten as though they had not been, but that the light which has faded from the walls of the Academy is one which a million Koh-i-noors could not rekindle. . . ." When, later that year, Turner died, Art seemed to Ruskin to have died with him. How true the prophecy Constable had uttered in 1822, "Art will go out. There will be no more genuine painting in England in thirty years." Had he not foretold the death of Turner to within a few months? The sun, "the sun which was God," had been quenched; and the world was in darkness.

Melancholy now hounded Ruskin, and sometimes bitterness was on his tongue. In moments when the public nodded multifarious heads before his eloquence, he railed that they loved his pretty phrases but neglected his principles, dearer to him than all the verbal music in the world. Indeed, for verbal music or pure poetry he had the limited appreciation of the moralist. Something there had to be, more than witchery of sound in literature, besides the harmony of color in painting, to evoke his admiration. It was the same something Thomas Carlyle, whose disciple he became, sought beyond the work of a genius, in making his estimate of the man — though, unlike Carlyle, Ruskin would

JOHN RUSKIN

FROM A PENCIL DRAWING BY G. RICHMOND

never have passed by a museum containing statues of Michael Angelo, and, while contemplating a life of him, have said: "His sculpture, mon? We need only glance at *that*." That something was art's significance toward universal good. There was a difference between master and disciple. Where the one, a moral, upright man, strove to love humanity only to curse mankind, Ruskin, in his inability to settle his affection successfully on one dear being, loved the whole world, which he would have reclaimed from evil and ugliness.

Disillusion came early. Man, he found, was much more concerned with the things that gave him his bread and butter. Neither parables nor sounding oratory had power to keep him interested more than a polite moment. Formidable causes underlay this indifference. Ruskin set out to study them as painstakingly as he had studied the veins of rock and leaf, still cherishing, as much, if not more, the belief in the regeneration of mankind through beauty.

It was at this time his attention was called to the Pre-Raphaelites. Millais, the heretofore successful young cockerel, felt he was getting a little too much of a plucking simply because he had adopted the ill-fated monogram of the brotherhood. His father and mother suffered; his enemies rejoiced. He was beginning to get tired of it all. One night, after reading what the *Times* had had to say, he went, irate and vociferous, to the mild Coventry Patmore. "You've got to help us," he cried, waving the blasphemies of the press. "Listen to what the fellow says about our paintings—'faces bloated into apoplexy or extenuated to skeletons . . . color borrowed from the jars in a druggist's shop . . . expression forced into caricature. . . .' It's nothing short of malice! You must go to your friend Ruskin and ask him to take the matter up!"

Patmore went at once to Ruskin, who was already in sympathy with the young men's strivings. Like him, they, too, were working toward the goal. A few days later the *Times* published a letter by "the Author of *Modern*

Painters." With his impartial logic, Ruskin showed where the critic of that paper had followed the hue and cry, and concluded: "There has been nothing in art so earnest or so complete as these pictures since the days of Albert Dürer."

The Pre-Raphaelites had won a powerful defender, and they were not slow to profit by him. Millais and Hunt wrote him a letter of thanks from Gower Street, where, one day, Millais received a visit from Mr. and Mrs. Ruskin, formal and elegant in their carriage. So delighted were they — especially Euphemia — with the charming, free-spoken, exuberant youth, unlike the middle-aged gentlemen of Ruskin's acquaintance, that they invited him to stay a week at Camberwell and carried him off with them then and there.

Margaret Ruskin sniffed the air ominously.

VI

GABRIEL AND ELIZABETH

THE Pre-Raphaelite Brotherhood was severing in body if not in spirit. Thomas Woolner, after repeated efforts to conciliate an unfriendly world with both verse and sculpture, found that though empty other folks' kettles are, artists' kettles are emptier, "good for nothing but tying to the tails of mad dogs." He had done his best in every possible way, worked out a sketch for the Wordsworth Memorial competition,—a grand design, the brethren thought it,—and in his spare time put in a fond touch or two on the towering clay model of what he hoped would be his masterpiece. It thrilled him each time he gazed upward on his representation of the victorious present striding over the past, and it was with paternal tenderness that he swathed "The Generations" daily in damp cloths. Unfortunately, another received the memorial commission, and in a fit of dejection Woolner put an end to whatever he had in progress, even his gigantic clay model. Again he essayed his hand at poetry, but it did not satisfy him. With sulphurous rhetoric, he burred his grievance. "Poetry is not my proper wurrk in the wurrld. If a man undertakes to plough a field, but shies off with a gun in his hand and brings back any amount of game, would his master thank him? Unless I take care, my master Conscience will have something to say I shan't like."

And so, on the advice of Tennyson, he left art for the gold diggings in Australia, forsaking the empty kettle in the hope of filling a gold-pan. He was not unique in following the lure of the precious ore. Since May of 1851 when Hargraves, the miner from California, had made the Macquarie plains resound with his cry of "Gold!" men arrived by the thousand from all parts of Australia. Thick as ant files, they streamed with their packs on their shoulders through the roads from town to settlement. Industry was abandoned, farming entrusted to providence and the skill of the women, and domestic animals left to run wild. From all parts of the world came ships teeming with immigrants, and after their crews landed it was often a matter of weeks before sufficient hands could be found to replace deserting sailors for the voyage back. Hundreds left England weekly for the colony of Victoria. So great the boom resulting from the gold rush that within six months Victoria was made a separate province. Thither Woolner and his friend Smith went with the rest of the discontented, adventurous souls who looked back on England with regret—and hope—in their eyes.

The brethren bade them an affectionate farewell with promises of frequent correspondence. From the shore Madox Brown watched the ship diminish on the horizon and was full of bitter reflections—on Woolner, on himself, on England's manhood that had to abandon her to keep body and soul together. Things were not going well with him, either. His work, into which he put the best that was in him, for which he suffered sunstroke to get true daylight on a field, and braved December chill for crisp outdoor effects— his work that was his life received cold cheer from those who succumbed to the blandishments of falsehood. Less fortunately situated than Woolner, he had a wife and babies to think of. Little country-bred Emma, scarcely out of her teens, was so unlearned in household economy (unlike his first wife who had been years older than himself) that the steepness of grocers', fishmongers', and bakers' bills gave poor Brown many a reason for tearing his hair. Perhaps he, too, might be forced to give up his work. In the ship that bore his two young friends he could see himself, an emigrant, looking his last on England. But his were momentary fits of depression. Palette on thumb and Emma lovely though "uncultivated" posing for him, he forgot his disappointments.

Christina, in a rare fit of levity, celebrated the fortunes of the P.R.B.: —

> Woolner in Australia cooks his chops;
> And Hunt is yearning for the land of Cheops;
> D. G. Rossetti shuns the vulgar optic;
> While William M. Rossetti merely lops
> His B's in English disesteemed as Coptic;
> Calm Stephens in the twilight smokes his pipe,
> But long the dawning of his public day;
> And he at last the champion great Millais,
> Attaining academic opulence
> Winds up his signature with A.R.A.

Not a word of Collinson; he might never have been one of the brethren. Christina, now that she had lost him, had made an effort — too great an effort — to put him out of her mind, and she had not succeeded. One day she had met him in the street as she was walking arm in arm with William, and she had fainted. The diamond sharpness of her breastplate protected from without, but its asperities stabbed a heart of flesh.

Frederic Stephens and William Rossetti, like Woolner, remained non-contributing members of the brotherhood so far as art production went. Both had taken up criticism, and with the help of friendly journals became the mouthpieces of the P.R.B. Only Millais, Hunt, and Gabriel were active. Millais early received the associateship at the Royal Academy, — the friends thought in order to divide their forces, — the conventional honor abashing those who would have attacked. Hunt, obsessed more and more by his moral mission as an artist, and encouraged by Ruskin, looked longingly toward the Holy Land where, he was sure, he would find the true inspiration. Meanwhile he worked in

secret and alone, of his own faith striving to make a light
for the world.

Gabriel painted water colors, light-fused as jewels and as
rich.   He yearned for no Palestine out of London, for in his
studio at Red Lion Square, which he shared with Deverell,
lands of glory unfolded themselves before him.   Golden
ages played a pageantry in his mind, and out of them he
brought knights and princesses to visit him.   Damozels
soothed him with the music of airy instruments, twined themselves in living wreaths, combed out their rippling hair, held
him with the spell of their eyes.   Dante's Florence was the
land of his desire.   In twilit moments he saw himself the
poet, and one, a radiant girl, a more beautiful, because a
living, Beatrice.   No need of his traveling far for his inspiration.   It was there within a pace of his easel; he could
lean forward on the pretext of arranging a fold, and burn his
fingers with the warmth of the body beneath.   He had only
to lift his eyes, to shut them quickly from too great a beauty.

Christina, away with Maria on a short vacation, caught her
breath sharply as she read a note from Gabriel, unrestrained,
even for him, and she could not help fighting against a pang
of jealousy toward Elizabeth Siddal.   "Since you went
away I have had sent me . . . a lock of hair shorn from the
beloved head of that dear, and radiant as the tresses of
Aurora, a sight which may perhaps dazzle you. . . ."
Christina's hair was dark, a waveless brown, as undis-
tinguished as a lark's wing.   Gabriel had changed it to
gold in his paintings of her as Mary, Virgin; for the Pre-
Raphaelites preferred golden hair.

Perhaps the predilection had first been Gabriel's.   Even
before he had begun to put his dreams on canvas, he had
been haunted by the image of a girl of wonderful beauty,
lithe-limbed, with a long full throat and hair glancing in
motion as a sunlit sea.   Women's hair intoxicated him.
Chaste in his body as a Saint Anthony, he was more bitterly
tempted than the hermit by the devil of his own voluptuous

imagination. All the emotions of love and sorrow had been his by the time he was eighteen, not by those experiences which leave a youth ripe for life, but by the powers of a mind that lived more in itself than in the world. The cordial "stunners" who flirted with him in the restaurants got in return only good-hearted smiles and a show of gallantry. He was no more touched by them than if they had been the pretty animals he loved to watch at the Zoo. Amused, yes. But only his dream love kept him in tormented sleeplessness.

He knew her every feature. She was the maiden he had loved, whom death had taken away, and who now leaned out from the gold bar of Heaven with three lilies lying as if asleep along her bended arm and seven stars circling her hair, as

> . . . the souls mounting up to God
> Went by her like thin flames.

He could see her eyes, deeper than the depth of still waters, gazing upon him from her far height.

> Yet now, and in this place
> Surely she leaned o'er me — her hair
> Fell all about my face.

He knew it could not be. She was in Heaven, watching time "like a pulse shake fierce through all the worlds" as she waited for him and prayed for the day when she might ask of God the boon

> Only to live as once on earth
> With Love, — only to be,
> As then awhile, for ever now
> Together, I and he.[1]

In his imagination he had known with his love the sweets of daily living—the seclusion of a warm room

---

[1] "The Blessed Damozel" and other Rossetti poems that follow are quoted, except where indicated, from the *Collected Works*.

with the rain pelting the windowpane and they within, alone with their joy; the happiness of walks in a silent wood; they had tasted the freshness of living waters, and he had painted her portrait

> 'Mid mystic trees, where light falls in
> Hardly at all; a covert place
>   Where you might think to find a din
> Of doubtful talk, and a live flame
> Wandering, and many a shape whose name
>   Not itself knoweth, and old dew
>   And your own footsteps meeting you.

Your own footsteps meeting you . . . eerie foreshadowings of death. There was an old belief that when one met one's image face to face it betokened death. He had come upon instances of it in his wide reading: —

> Ere Babylon was dust,
> The Magus Zoroaster, my dead child,
> Met his own image walking in the garden.

Shelley . . . The weirdness of it stirred the hair of his body. By some inexplicable sense he felt he was fated to love and to be robbed by death. Always the motive of loss recurred, a tolling bell beneath the surface of his consciousness. He heard it there, trembled at the warning, but felt as helpless as the doomed mariner who sees in the dimness the phantom bark.

He heard of Elizabeth Eleanor Siddal one night while he was dining at Holman Hunt's. Suddenly the door flew open and Walter Deverell burst in upon them with the eyes of one who had seen Pan. It was several minutes before he ceased his excited walking to and fro, planted himself before them and cried: "What a stupendously beautiful creature I've found! Magnificently tall, with a lovely figure and stately neck and a face of the most delicate modeling. . . ."

Before they could say a word he gave all details in the painter's jargon; at one point Gabriel's pupils flashed with the inner lightning of recognition. "She has gray eyes and her hair is like dazzling copper, and it shimmers with light as she combs it down."

On and on Walter talked. The "beloved disciple" had made a signal discovery and he was anxious to have them share his enthusiasm. What Gabriel and Hunt gathered from his outpourings was that Elizabeth Siddal was not a professional model but a milliner's assistant. Walter had accompanied his mother to a bonnet shop in Cranbourne Alley; while she was choosing her headgear Walter, embarrassed and bored, had peered behind a screen at the sound of girls' voices; and then came the vision—the perfect Viola for his Shakespeare painting. "Not only Viola—she's all of Shakespeare's heroines rolled into one. Ophelia, Sylvia, Rosalind, Juliet. . . ."

Yes, but how was he going to get her to pose?

That was already settled, and he told of how he had given his mother no peace till she had gone back to the bonnet shop, talked to the girl, and had her promise to sit to him.

And Elizabeth Siddal became the favorite model of the brotherhood: Holman Hunt's Sylvia, Millais's drowning Ophelia, Dante Gabriel Rossetti's Beatrice—most of all, Dante's Beatrice.

Elizabeth was just seventeen when Deverell discovered her, a fairy creature imprisoned in the shoddy garishness of the cheap London shop. The brethren gasped when he brought her to the studios. It was not that she was beautiful in the accepted sense, with the classical features he had led them to believe she possessed. The oval of her face was a trifle too round, her nose a little large of nostril. Were they gray, her eyes, as Walter said? Not gray, but green, the green of the sea when the sky mixes with it, the shade of an emerald and a sapphire, if they could be merged without letting the sun through for that would have given a sparkle where there was none. The heavy lids cast a shadow over the orbs set wide apart. Yet even those rare moments when they looked straight out, they were dimmed by an invisible cloud. Was it shyness or the veil of adolescent wonder? Or some secret ill? The young painters looked at her critically. Yes, she would do, but her chief lure, especially for Gabriel, lay in the two great folds of red-gold hair which in the light framed her face in glory. All the brightness that was not in her eyes sparkled in that vigorous hair.

Elizabeth had nothing of the circle's culture, but she did have a willingness to learn, and the wisdom to listen in silence when the conversation floated far above her head. Painting and poetry which were the life of the group were wholly unknown to her but for Tennyson, some sheets of whose poems she had brought home wrapped round a pat of butter. However, the P.R.B.'s could overlook anything for beauty's sake, and Elizabeth had enough of it to justify their willing blindness. Besides, she was young and quick and eager to become their equal.

The opportunities for her at home had been scant, her father, a Sheffield cutler, earning hardly enough to support his family; and that little, with what the children brought in, he sank in endless suits to reclaim some obscure title: Jarndyce and Jarndyce in real life. One of the children was "an innocent," and thus a double burden. Only her sister Lydia was sufficiently interested to find out who were these queer artists who had adopted Lizzie. She had none of the young girl's beauty, so the brethren merely dubbed her "the Roman" and tolerated her for Elizabeth's sake. Neither of the girls had had much schooling. Elizabeth, however, could read well, spoke with wit and intelligence, though with a slight, self-conscious sibilance, and wrote without disregard to spelling—to the relief of the punctilious William Michael.

Before long she became Gabriel's exclusive model. More

Ophelia

BY J. E. MILLAIS, P.R.B.

(Posed by Elizabeth Siddal)

aware of her latent talents than the others had been, he spent hours guiding first her pencil, gradually her brush. As he leaned over her shimmering copper hair in heavy wings about her face, and closed his hand over her fingers, he learned as much as he taught—learned that here was a damozel of flesh and blood whose hair was more fragrant than the flowers of his imagined pleasances, whose hand, warmer than the touch of dreams, set the pulses beating at his temples, whose changing blue-gray eyes were now stiller than still waters of evening, now coruscating with meanings he trembled to read.

Elizabeth studied, posed, and made progress. Her little drawings, which, reflecting Gabriel's with the naïve and un-developed likeness of child to parent, possessed, besides, a freshness of invention, filled him with wonder. Too, like all who came in contact with him, she began to write poetry. In the half-dream wherein master and pupil shut themselves, the months glided imperceptibly into years.

Madox Brown, living in disappointed seclusion, received Gabriel's confidences. "I knew from the moment I met her that my destiny was defined." Christina knew it, too. Since the appearance of that star, her own light was dimmed. Her brother no longer asked her to sit to him, nor the others, either. Little by little she withdrew into herself and her writing. Gabriel, who had given her a taste of the world, had now taken it from her; the delight, so soon turned to bitterness, was still fresh in her memory.

Sometimes her youth protested against the nunlike rigor of her living. Others were joying in life—why should not she? On learning that Elizabeth was painting, she became ambitious to surpass her. For several months she attended a night art class of which Brown was master. Painstakingly she copied the wood shavings the students had as models before them. At home she tried to do portraits. Instead of encouraging, Gabriel twitted: "Take care not to rival the Sid, but keep within respectful limits . . ." She

gave up the school and exercised her bent only to paint
borders about fair copies of her poems, and sometimes to
color sprigs on notepaper at one shilling per sheet, "for
the good of the house." She hardly went out now except
with her mother and Maria. Her clothes were getting
shabby, though she kept them so well; but, with the Professor too ill to work, it was no time for vanity. Still, she
winced when Gabriel boasted with a lover's inconsiderate
pride: "Lizzie has lately made herself a gray dress, also
a black silk one, the first bringing out her characteristic as
a meek unconscious dove while the second enhances her
qualifications as a *rara avis in terris.*" Christina had no
skill with the needle. With the income from her poetry
amounting at best to ten pounds a year, neither had she
the means to indulge her elegance. Unconscious dove—
rara avis — none of these was she, but only a dun little
pew-opener.

She could have wished, however, to see more of her
brother, whose ways had grown extremely secretive. For
a while William alone knew where to find him, and then
only to be relieved of all available "tin." Christina guessed
the reason for his aloofness; sometimes she grew petulant
with William for his connivance. "If his whereabouts is to
be kept secret, pray do *not* let me have his address."

Other things about Gabriel the family could only surmise. He was having a hard time as a professonal artist,
especially since he was now recognized as a dangerous
iconoclast. The painting on which he had built all hopes
of financial plenty came back from the gallery unsold; he
had to pay for his studio, buy colors, and get enough to eat.
Money was not forthcoming except from William's lean
pockets and in the form of loans from Madox Brown, who
could ill afford to play banker. Moreover, Gabriel was in
love, with growing ambitions and an increased appetite.
Desperate with failure and the scorn with which his "Catholic
Art" had been dismissed by the reviewers, afraid besides of

not cutting a provident figure as a lover, he set out one day to offer his services to the North Western Railway as telegraph operator, knowing as much about telegraphy as a good navvy knows about art. One of the employees explained the instrument with its intricate keys and symbols, while the applicant stood by politely. The demonstration over, Gabriel thanked him kindly, and went as fast as he could go; while, unheard of him, the guardian angels of a million railway passengers thanked the Lord and followed his receding steps with eyes of gratitude. Never again did Gabriel attempt to enter the lists as a wage earner.

Then unexpected help came. Brown's patron, Mac-Cracken, was so struck by the contrast between Pre-Raphaelite art and the mileage of canvas at the exhibitions that he purchased as many of their works as he could afford, among them the "Annunciation" — long become to Gabriel "the blessed white daub" and "the blessed white eyesore," for its insistence on remaining with him. Gladly he bade good-bye to it, and also to "sacred" subjects, though he had it to thank for providing the wherewithal for Lizzie's "unconscious dove" dress and the black silk.

Gabriel was not a patient worker — rather, since he was not content with anything short of perfection, and perfection required time, he began ambitious subjects only to lay them aside. Now, with Lizzie to draw from, he drugged his senses by capturing one lovely aspect after another, letting the work of painting wait. Occasionally, he finished a water color to keep the wolf from the gate of his paradise.

"His head and beard grow finer every day," wrote old Bruno to a P.R. friend in Rome, "and he has made some designs which are perfectly divine . . . but paint he *will not*. He is too idle." His own industry made Brown notice the more Gabriel's apparent laziness. Again he wrote to his friend, drawing up a list, "Pictures commenced and put by: Madox Brown 2, Hunt 3, Millais 2, Rossetti (the put by is for Rossetti) 6. Got abused in the papers, everyone including Millais and Rossetti, although the latter very unjustly, seeing that he has done *nothing* to merit it."

Meanwhile Woolner's chops turned out tougher than he could stomach, as his letters proved, groaning with nostalgia and desperation from that topsy-turvy country "where trees shed their bark instead of leaves and cherries grow with their stones outside." Together with his mining, however, he had managed to work up a little art business to make ends meet, by executing portraits of the Australian gentry, and the better to impress his patrons with his importance, he asked the brethren for tangible testimonials that he was of their persuasion, "since your names appear so often in the homepapers." Besides, he was pining for a sight of them if only in effigy.

One morning, therefore, the "Pre-Raffs" gathered at Millais's studio and sat to each other — Millais drawing William Michael and Stephens; Hunt, Millais and Gabriel; while Gabriel began to make a leisurely masterpiece of Hunt. Twilight fell, and still Gabriel was drawing the wilting Hunt. Finally, the picture had to be sent to Woolner, unfinished as it was.

"It makes me look at least twenty years older," complained Hunt.

"It's very like Rush, the murderer," commented William Michael.

VII

VARYING FORTUNES

AFTER Ruskin had written to the *Times* defending the
Pre-Raphaelites, he was not satisfied that he had done
enough. Here, within his day, was a group of young men
—mere boys—working out the principles of art he had
been laying down since 1843, himself then a youth hardly
older than they were now. Perhaps a spark of his own
fire had caught and thrived in their eager minds; perhaps the
same forces that had influenced him had wrought their
miracle in them. Certainly a new and wonderful spirit was
blowing as a wind across British art, quickening something
that had long lain fallow. John Ruskin was not the man to
let the wonder pass without hosannas and uplifted arms.
His praise grew in size and volume and took the form of a
pamphlet.

Championship from so eminent a man came not without
its fruit. Ruskin had considerable power. Besides his pen,
which he wielded as foil and sceptre, he had wealth which
could speak with persuasive tongue to ears too gross for his
message. He had, moreover, a wide circle of influential
connections who relied entirely upon his judgment. An
object had only to be praised by Ruskin to win admiration,
and, in the case of art, a purchaser. Nevertheless, there
were critics too long in the harness to have anything but
kicks for the new freedom. Others, proud of their independent thinking, preferred mulishness to justice. Still
others sincerely mistrusted innovation and grazed comfortably in the old pastures. Criticism, however, changed

in tone—and in what touched Millais, A.R.A., became even respectful. Ruskin's defense had at least one important result, in that it assured the brotherhood of an income sufficient to make the youths persevere. Not that they ever had more than the scattered fruits of plenty.

There were times when to the dejected Hunt almost anything seemed better than continuing in a thankless pursuit. Desperate thoughts then came to him of learning farming and cattle-raising from his yeoman uncle, and going off to Canada as a settler. There, away from the petty jealousies that grudged him even his well-earned triumphs,—the Liverpool prize, Ruskin's praise,—he would fulfill himself in an honest, toilful life, his hours of rest sweetened by a wife and young ones whose portraits, painted by his calloused hand, would line the walls of the backwoods cabin. But in a moment he opened his eyes to a brighter light, beckoning as a star toward Palestine.

Millais had neither the fits of dejection nor the visions. If not born with a silver spoon in his mouth, it was with the seal of assured success. He was one of those destined to walk as gods over the earth, with a god's triumphs and a little of pagan nonchalance. "Millais's luck" became a byword. Remarkably handsome, with a fine head,—"of an angel," Gabriel said,—he won friends by his presence alone. No disappointments, no harsh struggles had embittered his youth, therefore he was genial, expansive, charming. Therefore, also, he lacked depth and thoughtfulness: in the power of profound thinking he was Hunt's antithesis. Impulse came easier to him than reflection, a quality which in his painting already showed itself in a dangerous facility. Then, too, his feet hugged the ground too close for his head, like Gabriel's, to be lost in the clouds. Of the group, he possessed least imagination and most realism, in his case a virtue rather than a weakness, for what he lacked in poetry he more than made up for by the vividness of his renderings. This realization of fact in even the most Pre-Raphaelite of his works brought him nearer to his public and won him popularity where his friends were still fighting for recognition.

John Ruskin and he soon became friends, though Millais had his views about art which did not always conform to those laid down in *Modern Painters*—a book he would not read. Nevertheless, to the older man he was a disciple whose fostering would help bring nearer the wonderful rebirth of art. Ruskin introduced him to wealthy buyers, preached to him, brought him home to his wife and parents, and gave him commissions. And then he invited the handsome Pre-Raphaelite to accompany him and Euphemia on a trip to Scotland.

Though the first few weeks were marred by incessant rains, there were still plenty of amusements. The young people were often alone, reading together and romping about in impromptu battledore and shuttlecock, while Ruskin, in the seclusion of an improvised workroom, studied the specimens of gneiss he had collected for his Edinburgh lectures. At last the weather cleared, and, the countryside offering itself in all the freshness of rain-and-sun-washed landscape, the recluses emerged.

Millais loved the outdoors with both a painter's and a sportsman's love. After hours of pedestrian exploring,—with Ruskin bending down to worship the upturning of a flower's face, and Euphemia, less reverent, gathering armfuls of bright-colored blossoms, herself brighter in the eyes of Millais than anything that grew,—the easel was set up, and he painted while Ruskin read or talked.

Everything, from the infinitesimal of a grain of pollen to the infinitude of a heaven in the sister glories of rising and setting, stirred in Ruskin springs of appreciation arid toward Euphemia. Enjoyment for him was not solely of the senses. The curling of a tendril, the purple of a thistle in its nest of metallic leaves, a lark's song, a rose's breath—they were all symbols to be enriched by the associations of a wide culture. Too, they were mirrors, to flash in un-awakened eyes, of the light that says, "Arise, it is day."

Euphemia sat for her portrait, and that done, for the woman in Millais's next Academy picture, "The Order of Release." Ruskin, grateful that his wife did her share toward bringing the dawn still nearer, failed to notice the gathering clouds. Then he, too, stood for his portrait, a sensitive-faced seer on a bit of worn rock, against a water-fall and darkling crags. His long coat, close-buttoned, fell as if it wrapped a shadow, so spare was he. In his left hand he held his hat, removed, maybe, that he might feel the wind of the rising storm; his right hand, leaning on a rough staff, admonished — was it Euphemia, whose laughter drowned some sweeter music? Down the stream he gazed, perhaps at some delicate water weed, swaying its anchored stalk to the tumult of the waters. "Just the sort of thing I used to do for hours together," he wrote his parents.

Mr. Ruskin nodded, pleased. Margaret scowled and held her peace, sensing mischief in this Scottish excursion.

It descended upon her son sooner than she anticipated. The idyll over, Euphemia, restored to the dullness of domestic life, packed her traveling trunk with sudden decision and took the train to her parents. No persuasion availed to make her return to her husband, though, in truth, he exerted himself not a jot more than was in keeping with decency. He had entered into the marriage without en-thusiasm; how was he now to show sorrow at what promised to be its end? The happiness of a common hearth had never been his with Euphemia; they had shared but little warmth. No lover of the fireside, she longed for the gas-light of the drawing-room, lured by a life she knew to be her rightful one. She had often gone out alone while he either worked in his study or suffered his mother to en-tertain him. Euphemia had always felt superfluous in his life, engulfed as it was by art and Margaret. Moreover, she had been shown her place early on their wedding trip, when he caught a chill sketching in the dampness of Salisbury cathedral; immediately he was ordered to Normandy, Margaret Ruskin taking the reins in her hard hands, and the faithful Anne following orders punctiliously and without question. It had been a nightmare for him, that weird, unconsummated honeymoon with a woman he could not love; his sickness came to him as a relief, and who knows how grateful he was to that body which, of weaker fibre than his will, could thus purchase him temporary freedom? Euphemia, through it all, decked herself in the clothes and jewelry provided by her husband, and found amusement where she could. Society finally became accustomed to seeing her without her husband. "Where is Mr. Ruskin?" a gentleman asked one night. "Oh, Mr. Ruskin? He is with his mother . . . he ought to have married his mother."

Sometimes, it may be, Ruskin had been troubled about the rightness of his holding so brilliant a creature, no more suited to his austere living than a butterfly. But he readily forgot his scruples in his work.

Shortly after she had returned to her parents, Euphemia brought a suit for nullity against her husband. He did not defend it: the union was dissolved.

After the publication of his *Notes on the Construction of Sheepfolds*, in which he made a fervent appeal for Christian unity, Ruskin became more deeply immersed in social questions. Nothing daunted that his address met with more of a sale among Cumberland farmers, who hoped to find in it valuable hints for improving their stock, than among the Christians for whom it was intended, he persevered in his propaganda, convinced that man, once educated out of his darkness, can be made to see the light. Herein he had a fervent associate in Frederick Denison Maurice.

For a number of years England's working classes had been looking for spiritual and material guidance toward Maurice, conspicuous in a movement opposing the stress on ritual and dogma of the preceding Tractarian generation. High Anglicanism unaided was not going to bring about the ideal society. Man does not live by bread alone, he granted with Kingsley and Arnold the elder, but without his daily bread and the facility for obtaining it, he cannot live at all. Maurice possessed two factors toward popular appeal, the gift of tongues and the recently acquired crown of a small martyrdom. Whenever he preached, he swayed the crowds as the wind sways the sea, and with the same effect of unrest. Nevertheless, since he offered bread as well as words, he had succeeded, little by little, in converting that unrest to a desire for self-betterment. In 1854, after losing his chair of divinity as well as his professorship because his published works had offended the established orthodoxy, he cast about for some activity to make that loss a gain. Half a dozen years before he had helped to found a school for the education of woman. Now he would create one for the workingman. And so, with the help of Ruskin, Kingsley, and Furnivall, the Working Men's College opened its doors at Great Ormond Street to teach the laborer art and Christian living.

Meanwhile the Pre-Raphaelites, no longer working as a body, were engaged in pursuing their individual fortunes. Woolner, finding the gold-pans of Australia could be emptier than his kettles at home, decided that after all the sculptor's chisel was pleasanter to his hand than the miner's tools, and, packing his dwindled goods, took boat for home. Galled rather than chastened, he fumed against the ministry and the aristocracy and men with handles to their names, "all devastators of the day, maggots in the wounds of us poor devils who have to fight the battle of life!" Stephens, of more temperate eloquence, taught the public what was Pre-Raphaelite and therefore to be admired. Hunt had left for the Holy Land, pursuing a vision that had haunted him.

Further still had voyaged Walter Deverell. His body, too weak for his spirit, fell prey to consumption. For

months he had lingered between life and death, not knowing that the doctors had given up hope. In his wretched
lodgings he had none to take care of him but his young
sisters, one of them a paralytic child of eight. A curse
had seemed to follow the family. First his mother had
died, and then his father, a learned but improvident man
who, bigoted in his atheism as others were in their faith, had
brought up his children to ridicule all religion. Walter
believed in nothing. What consolation another might have
had, was denied him — indeed, neither the pleas of the
churchgoing Millais nor the exhortations of Hunt had
converted him. He was tormented only about the fate of
the orphaned brood dependent upon him. The brethren,
without saying a word to him, made a collection among
themselves and sent in a stranger to buy his last picture,
relieving him for the nonce of financial worries. To the
last, Millais left his easel to stay at his bedside; Rossetti
amused him with fantastic stories. Then the unbelieving
youth, whom the gods loved, was taken away, leaving behind the first buds of a talent never to come to flower.

In the Rossetti household, lately removed to Upper
Albany Street, death had also paid a visit, when the old
Professor, long ailing, closed his eyes at last, leaving William
as the sole provider. Life at Upper Albany Street resumed
its quiet tenor, susurrous with prayer. Only now and again
when Gabriel paid his dutiful respects was there a flutter
of unusual life. Once, late in their acquaintance, he brought
Elizabeth with him. The women eyed her critically, dwelling on her flushed cheeks and thin, pale hands. They were
not pleased. They had heard from William, corroborated
by others, that the girl was ailing with a mortal illness;
ever since Gabriel had met her he had been spending what
little he earned sending her away for her health.

Christina, gently caustic, had let her brother know how
she felt about his Guggum, as he called her. The family
had thought, had hoped, indeed, that with his genius he

would have done better than to fall in love with a milliner's assistant. Perhaps Christina may have said more than was in keeping with sisterly solicitude; at any rate, for months after her meeting with Elizabeth the relations between her and Gabriel continued extremely frigid.

However the Rossettis may have felt, Lizzie had staunch admirers in the Browns. Emma, more than sister, was her bosom friend, so much so that Gabriel, jealous of men and women alike, and suspicious of feminine confabulations, turned unreasonably against her, afraid that she was making Guggum discontented with him. Lover's fears, yet in him founded on a sense of guilt. He had known Lizzie long enough for decisive action; their engagement had for more than two years been taken for granted; nevertheless they were no nearer marriage than at their first meeting. Little by little, in growing humiliation, Elizabeth resented its being mentioned. Shut in by a morbid sensitiveness, she took as a personal slight the cleverness of Gabriel's friends and found refuge in moods of silence out of which she watched him with the suspicion of her wounded soul. Every new friend was an enemy to her security, and, as Madox Brown wrote in his diary, she grew "thinner and more deathlike and more beautiful and more ragged than ever."

Sometimes Gabriel persuaded himself that his Bohemian life and the incertitude of his livelihood were the only arguments against an immediate marriage. Still, Lizzie was sharing greater hardships with him now, and he had to admit he was trifling with his conscience.

She was no longer his only model. A new quality had entered his work, less spiritual, if more real, which made him set aside his mediævalisms for the harsher aspects of contemporary life. Anxiously Lizzie watched the change, and more anxiously still the frequent appearance of Fanny Cornforth in his studio. It was not that she doubted Gabriel's love. He had proved it to her in tenderness and sacrifice, in the unselfishness with which he abandoned every-

BEATA BEATRIX

BY D. G. ROSSETTI, P.R.B.

(Posed by Elizabeth Siddal)

thing to nurse her in her recurring illnesses. Fanny Cornforth was exuberantly healthy, and Gabriel was a worshiper
of physical well-being. His artist's eye missed no beauty
in man or woman. Neither did Lizzie miss a flicker of his
enthusiasm. Time was when she would not have ventured
to doubt that his "Jenny" was only the fruit of a poet's
imaginings. But now, in the fullness of his manhood, would
he remain night long beside a beautiful girl and leave her
with, "Only a kiss. Good-bye, my dear"? Gabriel's mouth
was sensual under his light moustache. Elizabeth thought
of the brimming health of Fanny and was sad.

Nor was Gabriel happy. He had begun by loving
Elizabeth with a controlled love that made her the more
desirable for being the unattainable Beatrice. In his pictures
and poems she appeared as the elect of his soul, a being
marked with the poetic melancholy of unfulfillment. That
sublimation of passion, however, had been possible only because the body had maintained its chastity; for the influence
of Mrs. Rossetti, always dominant in her children, ruled
Gabriel's life long after he had broken away from home.
Over his mind it had had no ascendancy. Now his body
was claiming the satisfaction of his passionate nature, and,
no longer content with Psyche, desired Astarte.

In reality, Lizzie had never been unattainable except
in so far as it had pleased Gabriel's ideal. Fortunately, for
his art—since only by surrounding flesh with the nimbus
of spirit had he been able to create the impelling illusion.
In time he came to look upon her as a flesh-and-blood
creature and his passion was roused. There were no
obstacles of social position or religion to overcome. Lizzie,
if she had had convictions, had sunk them all in the depth
of her adoration for him, and from the time she became his
pupil, she also became identified with himself. The altered
relations wrought the expected change in him. Freed of
its constraining armor, the body exulted: the obverse of the
mediæval miracle took place. Where Pan put on a gown

and cowl and became Saint Satyr, the saint threw off his hairshirt and rediscovered the ancient pagan joy.

Lizzie, alas, was not always able to share it.   Now, when he desired her, she became unattainable by her mysterious malady.   Nobody knew what it was.   At first it had been attributed to overwork.   Again, the Browns thought her posing for long hours in a tub of water for Millais's Ophelia might have undermined her health.   There was also a superstition current among artists that anyone posing near or in water was doomed to early death; but neither Millais, in his zeal for realism, nor Lizzie herself, had thought anything of it.

The physicians had pronounced her ailment phthisis — how common it was among the young girls of those days! But Dr. Acland, Ruskin's Oxford friend, had found her lungs so little affected as to be nearly sound, and attributed her exhaustion rather to a creative energy long pent up and then suddenly overtaxed.   Ruskin, who had lately become Gabriel's patron, was ready with money and advice to help, as much for her sake as for the art she adorned.   She was invited with Gabriel to Denmark Hill, Camberwell, where Margaret cornered her and was grimly solicitous. "My mother has much medical knowledge," Ruskin imparted to Gabriel.   The lovely garden was placed at Lizzie's disposal, Ruskin assuring her that sunlight and the sight of growing things would restore her to health.   Quantities of ivory dust, said to be good for such cases as hers, were sent to the Blackfriars studio to be converted into jelly, and pieces of opal for Gabriel, that he might look at them through a magnifying glass and be cheered by their dancing lights.   Old Mr. Ruskin, impressed by his son's newly discovered "noble, glorious creature," shut an eye upon his extravagance and himself encouraged the buying of her water colors.   "To look at her she might have been born a countess," he remarked, to which, "Yes, George Fourth!" exclaimed mentally the irreverent Gabriel.   And so Lizzie became Ida, the Princess, in the family circle of Denmark Hill.

"You paint most beautifully when you paint from Ida," said Ruskin to Gabriel, engaged at the time on his modern picture of the fallen woman for which Fanny was posing — scarcely a theme or a model to appeal to the moralist. "I have naturally a great dread of subjects altogether painful," he explained. "I can be happy in thinking of Mary Magdalene, but am merely in pain when I think of 'Found.'"

Gabriel had chosen to portray the tragedy at its peak. A country girl, broken by the vice of the city, is crouching against a cemetery wall in the gray light of dawn, when she is recognized by her childhood lover, who is passing by leading a calf—symbol of the victim—in a cart to market. Vainly the girl tries to hide her face from him in shame; she has been found by the one man who would have had her pure.

Nature had been lavish in dispensing a voluptuous beauty to Fanny. In the lustre of eye and curve of lip, the whiteness of throat and breast, the full, firm moulding of thigh and limb, she was magnificent; and she knew as well, perhaps better than "Jenny," how to take advantage of her fairness. Married as she was to a drunkard, chastity would have served not at all to get her the pretty baubles with which, as needlessly as they would have decked a statue, she adorned her gorgeous body. Unspiritual as Lizzie was unworldly, she exuded passion. In her delicately rounded cheeks — for nature had given her grace as well as strength — the blood glowed with a flush that became vermilion in her lips. Her hands were soft and plump, and could grasp a man's hand strongly. And she was generous.

Gabriel had met her in the Strand, where she was cracking nuts with her teeth, scattering the shells about. Astonished at such cockney informality in one with the face of a goddess, he stared.   Her hair, golden where Lizzie's was red, spread in a sunlit cloud about her face, and as she turned, he could see the great knot of it gathered at the nape of her neck.   Unpinned, it might have covered her in a rippling cloth of gold. . . .   The girl caught his amazement, and, with a laugh, she pelted him with shells.   Encouraged by her hoydenish boldness,—he had lived so long with the Damozel's sanctities,—he went up to her and soon had her promise to sit to him.

Good old Bruno had no peace while Gabriel was working at his modern painting.   Not finding at Blackfriars the accessories for the background, though he did have the bridge, Gabriel packed up easel and paints and withdrew to Finchley, sharing Brown's hospitality as well as the Hampstead scenery.   It was no sinecure having him as guest. Brown, with his steady habits of work, recorded in hours and minutes at the end of the day, complained, "Rossetti . . . staying with me, keeping me up till 4 A.M., painting sometimes all night, making the whole place miserable . . . translating sonnets at breakfast, working very hard and doing nothing . . . I am to get him a white calf and cart to paint here; would he but study the *golden one* a little more.

"Gabriel gone to town to see Miss Siddal.   Getting on slowly with his calf.   He paints it in all like Albert Dürer, hair by hair . . . and all the time he wearing my greatcoat, which I want, and a pair of my breeches, besides food and an unlimited supply of turpentine . . . Emma within a week or two of her confinement, and he having had his bed made on the floor in the parlor."

Unsuccess had been steadily pursuing Brown.   Endowed with a fearless candor, supported by an unpliable backbone, he had succeeded in making a host of powerful enemies, especially at the Royal Academy where his pictures, when not rejected, were shamefully hung.   The climax came when his "Christ Washing Peter's Feet" was hid out of sight near the ceiling while Slosh triumphed on the line. On the opening day, when the President had come to offer his formal congratulations, Brown, fuming with indignation, turned his back and left the hall without a word, vowing inwardly never again to exhibit at the Academy, which became in his mind the very pit of the devil.

Where weaker men would have given up the struggle, he was pricked to intenser labor. How often had he dreamed of starting somewhere anew with Emma and the children! As on the day he had watched the ship bearing Woolner away, he had seen himself and Emma at the stern, emigrants sadly looking their last on a land that had been home. The water was frothing with wind, and their flesh was blue with the chill of winter. Wrapped in Emma's mantle, their infant child clasped its mother's fingers as she clutched her husband's hand for security. It was a haunting vision. To act upon it would have meant defeat. Therefore he expressed the sadness of his soul in the noblest way he knew: on canvas, in "The Last of England."

The year 1854, that of Sir Joseph Paxton's palace of crystal and iron, began auspiciously for the Pre-Raphaelites. Before setting out for the Holy Land, Holman Hunt had completed for the Royal Academy exhibition two paintings, one of which was destined to stir all England. He had begun it in 1851 when, with Millais and Charlie Collins, he had taken lodgings at Worcester Park farm to paint directly from nature. Collins had professed himself a Pre-Raphaelite by a picture portraying a nun musing on love in a convent close—a painting which Ruskin had praised, for, among other things, the fine drawing of a water plant. At that time, wishing to shake off a love that "had hipped him," Collins had turned to High Church mysticism, causing his friends no little worry. They had work of their own, however, and left him to his brooding while they went their separate ways to garner what natural wealth they could from the ripening autumn. There Hunt made the preparations for his ambitious religious painting which required the background of an abandoned, weed-grown orchard and a barred door, lighted by a lantern. For the effects he could work only at night, outdoors, by the flame of a candle. He went out, accordingly, after his two companions had retired, and worked until the first glimmerings of sunrise told him it was time to cease. The dark cold cramped his limbs; as a protection against it he had a sentry box of hurdles built, and, with his feet buried in a sack of straw, painted till winter made further work impossible. For three years he labored, assailed by doubts yet spurred on by an inner confidence, now working outdoors, now painting at the figure in his studio. Months before the opening of the Academy he scarcely slept at night, to the discomfiture of the local policeman, who eyed suspiciously the shining cracks round the darkened windows, and clasped his stick in self-defense each time a queer fellow with a lantern came down into the street and stood watching —maybe—the knots on the door. A "batty hartist," he was sure, and as such, best let alone.

Several times Mrs. Rossetti had come on mysterious visits, accompanying Christina; then, after remaining a few hours in the studio, as mysteriously had left. William, who knew, could have told that Christina was lending her sorrowful eyes for the face of the Saviour in Hunt's "Light of the World."

Ruskin stood in awe before it at the Royal Academy. Long he studied the white-clad Christ, carrying a lantern which threw its light, the light of conscience, upon a fast-barred door overgrown with weeds—the human soul. Among the grasses an apple, token of hereditary sin, had fallen from a tree. It was the very subject to move Ruskin profoundly. He remained at the Academy, watching its effect upon the people. Many sneered at it as a Pre-Raphaelite work. Others scoffed at the representation of the Saviour like a Diogenes with a lantern. Few understood it. He went home and wrote another letter to the *Times*, interpreting the symbolism, extolling the technique. "I believe there are very few persons on whom the picture, thus justly understood, will not produce a deep impression. For my own part, I think it one of the very noblest works of sacred art ever produced in this or any other age."

"Just like Ruskin, the incarnation of exaggeration," grumbled Brown. As it was, the painting was reproduced in great numbers, finding its way into the homes and faith in the remotest corners of the Christian world.

The exhibition pointed at yet another triumph. Nearly half the walls were covered over by imitators of the Pre-Raphaelites.

VIII

RUSKIN AND THE LOVERS

Those who knew Ruskin and Gabriel wondered how long their friendship would last; and with reason, for never were two men less framed by nature to be elective affinities. Madox Brown watched with his tongue in his cheek, grinning at every proof of Ruskin's affection, or grunting his pleasure at Gabriel's ability to work toward his own advantage — and, of course, his friends'. Indeed, no sooner did a new hope present himself, than Gabriel, after striking his own bargain, brought him, enwhirled in a wind of speech, to the home of his neediest brother. The patron would scarcely be over his wonder before he found himself driving home in a four-wheeler — with a lighter check book, and new portable property on the seat beside him.

Gabriel had already tried to enlist his new friend in a number of causes. Charles Bagot Cayley, an old student of Professor Rossetti's, had just published a translation of Dante. Promptly, Gabriel wrote to Ruskin. Would he read it and give his opinion? The eminent critic read, but he could not give any judgment that would have sent the public flocking to the booksellers'. "I think Mr. Cayley has failed simply by endeavoring the impossible," he pronounced. "You call this a literal translation. I open it at random, and I come upon the reading of the exquisite *Come i gru* . . . Now observe — 'And as the cranes, chanting their lays, *do* fly.' This '*do* fly' is bad English. . . . I write this for *you* only, because I think your taste is as yet unformed in verse." A reply not couched in a manner to soothe.   But if there was anything Ruskin valued above friendship, it was intellectual honesty.   An opinion with him had the force of an oath sworn before God.   Sometimes he feared he sinned on the side of harshness, and then he sought to justify himself with touching candor.   "I am very self-indulgent, very proud, very obstinate, and *very* resentful; on the other side, I am . . . nearly as just as I suppose it is possible for man to be in this world — exceedingly fond of making people happy, and devotedly reverent to all true mental and moral power."   He did not see the mental power in Cayley; and therefore, even at the cost of Gabriel's displeasure, he could not praise.

Happily, Cayley was too far removed from the life about him to take either praise or blame with anything but a nearsighted scholar's stare.   His world was bound for him between the covers of a book; a room with well-stocked shelves was the universe itself, out of which he scarcely ventured without dread of cataclysm.   Before Professor Rossetti's death, he sometimes visited at Charlotte Street, pored with him over some old book, and later, in the sitting room, spilled tea over his shirt front as he watched Christina work at her worsted.   He had known her as a budding girl; now she was a woman.   In the lamplight, he would stare at the shining path the glow made on her smooth hair; in his room, the bars of light repeated themselves between his eyes and the book.   He would rub his spectacles; and when he put them on again, all but the printed lines had vanished.

Nobody had seen much of him while he was engaged in his translation.   But when the chaos of sheets had found order between book covers, he was visible in the world again, shyer and more myopic than ever.   His face wore a lost, abstract look, which concentrated itself with startling intentness whenever anything interested him, as if through an effort of will he suddenly called back his soul.   No wonder Madox Brown, after a visit at Gabriel's, recorded,

"Heat intense and lots of strawberries. I forgot Cayley who looks mad and is always in a rumpled shirt, without collar, and an old tail coat."

Indeed, Cayley could never have been held up as a model of elegance and deportment even by one less respectful of the world's good opinion than Brown. The scholar's costume, however, shabby and outmoded though it was, sorted well with the intellectual cast and furtive humor of his face —an ingenuous humor that kept the corners of his mouth smiling and his eyes intermittently flashing as at a blithe something known only to himself. He had little enough, certainly, to rejoice him in practical matters. Until recently, he had fulfilled, as scrupulously as his scholarly habit would allow, his duties at the Chancery Lane Patent Office; then a farseeing friend had persuaded him to invest his capital in an enterprise for adorning railway stations with advertisement posters. In less time than it takes a shark to gulp down its prey, Cayley's funds had been swallowed by the scheme. The friend had seen too far ahead; Cayley, not far enough. He had now only his scholar's hands and his scholar's mind to help him through a bewildering life.

In Brown's case Gabriel's efforts to swing Ruskin thitherward had been equally unsuccessful. With his cantankerous antipathy toward anything authoritarian, Brown responded with scarcely more than a growl toward the critic. Ruskin, equally cantankerous, made chill overtures. Brown's work, with its striving for fidelity, sometimes at the cost of beauty, left him cold, and he made no attempt to conceal his feeling. Friction and fireworks, therefore, were expected when, the day after the strawberry and Cayley party, Ruskin came to Chatham Place where Brown, in shirt sleeves, was smoking a comfortable pipe.

"There, while I go on smoking," Brown was fond of repeating, "he talks divers nonsense about art hurriedly in shrill, flippant tones. I answer him civilly, then resume my coat and prepare to leave. Suddenly he says, 'Mr.

Brown, will you tell me why you chose such a very ugly subject for your last picture?' I, dumbfoundered at such a beginning and satisfied that he intended impertinence since he had *praised* the subject to Gabriel a few days before, replied, 'Because it lay out of a back window,' and turning on my heel, took my hat and wished Gabriel good-bye.''

Turning on his heel was Brown's reply to whatever ruffled him. Not for him to hang on anyone's skirts for rightful recognition, nor was Ruskin one to take affront lightly. Consequently, the discord of their first interview resolved itself into no harmony as they saw more of each other.

The family circle of Upper Albany Street was soon brought to Ruskin's acquaintance. William and Maria were invited to dine at Denmark Hill, where the covers were taken off the paintings in their honor, and the garden thrown open. Ruskin even went out of his way to get William an additional post as art correspondent on Stillman's American paper, the *Crayon,* and found him remunerative odd jobs to do. He was so kind, indeed, that Maria's obdurately sainted heart was touched with human affection. Many a night his name was in her prayers. By day, when he came to Upper Albany Street, she tied a lavender ribbon round the neck of her holiday fichu. Ruskin, gentlemanly courteous, was entirely unaware of the flutterings his presence roused in her breast, so that whatever hope had there been awakened was stilled again: after death, perhaps, the chrysalis would wing a happy flight in heaven. Meanwhile plain Maria tried not to speculate on what might have been, and assured Christina that love on earth is only a brief foretaste of the bliss in eternity. For the sake of that bliss she kept herself pure and acted only according to God's word. No unholy thing was suffered to offend her sight, nor would she hearken to the voice of temptation. So fixed did she become in her ideal of holiness that when she was shown Blake's prints from the Book of Job she shut her eyes in horror at a work that went counter to the Second Commandment. No persuasion in the world would make her enter the mummy room of the British Museum, fearful that the Resurrection might take place while she was gazing at those "solemn corpses." Christina looked up to her sister and was edified, storing such little examples in her mind as stepping-stones still to mount in her own salvation.

Ruskin did not respond to Christina. The quiet, self-possessed young woman who insisted upon being taken as she was disconcerted him. She was dark—he preferred the fair in women; she laughed but seldom, and he was then in need of gayety. Since Euphemia's suit, the world had found much to roll on the tongue of gossip—whether true or not deprived it of none of its tang. He was rumored an eccentric, a Bluebeard, impotent and a satyr at once; and because he said no word in self-defense, the absurdest of lies found credence. Even his interest in the workingman was misunderstood. Goaded by insult, he would have taken the sphere of his philanthropies and, a wrathful demiurge, flung it into chaos; his mother's teachings and his father's uprightness deterred him. Then, too, his love of man, in man's despite, was a need to fill the void of his companionless life.

Elizabeth attracted him because she was young, unworldly, in need of protection, and—unhappy. He realized her unhappiness from the moment he was aware of the extent of her love for Gabriel. He, too, loved Gabriel, as everyone did who came in contact with his vivid personality. Therein lay the root of her unhappiness. Ruskin had learned of the long engagement. He had seen Lizzie's eyes downcast with fear of what she might read in Gabriel's whenever Fanny Cornforth or some new model came into the room. She was jealous because she was not sure of him. For that matter, Gabriel, in his reckless expansiveness, sometimes did not seem sure of himself. And yet he professed to adore Lizzie. Again, since the early days of the brotherhood, Gabriel had made himself a number of intellectual friends. William Bell Scott envied and admired him. Browning invited him to his home and, with sincere flattery, quoted to him lines from "The Blessed Damozel." He was attaining a reputation which brought his name before all London. Lizzie did not always fit in with his friends. Ruskin had seen it — and he had seen, too, how much it hurt her. A man's fiancée, after an engagement which does not promise to culminate in marriage, is soon put into the same class with his mistress; in the Bohemianism of Chatham Place life, the shift was a simple one.

Perhaps if Lizzie were made to assume a new prominence in her lover's eyes, or if he, Gabriel, were released of some of his financial burden . . . On the impulse of his inspiration, Ruskin wrote Gabriel a letter whose contents made him communicate them in hot haste to Brown, who in turn recorded them in his diary: "Ruskin . . . made two propositions to Miss Siddal: one to buy all she does one by one, the other to give her £150 a year. . . . D.G.R. in glee." "Meanwhile I love him and her and everybody," Gabriel exulted. "Lizzie will take tea, perhaps dinner, at my mother's to-morrow." The "meek unconscious dove" would be made to show her worth.

So far, Ruskin's plan had worked. Gabriel, nothing loth to have Guggum earn money on her own account, rode over her objections that Ruskin was helping her for his own sake. Sensitive to a fault, and proud, Lizzie insisted, nevertheless, upon having the assurance from Ruskin himself, and despatched a letter to Denmark Hill which immediately brought an answer.

"Perhaps I have said too much of my wish to do this for Rossetti's sake. But, if you do not choose to be helped for his sake, consider also that the plain *hard fact* is that I think you have genius . . . I should simply do what I do . . . as I should try to save a beautiful tree from being cut down, or a bit of Gothic cathedral whose strength was failing."

And Lizzie's health was failing. A new attack which definitely indicated phthisis made rest and change of air imperative. "If you would be so good as to consider yourself as a piece of wood or Gothic for a few months, I should be grateful to you," Ruskin urged in touching mock-gravity. The arrangements for the yearly subsidy were duly made, "And," he wrote to Gabriel, "in case I should be run over, or anything else happen to me, I have written to my lawyer to-day, so that the plan cannot be disturbed by any such accident."

Although Gabriel was now assured of greater financial security, what with the instructorship Ruskin had obtained for him at the Working Men's College and the commissions he procured him, he said no word of marriage. Ruskin, solicitous to womanishness, ceased hinting and spoke outright. "I should be grateful if you thought it right to take me entirely into your confidence, and to tell me whether you have any plans respecting Miss Siddal which you are prevented from carrying out by want of a certain income."

Gabriel bristled. No one was going to help him make up his mind. In his usual way, he replied not at all rather than commit himself. But Ruskin would not be put off. He had seen lives blighted by avoidable sorrows, and Gabriel, whose genius he believed in above that of all the painters he knew (Turner being dead), was walking in the shadow of a cloud he could outrun. If Lizzie were to die and Gabriel remained with the serpent of conscience devouring heart and mind, what message could he sing to mankind? What beauty could he give to a world gone black forever? The pelican Ruskin plucked at his breast. "I once had affections as warm as most people; but partly from evil chance, and partly from foolish misplacing of them, they have got tumbled down and broken to pieces . . ." Then, coming to the point, "I daresay you do not quite like to answer my somewhat blunt question," he said. "I did not know how best to act for you, and what to propose about sending Miss Siddal to Wales or Jersey . . . and also because I thought that the whole thing might perhaps be much better managed in another way, and your own powers of art more healthily developed, and your own life made happier."

But the whole thing was not at the time managed in "another way." Gabriel continued in his care-free life, keeping his room — to Ruskin's exasperation — as much of a litter as ever, indulging in weeks of inactivity and then suddenly producing a glorious water color that Ruskin could not bear to part with. Lizzie drew when she could, and added to her wardrobe, making Brown remark — perhaps for Emma's ears — that he had seen Guggum "beautifully dressed for about three pounds, altogether looking like a queen."

And so, to the end of the year, life at Blackfriars went its irregular pace, Lizzie glooming as Gabriel alternately threw his heart at her feet or neglected her for days in his passion for his work — and his model, her jealousy prompted. She grew frailer and more wraith-like with the coming winter. At last, accepting Ruskin's offer, she left for Nice, — taking along Mrs. Kincaid, a cousin of Gabriel's, to chaperon her, — and thence to Paris, dream of her bonnet-shop days.

No sooner had she gone than Gabriel, wild with longing, spoke of joining her. "Positively if you go to Paris, I will," scolded Ruskin. "First, I can't have you going . . . near Ida till you have finished those drawings. Besides, you can't do anything now but indoors, and the less you excite Ida, the better. But you won't go, I'm sure, when you know I seriously don't think it right."

The drawings still required days, weeks, of work; and letters came from Lizzie saying that with the help of Mrs. Kincaid she had gone through all her money. It was no

time to humor Ruskin — rather, now was the time to soothe
him the right way. In a frenzy quickened by necessity,
Gabriel began an entirely new picture, worked at it by daylight, and again till dawn paled the flames of the lamps, and
added the final brushwork before the week was over. Ruskin, delighted, bought the "Francesca" for thirty-five
guineas.

Immediately Gabriel started off to join Lizzie, leaving
Ruskin to shake his head. He was sure they did not mean
to do wrong — "Besides," he pleaded for them, "they don't
seem to know what *is* wrong, but just do whatever they like
. . . as puppies and tomtits do."

Within a week Gabriel was back in London, and straight
to Finchley to tell Brown the news. "There's nothing at
the Beaux Arts comparable to Ingres and Delacroix.
They're real stunners!"

Brown nodded. "I've always stuck up for Delacroix . . ."

Then, talk of Lizzie. "Why does he not marry her?"
Brown pondered.

PART TWO

"As dreams are made on . . ."

IX

MORE YOUTHS AND MORE IDEALS

At Exeter, Oxford, something was brewing. Almost daily
a number of youths congregated in one of the rooms, whence
sounds, not exactly those of divinity students, assailed the
ears of passing members of the University. William Morris and his friend, Edward Coley Burne Jones,[1] both studying for the church, had received revelation — not from the
Holy Book or the inspired rhetoric of their dons, nor yet
from the still, small voice, but from the world whose lures
their masters had tried to keep from them.

Exeter was no nest of angels, however. Unlike Balliol,
where Jowett's influence had made itself felt among masters
and students alike, Exeter was far from exemplary as an
institution of learning or of life. Undergraduate wildness
was a little wilder, neglect of studies not a thing unheard
of. Many an aspirant to holy orders, when not carried
away in the whirl of fast living, may have written back to
his mother as Morris did: "If by living here and seeing evil
and sin in its foulest and coarsest forms . . . I have learned
to hate any form of sin and to wish to fight against it, is
not this well too?"

Excellent logic for a would-be churchman, yet betraying
disillusionment. He was not of those who believed in
losing himself in order to be saved, therefore he could only
play the rôle of spectator in his university life. Happily he
had a companion of his own way of thinking in Ned Jones,
and the two together, with a number of congenial fellow

[1] Jones adopted a hyphen later — when he became an artist.

students from Pembroke, formed a coterie devoted to "higher things." A deep friendship had sprung up between Jones and Morris. Both had a Celtic strain in their blood, a poetic, and in Morris a sometimes gloomy, imagination, and a love of romance which for them reached its sublimest in the Arthurian legends. The *Morte d'Arthur* was a treasure-trove which made their days golden and whose inexhaustible bounty they lavished on willing and unwilling alike, for their own delight in it. Tristram and Pelleas, King Arthur and Gawaine, Launcelot, the sinful knight, and those ladies whose names were sweeter than honey in the mouth: Guenevere, Isoude, Ettarde — these figures of a bygone day, who had loved, sinned, and suffered, walked with them hand in hand, and at night visited their dreams.

William Morris, like the child whom the fairy realm claims for its own, had always been obsessed by the memory of a lost world, more beautiful than the real, which he might perhaps some day regain. It was wooded with hornbeam and ageless oak, interspersed with thickets of holly. Beneath its shadows armor gleamed in scarce beams of light, and the sound of steel wakened the close silence. Sometimes the note of the horn prolonged itself, a scarlet lightning from end to end of the landscape; a white doe bounded, the hounds panting in pursuit, and then the hunters, gay in vermeil and green. Beneath flowering bowers the white slim hands of women wrought with colored silks on their embroidery frames, making more lasting flowers grow with the touch of their fingers, while young girls sang and danced in rings of living and more wondrous blooms. But let none imagine in the Morris of Exeter a willowy damoiseau sustained by dreams and fragrance. He was a short, stocky youth, strong and broad-shouldered, with a manly countenance out of which his eyes gazed clear and blue. His friends' sisters thought him handsome, though the feminine taste might have desired a trifle more care in the rumpled locks, and the fit of his waistcoats.

As a child he had scoured the Essex countryside, seeking something — he could not say what. He would return with rubbings from worn inscriptions, his talk full of the sights he had seen in the Norman churches, rich in old carvings and brilliant tapestries. Then it was as if his lost world opened before him. When his father gave him a suit of armor, the child rode proudly in it all day long and no persuasion would make him take it off till bedtime. He had found his proper garb.

Yet even as a child Morris had been no idle dreamer. Though he was enchanted by his armor and pony, he had eyes for the realities about him, a faculty that remained his, guiding him with its thread of common sense through the mazes of his dreams. Thus, while relishing his fairy tales, he also paid heed to the precepts of the two maiden ladies who educated him through his boyhood; so that when he entered Marlborough College he was a sturdy lad full of muscular and mental energy, none the worse for a too active imagination.

The environs of Marlborough held a new wonder for him in their ancient barrows, stone circles, and Roman ruins. Savernake forest became his joy, as Essex had been. Soon there was not a yard of ground with which he was not fully familiar, no pool of water left by the rains in a root-hollow that he did not know from the reflection of intertwining branch and cloud to the upcurled leaf floating upon it. He had the same love for growing things as for human beings, and the death of a friendly old tree was as much an occasion for mourning as the death of a companion. But there was nothing he loved so well as a true English landscape, twisted with pollards and thick with holly, like Epping forest of his childhood, unchanged for a thousand years.

The Morrises were well off. At the death of his father, who had held a partnership in a firm of brokers, William, as the eldest son, was left comfortably provided for, free to choose any respectable position open to him. Mrs. Morris aspired to aristocracy; since, before his death, her husband had obtained a grant of arms from Heralds' College, her aspiration had something tangible to work for. William himself boasted of that heraldic grant. Through some quirk of his active brain, he came to associate the Morris arms with the White Horse of Berkshire Downs, which became a sort of patron and totem, to be respected and propitiated. No knight of Arthur had been more assiduous in a quest than the youthful William in his yearly pilgrimages to the White Horse — pilgrimages undertaken in the grand manner and with proper devotion. After all, it was a link to the bygone day, the lost world.

Edward Jones, whose mother had died to bear him, came of more modest beginnings. His father, a frame-carver, had had no grant of arms, and his chief ambition was to provide Ned with a calling. As a child, Jones had loved to play with pencils and draw funny little pictures that the family laughed at, but discouraged. He was not going to be an artist but a man of God. And so Jones and Morris entered Exeter on the same day.

He was a slight youth, Ned, with straight, fine, colorless hair, small penetrating eyes that suddenly twinkled with fun, and features that were pleasant without being regular. In repose he possessed an eerie, delicate beauty. As a rule he was quiet, in contrast to the quicksilver activity of Morris, who could not remain in the same position for ten seconds at a time. He dressed neatly, brushed his hair until not one strand stood out of place, and spoke in a gentle voice rippling to laughter at some prank of his own — for he was not above a practical joke.

One long vacation Morris traveled through Belgium and Northern France, coming back incoherent with enthusiasm for the things he had beheld. The glories that Ruskin had been describing he had seen with his own eyes. He would not be a minister; there was something in him that made him burn to design tapestries, build cathedrals, write of beautiful far-off things. "Anch' io son poeta!" Who had said that?

Ned became infected with his fervor. He, too, of late, had been in the clutch of unease; more and more often, in the midst of the lectures, he had let his pencil stray; and when he looked, there on the margins of his books smiled lovely faces beckoning to a world that was full of beautiful things. Others were doing them. He had seen some of Rossetti's water colors and had found in him a spiritual kin. Ned and Morris had read his poems. One day Morris had discovered in himself a gift for writing, so that each time the little group from Pembroke met, he had a new fytte to read them, of fair ladies and brave knights.

The following year Morris again spent the long vacation abroad, this time together with Ned and their friend Fulford. They traveled light, the only item in excess of their necessary luggage a volume of Keats. Just as, years before, other youths had found their inner voices echoing to the poet, they too were moved. One night at Havre, Jones and Morris reached a momentous decision. No more studying for the church. Morris would become an architect and build cathedrals like those of Northern France; and Jones would be a painter. Then and there Ned made the choice of his master: Rossetti.

The winter of that year he went down to London to see him. He knew he could find him in the evening at the Working Men's College. For a long time he walked about Great Ormond Street, watching the masons going in "with upturned fervid face and hair put back," trying in his indecision to forget the cold. A high-shouldered little man with pointed features walked past and then went into the school. Other men followed, some carrying boxes which made Ned's heart leap. Would he ever have a paint box all his own? The night was getting chillier. People had ceased going into the building. His heart thumping with excitement, at last he found courage to enter.

Within, a monthly meeting was in progress, during which

the heads of the various departments explained the conditions of the school. For a nominal fee anyone could gain admittance and break bread and drink tea with his neighbor. Ned lost no time in paying his modest pence. He took his place on a bench at a table, received his helping of thick bread and butter from friendly people whom he did not know, and waited. A man, evidently of the faculty, introduced himself as Furnivall, and Ned told him who he was and why he had come. Furnivall in turn presented him to a plain young man with thin hair and whiskers from ear to chin; but everything about him was enhaloed for Ned. Did not this happy mortal know Rossetti? "Please point him out to me when he enters," Ned whispered. Lushington doubted, however, that Rossetti would be there. He hated that sort of thing — speeches, meetings. Yet he might come; and Ned, putting all his desire in his eyes, watched the door. "Come to my rooms," Lushington invited him, "and I'll have you meet him some night." Still Ned watched the door, his mind in a fog of excitement. The little man he had seen outside came in and addressed the group on Macaulay's new volume, condemning in Carlylean epithet the attack on George Fox. It was Maurice himself, the Christian Socialist. Perhaps right before him in the flesh might also stand Rossetti and the prophet Ruskin, whose words on art had filled his ears at Exeter to the exclusion of the divine call.

Again the door opened. Ned sat up and stared. Surely this must be he. And that same moment, as his blood tingled from the shock of adoration, Lushington whispered, "Rossetti has just come in."

Ned had not expected to meet anyone so young. Rossetti could not have been more than twenty-seven or twenty-eight, in spite of his beard and moustache. And he had done so much in so short a time! How could he, Edward Jones, ever hope to accomplish anything when at twenty-three he was where he should have been at fifteen? Art is long . . .

everybody said that.   Even Maurice was saying it now, in a different way, as he urged the London navvies to improve themselves.   He, the Exeter student, had done less than these laborers, who had had the advantage of him by the practical guidance of such admirable men.

He studied Rossetti.   The deep-set eyes gazed straight ahead, but with a look that Ned could feel saw nothing but what the active mind unreeled.   His eyebrows were arched and dark, and had between them, over the bridge of the nose, a deep furrow that gave the whole face an expression of concentrated thought, of brooding, even.   He was of medium height and compactly built, with small hands and feet.   Ned was especially impressed with the hands, very delicate and very white, although the complexion of his face had a pale olive tinge.   Over his forehead, nobly high, slightly higher above the left temple, his chestnut-brown hair parted, falling in loose waves.   His beard was of a lighter brown, and crisp, with here and there a glittering wire of auburn.   (*Rossetti*—"the Reds"?)   He slouched, rather than sat, and listened—though not attentively, by the drumming of his fingers—to the various speakers.

Ned knew that here was his true master: not Ruskin whom he revered, not any of the other Pre-Raphaelites whose paintings he had seen in High Street, Oxford, at Mr. Wyatt's shop—but Dante Gabriel Rossetti, who had opened wide for him the door of imagination with a small illustration in a book of poems.   It was a little thing, which Rossetti may not have thought much of, that picture of the "Maids of Elfin Mere," from Allingham's *Day and Night Songs;* but when Ned had first seen it, he had been smitten by the haunted loveliness of the singing maids, by the mood of magic Rossetti had been able to transmit to the dead paper. In those maidens Ned had recognized the denizens of his own lands, as he now saw in the artist the Virgil who should be his guide.

He scarcely knew how he got into Great Ormond Street

again. The place was deserted and chill and dark, for it
was late. Not a light filled the windows of the college;
everyone had gone home. Ned wandered through the
black streets like one lost in the fogginess of a dream. Rossetti, Maurice, the Maids of Elfin Mere. . . . With a
pang, he recollected the one reality: he had been too shy to
approach the great man, and now he would be going back
to Oxford with as little accomplished as if he had never
left it.

But Ned's accounts of the masters he had seen face to
face were glowing enough. He described the school, with
the men drinking in the messages of salvation, their hard
hands eager to create such beauty as in the Middle Ages had
been theirs to wrest from wood and stone. England might
yet see another day of glory.

Fervent with zeal to reform through art, according to
the teachings of Ruskin, the two friends decided to delay
no longer the resolution they had made at Havre. Morris
had passed his finals. Instead of continuing his studies,
he took the nearest way to the offices of Street, the architect.
Now was the time to lay the corner stone for his cathedral
of the future. Street took him as a pupil, and set him to
measuring and conning—tasks as tedious as the scaling of
a mountain, and as disenchanting, to one who had hoped to
find the close view as enrapturing as the distant outlook.
But Morris, in his stocky body, had the energy of a giant.
If he wearied of one kind of work, he relaxed by taking
up another. So, when his eyes tired of the architect's
prints and the dreary office, he shut himself in visions of
his lost world. Back in his rooms he filled page after
page with prose and verse which he promptly brought to
his friends.

Eagerly they listened as he unfolded each tale of bygone
places, to the jingling of his watch chain and keys. Not so
long ago, in London, another group of wide-eyed youths
had hung on the lips of one of their fellows. Dante Gabriel

Rossetti since then had made many a forward stride, little knowing that any should follow in his way. He was not a little flattered, therefore, when six years to the day of the *Germ's* birth the *Oxford and Cambridge Magazine* came, like a shoot of the seed long sown, to his studio at Chatham Place.

Not much later, with fear and trembling, Ned went to Lushington's rooms to meet Rossetti. There, "satisfying all his worship," he found him, in a crumpled, plum-colored frock coat, but still divine to the adoring youth. They were quickly friends. "He is one of the nicest fellows — in Dreamland," said Gabriel of him, how truly. Just then, however, Ned was treading a blissfully real paradise, watching Gabriel at work or walking the streets with him, wondering what the dull people of London found to interest them that they had no eyes for the god in their midst.

Ned became his pupil, and, through him, Morris also. Street had removed to London during the summer, and the two friends divided their time between Blackfriars and Oxford, where the magazine, under Fulford's editorship, paid for by Morris, had passed its sixth month of life. Morris, of course, was a prolific contributor. Shrewd, humorous Ned saw where at times an insidious artificiality threatened to creep over the robust stock of Morris's creation: there was too much harping on "true love" and knights and ladies, too much sweetness. One day, it fell to him to correct the proofs of a more than usually mediæval tale of love and prowess. Slyly he interpolated a little adjective before lover and lady, and so the tale went to press. What roars and invectives, what tearing of hair, when Morris discovered that his romance had been transmogrified to the silly antics of an ancient dame and her passionate, if superannuated, lover!

A change came over Jones after his association with Rossetti. "He wears his hair so long and is not so neat as he used to be," commented a young lady of his acquaintance.

"He looks an artist." She said nothing of Topsy Morris, whose hair and linen not even the Rossetti influence could render more artistic.

Ned *was* an artist; and Gabriel never tired of praising the purity of his pupil's drawings. "There are not three men in England who could have done that . . ." Of Morris he had no great expectations as a painter, but still he kept him at the easel, where the young man, who had now abandoned architecture to dedicate himself to art, marched back and forth doggedly, his lips tight and his hand bristling with brushes, as he tried to get some resemblance between the model and the figure on the canvas. The details of design, however, he loved. No winding tendril had more grace than the incidental patterns in the gowns of his women and the festoons with which he loved to deck the margins of his paper. Gabriel spurred him on. And Morris toiled and sweated. How painful his struggle, only those knew who could read between the lines of his mediæval tales. It was no empty imagining that made one of his heroes say, "Then I tried to learn painting till I thought I should die, but at last I learned through very much pain and grief."

At 17 Red Lion Square, the studio that Gabriel had occupied with Deverell in the early Pre-Raphaelite days, Ned and Topsy set themselves up as artists in fine style, Morris's allowance permitting of refinements impossible to the starved purses of the earlier tenants. Brasses of old knights and drawings of Albert Dürer hung about the walls; such tapestries as the London shops could afford brought the illusion of antiquity, and a pet owl, installed on a roost, did service for the tercel gentle no well-regulated knight of old would have been without. Most marvelous was the furniture, designed by Morris and entrusted to the skill of the local carpenter, under threats of dire calamity if he deviated to the extent of a sixteenth of an inch from the specifications. An enormous settle with virgin surfaces tempted the two housemates to devote leisure hours to covering them with painted story: the result, an astonishment to the eye.

Gabriel, visiting there, looked about and goggled his eyes. Such magnificence was unheard of in Pre-Raphaelite studios. Poor old Brown's was a very cubicle of a room, with the canvases lying about, and the lay figures sprawling in various states of repair. Brown himself curled their wigs with the tongs, made them hats for his historical pictures, and draped them in "togams." (In vain William Michael called his attention to Latin cases. Togam it was, and togam it remained.) Then, too, he had a peculiar notion of the decorative effect of pieces of string, carefully unknotted from a bundle, wound about the fingers, and then slipped over a convenient nail on the wall. Such festoons were as common at Brown's as tapestries in Red Lion Square.

Gabriel brought his wonder to Finchley. "You should see Topsy's crib, Bruno! He's rather doing the magnificent there . . . tables and chairs with succubi and incubi. . . ."

On beholding such lavishness, it was not long before Gabriel "was doing the magnificent" by his impecunious friends. Morris was escorted to them and, under his guidance, made to play patron for the adornment of the mediæval studio. A small painting of a hay scene was purchased from Brown; odds and ends from another. The members of the writing clan were introduced, and their works suggested for the magazine. But it was no one-sided affair. Through Gabriel Ned began selling his drawings, and Topsy won Ruskin's praise for his illuminations.

"He's better than anything modern I know," prompted Gabriel to the listening ear.

"Better than anything ancient," said Ruskin. If only he had taken kindly to Brown, whose growing family could well have profited by the bounty of patrons!

Besides Lucy, by Brown's first wife, there were Cathy and

Arthur and Oliver—"Baby Nolly." Lucy was already in her teens, an intelligent girl who loved to potter about in her father's studio; but she was growing up with a dangerous lack of womanly education. At least, so Brown thought. One night he went to the Rossettis to see if Maria or her mother would undertake the charge of Lucy through her adolescent years, Emma being so young and so busy with the other children. There he found William and some of his clever friends talking such highflown nonsense about art, to his thinking, that he walked out of the house in high dudgeon without broaching the subject. Emma's soothing presence made the next venture a success. Mrs. Rossetti consented to take forty pounds a year for the girl's maintenance,—*nothing* for the instruction,—and Lucy joined the pious household. "A blessed thing for Lucy," Brown reflected, little knowing the girl was to profit more by William's freethinking than by the women's piety.

Lizzie meanwhile had come back from her trip improved in health, and Gabriel's love put forth new leaves. Never before had he seemed to care for her with such passionate intensity. They went out a great deal, Gabriel decking her in Indian opera cloaks and antique jewelry, as if to make her more beautiful, that her radiance might sear from his eyes other images lingering there. One midnight he burst in upon Madox Brown.

"I'm going to marry Lizzie at once," he said, "and then off to Algeria." Why Algeria?

Something, a dread of his straying passions, was urging him to the step.

X

"SLOW DAYS HAVE PASSED . . ."

Slow days have passed that make a year,
    Slow hours that make a day,
Since I could take my first dear love
    And kiss him the old way;
Yet the green leaves touch me on the cheek,
    Dear Christ, this month of May.

I lie among the tall green grass
    That bends above my head,
And covers up my wasted face
    And folds me in its bed
Tenderly and lovingly
    Like grass above the dead. . . .

ELIZABETH paused again and again during the copying of
the verses she had composed after a day in the woods. It
hurt her to bend over the writing table, and her breath came
in short, quick gasps. Every exertion fatigued her now,
though she had come back almost a new person from her
trip. But it was ever so. The benefits of her rest cures
were always short-lived. A week or two in town again,
and she became the invalid. With a sigh she bent over as
she wrote the last stanza in the thin copybook of her verses.

A silence falls upon my heart
    And hushes all its pain.
I stretch my hands in the long grass
    And fall to sleep again,
There to lie empty of all love
    Like beaten corn of grain.

Gabriel then, knowing nothing of her pain, had been joyous as in that May—how long ago! —when they had told each other of their love. Dear God, had it ever been? But here was the iris, dry now and without fragrance, that he had tucked in her hair when he and Barbara Smith and Mary Howitt had made sketches of her. Then the women had left for Barbara's cottage—they had known what they were doing—and they two were alone. She had known he loved her. He had said it to her in many ways, as she had told him with every look of her eyes. Their hands more than once had met and stayed, and sometimes, for hours, they had sat cheek to cheek beside the darkened window at Blackfriars, watching the shadows of people passing to and fro on the bridge. But they had never spoken. That day at Hastings . . .

They had walked to the woods together, hand in hand. The branches met close overhead and they felt there more secluded than even on those nights at the studio. Still they did not speak. And then they walked on to a spring, and they leaned over, and together they moistened their parched lips. And suddenly from the hills came the rumble of thunder, and dull raindrops smote them on the cheeks and hands. Fate, the potion, tears? She remembered shivering with sudden cold. Not long since she had read of two, and of the magic drink that had brought them love and death. Then, as the heat rumbled louder in the hills, Gabriel had clasped her to him, and for the first time he spoke.

In the rain they walked slowly home, silenced by a sadness she knew to be sweeter than the sweetest joy. The leaves and flowers, the wet earth, enveloped them in a breath that made them reel. A haze denser than the rain transformed the world to the shadows of a magic glass, themselves the only living beings in it. She could not remember what they said to their friends, or what passed at the cottage until those hours at dusk when once more they were alone. Again he told her of his love, and it was as if a stream of life had been poured through her veins. And she had listened, not daring to meet his eyes, but gazing through the pelted windows out upon the pastures, as blind with rain as her senses with the flood of her passions. And like children they had carved their names on the glass.

Next morning all was peace. She could recall only the coolness of the summer room with flowers newly opened in their boxes, and bird song fresh as the new day through the open windows. Softly Gabriel entered. Her heart had beat fast with a new emotion, and until his hand touched hers she had not the strength to turn to him and to touch his lips with a kiss appeasing as the new morning. And she knew herself his forever.

But he had not always remembered that since that night and that morning they should have been knit as two souls in one body. Time and again he had let his senses stray. She had never had proof, but she had caught sometimes in his eyes an ardor that should have been for her alone — not for his work, not for any dream, not . . . not for any woman, but for her alone. In their intimacies little foreign arts crept in that caused her agonies of suspicion. And when she had spoken he had always denied.

Perhaps it was her sickness that made her watch him with narrowed lids. But O dear God, she loved him so — loved him to hate and bitterness. The world was so full of loveliness in the bud, where hers was consuming in lasting fever — and he was a man of flesh and blood, after all. For months and months he had been working on his painting of the fallen girl; for days at a time Fanny had been locked in his room with him. The painting was not finished and Fanny still came, making free of the studio, dressing and undressing, looking at her, when they chanced to meet, with ill-concealed mockery. And well she might, the cockney wench, with her cheap but becoming finery following the

French fashion; she could have nothing but humorous contempt for the lean, red-headed model who did n't know enough to steal and sell, to get herself decked like any lady of them all instead of appearing in those queer clothes of hers.

How often had Lizzie asked Gabriel to send the girl away, to have nothing more to do with her! And he would promise. But she always reappeared, handsomer, merrier, more arrogant than ever. There was some reason why he could not get rid of her. She surprised it in their quick glances, in private whisperings that became genial, too genial, conversations as she opened the door.

To soothe her pride she had resorted to a pretense of indifference, and grew sarcastic of love, flaunting her verse before Gabriel, though every word cried out her jealous pangs. In vain she taunted:—

> Oh never weep for love that 's dead,
>   For love is seldom true,
> But changes his fashion from blue to red,
>   From brightest red to blue. . . .

Her love did not change its fashion—how she wished she could have wounded Gabriel as he wounded her! —and it was too slavishly true. From the time she had met him she knew she was doomed. He had been fiercely jealous, and she had had to cease posing for Millais and Hunt and for poor Deverell. He was jealous of Ruskin, who was so noble a man. He resented even her confiding in Emma. But, dear Lord, she needed an understanding woman to whom to open her heart. His family had never accepted her. Christina, Maria, William—no, their cold civility showed more plainly than rudeness how they felt toward her. Only the strength of Gabriel's love had borne her up through it all, for he *did* love her. She was everything to him. Had he not sworn it in the most solemn moments, when God surely must have listened? It was her suffering that made her suspicious. Gabriel was innocent. He loved her, only her. . . .

What gladness had been hers when Gabriel, dear, innocent Gabriel, had laid her head on that sweet grassy bank and spread her hair on either side, making the newly opened wood flowers look through. He had called her fond, foolish names, and he had said, "Close your eyes." And she had closed her eyes, and in that shutting-off of light and his face she had tried to imagine what it would be like in the grave. Then she had thrilled to the warmth of his kiss, creeping up her throat to her lips, and she had known what it was to be called back to life. No, no! He had never been false. It was only her broken health oppressing her with black fancies. With his arms around her and her head on his breast, she would regain the faith to believe in him. What if she could not give him the love she gave so long ago in the fullness of her girlhood? What if she had only a sinking heart and weary eyes and a faded mouth that could not smile? Her spirit had the strength her body had lost. Sometimes she thought that if she were to die,—and death was never far,—her love of him would make her break through the grave, to haunt him night and day, like those unhappy girls in the old ballads whose lovers had betrayed them. Men betrayed. How could she be sure that Gabriel was not like those faithless lovers? What certainty had she that this moment, when she was rending her heart between faith and doubt, he was not giving her a definite answer—in the arms of another? Fanny, or Hunt's pretty model—Italian, too, they said. It was not morbidness alone that made her suspicious. What of those things his eyes had shown? He was absent often from London. With his new friends he would stay weeks at a time at Oxford. Work to be done, he said, and spoke of Ruskin's friend, Benjamin Woodward, the architect. Work, work. . . . He had pleaded for his work whenever she would not have Fanny sit to him. Work. . . .

At Upper Albany Street, however, the glow of a new rising colored the diamond with a ruby tinge. Christina, painting her sheets of notepaper, knitting, or going about her household duties after Lucy had been given her daily lessons, looked on the world with eyes a-shine. She hummed softly now over her tasks, and her lips moved with words that were not prayer, so cheerful the curving at the corners, so tremulous the desire lurking there as if ashamed. When she was alone the murmur rose sometimes to a cry, breaking in the lonely room like the cascade of notes of the skylark's soaring. It was another dawn for her, a new birthday, and like that lark she sang.

> My heart is like a singing bird
>   Whose nest is in a watered shoot:
> My heart is like an apple-tree
>   Whose boughs are bent with thickset fruit;
> My heart is like a rainbow shell
>   That paddles in a halcyon sea;
> My heart is gladder than all these
>   Because my love is come to me. . . .

The little nun had visions of delight wherein, closing her eyes to the beatitudes of a Christian Heaven, she reveled in a pagan Elysium. She was no longer the drab recluse, living in a dingy house in a dingier London quarter, but a thing of light and air and fragrance whose footstool was the whole earth, whose limit the infinite sky. A change had come to pass in her, raising her to queenly rank. The wondrous things her brother Gabriel's sensuous nature brought to reality were to be hers, too: the regal dais hung with purple and adorned with fair adornments, all that life held of beauty and delight which so far she had put away with a love that had been. Over and over again she called up the wonderland in her heart which a new love had created, until, in a frenzy of joy, she felt tingling within her the blood of a bacchante and crushed against her lips red drops of pomegranate and grape. Avidly she savored them in her imagination, stilling the voice that whispered it was sin.

James Collinson had not been forgotten, however,— Christina could never forget,— but in her quiet, well-ordered life she had put away the memory of him like a flower in a book, the sight of which, in the turning of her days, brought back a breath of the unwasted bloom. Pain had been hers, and hours of deep regret when she wept in silence her lost days. "Come to me in the silence of the night," she begged of the time that was. "O dream how sweet, too sweet, too bitter sweet!" And the vague longing for a return of the old days became a fleshly yearning for a human touch, a nearness with a definite being. "Come back that I may give pulse for pulse, breath for breath!" As with Gabriel, passion in her became spiritual exaltation, except that in her virgin close it turned within itself for completion; ecstasy was hers, more wasting because it was only of the imagination.

She knew she would not have been happy with Collinson. Where she was as unbending as the oak of the family motto, he bowed with every impulse. Since his last conversion he had undergone many changes of heart, the last leading him to matrimony. Christina had learned of it and had spoken no word of pleasure or pain. But now, in that chamber of her heart so long shuttered, she felt free to let the sunlight enter, and with the sunlight the shadows of men, as once, in the noonday of her life, when those shadows had been raimented in the colors of her adolescent dreams. Had Gabriel and William not been so far above Collinson, or had they at least not been her brothers, by now there might have been children on her knees. A withdrawn life was not what she would have chosen. In vain she tried to match the upheld sanctities of mother and sister. The wasting of her body showed how cruel the struggle, though none had known. Only the recurrence in her verse of the delights of desirable, material things, her descriptions of fruits and flowers, her relish of imagined bounties, even when they were spoken of as attainable in Heaven, betrayed how keen her yearning to possess them on earth.

Charles Bagot Cayley was scarcely the lover to turn a girl's heart to a singing bird, a fruited apple tree, a rainbow shell. Christina was now a woman of twenty-seven, and already threads of silver in her glossy brown hair warned her the time of her flowering was nearing its close. The first birthday of her heart had opened auspiciously and had set in darkness. The second, come with the gray light on her brow, would burst into an eve of glory.

No young girl would have looked twice at Cayley, nor had Christina in the days when he was twenty-four and she seventeen. Then the retiring old-young student who, when he arrived to closet himself with the Professor, dared not raise his eyes upon the womenfolk, who surrendered his hat with the unwillingness of a king relinquishing his crown, who accepted a cup of tea with hems and haws of embarrassment and gulped it down scalding the more quickly to get out of female company, who smiled nervously when he caught one's eye and never sat but at the edge of his chair, the unfledged buzzard who blundered against everything, the mole who rooted among books — what had he been to imaginative girlhood but a specimen of natural history, or, at best, one of the Professor's "lessons"? Moreover, he was tremendously learned. The Professor had never tired of extolling his *bell' ingegno*, which ran in the family, evidently, considering the wonderful things his brother Arthur was accomplishing in mathematics. But whether Cayley had a fine mind or not, whether he had Hebrew and Greek, Latin and even Iroquois, in his phenomenal cranium, it had counted for nothing to Christina, awaking to the exciting world Gabriel was beginning to show her. Then had come those glorious youths . . . and James. And Cayley had hibernated amid his tomes, nobody but the Professor caring why or wherefore.

It was a different Christina who saw him again, years later, just before the Professor's death, and she saw him differently. To her, sobered yet life-hungry, the scholar who had not aged because he had always been old, — or young? — the mild, sweet man who could look at her with the adoring wonder of an adolescent, brought a challenge to live. She was still young; men could love her, for did not Cayley tell his love with every shy look of his eyes? Why need she always lower hers to disentangle sudden knots in her worsted? Then Cayley vanished as suddenly as he had come, but love and a new interest in life remained with Christina. She went out visiting again, and at a friend's home, where all had arrived in costume, she even put on a Syrian dress.

Now Cayley reappeared and came often to Upper Albany Street, seeming to discover a great attraction in William. But Christina knew he came for her. His odd little gifts told her so, and sometimes, most inarticulately for one who knew all the known tongues, he said as much in blunt, Anglo-Saxon words. Yet those words reached deeper than deepest music, leaving her body vibrant with frightening emotions. The nun returned to the world.

XI

SIR ISUMBRAS, THE NIGHTMARE, AND THE CRITIC

THE Critic, revisiting the Royal Academy a week after its opening in 1857, twirled his moustaches, steadied his eyeglass, and strode from canvas to canvas, peering at the signatures. The name he sought was certainly not there, nor had it appeared in the catalogue. But one could never be too confident with the tricks those Pre-Raphaelites had up their sleeves. Dante Gabriel Rossetti, spoken of in whispered awe by his admiring brethren, was evidently not represented in that year's showing either, though, to be sure, he had not dared for the past half-dozen years to fling his lecherous asceticism in the face of the public — thanks, certainly, to the campaign of ridicule Mr. Critic and his fellows had been conducting for the purity of British art.

Rumor ran that he was too conscious of his excellence to place his work at the mercy of the long-eared tribe at the Academy; that the imagination in his allegorical sketches, with their exuberant color and chaste drawing, would have been cast as a pearl . . . However it was, Dante Gabriel Rossetti was not represented. Nor were the three mystic letters in evidence. No, thank God! There was no more parading of crude effrontery, no more banding together of the young and misguided to overthrow an art which had for its corner stone Virtue and Decency and Convention — the foundation without which Society would crumble.

The brotherhood had been drowned, drowned like a cat with the rock of British criticism round its neck. Drowned?

Mr. Critic looked at the two canvases signed by Millais, A.R.A.   Not drowned, in his case, but belled, belled with a golden trinket that chimed prettily to the approval of John Bull.

There was hope of Millais.   With his paintings of the previous year he had won over the great British public, lover of fine, healthy subjects.   England had been concerned with war; he had given her timely pictures, war scenes and scenes of peace.   Of course in "Blind Girl" he had had some poetic nonsense, — "with sweetmeat rainbows and lollipop colors," as a brother critic had said, — and also in "Autumn Leaves," where a group of girls were burning dead leaves in a heap.   The year's spring?   Memories? Some such nonsense.   But then, the "Child of the Regiment" and "Peace" had been excellent, solid subjects, truly British, though nothing like "The Order of Release" of 1853, which had required a policeman to move on the crowd.   Millais's luck. . . .

His chief painting this year was a large one, with virtues, and Mr. Critic had deigned to give it a sentence of staid praise.   After all, John Everett Millais, Associate of the Royal Academy, was a personality distinct from Millais, P.R.B.   Granted, there were Pre-Raphaelite effects in "Sir Isumbras at the Ford" — indeed, a sympathetic fellow critic had pronounced it the best thing any Pre-Raphaelite had ever produced, in spite of Ruskin's "This is not a fiasco but a catastrophe."   (But then, Ruskin had reasons.)   True, the "Roman-nosed horse" which Sir Isumbras mounted did look as if it might leap out of the frame, and the knight's armor was painted with ridiculous antiquarian precision. The little girl, sitting before him, looking up with awe into his face, was only a peasant lass, but she was very pretty. And that curly-headed urchin sitting behind the knight and holding him fast — though he did have a bundle of faggots on his back instead of something picturesque, say, a brace of partridge, still he seemed so well-bred that he might have been a gentleman's son. Also, the moral was edifying. Help the helpless, he took it to mean — a Christian sentiment.

But Mr. Critic could not appreciate the popish detail that Millais had seen fit to thrust into the picture: those superfluous and distracting nuns — the Rossetti influence, surely, as was the general twilight of the painting, too mystical and untrue to British art with its frank light and shadow, a third of the one to two thirds of the other, according to academic rule. Millais was still young, however. He would outgrow that nonsense and paint canvases that the nation would be proud to own. His pictures now told a story, and no head scratching was necessary to find out what they meant. And they were fetching stupendous prices!

Mr. Critic was disappointed to find no new work by that other Pre-Raphaelite, Holman Hunt, whose chief picture, like Wallis's "Chatterton" the previous year, had set all London buzzing. He, the Critic, had distinguished himself wielding his subtle satire, the keen blade in the gloved hand, against Hunt's atrocity, "The Scapegoat." Scapegoat indeed! That's what he had tried to make of the British public. And the pretentious fellow had gone all the way to Palestine to bring back — what? A purple canvas with an ugly old goat standing uncomfortably in a waste salt landscape — the shore of the Dead Sea, was it?

He shivered even now to think of it, though his shiver was not unmingled with a thrill at the triumph he had achieved flaying it. A short, sharp bark of merriment escaped him at the thought of Gambart, the Jewish dealer, who had ordered a religious picture which the public would have swarmed to see, only to get an animal in a dismal marsh. "Here I commeesion a religious peecture, and he breeng me back an horreeble old goat. Ze scapegoat? Nevair heard of heem! What do ze public care for ze scapegoat? He have no business painting animals!"

The Critic had been present when two fashionable ladies were standing in obvious bewilderment before the canvas.

"The Scapegoat?   Hm . . . a peculiar beast."

"A Syrian animal, doubtless.   Look at his funny long ears."

No, it was only Pre-Raphaelite.   Even at that, Sir Robert Peel had graciously offered to buy it for his private gallery, where it might have hung as a pendant to an animal subject by Landseer.   Hunt had refused to sell it, out of vanity!

The man was still hopelessly Pre-Raphaelite, with his morbid symbolism and subjects which required people to think.   People don't want to be made to think when they look at a picture.   That is not legitimate art.   It is art's purpose to amuse and to uplift.   What uplifting could result from the picture of an agonized goat with red worsted tied round its horns, even if it did represent atonement or the suffering of the Saviour, or — he didn't exactly know what.   The subject was decidedly unpleasant, and he had not been unique in finding it so; on the contrary.   He had taken care to con the published opinions of others before he had laid pen to paper.   His friend of the *Art Journal* had described the goat as "an extremely forbidding specimen of the capriformous races," and pronounced the picture "useless for any good purpose, meaning nothing, and therefore teaching nothing."   Another had pulled Hunt's leg about that absurd symbolism.   "Of course the salt may be sin and the sea sorrow . . . and so on, but we might spin these fancies from anything, from an old wall, a centaur's beard, or a green duck pool."   That was good about the centaur's beard.   But the wittiest thing had been said by that M.P. who declared that Hunt's picture was a first-rate portrait of Lord Strafford de Redcliffe.

Nevertheless, the fellow had a knack of making his pictures talked of.   What a stir his Christ with a lantern had made!   But that seemed a trick of all the Pre-Raffs — to make themselves or their paintings talked about for some reason or other. Rossetti by his aloofness, Millais, well, by a little scandal, and Hunt by his strange subjects. Would *he* ever be an Academician? Mr. Critic thought not.

Later in the day he caught sight of a confrère in front of a print seller's window. In fact, he saw not only one, but a group of confrères, distinguished from the lower orders by a wealth of cravat, an abundance of beard, and pockets stuffed with cuttings. A crowd was gathered about something — a picture? A placard? Was Thackeray dead? Or perhaps the Laureate? But the people were laughing and winking, and nudging one another. He elbowed his way to the front. Martin, his friend, greeted him, and, pointing to a lithograph exhibited in the centre of the window, laughed. "Did you ever — !"

Mr. Critic peered through his eyeglass and for a moment could make nothing extraordinary of the picture, portraying an ass with three riders on its back and some figures in the distance. Where had he seen it before? "The Nightmare," it was called, and it was unsigned.

He pricked up his ears to the talk of those about him who were trying to identify the three riders on the ass's back. "Disraeli's the one in front, and Sir Robert Peel the big chap in the middle, and that little one, there, the hindermost — that's Russell, that is. . . ."

Martin spoke. "There'll be a lawsuit, if I know Ruskin *père*. But it's deucedly clever, don't you think?"

"Ruskin? I don't understand."

"Why, dear fellow, don't you see?" A square-nailed forefinger left a smudge on the glass. "Look on the ass's rump, the brand. . . ."

"J. R. Oxon. You don't mean John Ruskin — the *ass* is John Ruskin?"

"That's exactly what the clever devil of an artist labeled him."

"And that's Millais in the middle — couldn't mistake

THE NIGHTMARE

A SKIT ON "SIR ISUMBRAS" AND THE P.R.B. BY FREDERICK SANDYS

the coxcomb—and that little person in front is Rossetti, and that thin-whiskered chap clinging behind with his bundle of paintbrushes—is n't it Hunt?   Why, it 's a skit on Sir Isumbras!"

"Precisely!   Look at the paint pot hanging from the saddle.   He has put P.R.B. on it so there would be no mistake.   John Ruskin, the ass, carrying the Pre-Raphaelites over the ford."

"And those figures in the background—what 's the legend?   Yes, I see.   They 're Raphael, and Titian, is it? — and Michael Angelo begging to be carried across, too. Fiendish clever!"

"Extraordinary how he got the likeness in the ass, though."

The staring, long-nosed beast did bear a distinct resemblance to the eminent author, even to the drooping surliness of the underlip, a disfigurement in Ruskin which had resulted from the bite of a dog in childhood.   Margaret Ruskin had never got over it, though her piety had made her see in the mishap a valuable experience for her son, on whom she never ceased to inculcate the lesson that the body's trial is the soul's balm.   Now, by the clever malice of an anonymous artist, the celebrated Ruskin was made to splash quadrupedantically over a ford, bearing on his back the three leaders of the Pre-Raphaelites whose cause he had championed!

"Rather laid on with a trowel," remarked Martin to the Critic as they walked away, "putting Millais astride his back, considering Ruskin's wife—"

"Is now Mrs. Millais?   Oh, but I have it on good authority that Ruskin really wanted to be rid of her.   Someone told me, who knows Furnivall, who knows—"

"Maybe.   He must have been a trying husband to live with. . . . Is it true Ruskin used to make note of all her peccadillos and read them over to her every Monday?"

"I 've heard that, too.   And my friend also said that

Ruskin invited an Italian count to stay as guest in his house, thinking his wife might fall in love with him and leave Millais alone."

"Yes, I know that story. Only the count was attracted to her jewel box and eloped with it instead — and the chambermaid, too, was it? They say Ruskin thought only of Millais's art."

"Oh, I have it on the same authority that after his wife left him Ruskin still posed for the portrait Millais had begun in Scotland, Ruskin standing without saying a word, the young fellow painting away. I wager he used big brushes to finish the job."

"Old Ruskin threatened to slash it with his penknife, he was so mad, and it had to be smuggled to Rossetti's studio for safety. Anyway, I think it is a little raw putting Millais on Ruskin's back like that. A chap who works at Smith's, the printer's, told me Old Man Ruskin was there storming and threatening the house with all kinds of mischief if Smith did n't divulge the artist's name. I tried to discover it for myself — a good find for my review, you know, but I 've had no luck."

They parted at the turning, moving aside for a long-haired young man in a resplendent white waistcoat and studs. On his way to beefsteak and pudding, the Critic wondered whether he had not been too lavish of praise in his sentence on "Sir Isumbras."

The white waistcoat pressed through the crowd, made his way to the shop, and mounted to the office.

"Umph . . . good day, Mr. Smith."

"Good day, Mr. Sandys. What can I do for you?"

"Quite a . . . demonstration outside, I see. Umph . . . they rather like Frederick Sandys's little picture. Mr. Smith, I 'd like an advance of . . . umph . . . twenty-five pounds."

"But we 've paid you in full for the caricature, Mr. Sandys."

"Right, sir, but . . . umph . . . I was thinking you might give me an advance on my next opus — say, thirty pounds."

"I 'm sorry, we could n't advance such a sum, Mr. Sandys. It 's against the firm's principles, you know. Moreover, we 're likely to get into the law courts. Ruskin's father has been here, offering five hundred pounds if we would give him the artist's name, and —"

"Five hundred pounds!" gasped Sandys. "At that price . . . umph . . . I 'd tell the old gentleman myself. Five hundred pounds!" He made a deep obeisance before an imaginary third person. "Frederick Sandys, your humble servitor! I 'd out P.R. the Pre-Raphaelites for five hundred pounds!"

Smith smiled. "He did n't offer to give *you* five hundred pounds. He is probably reserving a good stout cudgel —"

"That 's the way with us poor artists! Cudgels and poverty . . . umph . . . while others get both the fat and the lean! Oh, about the advance you mentioned . . . umph . . . better make it forty pounds, Mr. Smith. Laundry bills have to be paid," he tapped his snowy waistcoat, "and a man must eat solid food now and then, even if he feeds on dreams."

"Here are ten pounds, Sandys," said Smith. "You promised me three days ago when I gave you a loan —"

"Thank you, Smith," called Sandys from the door, waving good-bye with the notes in his hand.

In the corner of a doorway he picked up a pretty young girl who had been waiting for him. "Throw the paper away," he said. "No, better fold it up for the next time we send it to be washed. Any spots on it yet?"

The girl examined his waistcoat and shook her head.

"Good. Now let 's go and have something to eat."

XII

HERE AND THERE

OXFORD was undergoing an æsthetic change. For some time a museum had been a-building after the designs of Benjamin Woodward, to whom Thirteenth-Century Gothic stood for the ultimate in architecture. Ruskin took an active interest in the new temple, supervising the sketches for the decorations that no sensuality might enter in to divert people's thoughts; and, the better to ensure the success of the work, made the young architect acquainted with the Pre-Raphaelites — more accurately, with Gabriel. In no long time Pre-Raphaelites and their disciples were working at the museum, Woolner on a figure of Bacon, Alexander Munro, a brother sculptor, on Galileo, while Gabriel, the Samaritan, enlisted the services of other needy artists who were likely to find a modest honorarium sufficient to their wants. Long after Munro had finished his Galileo, Woolner was still using his chisel delicately on Bacon, holding that the greater the man, the longer the time required to perpetuate him in stone.

Funds for the decoration of the museum were limited, however, so that the prospect of completing it was many years removed. The young men worked with good will, none the less, to the delight of Ruskin, ever ready to see in their labors a revival of the blessed spirit. Youth, youth, all ideals!

Meanwhile in London the Pre-Raphaelites got together an exhibition of their works at the instance of Brown. Rooms in Russell Place were hung with backgrounds that would not jar with the vivid yet subtle colors, and seventy-one works were hung up for public view.

Brown had a fine showing—twelve pictures, including "The Last of England" that had been awarded the Liverpool prize the previous year. (With what anxiety had he written in his diary, "I hope fortune will favor me . . . or I fear it will go hard with Emma and the chicks." Now, in the summer of 1857, the money was all gone, and worries began anew, with the heart made sick by hope deferred in the persons of purchasers. "The distiller promises to call again with his wife, and if he buys I make a vow to purchase Nolly a perambulator.")

Holman Hunt contributed four pictures and photographs of his designs from Tennyson. Wounded by the treatment "The Scapegoat" had been accorded, he would not show it there. Frustration was plunging him deeper into abstract conceits which, remote from public appeal, hazarded his chances of becoming an A.R.A., a distinction he had been coveting since Millais had acquired it. The brotherhood, after all these years, seemed a bit of boyish daring that had had its time and now must give way to the serious work of maturity.

Distinct from the rest of the Pre-Raphaelite productions, Rossetti's water colors glowed for the quality of their imagination. Where Millais's invention was taking on the vapidity of sentimental anecdote, so popular with Victoria's subjects and now quite obvious in the two paintings he was exhibiting, and where Brown's bore the strength and also the weakness of his Hogarthian realism, Rossetti's was like poetry made visible. ("Why don't you frame your sonnets?" an artist wit was later to ask.) He did not show his modern painting. To Brown's exasperation several generations of calves that had posed for it had been converted to beef, and still Gabriel's canvas remained unachieved. Fanny came and went, wheedled money for gifts, grew daily more sumptuous, and inspired him with studies of fleshly beauty that contrasted strangely with his ethereal Beatrices. Always one face looked out of these dreamy canvases, sad with a sorrow beyond life. Gracile as an osier, the lovely body leaned, or stood, or drooped, the white neck reared, the head heavy with coils of deep copper hair. It was the hair of the Pre-Raphaelite women, which in other paintings set the public on edge and closed the purses of the dealers. Even the sober *Athenæum* had indulged in levity at the expense of Millais, who, it said, "must have been staying at the village which Goldsmith immortalizes as 'Sweet *Auburn*, loveliest village of the *plain*,' for plain people with red hair seem this year his idiosyncrasy." "Please, please, a truce on red hair!" others cried.

With Rossetti's water colors hung a number of drawings from Moxon's illustrated Tennyson — the Pre-Raphaelite Tennyson, it came to be called. The Laureate had been pleased, on the whole; not so poor Moxon, who died, it was said, of the vexation and worry those infernal artists had caused him. Nothing seemed to delight the Laureate nowadays, not even the tribute of a beautifully illustrated edition of his works.

The unjust criticisms that had assailed "Maud," the poem in which for the first reckless time he had spoken with genuine passion, had shaken his faith in himself, and things that would have given him joy left him cold. Was his, the voice that should exult in the storm and thrill to the hushes of passion — was it to chirp forever like a guest at a polite matinée? He loved the cadences of his verses, the gossamer of his fancies, spun fine with sentiment and jeweled with dew of tears — webs in which delicate ladies' hearts throbbed captive. With his splendid giant's body, he had also an herculean power; but it was harnessed perforce to the demands of a prissy Omphale, his public. For once he had struggled free, and the wench showed fickleness; it was late for him to curb her to his will. He should have done it in youth, early, when there was strength either to succeed

or to fail. He was already beginning to feel weary. Did
Omphale want sweet counterfeits of passion? She should
have them. Too late, too late for him to make her over.

Lizzie had also made a number of sketches for the Tennyson. But whether Moxon had not been struck with them,
or whether Elizabeth Siddal's was a name too little known
to bait new purchasers, they were omitted from the book.
At the exhibition they appeared, next to Gabriel's, like a
shadow to his light, and morbid where his were poetic.
Ruskin had often blamed Gabriel for making Lizzie over-
tax her imagination. "You're letting her wear herself out
with fancies, and she really ought to be made to draw in a
dull way, sometimes, from dull things." "The Haunted
Tree," part of her exhibit, he disliked intensely, so much,
indeed, that he had turned governess and begged her not
to paint any more unpleasant subjects like it, for her soul's
sake. "You're a good girl," he nodded when she promised
to obey him. "You *will* break off those disagreeable ghostly
connections." But he might as reasonably have asked her
to build her frail body anew, or keep her mind from brooding over Gabriel's infidelities.

Besides the Pre-Raphaelites, their sympathizers found
wall space: Seddon, who had died earlier in the year, Inch-
bold, Hughes, Windus, whose "Burd Helen" had won a
public letter from Ruskin; Martineau, Bell Scott, the poet-
painter drawing-master, so embittered by his failures that
he was affronted by the success of his friends; Boyce, Campbell, Collins, Arthur Lewis, Bond, J. D. Watson, Brett,
Davis, Wolf, Dickinson, and Halliday.

But for the few instances where Omphale was consciously
propitiated, Pre-Raphaelite work, thus far, had not modified
its dictum of absolute sincerity in the portrayal of actual-
ities. Hunt's models who had broiled in the sun of Jeru-
salem could have testified to that striving, and Gabriel's
calves, too, that had kicked and fought all the time they had
remained tied up for art's sake. As for Brown, he was more

exigent for truth than any of them, stopping at nothing to gain his end. If he saw a street Arab and any part of his outfit might serve in a painting, Brown promptly bought it. Not so long ago he had brought out all of Heath Street when he appeared with a costermonger's truck fitted up with rods and curtains, easel and paints, and a canvas six and a half feet long, all of which he trundled himself to the chosen spot: he was working on a Carlylean concept celebrating the nobility of labor; fine specimens of the British navvy were there engaged in digging up the street. What better opportunity? Certainly nothing could afford to be overlooked in an undertaking of such magnitude. He was going about it very *seriatim*, he gravely informed William Michael, who humorlessly instructed him as to the precise meaning of the Latin. But, William or no William, *seriatim* remained the elegant way of saying "seriously" for Brown.

The press noticed the exhibition favorably. Gone the day when the innovators could be laughed at. Their work, in spite of the Academy's discrimination, had asserted itself as vital and healthy, and, though it could be kept off the walls, it managed to sneak in through pale, sanctioned counterfeits. Mr. Critic, finding that the arbiters higher up had modified their lay, made echo with his penny whistle: no profit tooting an individual note.

"Pre-Raphaelitism," said the *Athenæum*, "has taught us all to be exact and thorough, that everything is still unpainted, and that there is no finality in art." At last a confession of indebtedness.

His wonted ill luck attended Brown. His painting, winner of the Liverpool prize, was attributed to Holman Hunt, so that even public recognition was denied him. On the whole, however, the Pre-Raphaelite exhibition did little more than bring the names of the school before a wider circle at a time when the individual members had become settled in their personal interpretations of the function of art. But for the name that bound them, there was as little

The Last of England

BY FORD MADOX BROWN

in common between the painting of Millais and Rossetti,
or, for that matter, of Millais and Hunt, as between the
Academy President's and Brown's.

For nearly two years, ever since William Michael had
been contributing to Stillman's paper, the brethren had been
in close touch with literary and artistic movements in the
United States. A strange, inchoate book of poems called
Leaves of Grass, by one Walt Whitman, while shocking all
literate America, had succeeded in crossing the ocean, reaching William Bell Scott at Newcastle. Now Scott, though
ready to cry "plagiarism" if any dared to treat of a universal
subject after he had done so, could recognize merit in the
work of a stranger. And so, no sooner did he discover the
new oracle at a secondhand bookstall, then he communicated
his find. "It's a revelation," he declared, "although an
ungainly and not a little repulsive one."

He sent the volume on to William as a Christmas box.
"It struck me you were the man to like it. Obliterate . . .
half a dozen lines and half a dozen words, ignore the author altogether (!) and read as one does the books that express human life like the Bible, and one finds these *Leaves
of Grass* grow up in a wonderful manner."

The book passed from hand to hand. Of an evening
select bodies gathered at Chatham Place and listened to
Gabriel intoning the surging, overwhelming lines.

Of life immense in passion, pulse and power
Cheerful for freest action form'd under the laws divine
Of Modern Man I sing.

Scented herbage of my breast,
Leaves from you I glean, I write, to be perused best afterwards,
Tomb-leaves, body-leaves growing up above me above death,
Perennial roots, tall leaves, O the winter shall not freeze you deli-
    cate leaves.
Every year shall you bloom again, out from where you retired you
    shall emerge again. . . .

One day Ruskin brought another American to the Pre-Raphaelite exhibition, Charles Eliot Norton of Cambridge, Massachusetts. Norton, with his interest in Dante, found much to admire in the work of the P.R.B.'s, particularly in Gabriel's, and, when he went back to America, invited him to contribute to the first number of the *Atlantic Monthly*, which was about to appear under the ægis of his friend James Russell Lowell. Gabriel sent "Love's Nocturn" and the names of Morris, Scott, and Allingham as fit to grace the pages of the new magazine. Lowell, however, found Gabriel's verses too foggy for the American reader, and declined to publish them. "I have no doubt they really are so," wrote Gabriel with a sting to his courtesy, "and it is not much use extending their sphere of perplexity." Still, he could well afford to take the rejection lightly, for Norton had been generous in other ways. Besides commissioning a portrait of Ruskin and a water color, he had bought Lizzie's "Clerk Saunders."

There was to be a closer connection with America. Captain Augustus Ruxton, a retired army officer, an art enthusiast though no artist, was seized with the idea of holding an exhibition of British art in the United States, and accordingly invited the radical Pre-Raphaelites to help him. Crafty Gambart, thinking it might prove a profitable venture, joined forces with the Captain, and by the middle of October the exhibition opened in New York. For two months Brown, again tormented by the urge to start life anew, fought with the idea of joining Ruxton in America, but at last decided to let him take care of the hanging of the pictures without his help.

The year 1857 was fraught with financial disaster for the United States. Every day brought news of some sinister crash in the stock market; money was nowhere obtainable. In New York the unemployed stalked in hordes about the streets seeking work that was not to be had, while their wives and children stood in line waiting for the crust that would keep them alive yet another day. At night the park benches swarmed with the homeless, their only shelter against the increasing chill the newspapers stuffed between their flesh and their tatters. Organized charity was powerless against the formidable march of hunger.

It was not only the poor that suffered. "I saw a wretched animal yesterday," wrote Ruxton to William, secretary for the enterprise, "who had been obliged to vacate a palace in Fifth Avenue, without so much as enough to pay for a bed elsewhere."

The exhibition could not have been undertaken at a more inauspicious time. The Captain was charming and engaging, however, and found no lack of obliging ladies to help him. Stillman, Durand, and the President of the Academy in New York supervised the placing of the pictures, and six galleries were filled with British work, a goodly portion of it, professedly or not, Pre-Raphaelite.

Brown's "Lear" and Hunt's "Light of the World" attracted admiring crowds. One man, pointing to Hunt's painting, remarked as the galleries were being lighted: "Never mind the gas. The picture will light us up."

Little was sold, Brown, among the few who disposed of anything, realizing about thirty pounds for his trouble and receiving his work badly damaged from its various transportations. Ill luck prowled still at his elbow, and it came companioned with death when Baby Arthur fell suddenly ill. The distracted father had not even money to bury him, and to the grief and the loss was added the humiliation of borrowing. And the little body was carried away, leaving behind lifelike shadows of the child in many a painting. In the foreground of the Carlylean canvas, he looked out, a round-eyed cherub of a few months, his little fist in his mouth, his downy head unfledged. On the shoulder of his smock a black bow denoted mourning — there for his mother, for he represented one of the waifs of life. Now the dark knot held a new meaning for Brown, but took from him none of his courage. "Work" was going to be his masterpiece. To that end he forgot himself, life and its trials, and, in the hours when he was too much exhausted to paint, read over and over again Carlyle's words:—

"The spoken Word, the written Poem is said to be an epitome of the man; how much more the done work. . . . Whatsoever of strength the man had in him will lie written in the work he does."

"Work." It would be a tribute to the millions un-named who toiled, meagrely rewarded, often despised, though their calloused hands held up the foundations of the world; to those others who created new worlds with blood and brain, only to be themselves destroyed by those whose visions they enlarged. The lowliest and the highest, both would be glorified, for each in his way had epitomized himself. In that painfully growing painting, Brown's own strength would lie written.

XIII

THREE OLD MEN AND A BOY

To Rydal Mount, one day in 1849, had come a lady with a puny red-haired lad of twelve. It was not to admire the beauty of the Lakes or the woods and mountain of the region which always attracted visitors, but to see William Wordsworth, the Poet Laureate. A strange pilgrimage for a lady and a boy, visiting a household three of whose members were old, old people. But Lady Jane Swinburne was no usual fond mother, and her son Algernon Charles no ordinary boy. He was already well acquainted with the Laureate's poetry, and, moreover, had ambitions of his own. So to the old house the two made their way, Lady Jane understanding well the agitation that brought the boy's hand to a flutter in her own and stiffened with manly resolve his narrow, sloping, too-girlish shoulders.

Life had brought many and unpredicted changes on the poet. By slow, deep strokes the same hand that had chiseled the rebel face of youth to the wary conservatism of old age had hewn his soul to a like model. Long since had died the Wordsworth who had been a revolutionist in France, who had found a people uprisen in the cause of freedom, noble to godhood. Long since, too, had died the lover of Annette Vallon, who, while she had taught him French, had also wakened his senses to their first bliss. Once he was back in England, Annette had been forgotten with the daughter she had borne him, and, more slowly, the love of freedom that had made him feel the divinity of mankind. Then he celebrated an English Lucy upon an

English soil,—a tangible charm to exorcise the ghosts of memory,—married, with conventional romance, a childhood sweetheart, and settled down to a decent conservatism. Years later, when Annette's daughter needed her father's legal assistance to marry, Wordsworth was jerked back to the past. But his sister Dorothy, as always before, spared him by seeing to the unavoidable nuisance herself. Since 1798, when the first-fruits of his humble muse appeared with his friend Coleridge's flights to the supernatural, he had written steadily, enjoying no surfeit, but suffering no want by the considerateness of a watchful Providence and the management of Dorothy and his wife. Nothing interfered with his creativeness, and so he wrote on, of Nature, and simple folk, and of God Who is in His works. When his friend, the Laureate Southey, died, Wordsworth succeeded him. But to England's youthful bards he was a lost leader.

> Just for a handful of silver he left us,
> Just for a riband to stick in his coat. . . .

They must look elsewhere for light. Robert Browning sought it in the rock-bound pharos of Self, steadfastly burning mid the ocean of humanity.

Dorothy, with the oncoming of years, had lost the sparkle of her observant eyes and sunk from an old maid to an old woman. Her devotedness to her brother remained constant until the time when, the light fading from her mind as from her eyes, she stood in need of sympathetic understanding. She became a living shadow of her noble old self, seeing her brother and the world and life pass as even more unsubstantial phantoms before her dimmed mind. Long ago she had been young, and there had been one she had loved with womanly love. But they had met too late. Now, cared for by those who had been her sole care, she waited, unhoping, for the close of her darkened day.

Wordsworth received Lady Jane and little Algernon. Whether he was flattered by so young a visitor whose head had already been touched by the light of his poetry, we do not know. But, after Lady Jane had spoken, he said with truth that there was nothing in his works that could do the boy harm, and that there were some things that might do him good.

Lady Jane brought him her son none too soon, for the following year the venerable Laureate died, leaving a lasting memory of himself in the heart of the impressionable boy. But Algernon's true accolade came from Samuel Rogers.

The laurel wreath falling empty with Wordsworth's decease, Rogers was invited to place it on his own hoary head. At eighty-seven, however, with the fame of his first book antedating by three years the fall of the Bastille, he felt too much the survivor of a past age to receive the honor rightly due a man with life still before him. He declined in favor of Tennyson. Nevertheless, for those who savored the graceful precision of a bygone day, he towered, a splendid giant. His works were well known at the Swinburne home, especially his *Italy*, which Turner had illustrated with delicate vignettes. Lady Jane, in love with everything that touched that fair land, darling of England's poet minds, had from Algernon's childhood fostered in him her own affection. And he had responded, reading at her knees Ariosto's poetic errantries before he had ever heard of the English bards.

With Rogers's eighteenth-century verse much of his reputation had reached the Swinburnes. He had known Shelley and Byron; before them Fuseli the artist, perhaps Blake. Though the sting of his snake tongue was notorious, his generosities, too, were widely known. Even Wordsworth, in a needy moment, had proved the value of that friendship when Rogers obtained him his remunerative sinecure of stamp distributor. Lady Jane felt her son could only profit by meeting such a man.

She went with him, therefore, on a second pilgrimage,

this time to a sumptuous mansion in St. James Place. Rogers received them in his chair, for he had suffered an injury and was unable to greet them with the obeisance he surely must have made. Grandly hierophantic he looked, with his great old head and venerable frame, in the midst of the treasures he had accumulated from the proceeds of his banking business. Some had once graced the halls of the Palais Royal of France; each would have ransomed an emperor.

The patriarch, shrewdly observant, easily divined the acute sensitiveness of the lad before him, with his twitching hands and feet, the long-maned head too large for his body, and the fine eyes under a span of forehead. They talked a little of books and art, Rogers listening, nodding, ora-clizing in his suavely modulated voice.

"My son," said Lady Jane, "thinks more of poets than of any other people in the world."

The hierophant caught his cue. Bending forward in his chair, he laid his hand upon the curling red aureole. "I prophesy that you, too, will be a poet."

Whether, back at Capheaton in Northumberland, Alger-non took his grandfather's fleetest blood-mare and rode her madly through the countryside in the exultation of his ded-icated soul, no one knows. Certain it is that from the mo-ment of the prophecy he saw himself of the poetic line. Not that he had as yet passed tentative fingers across Apollo's lyre. He had read, not too widely; but that taste of books had been enough to make him find himself.

From earliest childhood Algernon had imbibed the in-fluence of still another old man, Sir John, his grandfather. It was at the ancestral seat, in its moor-bound setting, that Algernon spent his vacations, matching the old man's wild horsemanship, swimming in the waste chill waters, and listening to fantastic tales of the glory of past Swinburnes. As a border family, Sir John told him, they had made the country gasp with their feats. In later years, when Mary

Queen of Scots had needed strong arms and staunch hearts to defend her, Swinburne blood had flowed in streams before her dainty feet. Always the Swinburnes had stood for the right, and he, even he, Sir John, had often in his day run the risk of impeachment and execution for upholding the rights of man against tyranny. Yes, the Swinburnes had known what it was to leave their hearths and eat the hard bread of exile. Even he . . . With the elegance of a courtier Sir John related his adventures as a paladin of freedom, carelessly coupling with his name Voltaire's, Mirabeau's.

And so, at the old man's feet, Algernon's fancy stirred to the glories of his blood. Mary Stuart, the red star of his thought, lighted him to ways of romance, and, with large catholicity, was allowed to burn side by side with the torch of republican ardor. Everything Sir John told him he believed. Swinburne blood had not only been spilled for Mary; she had remained for succeeding generations the sun of their devotion. He, too, was bound in fealty to adore her. For the old, lost cause, new causes would be embraced; he would distinguish his honored name.

It never occurred to him to seek into the truth of his family history, or to reconcile his fealty to a dead queen with his revolutionary spirit. From other quarters he sometimes had inklings that the blood and lands given up to Mary were figments of his grandfather's dotage; that Sir John himself, though he had known one of the chief figures of the French Revolution, had never come within visual acquaintance of the henchman's axe, and that his republicanism was of a pleasant, armchair kind. Yet what could so old a man do now but fire the mind of youth? For Algernon, Sir John had lived as an intimate with Voltaire and fought with Mirabeau in the cause of liberty, and now was passing the torch to him, more than ready to receive it. Italy was gasping in the clutch of tyranny. Mazzini, the apostle of her liberation, called for soldiers. No Swinburne could be deaf to the summons.

So far all that Algernon could do was to hang up a picture of the Italian patriot in his room at Oxford and declaim revolutionary verses before it with frenzied gestures and weird dances. And he could abhor Napoleon III, archetype of the foe of freedom. His fellow students heard the declamations, witnessed the dances, and listened to the invective against Louis Napoleon, with hotter words preaching his assassination, and they kept safely aloof from the flame-headed advocate of regicide.

When Algernon was not with his grandfather amid the patrician refinements of Capheaton, he stayed with his parents at East Dene in the Isle of Wight. He was seldom with his father, the Admiral, for the good man, Britishly abhorrent of anything hinting even vaguely of effeminacy, avoided the salon where his daughters played endless sonatas, and sought refuge in his garden workshop, contriving all kinds of ingenious mechanical marvels in hours of solitary bliss. Algernon shared little with him but a love of the sea and the color of his hair — perhaps, too, an intolerance for music that came out of instruments. When Lady Jane was not chanting to him out of French and Italian poets in her cadenced drawl, he was usually roaming about outdoors, where the variety of landscape, now sloping into meadowland, now menacing with cliffs, carried him far from the pianoforte virtuosity of his sisters.

Early in life he had begun to look upon himself as an elemental portent, one with speed and fire, air and moving water, whether the dark depths of the northern ocean or the gentler southern sea. As he watched the rhythm of the gulls, hurried by the wind over the endless waves, he envied them their flight until, his own light body stripped of clothes, he came closer to the sea than any halcyon, sank himself wholly in it, embraced and repelled, returning at last to the shore exhausted but triumphant. Another thing he loved — the shrieking impetus of the wind whipping his face, blowing his hair till it stung at the roots, flapping his clothes like useless wings. And then he wished that like a sea mew he could fly.

Once, after Eton, he set out secretly from his parents, who would have forbidden it, to scale a cliff no one had dared attempt before him. Like a creature of the scaurs, he clung with feet and hands to the jagged rock, finding foothold where the fearful crowd below could see none, swaying, teetering, but bravely clutching on, till, with a cry shrill as an eaglet's, he proclaimed his victory. When Lady Jane was told of it, she thrilled with fear, clasping silently to her breast that strange, elfin thing who was somehow her son — so puny, so girlish, and yet so brave.

Algernon had been a desultory student. Toward the end of his career at Eton, for some mysterious reason he had had to be called home by his parents, and no urgent invitation came from his masters that he be sent back to school. Adolescent turbulence? Mischief? He had distinguished himself by no scholastic achievement except the winning of the Prince Consort's Prize for French — nothing to wonder at, what with Lady Jane's drilling and his exhaustive reading of French literature at Capheaton and in the library of his uncle, the Earl of Ashburnham. He had mingled with few of the boys at Eton, having scarcely a friend, and wanting none. The odd little creature, squeezed into his tightly buttoned coat, elaborate in his courtliness and unexpectedly violent of speech, was not of the stuff to make a popular favorite. He joined in few of the sports, preferring to crouch cross-legged in a window nook with a volume of Restoration plays on his knees, or to pour forth torrents of verse. Rumor had it he wrote it, too, in imitation of Sappho, and Landor, and Victor Hugo.

When the Eton housemaster had shown no inclination to recall Algernon to the fold, the Admiral had sent him with his uncle, the earl, to travel abroad. He returned quieter, with a look of wondering awe in his eyes. The sea, that he had watched mysterious and still in the north, gently rebellious in the south, had shown another, a terrible aspect of herself on the passage from Ostend to Dover. He felt the more her son.

He was almost nineteen when he entered Balliol. Newman's influence still hung like an aura of incense about the Oxford cloisters, but, though Puseyites and followers of Keble endeavored to carry on their High Church propaganda, the old spirit was waning among the students. Keenedged intellects were already cutting into what had been deemed inviolable, and even the Word of God was being questioned in the light of the revelations of science. It was time for a new gospel, one that could be demonstrable to the doubters and fitted into the test tubes. Man had it in his power to produce it. Man was mighty. He might be, he was, God.

And so, through the mist of the Catholic Revival, rationalism was pushing its edge. To the devout it was an auspice of evil that would wipe out religion and fill the world with the lurid glare of materialism. Where would man be if God were not? "In the beginning God created the heaven and the earth," they affirmed with faith. "In the beginning was a ball of fire whirling in space. For millions of years, until it cooled to bubbling, primeval ooze, there was no life upon it," answered the geologist. The religionists hung their heads, unwilling to give up the belief in which they had been nurtured, yet unable to disprove the facts that were daily being made more evident. They had been taught to love man and the world because God had created them. How could they now hold to their faith of the divine Maker?

But, where the believers were shaken in their certainties, the others gained consciousness of man's power. There was pride of self in the new science. Man had not fallen, an abject rebel, from Heaven, but by ageless, arduous steps he was ascending to it. With the knowledge he was acquiring, he was bringing the universe closer within his hold.

In time there should be little he could not accomplish to ease his span of life and ennoble it. Social inequalities would be wiped out: one man would stand, the peer of his neighbor, to fulfill himself to the utmost for the good of all. No more children stunted in the factories. The reign of man on earth was at hand. In 1856-1857 one Karl Marx published his "Communist Manifesto," with other sociological articles, in David Urquhart's *Free Press*.

The poets, taking up the refrain, still incoherent and misunderstood, proclaimed the new truths to the world, and the world waited. Tennyson's prophetic "Locksley Hall" had appeared as early as 1842.

Meanwhile, at Oxford, youth was going its way, forming its smaller circles on the wider surface of university life. As Morris and Jones had banded together at Exeter, other groups formed at Balliol, one, the "Old Mortality" headed by the magnetic John Nichol, finally winning over, or rather accepting, Swinburne.

A dangerous preceptor was Nichol for a youth ignorant of life and with a mind ready for the shaper. Alarmingly extreme in his modern views, making agnosticism of the new freedom and violent republicanism of political reform, Nichol, by his seniority over Swinburne, which lent added force to his dogmatism, soon had emphasized the best and the worst in his disciple. What enhanced his authority in Swinburne's eyes was the fact that he knew Mazzini. In the light of such glory Algernon's brains were inflamed to frenzy, and an astonishment to all beholders became the Corybantic rituals he performed before the patriot's shrine over his mantel.

Alas, not republican fervor alone quickened his heels and inspired his effusions. Mazzini's effigy often looked down on toasts of whiskey and soda, whose bubbles, exploding against unaccustomed lips, shocked Swinburne like minute bombs of revolution. Nichol had a Scot's head for drink. The more glasses he emptied, the greater his assurance and the resulting dominance over Swinburne. Coming as he did from Glasgow's sophistia, he was past master in an art of which the younger man was never to exceed a disastrous novitiate. Still Algernon drank and orated and read, and when his sight, in spirituous prankishness, showed him two pages of script where he required but one, he clapped one hand over one eye, and then followed the words without difficulty. The uninitiated thought him troubled with some peculiar eye disease, but Bacchus smiled.

On January 14, 1858, the telegraph wires were a-buzz over Europe with the news of a fanatical attempt on the life of Napoleon III. He had been attending a performance of *Un Ballo in Maschera*, when, upon leaving the Opéra to enter the imperial carriage, a bomb exploded, missing him by miracle. Ironic poetic justice had doubtless prompted the *carbonaro*, Felice Orsini, to make his desperate move after the spectacle of King Gustave's assassination had unfolded itself before Napoleon's eyes. Censorship in Italy increased in severity, and indeed all countries were urged to fend off the danger of republicanism. Immediately Naples refused to sanction the representation of Verdi's opera at San Carlo, urging the master to adapt his music to another, less inciting libretto. Verdi refused. It was not for nothing the youth of Italy flocked to the opera houses, acclaiming him a champion of liberty. But no city in Italy dared set the example of regicide before an inflammable audience. At last Rome took the risk, after the scene was changed to the New World and Gustave to Riccardo, Governor of Boston.

Algernon's republicanism gave growing cause for professorial alarm. Now not content with enacting his revolutionary mysteries for a select audience, he delivered public harangues as remarkable for their fire as for the Rabelaisianisms that enriched them. A portrait of Orsini found space on his walls, and thus two ikons received double worship.

Jowett, watching over Algernon as once another young firebrand had been watched at New College, had reason to shake his head as with dismayed tolerance he murmured, "Youth! Youth! It's all youth!" University authorities, however, were not always willing to accord it special privileges, and the gentle master dwelt with melancholy on Shelley's ignominious dismissal. The same error must not occur again.

He recalled with pleasure the first canto of Algernon's "Queen Yseult" that had appeared in *Undergraduate Papers,* the organ of the "Old Mortality." Fine youths, talented youths, all of them: Nichol, Green, Luke, Dicey, Birkbeck Hill, Bruce. Nichol and Swinburne made him uneasy — especially Swinburne. Something not quite of normal youth tormented the lad. He was so different from the athletic population of the university, with his restless, fragile body and faun's head — and uncontrolled passions. Adolescent bubblings, certainly, like those rumors of perverse floggings and drinking — and other things. Mere bravado.

Algernon showed promise. That article on Marlowe and Webster he had published — it revealed good scholarship and a sound, critical mind, if somewhat erratic. But Jowett thought with less pleasure on Algernon's review of a nonexistent book, Ernest Wheldrake's *The Monomaniac's Tragedy,* a hoax which the imp seemed immensely to relish; and on his tirade against church imperialism, winding up with excoriations on Napoleon III. He had heard — and indeed who had not heard of it with Algernon's shrill boasting? — that a few months after the Emperor's escape from death, while the Swinburnes were driving through the Bois with their son during the Easter vacation, the imperial carriage passed by. Admiral Swinburne and Lady Jane bowed. Algernon, on the other hand, stiffened his little body, and, without removing his hat, glared his defiance. "Youth! Youth!"

New contacts had in the meantime come into Algernon's life. Dante Gabriel Rossetti, whose poems had been circulating among the students, had been a frequent guest at the university since the autumn of 1857. On the first day of November, Algernon met him, Morris, and Jones at the Oxford Union, where, sponsored by the fertile Gabriel, an extraordinary undertaking was in progress.

XIV

OXFORD

BENJAMIN WOODWARD's Veronese Gothic buildings were slowly achieving the harmony both he and Ruskin thought in keeping with the surroundings of the university, and it was with pride akin to that of Renaissance builders that they watched each detail budding forth under the hands of their workmen. Arches of the noblest framed space to easy curves, restful to the eye and bidding the spirit look upward. Over the porch sculptors were hewing stories out of stone. And in the Debating Room of the Union wonderful things were happening. Each time Ruskin crossed the threshold he breathed deep of the smell of paint and turpentine as if it were the air of his beloved Swiss mountains, or, better yet, of Fiesole, long ago, when Brunelleschi's cupola was but a calyx of the blossomed rose, below, in the vale of Florence.

Woodward had had dreams of granite and serpentine and porphyry to clothe the skeletons of the columns he had conceived, and Ruskin had seconded him. But the dons' reality was of a brick and mortar cast. There was no money at Oxford for architectural luxury. Moreover, who had ever said they wanted Gothic in the town, such new, peculiar Gothic, on which simple masons hewed their decorations as they saw fit? Why, only the other day a sober member had watched an Irish terror chiseling base simians over a stone lintel; when he had protested, the man changed them to cats, and, when he had decried against the felines, altered them again to ugly birds, each bearing the face of a university don. "Yes, they're howls and parrots," screamed the irate O'Shea. "Howls and parrots! Members of the Con-wocations and dons! Howls and parrots!"

Such outbursts did not tend to ingratiate the university members. As a result, the allowances shrank still more. The pillars that were to have been covered with serpentine remained of rude brick. Nevertheless, neither Ruskin nor the architect was discouraged, and, the better to demon-strate the nobility of labor, Ruskin took off his coat, rolled up his sleeves, and himself erected a pillar, brick by brick, to the amazement of laborers and university men. For a day the tenor of life was off key, but John Ruskin was happy — happy that he had done useful work with his hands and inculcated a moral lesson as well. What matter if the column had to be taken down and made over by a bricklayer? What matter if Oxford intellects held fore-finger to temple when they spoke of Ruskin's feat?

What he had envisioned was coming to pass — not in London, as he had hoped, for London, alas, was beyond re-demption; yet, no matter where, a glorious thing will ever be glorious. Only London, that needed beauty most, was readiest to do without it. His work with Maurice at Great Ormond Street had caused him of late more disappointment than pleasure. His classes were always crowded, it is true, and whenever he lectured to the workingmen he was wildly acclaimed. It was not acclaim he wanted. The louder his "pretty speeches" were applauded, the lower he bowed his head, knowing he had not been understood. In vain he wove his message with simple parables, that their minds might grasp his meaning. Like children to whom one would point a moral with a fable, they were amused but not instructed. He had had to admit to himself that the sense of beauty which his teaching chiefly regarded was, through no fault of theirs, either lacking or perverted in the men he would have taught. "And thoughts respecting beautiful things," he would muse, "are unintelligible to men when the eye has been accustomed to the frightfulness of modern city life."

Religion was beginning no longer to comfort him, though there had been little room for comfort at best in the rigid Sabbatarian training Margaret Ruskin had imposed upon him. The pagan, irresponsible Gabriel had done not a little to jar the pedestal of ethical superiority on which Ruskin had been taught to settle himself when the mire of the world had threatened to stain his boot. "And yet," he had had to confess, "and yet he is a good sort of person." Except with regard to that unhappy girl. But he still had faith that all would be well in the end. Who was he to judge a man of such genius as Gabriel had?

The painting of the hall had been begun in the autumn of 1857, and a great to-do there had been about it. Gabriel, on one of his visits at Oxford, had cast his eyes over the newly finished room and its magnificent expanse of walls begging for paintings. For him to think of a thing was to act upon it. Immediately, Woodward was apprised of how fine it would be if walls and ceiling were frescoed with, say, scenes from the *Morte d'Arthur*, perfect subjects for the simple character of the interior. But who was to do them? And how was one to get the money? Mere lack of funds could not discourage Gabriel. To begin with, he was earnestly eager to experiment in a style he had always admired. Again, he liked the life at Oxford among youths who made a sort of god out of him. And then, there was Jane Burden.

Morris had already written reams of mediævalist verse about her, and she had sat to Gabriel for her portrait. (Guenevere and other romantic names he had written round the margin enclosing her exotic loveliness.) Oxford made him, now nearing thirty, young with the fervency of his early youth. That same fullness of heart that had given him ambition to win the world was his once more, with the added zest of acknowledged leadership. These young men flattered him with imitation. They affected his way of speaking, called all beautiful women stunners, and burst into rhapsodies over that most adorable of God's creatures, the wombat, which most of them, except for Topsy and Ned, had not even seen at the Zoo. But what splendid men they were — Val Prinsep, that comely giant, and Spencer Stanhope, and Hungerford Pollen, the oldest of them, an unfrocked clergyman with his head full of Newman and Catholicism. In each, over whose brow trembled the flame of the ideal, he saw himself as he had been, and was content to remain with the vision. Home was not always reassuring to his self-conceit.

With his accustomed generalship Gabriel soon got together a number of volunteers to decorate the debating hall. They were to receive no money for their labors — fie on lucre when glory was the objective! However, since even the most ethereal of artists need solider stuff than heavenly manna to sustain them, it was arranged that the university should pay their expenses during the course of the work.

The planning began in good earnest. First, each one chose a subject from the Arthurian cycle as best suited to the architecture and their own poetic bent. All through the night in the university chambers Malory's tales rang out in Gabriel's rich voice, and when he was tired Morris succeeded him, thundering his stressed rhythm. More often he produced a bundle of manuscript and sang for them his own versions of Guenevere's sin, marking time with his restless hands. None of your Victorian primness for Morris. "He must be unhealthy in body and mind," he maintained, "who preferred puppets to living men and women." The characters of his poems, in spite of the word-tapestry that enfolded them like a pattern of *mille fleurs*, were animated by a deep life touched with his own intensity. It was the first part of his biography he was writing in mediæval masquerade.

The recognized poet of the circle, however, was Gabriel, though he had shown his work only to the limited world of coterie publications. "The Blessed Damozel," "Sister Helen," and the "Burden of Nineveh" had won him admirers, the last two none other than Ruskin, who, reading the anonymous contributions in the *Oxford and Cambridge Magazine*, felt upon the brink of discovery and wrote to Gabriel to find out their author. He was delighted when his painter-protégé turned out no inconsiderable poet. Indeed, Gabriel's poems, though fitting into the mould of current interest, the ballad-narrative at which every versifier tried his hand, were yet so individual as to be new. Nothing of the mysticism of "The Blessed Damozel" had ever entered into the literature of Victoria's drawing-room, while the pagan, Simætha-like witchcraft of "Sister Helen" was so foreign to polite society as to be shocking.

For ten years Gabriel had also been translating the works of Dante's poetic precursors. The bulk of them would have made a fat volume. His original poems formed a small, choice sheaf, many of them love tributes to Elizabeth, who, in his verse as in his painting, walked with the unearthly majesty of a Beatrice, "not as she was, but as she filled his dream," Christina had put it, a little acidly.

The themes for the murals once chosen, the hall rang with the hubbub of the buoyant crew. Besides Gabriel, Arthur Hughes was the only experienced artist among them, though Hungerford Pollen had done some decoration that had brought him to the notice of Woodward. But even they were novices in the art of fresco painting. Yet, if their equipment was limited, their enthusiasm knew no bounds. Ladders and scaffolds were erected, up and down which they clambered with ceaseless energy, singing, reciting, posing for each other, busy as could be. Not a minute did they hesitate to transfer their designs upon the scarcely finished walls, covered with a thin coat of lime that barely concealed the brickwork underneath. The figures of old romance woke momently to life, Morris's with a speed that was well-nigh magical. Sir Palomides's jealousy of Sir

Tristram was his subject, one of frustrate love which was beginning to crop up in his work with peculiar insistence. Since the appearance of Jane Burden his virgin emotions had been stirred. And it was no wonder, for the beauty of the seventeen-year-old girl had left no artist heart among them untouched. She was one of those destined to live beyond their ephemeral day for the ensorceling of ages to come, like Leonardo's smiling Lisa and Botticelli's long-limbed Venus not yet discovered by Ruskin.

Jane Burden in her un-English features held something that seized upon Gabriel like the summons of his weird. She had appeared, a materialized spirit in the box at the Oxford theatre, her head and shoulders, like those of some angel in an early painting, between earth and heaven. And to Gabriel she seemed both of heaven and of earth. The pale face, shadowed in the semi-darkness by the excesses of her luminous black hair, the wide eyes, lighted by an inner wonder, the full, firmly moulded lips—they were those of a supremely beautiful human creature; but a fascination hung about her, making of her girlish innocence the snare of a *belle dame sans merci*, an Arthurian witch, a sad goddess who was now only a fleeting visitor on earth. Every creative fibre in him had been quickened and he made no effort to conceal it.

Morris would not stand in the way of Gabriel. After all, he was their chosen sovereign, and who could blame anyone for failing to look beyond him to the retainer? Morris became curiously self-effacing. Still he could not silence his heart, and wrote many a stanza "in praise of my lady" in which he ingenuously betrayed the knowledge that another was preferred above him. He doted on her hair, her lips, her eyes.

> So beautiful and kind they are,
> But most times looking out afar,
> Waiting for something, not for me.
> *Beata mea Domina.*

Waiting for *something*, not for me. *Someone* he had not dared write. An association had been made in his mind, linking his *beata Domina* with the unattainable blessed damozel of another. That the other had fealties elsewhere he knew, but, true to his rôle of loyal follower, he felt his lord could do no wrong. Not yet had he overcome his adolescent worship, partly because he had still to find himself, and again because, even in his allegiance, he would not be outdone. Far from him the falseness of a Launcelot, alluring though it seemed as a poetic subject. Therefore he morbidly dwelt upon the despised, rejected lover, and painted him, and tried to lose in multitudinous activity a self he would not face.

His fresco of Sir Palomides was the first begun and nearly finished when the rest had barely laid in their grounds. But none had his energy, that renewed itself with every new labor. Not content with painting, he designed a suit of armor such as the knights of the Round Table might have worn, and enlisted the services of a blacksmith to forge it. The good man had never been called upon for anything of more delicacy than horseshoe nails; nevertheless with Morris's help he produced a coat of mail and a vizor. Morris promptly donned them, but alas, after the vizor was pulled down it would not lift, and fearful were the roars that came from within! It yielded only after concerted action, and Morris took it off for safety's sake. The coat of mail he would not part with the whole of the first day, but strutted about the grounds in it, struggled up the ladders to his painting roost, and even had dinner in it.

"Jones's picture is a perfect masterpiece," Gabriel told his friends. The mild, whimsical Ned had indeed made astonishing progress. A refined invention made up for what he lacked of technique, and in a short time he had acquired such skill that the dealers gladly gave him commissions, signed, importantly, Edward Burne-Jones.

Merlin in the toils of the Damsel of the Lake was Ned's

contribution to the murals. The rest told other incidents of the golden romance. Gabriel had chosen to depict Launcelot barred by his sin from entering the chapel of the Holy Grail. The sinful knight, fallen into a weary sleep before the shrine full of angels, sees in a vision Guenevere arise between him and the Grail. Her gaze is fixed full of deep meaning upon him, as she stands, her arms extended to a cross among the branches of an apple tree. Behind her the Maiden of the Grail holds in vain the chalice he is unworthy to receive. Guenevere's face was the face of Jane Burden; the face of the Maiden, Elizabeth's.

Lizzie did not accompany Gabriel to Oxford, and indeed she would not have been happy there. Betrayed hopes, jealousy, together with the mysterious ill that racked her, made her sharp and impatient with him. Sometimes she would obstinately refuse to see him. Earlier that year he and some friends had talked over with Brown a scheme for renting a building and forming an art colony, with the understanding that Gabriel and Lizzie would be married by the time the plan was carried through. Other artists were also to be invited, with or without their families. Gabriel communicated the plan to Lizzie, who was laconic and listless. Too often had he made similar proposals, without result, for her to believe in them, and he could not blame her unconcern. But when he mentioned that Hunt was to be co-tenant, Lizzie grew pale with indignation and refused with bitterer words than he had ever heard her speak. Then he understood that hers had been a difficult position. "I don't think he has acted lately as a friend toward me in her regard," he confided to Brown. ". . . She seemed last night embittered and estranged, whether for the moment or permanently, I cannot tell."

Lizzie's love, however, was too much her life for her to give up Gabriel, and again, as so often before, she forgot her hurt in whatever happiness she could snatch from their ambiguous position. Quarrels, anguish, partings forever, all led eventually to reconciliation and its short-lived bliss. Her health did not improve by these emotional upheavals. "Miss Siddal has been here three days," wrote Brown shortly after the recent misunderstanding. "She is, I fear, dying." It was not enough that the parlor at Finchley was turned to a sick room; Brown needs must go to town to console Gabriel, who was "so unhappy about Miss Siddal that I could not leave him." He had his hands full with the mad lovers, but, in spite of his help and advice, things were getting worse with them rather than better.

During the months the debating hall was a-painting, a small revolution had turned the venerable precincts to a Bohemia visited with uneasy curiosity by the dons. Those young men were doing a wonderful work, considering it was all for love; yet sometimes, when the shrewder members thought of the prodigious amount of food those spiritual artists consumed, the gallons of paint they splashed, and the exercises they indulged in, ruinous both to morals and to carpentry, they wondered whether it would not have been more profitable to have paid them for their labors and left them to God's mercy and their own resources. Matters were not improved when the red-haired firebrand from Balliol joined the sport. One evening two worthy members came to see the paintings, when they were transfixed on the threshold by the appalling talk that reached their ears. There was Swinburne on one side with Jones, and on the other Stanhope with a friend, all defending fiercely their conception of heaven. For five minutes the respectable gentlemen stood rooted to the spot, listening to descriptions of a rose garden full of stunners, kisses in Paradise, and more sacred intimacies. And then — they fled. Hungerford Pollen evinced qualms for his spiritual health, not to speak of his reputation, whenever he found himself carried against his will into some unusually boisterous escapade. "I greatly fear the disadvantage of appearing in such company," he confessed to his wife.

Ruskin was indulgence itself to his fosterlings, devils though they were. Good Dr. Acland had many a story to tell him of dinners ruined because of them, of all-night sessions of such vociferousness that sleep had become a stranger to Oxford. Notwithstanding, he was always going out of his way to be with the madcaps, unconscious of the title, "Rose of Brazil," they had conferred upon him, and of Ned's comment that "his pulse was only really quickened when osteologists were by who compared their bones with his till the conversation rattled." Poor Acland! And he thought himself so entertaining!

"You know the fact is they're all the least bit crazy," Ruskin explained. He was enchanted with the murals. "Don't annoy yourself about anything you owe me," said he to Gabriel in a burst of enthusiasm. ". . . If you like to do another side of the Union I will consider that as seventy guineas off my debt—provided," the preceptor spoke in him, "provided there's no absolute nonsense in it and the trees are like trees. . . ." Some of the decorations puzzled him, one particularly where Morris, endeavoring to avoid the difficulty of painting the figure,—always a trial to him,—had filled the foreground with gigantean stalks of expanded sunflowers. "Clever but not right," murmured Ruskin. But it did the heart good to see the stocky Morris in his painting coat and baggy trousers, perched on the scaffold many feet above the floor, painting away with a full swing of the arm at his golden palisade.

A spring captured in the fullness of its color did the Union hall appear to those who saw it. Between the sweeping arches, on all sides figures and flowers unfolded the legend of Arthur and his court of noble knights and ladies made for love. The whole room was a flower, with, alas, a flower's impermanence. Before the year was out the paint began peeling with the dampness from the walls, and dropped in petals of loosened flakes. With the next winter, the splendor had faded.

XV

FIRST–FRUITS

AMONG the volumes of verse that hopefully greeted the
spring of 1858, the *Defence of Guenevere and Other Poems*
set the Oxford group and its Pre-Raphaelite friends turning the pages of literary reviews and spying out that most
welcome of early birds, the customer at the booksellers'.
The poems were not new to them, for Morris had chanted
"Guenevere" for them over and over, as well as those
others which under a cloak of mediævalism had been too
keenly felt for forthright expression. However, the experience of seeing them printed between book covers thrilled
the friends equally with the joy of authorship. The literary
among them were immediately moved to bring forth their
first bound volumes, the little Northumbrian newcomer forsaking for the nonce his republican odes to add five more
cantos to "Queen Yseult," and Gabriel whipping into shape
his volume of translations.

Morris's début attained not even a *succès d'estime*, the
book, pulsing with more authentic passion than he was ever
again to command, falling cold upon an apathetic public.
Apathetic? A contented public, rather. It had its Laureate, who soothed their senses when he spoke with not too
much passion; there was Browning, whom it could abuse if
it could not understand. And, satisfying in his approved
way, there was Patmore with his celebration of married
bliss. His *Angel in the House* could be entrusted with
complete assurance to the Victorian virgin, while the *Espousals* might be sent as a wedding box, for not a phrase,

not a word, could have aroused the readiest of virtue's blushes. Yet even Patmore had not been without his days of tribulation. So bitterly attacked had been his first little volume that in despondence of spirit he had bought the publishers' remainders and destroyed them without mercy. George Meredith's *Poems* too might have met the same fate, had the book not cost the author sixty guineas that could well have been used otherwise in his unstable household: he hoped to get some of it back. Few bought it, however, and the critics scarcely noticed it but for one poem, "Love in the Valley," which brought him a letter of praise from Tennyson, lover himself of youth's first passions, though Omphale forbade.

History repeated its worn trick in Morris's case also. The book received scant notice and remained for many years mere lumber in the publishers' storerooms, Victoria's subjects willfully ignoring that something new, a rebirth of that wonder which in Keats had come to flower and died, lived again in their midst. Though the world was indifferent, that smaller and more real world of intimates hailed the book with corporate enthusiasm. Gabriel, writing to Norton, speaks of it and is sure the professor would like it. Browning says in a postscript to William Michael, "I shall hardly be able to tell Morris what I think and rethink of his admirable poems, the only new poems to my mind since there's no telling when."

Morris alone seemed unaffected by either praise or indifference. Other thoughts, closely linked with poetry and more closely still with life, kept him at Oxford long after Gabriel and Ned had gone. His activity was amazing. Now he was modeling, now making designs for stained glass, now carving stone. He tried his hand even at embroidery, making Gabriel guffaw at the news of it: "Topsy's taken to worsted work." Withal, he found time for thinking seriously of marriage.

At twenty-four, Morris was little more than a boy in actual experience. Intense activity, a boisterous heartiness in work and play, and an aggressively sane view of life kept him from brooding long on whatever did not quite dove-tail with his preconceived notions of the world's essential rightness. His secret doubts, a deep-rooted melancholy, a keen sensitiveness quicker to hurt than to heal, and a great heart aching for affection found outlet only in his writings. But never directly; his sensitiveness would not have allowed it. How could he stand naked before the world? "No man, healthy in body and mind . . ." Therefore he had his knights love and woo and suffer in his stead, speak elo-quently with his words and dare all with his passion. Lit-erature was his substitute life, just as Guenevere and all the lovesome ladies of his writings were Jane Burden as he saw her, now the frail queen in love with one other than himself, now the saintly damsel, clasping to her breast nothing more sinful than a spray of summer flowers. He could not, he did not wish to see life as it was, just as he could not bear to look at himself in a mirror. Was it that he was sick of that sham which is reflected upon life's sur-face as life, and sought his truth in the mind's fairer illusion? Or was it that the mirror gave back life too truly, "wart and all"? However it might have been, he created for him-self a niche in his lost world, hallowed it with all that was pure and comely, and retired to it from his everyday life, chaste and toilful though it was. Refuged, he did not suffer from the loneliness which his excellent spirits and boyish-ness hid so well from his friends.

Gabriel was still his master and guide, though he, the disciple, had forestalled him by entering into the lists as a published poet. Still, he had money, which Gabriel had not, a sesame which often enables a man to force many a door otherwise shut to him. Some day, when Gabriel would publish his poems, a marvelous thing would happen in the world. Gabriel was one of those who labor long but bring forth perfection, not like himself, Morris, who was impatient of form if but the spirit were there. It was irksome to polish a poem after it had been written; far easier to write it all over again. How different with Gabriel! No matter how old the work, or how finished, he still found room for improvement — his changes were always for the better. Somehow he seemed to follow the same procedure in his life — but only God knew whether with the same results.

One evening at a coterie meeting, talk had turned to the beauty of Jane Burden. Most of the youths were either in love or engaged, Ned to Georgiana — Georgie — Macdonald, a minister's daughter, Gabriel to Miss Siddal; Morris was the only heart-free bachelor, apparently. "I move," cried Gabriel at his loudest, "I move that Topsy marry Janey to keep the stunner in the family."

There is no record of what Morris said at the moment, or of what he did, whether he turned on Gabriel in chivalric fury at such unbecoming revelation of his heart's secret, or whether he sought to divert interest by giving another imitation of the eagle at the Zoo — climbing on a perch disconsolately and letting himself fall with a heavy plop. From his subsequent behavior, after Gabriel had hurried to Matlock at a summons from Lizzie, whose health had taken a turn for the worse, he felt like the knight who had stifled his own passion for the sake of his brother-in-arms whom he had deemed both loving and beloved, only to find at last that he had always been free.

On the twenty-sixth of April, 1859, he and Jane were married.

Meanwhile Gabriel worked out his peculiar problems. In London again, after Matlock, he nursed Lizzie and exercised his talents trying to please his patrons and himself, succeeding capitally in both. Ruskin's admiration of his protégé, whose drawings he coveted "even more than Turner's," had not diminished, though now and then he could not control a fit of pettishness at his domestic arrangements: his rooms always untidy, his days and nights a chaos, his affections — the less said of them the better. Something was wrong, surely, with the younger generation, an instability of thought and emotion, coupled with immense genius that made them angels walking on the brink of perdition. All, all of them were tainted. Recently at Wallington he had met Swinburne at the home of the Trevelyans, neighbors of that eccentric old baronet, Sir John.

The youth's enormous, devil-touched head, the elfin face with its vast dome and receding chin, repelled him, the lover of beauty; the rebel spirit, so out of bounds with the minikin frame, moved the student of nature to sympathetic understanding. "A dæmonic youth," he murmured. And indeed, there was the smell of sulphur about the demon who tore from his grandfather's to the Trevelyan estate two miles away, his mane and his mare's sweeping in the speed of his going, the air shivering to the shrill of his eldritch voice. Bell Scott saw him and heard him more than once while he was decorating the Wallington staircase with romantic paintings. For him the youth's advent had the "charm of sunshine or champagne."

Admiral Swinburne, however, had small reason to feel proud of his son's career. Things had been bruited at Eton and then at Balliol, vague rumors of imprudences imagined if not practised, that weighed upon the upright mind. After the Oxford Union painting, Algernon had been so unruly that Jowett had counseled rustication for a term. Accordingly the Admiral had sent his son to spend the spring and summer in Essex, trusting that the influence of Dr. Stubbs at the Navestock vicarage might purge him of wildness. There Algernon succeeded only in alarming the churchgoing village by appearing in Dr. Stubbs's garden with locks on end and a dressing gown of outrageous red, this vision of cardinal deviltry early Sunday morning furnishing the town with gossip long after his departure. Again he was urged to make an effort to fit into university life; again brandy and vice got the upper hand.

Perhaps during the hours of reflection in his garden shop, surrounded by the models he had made with his own hands, the Admiral may have suffered at the thought of his son, not brawny enough to follow him in a manly seafaring life, too irresponsible and unwilling to enter upon a dignified profession. The Admiral would not have objected to a lawyer in the family. But Algernon would have none of law; it was too tame and stuffy. He had always possessed a reckless courage and—it was pathetic—the ambition to rival the most muscular of men. Scarcely out of Eton, he had wanted to join the Dragoons—laughable, if it had not been so sad. People at East Dene spoke of the youth as a poet. What sort of poet could he ever become, reflected the artless Admiral, if he could not even take his degree? Relations between father and son became painfully strained, and Lady Jane observed with a pang that Algernon was more often at Wallington than at East Dene.

Diminutive, lively, tactful Pauline, Lady Trevelyan, had built herself, unaided by the saturnine Sir Walter, a select circle that had grown into a creditable salon. She had a taste for literature and painting, practised them both, and admired the young, struggling, and aspiring. It was her ambition to be a patroness of the arts, and, in a sense, the foster mother of genius. At nineteen, as the distinguished Pauline Jermyn, she had met, at a reunion of the British Association for the Advancement of Science at Cambridge, a stern gentleman of forty who lent a grim ear to all she said and scarcely left her a moment out of his appraising gaze. He quickened to livelier interest when he learned that she had read and corrected Dr. Whewell's history of the inductive sciences, a task that proved she possessed more than feminine intellect. Walter Trevelyan, scientist, botanist, and geologist, looked no further for a wife. The poetic interludes that came after, when the young bride sang in

ALGERNON CHARLES SWINBURNE

A PORTRAIT BY GEORGE FREDERICK WATTS

Wedded Love of the joys of marriage, and her industry in mastering water color, left Sir Walter a little cold, though he would no more have thought of interfering with her pastimes than he would have countenanced opposition in his biological experiments or his activity against the abuse of alcohol and nicotine. Many a time Lady Pauline had had fears of becoming a widow when in botanical devotion Sir Walter would eat messes of horrible black fungi gathered with his own hands in the woods, to prove to diffident society that they were not poisonous. Not content with trying them himself, he offered them to his guests, who would much rather have had him exert his generosity towards the wines of the wonderful cellar he had inherited from Sir Benjamin Richardson. A teetotaler himself, however, he discouraged drinking in others, and the man was indeed courageous who filled his glass a second time at Sir Walter's table.

Algernon had come to Lady Pauline hurt from his defeats. Sensitive herself, she read discouragement in the youth's pride, quick to fire. He was disappointed in his studies, in his lack of direction, in his poetry. Twice he had competed for a prize, this time offered by a nonresident member of Oxford for the best poem on the heroic seaman, Sir John Franklin, and once again, as in his attempt to win the Newdigate, he had failed. The announcement in the *Guardian* had set him to work in a fire of inspiration. In two days the "Death of Sir John Franklin" was completed — only to be rejected. Because he knew his poem could never have been classed with the prize-winning doggerel, the bitterness of defeat was the keener. His deepest enthusiasm had gone into play, and all his maturing genius, yet he had failed. Could it be that he was self-deceived? In his resentment he turned against Oxford and university studies, spending himself in sterile imitation of Elizabethan tragedy and Pre-Raphaelite dolor — and in drink, for, although John Nichol had left Oxford, his influence lingered.

Jowett had had occasion to shake his head more apprehen-
sively than ever. The school authorities, after the Oxford
Union scandals, and now, this, might be tempted to adopt
drastic measures. Happily they showed themselves lenient.

Algernon, however, smarted too sharply under his
ignominy to feel beholden, and it was a bridling *bête fauve*
that entered the drawing-room at Wallington. Lady
Trevelyan welcomed him with open arms. Here was a
wounded lion cub that she could nurse and tame and then
let loose before her amazed company. Algernon responded
gratefully to her ministrations. On gala nights in the season,
in the midst of select assemblages, he would be invited to
hymn his poems in the style he had derived from his mother.
Everything was forgotten during his poetic seizure: Lady
Trevelyan, with her understanding hazel eyes flashing encouragement; Sir Walter, dreaming of some new species of
fungus, grim in a corner, his long black wig enfolding his
face like a Florentine scholar's hood; the enraptured yet
disconcerted ladies, hiding bewilderment behind their fans
— everything was forgotten but the uncanny power that
possessed him.

There was something obviously abnormal, not only in
Algernon's appearance, but also in his movements. He
danced, rather than walked; his every gesture was explosive.
Lady Jane had noticed in the child the rigid throwing back
of his slight torso, and, in excitement, the ceaseless activity
of his hands. She had consulted her physicians, but they
had had no remedy to offer. Algernon was high-strung.
In time he might outgrow these little oddities, they said.
Adolescence had only aggravated them, and now, in Lady
Trevelyan's salon, that shaken body, the intense gaze,
oblivious of its surroundings, might have belonged to an
epileptic. And then that uncontrolled, shrill flow of dec-
lamation — it was unnatural, and not a little frightening.

The winter of 1860 saw Algernon settled at Grafton
Street, Fitzroy Square, a few steps from the British

Museum, thanks to his mother's womanly tact in convincing her husband that, after all, their son's life was his own to live. The Admiral, a fond father in spite of his sternness, settled a comfortable allowance upon him with freedom to live wherever he chose. Algernon chose the mad, bad, glad divine artists under whose influence he had fallen at Oxford. Soon he appeared in the dignity of print with two undergraduate plays dedicated to Gabriel. Dignity? He was alone to feel clothed in it, for the public, unlike the Eastern king's of the fable, refused to see him clothed in anything—indeed, refused to open its eyes at all. The critics, for all the courtesy of presentation copies, gave the book no mention except for one, who, like the boy in that same fable, cried aloud that the poet had nothing on. The volumes gathered dust unmolested on the stalls; never had there been such incuriousness in literary history. Even Morris's fledgling verse had not been so completely ignored. Swinburne's pride was stung, but he could twit his humiliation. "Of all still-born books," he would say, "the *Queen Mother* was the stillest," or again, gravely, "To date seven copies have been sold."

Yet there were beauties enough scattered through the plays to have warranted a passing tribute from the most uncharitable of reviewers, for Swinburne had taken no small pains to polish and deck them with whatever he had gleaned from his beloved Elizabethans and the Pre-Raphaelites. Not that he weakly echoed. His iterations, like his reading of another's verse, gave the substance transmuted by his individual characteristics, already strongly defined in the two plays. Where he admired, he was the mistress who did nothing but what would have pleased her lover. Feminine submission vied with a stubborn, exacting, if courteous, despotism, which, when inclined, he was not loth to exercise. During the writing of the *Queen Mother*, Gabriel had talked with too contagious enthusiasm of Wells's *Joseph and His Brethren* for Algernon not to have incorporated in his own the doubtful virtues of the unwieldy play which for more than a generation had remained forgotten, even by its author. Admiring Gabriel, he admired also his predilections. Even Denise, with her thick golden hair and swan-like throat, belonged to a Rossetti canvas. Rossetti's too, more than Pre-Raphaelite, the spice of graceful sacrilege,

> By God, how fair you are.
> It does amaze me; surely God felt glad
> The day he finished making you . . .

which, in his Wheldrake mood, Algernon could satirize, as in his parody of the damozel poet.

> Her bosom is an oven of myrrh to bake
> Love's white warm shewbread to a browner cake.

Admiration and satire, mystic ritual and sacrilege, self-abasement and fanatical rebellion, all were implicit in the first play. "Rosamond," however, struck the keynote of what was to be Swinburne's individual theme: love and hate, pleasure and pain, in inseparable alliance.

> I Helen, holding Paris by the lips,
> Smote Hector through the head: I Cressida
> So kissed men's mouths that they went sick or mad,
> Stung right at brain with me. . . .

So spoke Rosamond, "fair fool, with her soft shameful mouth," in the intoxication of that love that

> . . . makes the daily flesh an altar cup
> To carry tears and rarest blood within
> And touch pained lips with feast of sacrament.

Again the sacrilege, not parodied now, but earnest as a dark ritual.

A hell and heaven removed, this, from the lily mysticism of the damozel's yearning. Not in that strain did Swin-

burne speak, or was ever to sing of passion. No unattained
longings for his men and women, but fulfillment to surfeit,
after which nothing roused desire but the perverse. He
might, in moments of imitativeness, yearn chastely for Pre-
Raphaelite love, fuller of sighs than caresses. In his true
voice he preferred to dwell on "bitter touches of the lip,"
"mouths that bite their hard kiss through," and, with Henry
the King, cry,

> God help! your hair burns me to see like gold
> Burnt to pure heat; your color seen turns in me
> To pain and plague upon the temple vein. . . .

Ignorant as yet of actual passion, congenitally incapable
of normal appeasement, he wrested it from his imagination
—to the limit. His budding manhood had consumed no
ardors on an "impossible she," nor perforce sublimated them,
like Rossetti, first in his love of Elizabeth, made unattainable
through illness, later in his passion for Jane, unattainable
through his earlier pledged word; nor, like Morris, had he
compelled himself to resignation by his self-inflicted code of
chivalry. Whatever stressed the tenuous and Early Christian in the writings of the two men was justified by experience more than by adopted mannerism. Swinburne's
mediævalisms were scholarly affectations, pallid against the
high crimson of his sadic strain.

A few years later, in France, the compendious Goncourt
brothers had occasion to examine a young Englishman ad-
dicted to practices characteristically dubbed "le vice anglais"
by Gallic delicacy. So striking is the resemblance the word
portrait bears to the Swinburne of coming years, that it is
sufficient to fix him as a type. "A young man . . . with
temples swollen like an orange," the Journal records, "eyes
of a clear, sharp blue, an extremely delicate skin revealing
the subcutaneous network of the veins, and the head—
strange—the head of one of those emaciated, ecstatic young
priests that surround the bishops in the old paintings."

(Gabriel had used Algernon more than once as a model for his Christian paintings.) "He is an elegant young man, a little stiff in the arms, and with bodily motions at once mechanical and feverish, like those of a man with the beginnings of a disease in the spinal marrow; withal, he has excellent manners, exquisite courtesy, and a peculiar gentleness of behavior. . . . He talks and talks incessantly . . . and his somewhat singsong voice drills his cannibalistic words into your ears. . . ."[1] The stiffness of the arms, the mechanical yet feverish motions of the body, were Swinburne's; the courtesy, the gentleness, the flood of speech, all his. The *Queen Mother* volume betrays the Goncourt Englishman's prototype, still unsure, yet groping his way to a full expression of his nature. These are but lispings of the "cannibalistic words" to come.

Like a *deus ex machina*, a guide presented himself to him at Lady Trevelyan's—none other than Monckton Milnes (Lord Houghton), known in the early career of the Pre-Raphaelites as the editor of Keats. A littérateur, a dilettante, a man of the world, and an amateur psychologist, Milnes loved to play with men the part of destiny in Omar's checkerboard of nights and days, or, in keeping with the spirit of the age, of the scientific experimenter with his test tubes, combining divers human elements, passions, and weaknesses for the titillations the results afforded him. The ecstatic youth who poured forth whole books of European literature with the rush of a Niagara, who had the courtesy of a dauphin and in anger the language of Billingsgate, roused the experimental rage of the connoisseur. Here was a find for the inn of strange encounters, his home in Yorkshire. Here was a pretty chemical to make a whole laboratory of curious elements seethe and bubble in merry dance. The naked spot on Milnes's cranium flushed; the eyes peered hungrily; the thin nostrils quivered in the ambush of graying beard bordering his face. Ah, if he

---

[1] Author's translation.

could carry away this treasure to the wild gardens of Fryston, untenanted but for the companions of his choice, innocent of the influence of his wife, since not the most devoted of hostesses could stay the season in the damp of Yorkshire. There he would have Swinburne stand on a chair as he had seen him do at the Trevelyans', and, before a select gathering, have him declaim the most daring of poems. Milnes had a sharp appetite for the daring, though he himself never went beyond the writing of sentimental ditties, set to music by popular composers and sung by young ladies in unimpeachable salons. Another facet of his curious nature. . . .

It was not long before Algernon arrived as guest at the sprawling, ungainly building that was Fryston, lying in its acres of overgrown park like a dragon in wait for the unwary traveler. Within, it was hospitable enough, with its comfortable chairs before great, windy fires, and its generous bedrooms. Books closed in upon one everywhere, overflowing into the least likely places and vying for interest with curiosities and works of art of a decided genre. A cosmopolite par excellence, Milnes had rifled Europe for the decoration of his home, so that now, in his fiftieth year, he could boast of a sybarite's paradise. His erotic engravings, some excessively rare, were the envy of septuagenarians; his library of pornography spiced the talk of the clubs throughout Europe. Algernon was soon initiated into the exquisiteness of a Sapphic group by Pradier, and illustrated editions of the divine Marquis whose intoxicating poison Milnes had already poured into the youth's ready ears.

Then the refined cynic turned his prize loose in his sapiently arranged pleasure garden, and in the shelter of literature and art the seduction of a mind was accomplished. Not that Algernon was intellectually intact. The excursions of his curious genius had made it impossible. But it was Milnes's hand that pointed him down the bypath to the shadow where, from its pedestal, leered the face of his

Satanic Majesty, the Marquis de Sade. Algernon responded. From the first the Marquis became the Allah of his faith, with himself as the chosen prophet.

In the background the high priest smiled.

XVI

"SHADY HILL"

"Your 'Shady Hill' is a tempting address, where one would wish to be. It reminds one somehow of *Pilgrim's Progress* where the pleasant names of heavenly places really make you feel as if you could get there. . . . I find no shady hill or vale, though, in these places and pursuits which I have to do with."

So wrote Gabriel to Norton, back in his Chatham Place studio, Blackfriars. How, after Oxford, could he feel pleasure in the stench of the docks a stone's throw from the windows, the old hulls of ships rotting like things unburied, among the ooze and the slime and the jetsam cast ashore by the tides? And how could he find peace in the disorder of his life? A less naïf pilgrim, he had been groping his way toward a place whence he could see all things clear, his own puzzling self clearest of all: in vain. Whenever he seemed to see most clearly, he saw least of all; and he knew it, for the mists that blinded his true vision he himself raised up out of pleasant sophistries. It is scant comfort to know oneself self-deceived. In his excruciatingly tender moral mind, Gabriel had made him a hell as wasting as the fires of his own witch Helen; he saw himself consumed like the image, relentlessly, to the soul, and, like that image, was only melting wax in the power of that thing stronger than himself.

"What I ought to do is what I can't do." How often had he had reason to reproach himself when Lizzie's sad, spent eyes saw through him mutely! He knew what she read — scorn of himself for his passions too violently stirred (not by her now); torment of a word pledged which he would have unsaid; mutiny against fate and self and his sense of honor; and pity for her. She was now a confirmed invalid, going from one place to another in search of respite from her suffering. She had released Ruskin long since of his agreement; she had had so little to offer, and she was too proud to accept his help "as she would have accepted a glass of water when she was thirsty"—Ruskin's delicate plea. Strangely enough, Gabriel had been glad to have Ruskin's help cease. He could feel Lizzie more completely his own when he could supply her wants from his earnings—his own more wholly, now that he wished she had not come so early, and that other so late.

They say that when a prisoner, tried for his life, learns at last that the judgment is death, a peace settles upon him unlike the agonies of doubt and suspense that had made each day a punishment. Some such quiet settled on Gabriel when, that night in April, he knew Jane married. Was it a sentence of death? Then he would face it, knowing it had been marked down for him since the beginning of time.

He buried himself deep in his work, fulfilled commissions with extraordinary exactitude, completed his designs for the Llandaff Cathedral triptych, and even managed to get his translations ready for the printer. The publication of his own poems, the ballads and the sonnets to Lizzie, he put aside for the moment. Perhaps something of the bygone passion of them no longer struck true. Nevertheless he showed Ruskin some of his longer, more impersonal writings, reasoning that, as a critic in touch with the public, he would have the guiding reaction. However, things unknown to the rest of the world had also been happening to Ruskin, who answered in a moralizing strain unbearable to Gabriel in the state of his emotions. He had written to a man the weight of whose mind had been bearing down on a whole school of art, only to be lectured to by a schoolmistress.

"I do not think 'Jenny' would be understood but by few. . . . The character of the speaker himself is too doubtful. . . . He reasons and feels entirely like a wise and just man — yet is occasionally drunk and brutal: no affection for the girl shows itself — his throwing the money into her hair is disorderly. . . . I don't mean that an entirely right-minded person never keeps a mistress: but, if he does, he either loves her — or, not loving her, would blame himself, and be horror-struck for himself no less than for her."

Did Ruskin intend a lesson? "I don't mean that an entirely right-minded person never keeps a mistress . . ." A generous admission, coming from Ruskin, meaning more than it implied. "But, if he does, he either loves her — or, not loving her . . ." Words, words, words. But they burned worse than fire. Lizzie was no mistress; not the blessed damozel in her heaven was purer in his sight. *He* was the unworthy one, for he had committed the sin of the mind more heinous than any bodily betrayal. As always, his imagination carried him beyond the bounds of reasonable guilt-consciousness, prostrating him to the ground for pleasures keener in their imaged attainment than any realization. Mystic that he was, flesh and spirit held the same meaning for him, the one indistinguishable from the other in exaltation of body or soul.

> Lady, I fain would tell how evermore
> Thy soul I know not from thy body, nor
> Thee from myself, neither our love from God.

As the months passed in sight of the ordered domesticity of his acquaintances, he could not help making the contrast between their gladly borne responsibilities and his careless Bohemianism. Brown, not so many years older than himself, had grown children — Lucy almost a young lady, and Cathy and Nolly shooting up like plants in summer. The delight of Brown's heart they were, and he was never so happy as when he watched them working under his direction in his studio. Millais, Gabriel saw hardly at all. The tie of common interest had long grown slack. But everyone knew of his armload of beautiful babies whose faces began to appear in his paintings. Then there was Morris, so much younger than himself—Janey had hopes of making him a father. Delicate Ned Jones was planning for his coming marriage to Georgie. Even Christina was taking pains with her dress and wearing her hair in becoming braids circling her head—for Cayley's sake. Why was he barring himself from life? He was free to do his duty long deferred—by what vain hopes?

The spring of 1860 he joined Lizzie at Hastings after a long estrangement neither could explain. They were to be married in a few weeks. It was the risen ghost of the exquisite child of ten years ago whom he nursed to a semblance of health through weary nights and days, and a madman, aware of his madness, who tended her. Though abnormally squeamish in the presence of disease and pain, Gabriel helped her devotedly through her recurring attacks, feeling each time as if he had wrenched her from the arms of death. He carried her up and down the stairs of the little cottage, guided her steps like a child's when she was strong enough to stand, coaxed her to eat, even ever so little, on the chance that she might not bring up her food as she had been doing for days. It would have been a harrowing experience for any normal man; it was a cruel torment to Gabriel. He bore it with the fortitude of a martyr—indeed, his was a martyrdom, self-inflicted, that he might purge himself of his unfaith.

The starkness of a ballad was in the macabre betrothal, with Lizzie like the betrayed girl who came out of her grave to summon her lover to grisly nuptials—except that here it was the lover, strong and body-whole, who claimed his phantom spouse. Unnatural it was, and ill-omened. Morbid thoughts obsessed him. Long ago he had made a

sketch of an idea that had tracked him with sinister intent;
the picture of two lovers who, as they are walking through
a darkling wood, meet the shadows of themselves face to
face—a warning of coming death. The girl, aghast,
swoons, as her lover, supporting her with one arm, seeks with
his sword to thrust the phantoms through. "How They
Met Themselves." With disturbing insistence the sketch
obtruded itself into his consciousness, clamoring to be executed in spite of the overdue commissions lying unfinished in
Chatham Place. Lizzie was too ill, however, to permit of
his working, so he put it off to care for her with redoubled
devotedness.

She, poor girl, accepted his attentions with mute thanksgiving, not knowing, nor could he have explained, to what
they might be attributed. After he had come back so
changed from Oxford, she had nurtured a dim trust that
they would eventually marry, in spite of his swerving feet.
With every separation the chances seemed dimmer, until,
with untold anguish, she had settled to a confirmed faith
that death would come before. Then, that inexplicable
estrangement. . . . She was not of a confiding nature,
and, indeed, few would have appreciated the complexity of
the ties that kept her and Gabriel dangling over the gulf
in the hands of some capricious fate. In more than
Christian patience she possessed her soul, turning to the
world a face as enigmatic in its suffering as it had been in the
time of her short-lived joy. No one spoke of her engagement within her hearing. It would have been a cruel
jest. Only Emma was sometimes admitted into the secret
of her misgivings. And there was one other confidant,
the book into which she scribbled her verses.

How much it held in its melancholy little burden her
eyes alone had seen. The theme was always love—love
betrayed and come too late to the appreciation of the spurned
one's worth. Now she mourned her lost lover; now she
wept for herself as she would have had Gabriel weep for

her when she was dead. Inspired for him in his imagined grief, as if he had not at his command fair words enough, she made him a keening for his mouth. Some day, some day he would speak it, but she would have no ears to hear.

> I watch the shadows gather round my heart,
>   I live to know that she is gone —
> Gone, gone forever, like the tender dove
>   That left the ark alone.

But now, at last, miracle of miracles, he had come to keep his plighted word, and like heavy dreams her fears were lifted with the sunrise of his coming. Heroically she walked the weary way back to life, all-forgiving of the phantoms that had oppressed her — for what were they but phantoms in her present happiness: Fanny Cornforth, and the other, and the others. . . .

They were married quietly at Hastings, and Gabriel's mother and Brown, friend of friends, were the first to be apprised.

Little cheer gladdened the household at Upper Albany Street upon reception of the news, and truly his scribbled note far from expressed the ecstasy of a lover joined to his heart's desire. Between the lines stalked the rueful shadow of duty accomplished; once it showed its naked face. "Like all the important things I have ever meant to do — to fulfill duty or secure happiness — this one has been deferred almost beyond possibility." Woeful fulfillment! Better far had his habit of procrastination won out! The three women who felt they stood to Gabriel in the closest relationship would have been more than human had they accepted his step with equanimity. Lizzie was a dying woman; Gabriel, their son and brother, nearing the pinnacle he would surely attain. But now — now he would have to struggle on with a dead weight upon his shoulders.

His note to Brown hid much that was sad, in spite of the jovial all-hail of the greeting. "I am sorry I cannot give you good news of her health, but we must hope for the best. We go to Folkestone this afternoon. . . . If you are still with Top, best love to the Topsies." Scarcely an hour since he had left St. Clement's Church with his wife on his arm, and his thoughts were winging from Hastings to Upton, where Morris was building a miniature castle for his queen. But he — had he not come to his Shady Hill?

Their honeymoon in Paris was a happy time, at least for Lizzie, whose health bore up remarkably under the feverish pace of visits to the museums and galleries. Gabriel showed her every attention, and, knowing how delighted she would be, gave her a packet of notepaper with her new initials, E. E. R., stamped upon it. Only at times he fell into a brooding silence when he thought of the unfinished pictures in London, clamored for by Plint and Gambart, Gillum and old Marshall, pictures already paid for, and the money gone. He could not afford to be Bohemian now, not while Lizzie depended wholly upon him like a helpless child. And here he was in Paris, spending, spending, and earning nothing. Relentlessly, the sketch of "How They Met Themselves" kept hounding him. He looked at Lizzie, sitting spent in an armchair, her head thrown back as if by the weight of her massive hair, her long throat languorous, her cheeks wax-pale under the golden fringe of her lids. Her breast hardly rose with her breath. As in the olden days, he made one drawing after another of her, all of a face unsmiling in enigmatic poise. Finally, unable to resist the urgency of the *Doppelgänger* drawing, he worked on it through the last days of their stay in Paris, until it was finished. The girl, copied in face and form from the ailing Lizzie, resembled her like a twin.

Exciting days followed on their return to England: friends to be received, — not many of them, as Lizzie could not bear the strain, — home to be arranged; a pleasant prospect for Gabriel, who loved to build about himself an untidy nest of quaint and lovely things. But first he found lodgings for Lizzie at Hampstead, until they could obtain a house within their income. In the meantime Gabriel kept his studio at Blackfriars.

The Browns were the first to visit the newly married pair, and Swinburne, and Ned and Georgie Jones, themselves recently wed. In the less intimate circles gossip wondered why none of the Rossetti women came to see the bride. Ruskin, too, did not appear at the studio, but then, he had been abroad, and those who knew whispered he was in no mood for society. The Morrises, taken up with their home at Upton, and other more intimate events, were for the moment in seclusion.

In spite of Gabriel's efforts, no house was to be had at Hampstead. By a happy chance the second floor of the adjoining building at Chatham Place was available, and he took it at the instance of Lizzie, who preferred being there, even with the sickening exhalations of the water, than away from her husband. A communicating door was cut through between the studio and the living quarters. Happy weeks passed in decorating their little home, humble indeed in comparison with the magnificent Towers of Topsy, with their apple orchards, their turrets, and the huge painted settle that had been the astonishment of Red Lion Square. Yet if Topsy's Webb-designed domicile was "more of a poem than a house," as Gabriel said, his little home and Lizzie's was lovely, too. The fireplace, covered with blue glazed Dutch tiles of Bible subjects, welcomed with its simple comfort and made one think of the child Wesley learning Scriptures from just such rude painting, at his mother's knee. The wall paper Gabriel had designed himself, to serve as background for the many queerly shaped mirrors, vases, and knickknacks he had collected in his rummagings of out-of-the-way curiosity shops. The drawing-room, dedicated to Lizzie, was hung with her water colors. They had a bullfinch, too, in the sunniest room, and doves, to keep her cheerful with their song and cooing.

The summer passed and autumn was on the wane, and still no sign of old Mrs. Rossetti. It was the usual jealousy between mother and daughter-in-law. Mrs. Rossetti had been accustomed to having her children well under her thumb; her daughter-in-law she could not easily subdue. There was Lizzie's sickness to contend with, and also her will, not slow to manifest its tyranny where her hard-won happiness was menaced. The two women understood each other, but without love. Gabriel, like most men in such a case, did not know what fealty to follow, and so gave way to Lizzie and made explanations to his mother. "I hope," he wrote, while the apartment was a-furnishing, "I hope that we may manage to have your company in our new rooms. Nothing would give me greater pleasure, as nothing pains me more than the idea of our being in any way divided."

A change for the better came over Lizzie. Encouraged by it, she took up her paints and, as long ago, worked side by side with Gabriel. Continued effort tired her, however, making the brushes fall from her fingers and her head droop. Then she would watch him with dumb, far-off eyes. He knew, and knew that she felt, that the old days of hope were over.

PART THREE

"And our little life . . ."

XVII

OLD AND NEW

"The Pre-Raphaelite cause has been doubly betrayed by the mistimed deliberation of one of its members, and the inefficient haste of another; and we have to regret at once that the pictures of Holman Hunt were too late for the exhibition and those of Everett Millais were in time for it."

Thus Ruskin in his *Academy Notes*, the year of Sir Isumbras. Friends and enemies of the cause read the pronouncement with interest: anything that "savage Ruskin" said bore pondering. Dealers consulted with one another: to buy or not to buy? It would not do to take lightly the opinion of art's high priest. Critics repeated the query: to praise or not to praise? Meanwhile, since the initial issue of 1856, artists awaited *Academy Notes* with fear and trembling, not infrequently wishing its author at the bottom of some crevasse of the Alps he loved so well. "The little despot imagines himself the Pope of Art," complained Woolner (Ruskin disliked all sculpture), "and would wear three crowns as a right, only they would make him look funny in London." *Punch*, keen to the situation, voiced the Academician's lament.

> I paints and paints,
> Hears no complaints,
> And sells before I'm dry;
> Till savage Ruskin
> Sticks his tusk in,
> And nobody will buy.

In the case of the Pre-Raphaelites, Ruskin had all reason to be savage — at least, so he thought. He had championed them heart and soul when all the world was against them, popularized their school, found purchasers for them, confident that their movement would assert itself permanently; optimistic to exaggeration, he saw them spread their influence to life and humanity till the new generation turned sunward faces touched with a diviner light. But what had happened? After the first few years Millais had been guilty of the grossest betrayal by yielding to popular taste. Would he deny it? His choice of subject alone sufficed to prove it. What had he now comparable in poetry to the drowning "Ophelia," or in skill to the painting of the water reeds and flowering shrubs? Would he say his technique had improved? No, it had grown careless, careless because hasty, and hasty so that the Academy walls might not be without his work. He, Ruskin, had examined his paintings, one after the other, year after year. He saw, not progress, but deterioration, and an unforgivable betrayal.

He could not forbear making his moan to Val Prinsep during the exhibition of 1859. Prinsep reported it to Millais; Millais, stung to petulance, worried, moreover, by the pack of critics who had taken up the cry, complained to Euphemia. "He does not understand my work . . . too broad for him to appreciate, and I think his eye is only fit to judge the portrait of insects. . . ." Euphemia agreed with him and made sure to keep the newspapers from the old folks, who would have been needlessly pained. Johnny was too sensitive: he could not bear to have those who knew him as a genius discover that there were envious criticasters who did not share their view. Awaiting his return, she practised at the piano the pretty things he liked, to smooth his hurt. That Ruskin, with his pontifical airs! Only a man willfully blind could fail to see in the "Vale of Rest" the advance Millais had made. What if he had adopted a broader treatment in place of minute finish? That whole Pre-Raphaelite affair was a dreadful bore, and her former husband with it!

What Ruskin did not know was that nearly all the Pre-Raphaelites had long ago ceased to look upon their venture as anything graver than a schoolboy challenge. "The thing was a solemn mockery and died of itself," Hunt had said in 1855. True, but not wholly. The brotherhood as a body may have ceased to function after the meetings had been discontinued and the members dispersed, two geographically and one by the lure of his own wonderland. They were still bound by the solidarity of their rebellion. What had really taken place was nothing other than the assertion of individual talent over the rules imposed. Millais's may have been only a schoolboy mutiny incited by the fever of success and Gabriel's rhetoric; perhaps a temporary adoption of rosy glasses over his true practical vision. As time went on, and the mutinous spirit grew calm in the fair weather of recognition, the rosy glasses slipped from eyes that saw as others would have them see. After all, in the run of common living, rosy glasses are a hindrance.

Hunt's rebellion, however, had come from the conviction of his inmost being, strengthened by frequent self-communings, and later by Ruskin's support. A solemn mockery? He could not look at his paintings — few, and labored and painfully earnest — and cry them mockeries! Every brush stroke on the gems decking the vestments of his hieratic Christ, every detail of the landscape closing like doom upon the tragic atoning beast, confirmed mutely the sincerity of the early ideals. He remained a Pre-Raphaelite, in spite of his denial, because he could not be false to his essential nature.

For a number of years he had been unable to exhibit a figure picture, a failure which had contributed toward making Ruskin lose faith in his prophetic powers. He had brought back from the Holy Land few canvases and countless studies; his cruelly analytical conscience was like a hand that held back his brush whenever he would have painted. While his fellow artists were building fortune and reputation, he brooded in bitter impotence. Nothing he did satisfied the inner censor. He began to believe in a malignant spirit that set itself to impede the progress of his work because, in a certain sense, it was the work of God. Only after unimaginable struggles was he able to finish his "Christ in the Temple," the most ambitious work that had ever left his studio. Hunt was then thirty-three years old.

If the malignant one had done its utmost to keep the painting from being finished, it did not seem reluctant to wish it success, perhaps hoping, with the logic of devils, that pride cometh before a fall. It was purchased by Gambart for fifty-five hundred pounds, and exhibited by itself at a private gallery with handsome draperies behind it and curtains of plush at the grate to keep the crowds from approaching too close. Though Gambart had demurred at the price, he could tell by the hundreds of people who pressed to see it that he would get more than a profitable return. For months the street was choked with carriages. Ladies came to see it in their flowering taffetas and parasols, later in furs and shawls. Dickens complained that his Bond Street hatter had become madder than ever at the traffic that blocked the entrance to his establishment. Frederic Stephens watched with interest the sale of the pamphlet he had written for the gallery. One day, in the thick of the exhibition, hundreds were turned away by the triumphant announcement that Her Majesty and the Prince Consort had commanded the painting to be brought to the palace. On its return it received more visitors than before. It was a signal Pre-Raphaelite success, though the *Times* mentioned it not at all and the artist Dyce only sufficiently to say that it was three paintings in one.

The showing continued successfully through the winter, till the frustrate devil waxed wroth at the number of souls edified by the holy scene, and with a lick of its fiery tongue — some say it was the gas flame — set fire to the handsome draperies. Scores ran for the fire pails and found nothing but ice. The labor of many painstaking years would have gone up in flames had not a lady removed her Indian shawl and thrown the gorgeous extinguisher upon the fire. Even the devil could not but be touched by such sacrifice, and vanished in a puff of smoke. Months later it was discovered that the lady had been none other than Swinburne's Lady Pauline.

Meanwhile, with the original Pre-Raphaelitism, another was beginning to be linked that had as little in common with the school of 1848 as if it had never derived from it. As a matter of fact, it had not, for Gabriel's influence, not that of the group, was the fountainhead.

Up until 1860, Rossetti had been more or less conscious of his early affiliations and produced first his sacred pictures and then the water colors that had conquered Ruskin. Yet, even through the chaste conceptions of "Dante on the Anniversary of the Death of Beatrice," the "Tune of the Seven Towers," the "Blue Closet" that inspired Morris to a poem, there had glimmered perverse, subtly alluring innuendoes. "Lucrezia Borgia," a fit child of Delacroix had she not had the subtlety of Rossetti, "Bocca Baciata," for which, as for other sense-ravishing women, Fanny had sat, went hand in hand with the chaste ladies of romance. The Byronic inheritance was strong in Gabriel. It was gradually gaining the ascendant, both in the oils that marked his new period and in his verse.

It was not without significance that of the many paintings at the Beaux Arts he should have singled out those of Delacroix. No virtues of neat brushwork and high finish could have recommended the chaotic artist to the eyes of a Pre-Raphaelite: something deeper than workmanship captured the mind of Gabriel, a kinship perhaps of spirit, if not of genre.

Baudelaire, speaking of Delacroix, likened him to Poe. Both made their creatures move against green and purple backgrounds whence sprang "the phosphorescence of decay and the breath of the storm." The "Sardanapalus," the "Medea," the figures writhing in an orgy of violence and rapine in "La Prise de Constantinople," are things of the abyss whose counterparts in the world of men inspired the myths of horror. Medea, clutching against her swollen breasts the squirming bodies of the babes she had suckled, rises out of her cave-dim background like a torch from a pit, a dread embodiment of hate and love. Resolve glows in her terrible eyes, beautiful in their evil as her children's in their guileless wonder: the same eyes, the same flesh of her flesh, both born of love, both to be quenched by love-engendered hate. Her step falters. Killing them with the dagger in her hand is killing herself twice over. Will she have the strength? One look backward at her dis-honored hearth and she can pierce that dearer flesh through and through and through, each wound a bleeding mouth for every faithless kiss.

Medea with her dagger, Helen with her waxen puppet, both were sisters. Sisters too, but of a more luxurious be-cause more spiritual evil, the women who from now on began haunting Gabriel's creative hours.

The new school grew. Arthur Hughes, Charles Collins, and Windus had for years been recognized as disciples, though Collins had done little to justify his title as artist, what with his lack of skill and his anxiety to rival his brother Wilkie with the pen. Morris, Burne-Jones, and Val Prinsep, in so far as they painted, were followers of Rossetti's romantic art rather than of the Pre-Raphaelite tradition. So, too, was Frederick Sandys, to the discomfiture of Rossetti, who saw in the figures and conceptions of his erstwhile caricaturist more than a sincere form of flattery. Nearer the throne came the youngest of the disciples: Paton; Fred Walker, slight, small, and strung like a harp in the wind; Albert Moore, and a graceful, long-eyed Jewish boy by the name of Simeon Solomon. Wherever Pre-Raphaelite paintings were to be seen, they were sure to cluster, eager for the masters' secrets.

Simeon Solomon came of a family where art was second only to the synagogue. Old Mr. Solomon, a Leghorn-hat importer of comfortable means, had seen his wife's undeveloped talent come to fruition in his children. In 1858 Abraham's "Waiting for the Verdict" had been proposed for the Liverpool prize, which was given, however, to Millais for his "Blind Girl," much to the displeasure of the public, which had so admired Abraham's that chromolithographs of it were bought by the thousand. But Abraham's creativeness was of short duration. He died at Biarritz in his twenty-first year, the very day he had been made Associate of the Royal Academy.

Rebecca, too, inherited the family talent, and with it, from some obscure seed, a nature ever hungering for excitement. Now sad, now gay, she went from one extreme of emotion to another, quenching both at last in drink. With her marked Semitic beauty and her disregard for conventions, she easily became the centre of a motley group where morals existed only to be ignored and laws to be broken. Still, she found time to show paintings regularly at the Academy, where her "Peg Woffington" won its share of acclaim. Millais found her in her sober moments sufficiently trustworthy to be his studio assistant when the pressure of commissions required a skilled hand to make copies and paint in draperies. Yet, with her frank excesses, Rebecca was deeply religious, attending to her duties at the synagogue with the same fervor she put, scarcely an hour later, into the pursuit of pleasure. Mysticism, hedonism — she was the helpless pendulum between.

Simeon became the admiration of mature artists when, scarcely in his teens, he showed his early drawings. Rossetti saw them and envied the finished draftsmanship. The Academy a few years later exhibited them, when Burne-Jones speaking of them admiringly woke jealous worries in

Georgie, for whom none must dare surpass her Ned. In 1860 his picture, "Moses," evoked praise from Thackeray in the *Roundabout Papers* and made him famous overnight. But his finest works the larger public did not see.

Like his sister Rebecca, Simeon had received a double heritage of darkness and light, in him with the shadows darker and the light more radiant with promise. Those who saw the youth walking the London streets with the gracing step of an Eastern god hoped high for him, yet feared when they saw how fanatical were his religious observances and how easily he turned from them to mundane pleasures. He combined the features of a David and a Dionysos: the face of the half-holy, half-dæmonic beings of his illustrations. Like them, too, he bordered on the ambiguous. In the finely drawn heads he now made his means of artistic expression, their beauty furnishing their sole excuse, a dull sensuality glimmered behind the too-languorous large eyes, the lips curled as the petals of perverse flowers, the mingled hair, dark tendril twisting round fair, the throat full, as though throbbing with kisses given, passion-cries restrained. Outwardly those faces and bodies had the cold virginity of funeral marbles. It was only the soul, divined within, that was old in time-worn debauches. They were white vases holding within them the ancient fragrance of Lesbian roses, too long mingled with the breath of corruption. Swinburne snatched eagerly as the drawings passed from hand to hand, caught also fleet glimpses of Solomon's ephebic grace. It was still a year or two before the Jewish lad mingled as an equal in Pre-Raphaelite circles.

Other lights had appeared in art's horizon. In 1855, Thackeray, tapping Millais on the shoulder, pointed to an immense canvas at the exhibition and warned him, "Mark my words, that versatile young dog will one day be President of the Royal Academy." The canvas was "Cimabue's Madonna Carried in Procession through the streets of Florence"; the artist, Frederick Leighton. Millais tossed his curly crest.

The "Cimabue" created a sensation none the less, even in that most Pre-Raphaelite of years which saw Hunt's "Light of the World" triumph in two continents and Millais's glorification of the fireman bring him solid profit. No Pre-Raphaelite, however, had ever achieved the honor most signal in the eyes of the public. That honor was Leighton's when Her Majesty bought the painting off the Academy walls. In no time Leighton became a popular lion, and regal quarry he was. Brilliant, elegant, an accomplished musician, and handsome to boot, he brought to his native land the culture of the Continent's artistic centres. At twenty-five he had the lore of Germany and Italy at his brush-tip, and in his manners the urbanity of the cosmopolite. As for his art, it was difficult to place it in any school. Renaissance Florence, Rome of the Cæsars and of the Borgias, an Hellenic classicism, formed odd patches in his canvas, united by a mediævalism that was not of the Middle Ages but rather of the persuasion of Cornelius and Overbeck. Yet there was something which won admiration — a virility of imagination and treatment that promised better work to come. Again, because Leighton was a sculptor as well as a painter, he treated his figures "in the round," not always true of contemporary forms.

The year following his triumph, Leighton added no laurels to his crown, and Millais, the darling, breathed more freely. As season followed season and Leighton removed himself from Rome to London, and as success upon success came after, a trail of graces in the hero's wake, Millais knew he had to outdo himself to win over fickle fortune from her newest philandering. Ruskin, too, had hailed the conqueror.

A brief éclat was caused by one F. W. George with portraits 167 and 185 at the Academy exhibition three years later. For long hours the Academicians had wagged puzzled heads over the well-realized female figures, the fine color and knowing brushwork — certainly not the execution of a novice. One, it is true, sniffed suspiciously, smelling a rat, but after much deliberation it was decided to hang the pictures. No one could accuse the members of being ungenerous to strangers. Accordingly the portraits were well placed and better received by the press, until, to the mortification of the Academy, it was discovered they were by George Frederick Watts, at whose canvases the sniffing one would cry out, "Ha! There's a Watts! Let's sky it." And skied they had been, year after year, so that at the age of forty-one Watts was no nearer the associateship than the merest studio drudge. Now the prospect was more unfavorable than ever.

It could not be helped. After all, Academicians were men, hence, like other mortals, subject to error. Occasionally a trick could be palmed off on them, but it would not be repeated. They were inordinately cautious, therefore, before they decided to hang up a canvas, "At the Piano," by a certain James Abbott McNeill Whistler—an American, from what they gathered, of lively temper and brimstone wit. This time, fortunately, there were no mishaps. The newcomer was duly welcomed and the painting sold to John Phillip, R.A., who was certain he had acquired a masterpiece for the Velasquez qualities he detected in the handling of the charming indoor variation on a theme in white.

Nothing even remotely Pre-Raphaelite could be detected in the work of Whistler, who had come to London innocent of any "ist" or "ism" but with a dominating self-assurance and an armful of lively etchings of the Paris he loved so well. Indeed, few could have told which was the livelier, his quicksilver stroke or the vivacity of his mind. Those who enjoyed tracing influences even in an art whose rootholds are in the individual quoted Dutch and French masters galore. The treatment of this was certainly De Hooch, of that, Maes; his technique of the brush pure Gleyre. . . . (Whistler had studied with Gleyre.) Economy and brilliance of line went for nought. The artist read the reviews and exploded into a sardonic "Ha!

Ha! De Hooch, Maes!" In his wide-brimmed hat and white trowsers he prowled about the Thames making quick notes of Battersea Bridge and Putney, drawing busy wharves, barges, ginshops and taverns, as an eccentric barber's son had done before him. Like Turner, now ten years dead, he was beginning to win for himself the character of crack-brained, a character which he enjoyed for the leeway it gave him. Nothing makes for greater freedom than the reputation of having had Luna for godmother at one's birth.

And so, though he had been born in the unblemished town of Lowell, Massachusetts, he let the legend go unconfuted that he had been rocked in a Russian cradle, and embroidered worthily on the theme of his exceptional beginnings. Did it give pleasure to *hoi polloi?* Let them enjoy it to the full. For their amusement he was also known to leave his house carrying two umbrellas, a white and a black, against sun or rain. His pockets rattled with a supply of monocles which he would affix one after the other to a dancing, mischievous eye, to the discomfort of the observer. But, with his peculiarities, he was a dogged worker, puffing like Boreas at the dust of his etching plate — at his oils, too, though there was no dust to blow off — with the habit of concentration he had acquired during his Paris student days. Days of fun and labor they had been, and of penury, shared willingly by some pretty Mimi who watched with simple understanding the scenes and people of their common day springing to life under his quick, nervous hands. Many an old book in the quays' stalls had had its yellowed end-leaves abstracted by those same quick hands when coppers were scarce and the plates had to be printed.

Now London was noticing Whistler, though with a tenor of misgiving.

XVIII

"UNTO THIS LAST"

"Le pauvre enfant, il ne sait pas vivre," had said Couttet, the old Swiss guide, with a shake of the head as he watched the young author of *Modern Painters* risking his neck scrambling among jagged rocks, throwing away with both hands the energy he had come to save. It was Ruskin's first trip abroad in perfect liberty, with Margaret's admonishing "No, John Ruskin" an imagined echo, and his father's cautions forgotten. No wonder he fluttered blindly, a bird too long caged, meeting freedom like an adversary. "Poor child, he does n't know how to live!"

He had not learned how as the years went by. Freedom from parental repressions he had enjoyed from time to time, but it was a costly and dearly treasured freedom, paid for in the end with mental anguish for every infraction of Margaret's discipline. She was in his conscience like the white-hot needle in the eye of the decoy bird that cries out perforce the lesson bought dearly and in pain, as it longs vaguely for its clear, songless sight. Had it ever been his? Since his earliest childhood his parents had counted every breath he took, weighing like two righteous incubi upon his spirit. He had never had the strength, nay, the will, to tear himself free.

Fortunately there had been his work. In it, at least, he had been able to range more or less at liberty, though his triumphs were in a large sense his father's triumphs — did not James Ruskin make them so? — and his defeats the burdens, heavier burdens, of his parents. Did they not groan loudly beneath them for his chastisement? Often, in spite of his boast of spiritual integrity, he had had to make compromises for his father's sake. Adolescent rebellion seethed in his blood at an age when most men smile to see it in their sons.

Still, his father was an old man now. He had not much longer to live; besides, had he not wrought, built entirely for his son? Perhaps, some day . . . None the less the spiritual control was heavier than an iron chain. "You never had — nor with all your medical experience have you ever probably seen," he wrote to his friend Dr. Acland after old Ruskin's death, "a father who would have sacrificed his life for his son, and yet forced his son to sacrifice his life to him, and sacrifice it in vain."

What was true of his father was truer of Margaret, possessively tyrannical with the rights granted her by the Commandments and her aggressive femininity. She was all woman, a lingering example of a defunct matriarchate. John was her territory and her subject, from whom open disobedience, even now that his sandy hair was touched with silver, would have been as astounding as a newer revolt of an angel against divine authority. For she knew she derived her right from God.

In consequence of his limited knowledge of women, he was bewildered when life forced him into contact with them, and felt comfortable only in the presence of the very old, whom he treated like less austere, more terrene mothers, or the very young, by the magic of whose innocence he would have gained a glimpse of the childhood happylands he had never inhabited. Passion frightened him in art as well as in woman. He fled from young women unless, like Lizzie, — rather, Ida, — they were ill and helpless, or, like the plain Maria Rossetti, they had their eyes set too high on heaven to spare more than a slanting glance for beings terrestrial. He sought everywhere what he had been nurtured on, a protective, maternal love.

Endless was the correspondence he carried on with old women, first with the pitiful Miss Mitford, whose youth and life had been engulfed by a dissolute father as his by a virtuous mother, and years later with the two Miss Beevers, gentle maiden ladies who treated him in his best-learned rôle of the helpless child. With them he would be off his guard and feel safe. To Miss Mitford, until her death, he confided what he could whisper only to his soul, and the sweet, faded virgin, sheltered like a prim flower in her old-fashioned close, read, sighed, and understood.

But had she, in her white seclusion, really grasped the tragedy behind the lines he sent on Good Friday, while Euphemia, a week-old bride, was still wondering whether emptiness were all wedded life held? "Whatever faults she might discover in her husband, he could at least promise her friends.". . . Friends and friendship to compensate for the husband's love he could not give. And then, the anguished self-discovery. "I begin to feel . . . that these are not times for watching clouds or dreaming over quiet waters . . . and that the time for endurance has come rather than for meditation, and for hope rather than for happiness. Happy those whose hope, without this severe and tearful rending away of all props and stability of earthly enjoyments, has been fixed 'where the wicked cease from troubling.' Mine was not." No hope, none for himself in compensation for the happiness which he would not, could not give.

The sense of the hollowness of his work increased, and with it came inner whisperings like the hisses of Satan in the corridors of a soul left open to doubt. What had he done all these years with his gift—what but made pretty phrases against which men turned deaf ears? "A packet of squibs and crackers." What had he done with his life and his youth? Shed like the scarlet of a plucked rose, no more to bloom again. But the rose of his youth had never been scarlet; it had been a dull, waxen flower, struggling without sun in the cave of his Sabbatarian training. It could not have died, for it had never lived. Through youth and manhood he had been, because of his parents, a shadow among the living, doing what good he might, all-loving and unloved. One cannot love a shadow, however benefi- cent. Little by little his friends were slipping from him — was it that he could no longer hold them?

Happily for him the National Gallery needed his help to arrange the sketches and water colors Turner had be- queathed to it in his will. In a codicil Ruskin had been named his trustee and executor.

The task was no sinecure. Turner, as headstrong in mat- ters of life and death as he had always been in his work, had refused to call upon a solicitor, but had drawn up the will partly by himself in his colorful phrase and unique orthog- raphy, and partly by the help of solicitors' clerks. The result was as hazy as his own famous "Sun Rising in a Mist."

A gulf yawned between his original intention and the final execution. According to the provisions, he left a number of small legacies to his relatives; then he had be- stowed his two favorite paintings on the Nation, provided they were placed permanently between Claude's "Seaport" and the "Mill," forgetting that to the seventeenth-century master he owed not only the splendor of his color, but, in at least "Dido Building Carthage," the flattery of uncon- scious plagiarism. The remaining paintings he gave to the Nation on condition that they be shown in a special room to be known as Turner's Gallery. Finally came the pro- vision that embodied his most earnest intention.

Knowing, by his own usage, the adversities dogging the artist, he left the bulk of his estate, real and personal, to the founding of a home for the maintenance of "Poor and De- cayed Male Artists being born in England and of English Parents only, and of Lawful Issue."

It took many a clustering of solicitors' heads to arrive at

last at the conclusion that the will was too obscure for legal clearing. The provision on which the philanthropic man-scorner had set his heart was pronounced contrary to the Charitable Uses Act; his relatives contested it, with the result that they received nearly the whole of the estate, while the indigent and decayed male artists were cut off without a farthing for all their Britannic parentage and law-fulness of birth.

Ruskin had early surrendered his executorship. But the colossal labor of arranging the hundreds of sketches he undertook with a will, despite the curator's meddlesomeness and the outlay, never grudged, of his own funds for the assistance of his pupil, George Allen, and William Rossetti, in the deciphering of Turner's notebooks.

The labor was a thankless one. With the negligence of abundant genius, Turner had been in the habit of piling up his fresh sketches in the bottoms of drawers, stuffing them into books, cramming them into crevices like so much waste paper to stop up mouseholes, so that, what with his recklessness and the years of insidious damp in the Gallery storerooms, they were a ruin to make the very angels weep. In about a year's time all that could be saved were mounted, labeled in Ruskin's neat hand, and placed in sliding cases. Nevertheless, tongues of friends and enemies babbled alike. Ruskin, the squeamish Galahad, they said, the abhorrer of nudes, had destroyed Turner's most representative work — scenes of waterside brothels, sailors' haunts, ginshops. All of them he had burned without mercy, and made the artist an emasculate scrawler fit for a ladies' seminary.

Once more spiritual depression worried him in its fangs and he left England for the Alps and Italy to escape it. There, amid the sublime of nature and man, he sought heal-ing for his sick soul. The wound was deeper than he knew. A life of sensation was beginning to mean less to him. Not the Alps, not all the paintings of Italy, could cure the doubt that had dug sapping roots into his spirit. How was he,

the packet of squibs and crackers, to convince men that the
flash and the noise were but the means he used to make them
glimpse the fire and force of his consuming love for them?

At Rheinfelden he plucked a purple orchis and sketched
its ephemeral loveliness. With a shock he realized it was
the Sabbath, a day which his mother had taught him should
be consecrated to the service of God. Was sketching an
orchis on such a day doing the work of the devil? The
gloom of the Sabbatarian cave chilled him anew. How
could he, the lover of beauty, have lived so long in darkness and death? Too long! Too long! In a painful
surge of rebellion he groped his way out, to the sun.

As if the spiritual revolt had not yet been fully accomplished, he received added impetus to freedom in a Waldensian chapel in Turin. Again the cave, lightless, the abode
of death. Awful with self-righteousness, a preacher was
reveling in particulars of hell where all but Waldensians
would burn. They, only they, his flock and the flock of
other Waldensian preachers, would be saved — the rest of
the world damned to all eternity. Gasping for the purify-
ing air, Ruskin fled from the archangel of destruction, "converted inside out."

Converted — but to what new faith? Unlike the elegant agnostics of his acquaintance who grasped at every
scientific straw to save them from the ocean of confusion
churned up by new revelations, he let himself be tossed
about, knowing not whether toward safety or destruction.
Darwin's *Origin of Species* appeared in 1859. Ruskin,
together with Carlyle, fumed and held up opposing hands
in horror. Was this the vaunted open road toward the
superman, this, the throwing him down from a noble origin
to the protoplasmic slime of the brute? Was this physical
abysm the best hope science could offer? Ruskin shud-
dered. As it was, he had never had anything but contempt
for science.

What was it doing toward enlarging the horizon of man-

kind? It could place a crocus petal under the microscope,
amazing the mono-eyed fool with the intricacy of otherwise invisibly changing matter; but it did not teach him to
thrill to the wonder of a crocus field rising full-blown with
the first sun of spring and gilding the earth with the raiment
of a morning heaven. It could tear apart the throat feathers
of a dove to analyze the structure and the pigment, — tell
from the stuffed specimen the why and the wherefore of the
wing and feet, — assure you, too, that once, even as you
were no man but an ape, it had been no bird but some crude
anomaly, neither fish nor fowl. Where the lesson of the
bird of love, with a rainbow round its throat, and feet of
coral, touching even the dust of the earth with beauty?
Where the living, circling flight of this thing that was
matter — oh, so ably defined! — and yet lent the spirit of
the gazer wings? No, not in science could he find the true
faith. He could not be all-embracing in his aspiration like
his friend Acland up in Oxford, or like that mild eclectic,
Jowett.

Indeed, Jowett, soft, sleek, and round, was becoming a
power at the university. His voice, when he lectured to
the hope of the Empire, was sharp and incisive, now modulated to the aërial, now firm with his convictions. He had
little of Ruskin's poetry in his message. He parceled out
facts well buttressed with author and source, and left them
to make their impression upon his hearers. With benign
universality he brought together East and West in his verbal
symposia, making Plato and Aristotle rub elbows with Christ
and the Church fathers, Mohammed, Newman, and the new
lights, Darwin and Huxley. A man of wide sympathies
though few tenets, he caught eagerly at the inquiring spirit
of the age, seeing no barrier between science and religion,
indeed, mustering the forces of the scientists to champion
the new Christianity. There were those who accused the
classical scholar of calling the devil by a new name for
the sake of a hybrid faith, of closing his eyes to evil and

denying its existence in his effort to bring about Utopia — yes, of working with the hosts of destruction in the name of progress. He stood firm at Oxford, however, doling out his messages with even, lucid kindliness — but realized his intellectual promised land only in the pleasures of his Greek studies.

Ruskin knew not where to turn, for everywhere he saw ugliness, dirt, and squalor. Was God a just God who could suffer the inequalities that on all sides shrieked to heaven? Was there a God? The question gave him no peace. If there was no God, then it must be man, responsible for it all. The causes must be somewhere hidden in the débris of civilizations, poisonous roots to be uncovered, that injustice might no longer thrive on the earth. Fool that he had been, preaching beauty to a people starving for bread! Always the reproach obsessed him of his having given stones, beautiful, useless architectural stones, for bread. He frightened away sleep with futile inquiries. Why should people starve, they, the toilers, when there was so much bounty in the world?

The same energy he had put into the writing of his æsthetics he turned to the study of economic doctrines. Smith and Mill were oftener in his hand than sketchbooks and his beloved minerals which he yet longed to arrange on new white wool in their neglected cabinet. Carlyle, lonely Jeremiah, nodded encouragement.

In the late summer of 1860, Thackeray published the first of Ruskin's economic essays in the *Cornhill Magazine* — the "Roots of Honor," of *Unto this Last.* The subscribers lifted their brows over this novel excursion of the art critic and could make little of it. The next two papers caused them even more bewilderment. Not a few canceled their subscriptions at such heresies in their magazine, preferring to do without their pleasant pabulum than to have such unsavory doctrines crammed down their throats. Thackeray wrote hurriedly to Ruskin, apologizing profusely, but saying firmly he could publish just one essay more, and then an end.

Savage was the outcry throughout England, the echoes shaking Ruskin in his pacific seclusion. One might have thought he advocated moral dissolution, so scurrilous were the attacks upon his life and person. The *Saturday Review* would have none of the "eruptions of windy hysterics . . . the absolute nonsense" of a "perfect paragon of blubbering" full of "whines and snivels." It would not suffer the world "to be preached to death by a mad governess."

And yet there was nothing in *Unto this Last* that Adam Smith, Mill, Carlyle, or, for that matter, Plato before them, did not support. Ruskin simply arrived at a definition of wealth, and showed that its acquisition was permissible only under moral conditions of society, of which Honesty should be the foundation. (*An entirely honest merchant* was the highest tribute he was to pay his father on the slab where pious lies often triumph.) He stressed the essential points that youth should have the advantages of education, facilitated by the state; that manufactories and workshops for the exercise of every useful art should be run under government regulations, with homes provided for the old and incapacitated, and that wages should be justly distributed. What heresy was he preaching there, he asked himself? Was it a crime to cry for justice to all, a shame to plead for a more equable distribution of the goods of the world? When he heard himself maligned and saw his writings rejected, denied publication, when he knew himself pointed at with scorn and muzzled like a dangerous beast, he strode back and forth in his hotel room and groaned.

On his return to England his mother stumbled down the stairs and broke her thigh bone. To John, then, fell the charge of comforting his father through his marital anxiety and paternal bitterness at his son's fiasco, and keeping up his mother's spirits in her physical agony. She, staunch soul, could bear anything with fortitude, provided John administered the comfort of hour-long readings of evangelical doctrines. He read, chafing inwardly. No salve for his own blistered soul in that intoning, with the old solemn emphasis, of creeds he no longer believed in, or in being compelled to apologize for the things he knew at bottom to be right. With the critics baying at him on the one hand, and his mother, a fiercer hunter, hounding him to salvation as she saw it, he knew not where to find peace. "I find penguins at present the only comfort in life," he told Norton. "One feels everything in the world so sympathetically ridiculous. One can't be angry when one looks at a penguin."

It was wry-mouthed amusement. In the London streets, whose squalor ever shadowed wealth, gloom fell on him again. How could one bear to look at the upturned hand, at the peaked, starved face of the begging child, and then go home to luxury? His own wealth tormented him, though he lavished it on worthy and unworthy alike.

"Luxury is indeed possible in the future," he had written, ". . . innocent and exquisite; luxury for all and by the help of all." Ay, then it could be. "But luxury at present can only be enjoyed by the ignorant; the cruelest man living could not sit at his feast, unless he sat blindfold. Raise the veil boldly; face the light!" In vain, in vain had he exhorted. "Go thou forth weeping . . . until the time come, and the Kingdom, when Christ's gift of bread and bequest of peace shall be Unto this Last as unto thee . . ." Unto this last . . . unto the child with the upturned begging hand, unto the widow, unto the debtor rotting his days in jail.

"Foul socialist heresy," the mighty howled him down. God's in his heaven . . .

But there were some whom the message reached, and others who had no need of it, for they had it graven in their hearts by the finger of suffering and want. These, like Madox Brown and Emma in their none too plentiful home, opened soup kitchens for the starving of that dreadful winter.

XIX

WIDENING CIRCLES

THE Pre-Raphaelites were a clannish crew, fond of one another's company and of large gatherings where ale and speech flowed in equal measure. Ned at Great Russell Street and Algernon within walking distance saw each other daily, sometimes five and six times a day, to the embarrassment of Georgie, who would be haled forth from her household duties to play audience to each new stanza of Algernon's poems. Janey Morris in her miniature castle, ten miles away, enjoyed more privacy, but old Top at Red Lion Square was always in danger of being interrupted in his many activities. In the enlarged quarters of Chatham Place were held social reunions where Algernon talked outrageous de Sade to shock the intruding bourgeois, and lanky-bearded William Michael played the melancholy Gib-cat in dandified sleekness, listening, and storing away matter for future use. Was he not the custodian of the Pre-Raphaelite archives? His prematurely bald pate shone a polished reflector in the light of the candles and surrounding celebrity, and he purred melancholy content, though even now the spendthrift Gabriel mulcted him privately to help him defray expenses.

Millais and Hunt never came to these reunions, Woolner and Stephens seldom. "Academic opulence," bolstered up by Euphemia's social ambitions, carried Millais to flashier spheres; Hunt was too busy to waste time on earthly vanities, while Woolner had other relations. To the annoyance of Millais and Hunt, Stephens still seemed to favor the

Brown-Rossetti phalanx above their more aristocratic band, for great names and great people were more to their taste —genius nimbused in the glow of material success. If, therefore, they took off precious months from their easels to go on walking tours through Cornwall and Devon, the attraction had to be at least the companionship of Tennyson, nearsighted, willful, and obstreperously incognito.

Reputations on the left wing of Pre-Raphaelitism were still in the making; some, through the ill will of fate, were never to be made. Yet, however long fame delayed in reaching these, they were quick in giving it to others, even when they appeared reviled or without a name. Whitman's *Leaves of Grass* had become a handbook among them long before England or even America was aware of a new voice in literature. Again, Gabriel bought an outcast volume for a penny, and promoted the recognition of a future classic. For two years the *Rubaiyat of Omar Khayyam* had lain ignobly in Quaritch's storerooms, the publisher having lost faith in his ever getting back the pounds put into the printing of it. Laboring under the notion that some foolish bibliomaniacs might help him dispose of the lumber if he placed it on the street stalls, he made a display of the anonymous booklet and offered as bait the modest price of 1*d.* in thick black ink. Gabriel turned the leaves of the bargain, read at random, and dove immediately into his pocket. Then he went home and waved his prize before the visiting Algernon. Algernon bought a copy and told his friends; the friends bought and told other friends, who, when they went to Quaritch's a few days later, found that the crafty bookseller had doubled the price. By the end of the month the little book was selling at a guinea, and Algernon perched on chairs wherever he went, chanting the quatrains that broke like bubbles of wine, and whirled like motes in a sunlit wind.

Of Gabriel's treasured possessions the oldest, perhaps, was a manuscript book illustrated with sketches of a weird, disturbing beauty. He had bought it (with William's money) for ten shillings sixpence when even that sum spelled extravagance, but the nineteen-year-old bibliophile was not going to let mere dross, and borrowed dross at that, stand between himself and his desire. Palmer, the British Museum attendant, had no need to force the sale. That night Gabriel walked home with Blake's notebook stuffed in his otherwise empty pockets, and a head filled with visions. It was as if the mad poet and his host of singing morning stars were coming to inhabit with him his dreary little garret room.

At No. 6 Cheyne Row, next to the house occupied by Carlyle and his gossipy little wife, were living Alexander and Anne Gilchrist and their four young children. Alexander had started his career as a barrister at law. However, preferring the practice of literature to that of Chancery, he had won himself some repute as an author with his life of William Etty, and now, at thirty-three, was on the last few chapters of a study of William Blake. Someone told him that Gabriel Rossetti possessed a precious Blake manuscript. Diffidently he wrote to him. The letter was so well received, and Alexander so well liked, that before long the Gilchrists became favored guests at all the Pre-Raphaelite households.

The Gilchrists had been married ten years and showed in their relations a harmony that came of worship on the one side and practical sense on the other. Anne, a capable woman, handled her household with scientific exactness, in spite of her skill at the piano and the learned tracts she contributed to weighty periodicals, rousing the admiration of the neighboring dyspeptic, whose kitchen, alas, for all his wife's efforts, left much to be desired. Jane Welsh Carlyle, therefore, was encouraged in her visits next door, to learn the secret of baking bread that would not goad the gnawing lion at her husband's entrails.

Bread-making, and otherwise caring for her difficult

"Tammas," seemed, indeed, to take up all the hours Jane could spare from her fascinating industry of collecting and retailing the spicy morsels of London domestic life.

"You know the Duke of Malakoff," she would begin in an inviting whisper the moment a visitor crossed the threshold. "And Skittles. Oh, I hope you *don't* know Skittles—a *very* pretty and *very* wicked lady who rides about the park . . ."

The visitor did not know the naughty Skittles, and would willingly have made her acquaintance had not the philosopher, clad in his long brown indoor coat, shambled into the room at that point and beckoned his guest with his pipe to the hearthside, there to bewail the times and cover himself with ashes.

Even while Anne was standing over her to show her the art of baking digestible bread, Jane, bubbling over with news, exercised her special talents. "I went to see Fechter the other night and found myself—guess where! Between Lewes and Miss Evans. Poor soul! . . . She looks *Propriety* personified. Oh, so *slow!*" Up and down went her sharp little voice, juggling with the fireballs of scandal, particularly hot in the instance of the evangelical Marian Evans, known to the world as George Eliot, living *openly* in what the Church called sin, with a man who was the husband, my dear, the *legal* husband of another! Who would ever have imagined it of the Sibyl—and a most unattractive sibyl she was, too—who saw fit to edify the world with *moral* writings!

One scandal evoked another, as a highly spiced tidbit a compensating quaff. "And do you *really* approve of Millais's marriage to Ruskin's *wife?* I was at a dinner at Lady Goodrich's,"—Jane went everywhere, with or without her sage, and from tea time on flitted about the house in her high-heeled white satin slippers waiting for what invitation Providence might send,—"and what do you think—I had the good fortune to sit next to Holman Hunt. I asked *him,* of course, and he *defended* the marriage. But if because husband and wife don't *agree* they should separate, *many* marriages would be annulled."

She was equally garrulous in little notes that went flying like jays from Number Five to Number Six. "Nero is a much improved dog by sea-bathing with his master"—that after a vacation at Aberdour. "He snores less, scratches less, and is less selfish." Then again the problem of bread was uppermost. "I got some of the German flour," a note came, "and it is surpassingly beautiful, but Mr. C. can't endure to eat it! —it is so tasteless, he says. Perhaps he is right, and the flour, like women, can't be pre-eminently *beautiful* and pre-eminently anything else at the same time. . . . Also, I would like to have half a sack of *white* flour from the same man—if he would send the quantity—would he?" At that time Anne was nursing her eldest daughter through scarlet fever. But Jane's housewifely activities could no more be restrained than her propensities for gossip.

A sprightly little person, she had entered the life of Thomas Carlyle with the glamour of a brightly hued butterfly. What matter if the brilliant lovely thing had fluttered and flirted with the black-frocked Irving, his friend, her lover? He, Tammas, son of the mason of Ecclefechan, laid before her his forthright affection and future prospects. It was for her to take them or flit away. Jane, above him in station, took them with a stooping of her genteel little frame, a stooping she would never have him forget after they were married.

The trials that met the young bride at lonely Craigenputtock, her small property, whither they went that Tammas might write in peace, she made much of in voluminous letters to her friends. Baking was not the least of them, and her first experience had remained a symbol. All of one night she kneaded and pounded, watching at the primitive oven, waiting for the dough to rise. Hours she kept her vigil. The moon through the window had traveled the

length of the lonely kitchen; for some time the breath of
Tammas, resting at last from the gnawing of the lion, had
come to her, toiling below, like the far-off thunder of some
tyrannous Olympian.   The moon set and the streaks of
morning paled the coals.   At long length the loaf was baked.
In her joy and vexation, devotion and rebellion, she, little
Jane, who had been brought up on Greek and kept from the
vulgar knowledge of cookery books, broke into tears of
thanksgiving, sweetening her weariness with thinking of how,
centuries ago, one Cellini had travailed a whole night
through, burning his chairs to feed the furnace wherein his
Perseus was coming to immortal life.   Was she, Jane, less
of an artist than Benvenuto?   Was her poor little brown
loaf a meaner work in the eyes of One who judges of ultimate values?   Cellini's statue fed the eyes and souls of
generations.   Her wretched brown loaf fed her dyspeptic
Tammas, and gave him the strength to mould his thoughts
and wield his pen for the conquering of the Enemy, ignorance.   She, too, in toiling for him, won a share of his
glory.   Year in, year out, with youth and Craigenputtock
far behind, time, miles, had been marked by Tammas's
daily loaf, the pendulum of his pulse, the milestone of his
progress.   Now he was the monitor of the age, warning,
roaring, cursing as he blessed, blessing as he cursed.

In his studio Brown was painting him on his vast canvas.
Gaunt, dark, stooping, Carlyle loomed, his face furrowed
with physical and spiritual pain, his eyes farseeing, the
cavernous mouth snarling its optimism.   Not a pleasing
picture, but a good likeness—a prophet has no need of
beauty.

For more than five years Brown had been painting at
his apotheosis of labor, nor was it yet near completion, this
epitome of his life.   Meanwhile lesser artists were enjoying
the world's goods as he toiled in the bitter solace that his
infinite pains would in the end be justified by that reward
which is above transitory fame.   Emma, however, would

have been happier for some show of plenty in their pantry, most of all when the London crew arrived noisy and hungry for Finchley hospitality. The circle — Gabriel's circle — widened with every cast of his. One memorable evening at the theatre, surely to celebrate a sale, a mirthful company filled a row of seats, to the consternation of a programme seller who saw with misgiving the wild red head of a jumpy youth at one end, and, upon fleeing to escape it, a woman's, richer and fuller, at the other. Swinburne's red locks would alone have been sufficient for the confusion of a superstitious cockney. Swinburne's and Lizzie's spelled catastrophe.

These were happy times for the group, with life speeding by in fast, full days. Topsy, especially exuberant, could ill contain the joy of his recent fatherhood. It was a christening party ever to be remembered, therefore, that he held at the Red House. All of his friends were present — Gabriel, munching raisins as he sat like a king in the huge settle, Brown with more verbal slips than William Michael could record ("Of all her lovers I do think Mary Stuart had some feeling for Boswell . . ."), Ned, with mouse-like little Georgie, and "Carrots" Swinburne dancing among them in high glee.

In a long, chatelaine gown of rich fabric of Morris's design, Janey presided in her new dignity, looking, in the poem of her house, like the queen rose of its scroll. She had grown, if anything, more beautiful. What wonder Gabriel's eyes were often upon her! There stood his unpainted masterpieces. "Beauty like hers is genius. . . ." Not the world's supremest artists had been able to draw such music from the spheres of time as sang in her sweet presence. Hers was the loveliness that should live forever. He had the hand, the eyes, to capture it. He had the soul that from the first had vibrated to her soul.

For the moment, he, too, was happy. Poor Lizzie had received a new lease on health in her marriage, and, miracu-

lous though it seemed to him as to all who knew her, her
frail body gave promise of a new life. Daily he lived in
hope and fear and in a joy which he now tasted vicariously
in Topsy's elation. Indeed, the proud father was irrepres-
sible. At last, in the small hours, when even Pre-Raphaelite
owls needed sleep, mattresses were strewn about to accommo-
date the guests, and, when they gave out, some of the men
made their beds on the floor. Algernon, curling himself on
the sofa, settled into feline comfort.

With the new happiness came new responsibilities. Art
and literature, charming mistresses though they were, made
poor helpmeets, especially when there were wives to support, and now children. Brown could have given most
edifying harangues from experience. There was no denying
that the artist, unless he played pander to the public, could
starve to death in some rat-ridden attic and none be the
wiser till his carcass reeked its protest to heaven. Thus, in
the days of Victoria Regina. Now in the later Middle
Ages, how different things had been. In that far-off age
of gold, Morris expatiated, artists had been respected members of the community, doing all kinds of things, designing
every manner of decoration, from a shoe buckle to a cathedral window. Why could it not be so now?

"Well, why don't we form a company?" asked someone,
half in jest. "Come, let's each put down five pun toward
a company."

Lean as the pockets were, "a few pale fivers managed to
show their faces on the table." Morris, as the man of
capital, was elected manager, and so, partly in sport, a firm
was founded that was destined to banish Plush and Fuss
from the Victorian drawing-room and inaugurate the era
of art decoration. The affair marched with expedition, as
it could not fail to do with the volcanic Morris at the head;
by the spring of 1861, No. 8 Red Lion Square astonished
the passers-by with its painted front and a shingle marking
the headquarters of Morris, Marshall, Faulkner and Com-

pany. The "shop" made an ambitious beginning: two floors were taken, and part of a basement, up and down which a dozen men and boys could be seen carrying pails of dye, and tools, and all manner of curious objects. The members of the company were seven besides Morris, and included Brown, Jones, and Rossetti. "These artists," the prospectus announced modestly, "having for many years been deeply attached to the study of the Decorative Arts of all times and countries, have felt more than most people the want of some one place where they could either obtain or get produced work of a genuine and beautiful character. . . . They have therefore now established themselves as a firm. . . . It is believed," it continued, "that good decoration, involving rather the luxury of taste than the luxury of costliness, will be found to be much less expensive than is generally supposed."

What constituted the luxury of taste, the Firm was not backward in showing the pioneering purchasers of the upper classes. Would you have a drawing-room decorated or a chair upholstered? Take what the Firm offers you and make no objections, for you, poor man, have been mis-educated to a false notion of the beautiful and must therefore disabuse your mind by complete acceptance of our authority. "Comply or go elsewhere," was the attitude of the artists. Many complied, even when, in the beginning, queer-looking sofas projected wicked bases designed to break the shins of anyone who ventured near. There was a lavishness of decoration, an orgy of sage green in and out of season, that made many a drawing-room sicken to jaundice. But in time the mannerisms died out of themselves (though Morris's beloved green had a long, long life) and the Firm produced furniture and stained glass which, the following year, received the highest awards at the International Exhibition, sponsored by the Prince Consort. He, however, was not destined to see it.

In the forenoon of December 14, 1861, an anxious crowd

stood hushed at Windsor, watching the windows of the
silent castle. The Queen, within, at the bedside of Prince
Albert, hung upon each breath of the royal patient. They
knew he was near death; they knew it by the indefinable
quiet that lay over everything, though the winter sun shone
in fullest warmth lighting up each scant leaf of the ivy-
covered towers. But, under the glinting green, there too
was a shadow. A sudden movement heaved the crowd.
From a side gate the Prince Consort's own harriers broke
out and were hurriedly led away by an attendant. Had
they known?

That night the nation went into mourning.

Earlier that same year, when the Tuscan spring was
whitening to summer in the rose valleys, England had suffered another loss, though only those mourned who had
loved her and for whom she had sung her songs. Elizabeth
Barrett Browning was laid to rest in the Tuscan earth she
loved,

> The white-rose garland at her feet
> The crown of laurel at her head,

as one for whom life was a desert, gray miles long, with no
garlands and no roses, imagined her in the end.

XX

DEATH AND THE MAIDEN

LIFE at 14 Chatham Place had not changed since Gabriel's marriage. Fleet Ditch, under the windows, invariably sent up its stench in bad weather; the mud larks, in the hope of reward, just as invariably brought back the books which in his irritableness Gabriel pitched out of the windows. From the balcony he still watched the crowded Thames with its moving freight of barges, their coal fires on chilly nights, a floating processional shadowing as from a nether world the never-ceasing flow of people crossing and recrossing Blackfriars Bridge. It held a gloomy fascination for him, that continuous stream of strange humanity with which he felt not often kin.

Gabriel, never punctilious in matters of personal orderliness, saw no need for Lizzie's altering her ways, for so many years modeled on his own. They would go to bed whenever there was nothing more interesting, arise at noon to breakfast, and then Gabriel painted through the daylight hours while she tried to draw or read, pose or sit quietly, watching him with large, hollow eyes. People wondered why Gabriel made no effort to take his wife away from the miasmic air of Blackfriars, and accused him of indifference. As it was, he earned just enough to pay the doctors and keep the apartment going; and whenever he did send Lizzie away for her health she was so unhappy that the separation did her more harm than good. She liked the studio life, with its run of visitors and its freedom from domestic cares, that enabled her to go about dressed in long-sleeved, flowing gowns, uncrinolined to show the lines of her still lovely body: the Pre-Raphaelite lady.

Ruskin frowned more darkly than ever on the devil-may-care ménage. It was an entirely different setting he would have had for Ida, had Gabriel been less selfish and she more kind. But Gabriel was fiercely jealous, and, with that, self-willed. If Ruskin came at some early hour unbidden, he would refuse to get up or have Lizzie greet him. Past kindnesses in the face of the present importunity were lost sight of, and Ruskin went away, deeper in his growing despondency. Everything was forsaking him — his public, faith in himself. He gave his affection, — he, so rich in it, — and it was thrown back in his face. He hungered for love: it was denied him. In bitterness of spirit he would shut himself up in his Turner-hung study, the only bright room at Denmark Hill, and pen testy little notes, hiding nothing of his feelings and blunt to the point of rudeness.

"You are in little things habitually selfish," he grumbled, "thinking only of what you like to do — not of what would be kind." And, God knows, Ruskin had need of kindness now. "Where your affections are strongly touched I suppose this would not be so — but it is not *possible* that you should care for me, seeing me so seldom. I wish Lizzie and you liked me enough to — say — put on a dressing-gown and run in for a minute rather than not see me. But you can't *make* yourselves like me. . . ." How often had he had to repeat that refrain of his frustrations!

Such a letter was not designed to improve the situation, the more since, a gadfly's sting, it pricked a sensitive spot. Yes, Gabriel was selfish, but then, why should he get up hours before his time simply because Mr. Ruskin chose to make morning visits? Of late he had become too exacting, airing his views without consideration for the feelings of others. It was the prerogative of the reformer, but Gabriel was not of the stuff for making crucifixes, as one of the paternal proverbs would have put it.

"I fancy I gall you by my want of sympathy in many things," Ruskin confessed, "and so lose hold of you." It was a hopeless relation, the one as incapable of abstaining from sermons as the other of submitting to them. The wonder lay in their having remained friends so long. But Ruskin was tenacious where he saw the least tenderness, and Gabriel, in times of need, could be as gentle as a woman. After all, Ruskin had done much for him, for Lizzie. But *Noli me tangere* Gabriel bristled where his personal life was touched.

How different, this, from the gentle couple of Russell Place! There the protective love of the disillusioned man was repaid a hundredfold in care and endearments. Ned showed him his newest work, talked feverishly of his projects, asked for advice and accepted it gratefully, while Georgiana, "the little country violet with blue eyes and long eyelashes"—nothing was too good, she thought, for her husband's dear friend. The two quiet, fragile creatures were as eager to give love as Ruskin was to receive it, and in their modest place, charming with the refinements of their simple tastes, sweet with Georgie's housewifely care, he had the realization of his dream of home. He bought Ned's pictures as he had bought Gabriel's, took the new nest under his pelican wing, and found balm in their devotion.

Yet something about his old protégé attracted him as did no virtue in anyone else. Gabriel might be careless, irresponsible, untidy, selfish, unscrupulous—Ruskin could blame him no more than he could blame the thistle for not being a rose. Gabriel was a different sort of man from him, that was all, and Ruskin felt drawn to him perhaps for the very differences. In Gabriel's easy paganism he, but for the grace of Margaret Ruskin, saw himself. It was terrifying and wonderful. Gabriel entered no church except to see the treasures in it, seemed to believe in no orthodox God, had no reverence or passion but for the holy spirit of art.

He, Ruskin, on the other hand, tried to see God and moral values in everything.   Even his accesses of unbelief, during which he descended to the depths of the abyss, even they came of too uncompromising a search for perfection.   Religion, as the Bible had taught him and as his parents had lived it, was too narrow a vase for the boundlessness of the ideal he planted in it.   It cracked in imperceptible, deepening fissures.   He knew they were there and mourned because the vase could nevermore be whole.

Gabriel had no such torments.   Enough for him to take on faith that the earth moved round the sun, that the law of gravitation held in the case of a feather as in the case of a stone, that Greece and Rome had reigned and left their stamp upon the world; it was not for him to seek further. Poetry and painting joined the hemispheres of his perfect world, through which he journeyed without stepping beyond his studio boundaries.   Woman, mystically mediæval, inhabited the turreted castles and leafy bowers of all his continents.   And there were darkest lands where the unfathomable Lilith, daughter of lusts and vices intolerable, walked in the aura of her studied sins, leaving round each man's heart "one strangling golden hair."   Round his own heart that aureate chain was twined, tightening, as he found no solace in his marriage, with tyrannous pain.

Imagination in him took the place of his age's fashionable reason.   In vain might the geologists clink their hammers at the earth's skeleton, striking with every blow at the foundation stones of Genesis; in vain Darwin trace the origin of species; as futilely the philosophers build solider worlds on cobweb thought: they were all on other planets and did not touch him.   He was a pagan in his self-created country; what mattered it to him if the trappings were those of a mediæval archaism?   They furnished the background for his fancies and clothed the bodies of his women in sensuousness more refined than the most suggestive of nudities.   Candid nakedness left him cold, but a nudity showing through layers of silken gauze, as light through a mist, held for him a thrill at once physical and spiritual. He sought the exquisite of pain in pleasure with the urgency of a sadist, more passionately because more passionate than Algernon. More and more his poems and paintings had been assuming an obscurer symbolism wherein his heathen Christianity found it difficult upon which side to weigh. The fundamental paganism was yet there, for all that it was set amidst the traditional heaven and hell.

As in his work, so in his life. Immoral, without any trained control of his strong animal passions, without any guiding faith, Ruskin thought it. But that was the man, and not all the evangelical doctrine in the world could alter a hair of his head. He was best let alone, with a secret regret that oneself had not been so created. There would have been no vase, then, with deepening though invisible lines, which in the end might bore to its irreparable ruin. Who knows?

Ruskin might shake his head and disapprove, but he was never ungenerous of his help. When at length Gabriel's *Early Italian Poets* came out, Ruskin paid toward its publication, more joyously since the dedication honored Lizzie, about to become a mother. Sometimes, however, he showed a peculiar churlishness, a temporary blindness, that kept him from perceiving, or wanting to perceive, the most apparent beauties. He had never been sympathetic toward Christina, whose self-contained aloofness set up a barrier between her and one who sought always to be approached as the child. A fountain sealed, frozen over with the hard, sharp brightness of the diamond: no, she was hardly the woman, the maternal woman, to make the conquest of Ruskin's heart.

When Gabriel sent him, therefore, the neatly copied pages of her prospective volume, Ruskin put on his blackest of blinkers. The poems, though full of beauty and power, were also full of quaintnesses and offenses, he murmured.

The whole of Spenser, Milton, Keats, is written without taking a single license or violating the common ear for metre: why should Christina? "Your sister should exercise herself in the severest commonplace of metre. . . . Then if she puts in her observation and passion all will be precious." No publisher would take them as they were, said he. A publisher did take them, despite the pontifical pronouncement, and a year later they appeared as *Goblin Market and Other Poems* by Christina Georgina Rossetti. What Ruskin expected still less was the generous acclaim heaped upon this, the first successful book of the Pre-Raphaelite group.

Those were anxious weeks during which Lizzie's baby was awaited, though she, poor girl, bore up with the courage of despair, seeming, indeed, less fearful than Gabriel of consequences. With her own hands she sewed the baby clothes and chatted excitedly at the prospect of motherhood. She wanted the child as she had never wanted anything before; it would be a strong link to join with her at last the ever-wandering Gabriel. He, too, when free from harassing worries, speculated pleasantly on the new responsibility, though a baby hardly fitted into the disorder of Chatham Place. How strange a thing to think of his love and Lizzie's bearing fruit, as if the blessed damozel's celestial yearning had had earthly completion. Meanwhile Lizzie gained in wanness and mystery as she trailed her heavy body wearily to its time. The day came, a week passed . . . two weeks. Gabriel brought home a little wooden cradle, frilled and beribboned to frame the tardy cherub.

It was never to be filled.

The anguish of her frustrate body left Lizzie weak and her sickened mind dark with resentment. Back from the hospital, she sat for hours in her low chair, her feet inside the fender, her eyes fixed moodily upon the fire. Gabriel watched her, spoke, listened for a word that never came. It was like watching over a corpse. Shivering, he seized his hat and fled for a breath of air to clear his brain. Lizzie brooded on, unconscious. Why had she hoped and suffered if the fruit of her love was to be only the memory of a still-born child? Sometimes she would sit beside the empty cradle, rocking an imaginary baby, the child that was to have made Gabriel wholly hers. So Georgie and Ned found her one day, startling her to a cry, "Hush! Do not wake it. . . ." Do not wake the spirit child of the blessed damozel.

Her jealous suspicions throve darkly as the despondence over her futile travail increased. Now Gabriel could not leave the house without her interpreting each absence as an infidelity. Even her friend Emma was shut out of her secret life. Old Mrs. Rossetti and her two daughters rarely crossed the threshold of Chatham Place. There were the lost girls of the St. Mary Magdalene Home to be brought back to the right path. . . . Gabriel paid his filial duty calls alone, while William came more and more seldom, a neutral intermediary. None there for Lizzie to confide in. Besides, Christina and Maria would have made but dumb listeners to a tale that touched naked life so closely. What would it have meant to chaste Christina, this anguish over a baby dead on the threshold of life? Or to Maria, the half-nun, trudging surely toward the barren protective-ness of a convent cell? Less comprehensible still would have seemed the pain of Gabriel, who, when Lizzie offered the unused, tiny garments to Georgie Jones for her coming baby, wrote her pitifully: "Don't let her, please. It looks such a bad omen for us."

In spite of the frigid reserve that kept Lizzie apart by her own choice, a brother-and-sister attachment had devel-oped between her and Algernon from the day the startling youth had appeared at the studio to pose again for Gabriel as he had done at Oxford. Looking much younger than his years and possessing an inexhaustible fund of amazing conversation, he was a burst of radiance in the shuttered twi-light of her life. They seemed even to have a physical

affinity, the phthisic, ethereal woman and the youth, airy
as a sprite.   He was so attentive, so gentle, so understanding,
and, withal, so much the well-bred boy, once he succeeded in
keeping the omnipresent Marquis cooling his heels out of
the holy precincts.   He made her feel young again, as in
the days she had not known of beauty, and unhappiness.

When drugs failed to dull the neuralgia that bit her with
constant pain, Algernon read aloud to her from Dickens
and his beloved dramatists.   Then the scholar, so learned
in literature that Milnes used him to astound his jaded connoisseurs, became as simple as his listener in the enjoyment
of some delicious scene, and the champion of de Sade a
virtuous censor when, in his reading of Fletcher, he skipped
nimbly over passages too prickly for a lady, and that lady
the wife of Rossetti.   But Lizzie, in spite of the languors
imposed upon her by her invalidism and her Pre-Raphaelite
rôles, possessed a well of fun which needed only the faintest
light from without to set it sparkling — good English fun,
sometimes incomprehensible to Gabriel, who had to have
his wit tempered with intellect.   That radiance had to come,
however, from one as fundamentally young as herself.   To
good, solemn, pedantic William, she was and always remained enigmatic, as to all who saw her linked with her
poet-painter husband.   Nor did she exert herself to seem
less of a mystery.   She spoke seldom, and that brusquely
in matters that touched herself, smiled where others laughed,
and presented, in other words, a living version of her husband's painted creatures.   Even then she outdid them,
her brilliant hair, her deep, changing blue-green eyes, her
thin long hands seeming, by virtue of some dread witchcraft, to have taken the imaged beauty in exchange for her
own heart's blood.   Gabriel could not forbear astonishment,
therefore, when from the room adjoining his studio her voice
rang out in very human mirth to the sallies of his little
Northumbrian friend.

The verses Lizzie continued writing from time to time

grew painful in their sombreness. She had nothing now about which to rejoice. Gabriel, his physical demands grown more compelling, was drawing farther away from her for whom mere existence was made possible only by increasing doses of laudanum.

Small phials of the wine-colored appeasement stood always at her bedside. She could not have slept without the treacherous comfort that was breaking down her mind. Always she was steeped in a murky melancholy through which she would summon up the past, distorted by the fancies of the drug till her whole life seemed like an evil dream. Gabriel suffered most in her broodings. Had he ever loved her? There was a time he had in the silent wood, so long ago that it was like the memory of a dead life. It came back to her in the white vigils—the dim, open door of a remembered happiness. Groping, she entered, seeking to recapture the day and hour that had been. Like a prayer she worded her longing.

> In thy darkest shadow let me sit
> When the grey owls about thee flit:
> There will I ask of thee a boon
> That I may not faint or die or swoon.

She saw the wood in the hues of death, with the ill-omened bird hovering over it. She saw herself in its shadow,

> Gazing through the gloom like one
> Whose life and hopes are also done;
> Frozen like a thing of stone
> I sit in thy shadow — but not alone.

Death, who had so long claimed her, was casting over her the imminence of his wings. She knew and was not afraid. But with a greater power those first, few, rapturous hours called her back from the desired peace. When earthly life was done, would all things cease to be, the joyous with the sad, the good with the evil? No, she did not want oblivion,

though it could make as nothing all that gave her pain.   She
hoped for a continuance in a better world of that ephemeral
bliss with the man she loved.

> Can God bring back the day when we two stood
> Beneath the clinging trees in that dark wood?

The mysticism that had taken hold of Gabriel from his
youth became in her the assurance of a future life.   He may
or may not have written "The Blessed Damozel" as a mere
exercise of the Art Catholic; to Lizzie, ever the reflection of
his light, it was a glimpse of the true hereafter.   She dwelt
upon it, growing within herself, and towards him, into that
same celestial lady—an easy transition because of her frail
health.   Strengthened in her imagination, she wrote answers
to the poem, dramatizing each cruel attack of illness to her
last.

> Then sit down meekly at my side
> And watch my young life flee:
> Then solemn peace of holy death
> Come quickly unto thee.
>
> But, true love, seek me in the throng
> Of spirits floating past;
> And I will take thee by the hands
> And know thee mine at last.

So it would be, she incoherently assured herself in the more
hopeful hours.   Death would come to her, and then, in
the pearly dawn of a new life,

> She shall stand and listen,
> She shall stand and sing,
> Till three winged angels
> Her lover's soul shall bring.

Even that paradise was not without its serpent, and subtile
jealousy hissed in her ears, drowning the music of reunited
souls.   "True love," she had called him.   Had he ever
been true?   Even now, perhaps, as she was weaving her

heavenly visions, he was seeking a surer bliss on earth—
but not with her. What more had she to give? A living
corpse dragging down his virile strength. What wonder he
lingered where youth and health blossomed for his gathering? She had for him only the tainted lily, the lily that
Death himself was loth to take. How long, how long had
he let it stand!

Cruelly she lashed Gabriel with taunts she was too weak
in his presence to utter, covering the image of him with
reproach for his infidelities, whether real or imagined the
laudanum left no doubt in her broken mind.

> Ope not thy lips, thou foolish one,
>   Nor turn to me thy face:
> The blasts of heaven shall strike me down
>   Ere I will give thee grace. . . .
>
> And turn away thy false dark eyes
>   Nor gaze into my face:
> Great love I bore thee; now great hate
>   Sits grimly in its place.

Strong as her love, her loathing, those God-obscuring hours,
made of him a fiend and a vampire, a fearsome thing that
sapped away her life.

> All changes pass me like a dream,
>   I neither sing nor pray;
> And thou art like the poisonous tree
>   That stole my life away.

And for what? She had no answer; only a dull resentment.

Strained and unhappy their married life seemed to all who
ever met them, and Lizzie's growing instability gave color
to the belief. Their marriage had been but a promise fulfilled, the more intimate circle was aware. She had been
so ill that he had owed it to her, if only to give her
an easeful death and salve his conscience. He was not
for nothing the son of Mrs. Rossetti. Some praised him for

his uprightness, others disapproved.   What genius thrown
at the feet of death!   Of that other love, none but two knew
besides Gabriel.   And Lizzie—did she not know?   But
then, she suspected even where there was no cause, and would
be thrown into mute storms that impelled her to sudden,
unreasonable action.

A few months after her confinement, Gabriel had left her
staying with the Morrises while he went to Yorkshire to
paint a portrait, only to learn a few days later that she had
quit them without warning and gone back to the studio.
What had happened?   What fact or sudden divination had
made her flee?   Why had she returned to the lonely studio
and not a halfpenny of money in the house, rather than
remain at Upton with its lovely garden and Janey's baby—
and Janey?   He had many thoughts, all of them disquieting.

Nobody knew what to make of the fantastic household,
with a strongly passionate man married to an invalid whom
he worshiped, painted, was jealous of, and betrayed, and
a woman of angelic purity of aspect, striving, even against
death, for such bliss as angels have no need of—loving,
hating, and knowing herself betrayed.

Then one day an unforeseen trick of fate put an end to
their friends' wondering as they read in the only newspaper
that reported it the bare account of the

DEATH OF A LADY FROM AN OVERDOSE
OF LAUDANUM

On Thursday Dr. Payne held an inquest at the Bridewell Hospital on the body of Eliza Eleanor Rossetti, aged 29, wife of Dante
Gabriel Rossetti, Artist of No. 14 Chatham Place, Blackfriars, who
came to her death under melancholy circumstances.   Mr. Rossetti
stated that on Monday afternoon (February 10, 1862), between
six and seven o'clock, he and his wife went out in the carriage for
the purpose of dining with a friend at the Sablonière Hotel, Leicester
Square; when they had got about halfway there his wife appeared
to be very drowsy and he wished her to return.   She objected to

their doing so, and they proceeded to the Hotel and dined there. They returned home at eight o'clock when she appeared somewhat excited. He left home again at nine o'clock, his wife being about to go to bed. On his return at half-past eleven o'clock he found his wife in bed utterly unconscious. She was in the habit of taking laudanum, and he had known her to take as much as a hundred drops at a time and he thought she had been taking it before they went out. He found a phial on a table at the bedside, which had contained laudanum, but it was empty. A doctor was sent for and promptly attended. . . . He saw her on Monday night at half-past eleven o'clock and found her in a comatose state. He tried to rouse her and could not. . . . He and three other medical gentlemen stayed with her all night, but she died at twenty minutes past seven o'clock on Tuesday morning.[1]

Gabriel broke down completely. Let alone the horrible shock of finding Lizzie dying,—no one would ever know whether by accident or willfully,—the thought that he, innocently or not, had contributed to that death laid accusation upon him. What if Mrs. Birrell, the housekeeper, and her daughter had testified at Bridewell "that her husband and herself lived very comfortable together," that Lizzie's sister told the judge "she knew of no harm to her"—had there really been happiness for them in that unwholesome studio that was so seldom home? Could he have sworn, unperjured, that he had never wished her better dead? "They dined with me on Monday," Algernon had said in the solemn chamber. "I saw nothing particular in the deceased except that she appeared a little weaker than usual." Always the friend, implying in this subtle way that Lizzie, in her weakness, had not been aware of what she was doing, and, instead of finding release from pain, had found it from the keener pain of life. For yes, ah, yes, it was crueler to live on than to lie at peace as she had lain before they carried her under the aspen of Highgate, with only the black seal of the poison on her lips to show that *she* had lured Death, the bridegroom. In vain the jury, overthrowing

[1] *Daily News.*

the suspicion of poisoning or suicide, returned a verdict of accidental death; *he* in his mind could never feel guiltless. Perhaps not that night or any recent night had he given her cause to surrender to oblivion; the guilt was in his soul whether the world saw it or not.

And the world was ready enough to see according to its lights. Some said that after he left his wife at nine o'clock he did not go to the Working Men's College, as he had told her, although it was his night there, but went instead to another woman with whom she suspected him in love. Fanny Cornforth's name was whispered. Driven by jealousy, Lizzie had then taken her life, leaving him with the burden of her death upon his conscience. Others, more generous, believed that Gabriel had really gone to his class,[1] but that Lizzie, in her sick imaginings, construed his absence as betrayal and determined to find peace where alone she knew it to be. In the minds of many, despite the jury's verdict, suicide was more than suspected. Even Algernon, though relieved of the shadow of the law, was cryptic in his references to the woeful facts. "Happily," he wrote to his mother after the inquest, "there was no difficulty in proving that illness had quite deranged her mind, so that the worst chance of all was escaped."

The worst chance of all? What was it? Had he feared it for Lizzie's sake, whose body might have suffered the indignity of the operating table or burial in the unhallowed plot of the suicides? Or for Gabriel's, who had been so near suspicion of murder?

The blurred uncertainty of a harrowing dream fell upon Gabriel after the hectic hours when he had walked from one end of London to the other to get help for his dying wife. But even when Dr. Hutchinson gave up all hope, after endless hours, he could not grasp it was the end; not then, nor when the undertakers had come and clothed her for death, and she lay still and meek, as she had always been. The

---

[1] William Michael notes specifically in his diary that Gabriel was returning from the Working Men's College when he found his wife dying.

laudanum — it sometimes left its victims in a coma for days: perhaps it was only working itself out in a sham death.   In a burst of hope he rushed down Bridge Street for Dr. Hutchinson, who humored him — one must humor a man crazed with grief.   The doctor stood at the coffin head. No, she was dead. . . .

Among her poor little writings, one was found of more significance than all.   The script, never steady, rambled painfully over the page, the letters themselves twisted like things in pain.   They had been traced by one whose sight, dimmed by the final shadow, had still one crying accusation to leave behind.

> Life and night are falling from me,
> Death and day are opening on me . . .
>   Lord, have I long to go?
> Hollow hearts are ever near me,
> Soulless eyes have ceased to cheer me:
>   Lord, may I come to Thee? . . .

The veiled reproaches reached their target.

While the coffin still lay open, Gabriel, stricken with re-morseful anguish, took the sole manuscript of his poems, the poems written to her, read to her, inspired, even before she came, by the presage of her, and laid it between her cheek and the folds of her hair.   And a double loss was buried beside his father's grave in Highgate Cemetery.

At Upper Albany Street, whither Gabriel turned for refuge from himself and the ghosts of Chatham Place, Lizzie's bullfinch sang in the sunlight as if death could never be.   Who knows?   Perhaps there is no death.   Perhaps, after that sad sleep, the blessed damozel — Beatrice, Eliza-beth, one under all these names — awaits, in the ramparts of God's house, the day when the false are true, and, purged of all mortal frailty,

> He and she and angels three
> Before God's face shall stand. . . .

XXI

LOVE COMES TO THE PROPHET

"The loneliness is very great and the peace in which I am at present is only as if I had buried myself in a tuft of grass on a battlefield wet with blood, for the cry of the earth about me is in my ears continually, if I did not lay my head to the very ground." Down, down, in hard humility.

Charles Eliot Norton was far from cheered by such letters from his friend Ruskin, who, more than with any other man, laid his heart bare before him. Shady Hill, that had seen the American scholar born, had endowed him with a symbolic largeness of spirit, which, like the hospitable oak, welcomed the wounded from the world's storms. Norton's life had been singularly pacific. Of a gentle, studious nature, he had been fostered in an atmosphere of urbane culture further enlarged by foreign travel. He came of sturdy American stock, independent in religion, — his father was a Unitarian and professor of sacred literature at Harvard, — devoted to the family and respectful of the arts. Besides, he had a quiet tact that made the most reticent open out to him, knowing they would find a sympathy as wide as it was unostentatious.

Ruskin and Norton had met on their travels, and a spontaneous friendship had sprung up between them, nurtured by a common admiration of early Italian art and literature.

Norton was engaged in his translation of the *Divina Commedia* when Ruskin's painful letter reached him. Grief and turmoil, full-winged, were circling the world, angels of destruction. In his own country civil war had been raging, begun bloodily with the bombardment of Fort Sumter, continuing more bloodily through the first and second battles of Bull Run, until it seemed as if the conflict between the sister states should not end but with the sacrifice of their finest lives. For a few dread days there had been danger of war between England and America when two Confederate commissioners were seized aboard an English vessel, but the danger had been averted by their surrender. The scholarly evenness of life in the university town, as elsewhere, had been jarred, none finding it in himself to stand by in a contest that touched the very keystone of the temple of government.

"I give my time and my work for the cause for which we are contending—the cause of justice and liberty," wrote Norton to his English friends, "and I am happy to bear my part. . . ." Like him, others, North and South, gave of themselves for the thing they thought right.

The young men falling in and arming,
The mechanics arming. . . .
The lawyer leaving his office and arming, the judge leaving the court,
The driver deserting his wagon in the street, jumping down, throwing the reins abruptly down on the horses' backs. . . .
Squads gather together by common consent and arm.

But he, Walt Whitman, did not arm. His conscience was against the taking of human life, even in the cause of freedom.

Arous'd and angry, I 'd thought to beat the alarum, and urge relentless war,
But soon my fingers fail'd me, my face droop'd and I resign'd myself,
To sit by the wounded and soothe them, and silently watch the dead. . . .

Nearly three long years, and still he watched and there was no end. A war, cruel in itself, was rendered crueler by the hardships of nature in the bitter winters and the distances of vast country. Three rivers stretched their lengths in flood and drought, ice and heat, in the embattled territory; changing climates took their toll of the dead. America bled, a Titan turned against itself.

It pained Norton to read what Carlyle and Ruskin had to write of the conflict, siding, as they did, with the South, and justifying, with extreme logicality on Ruskin's part, a slavery which from the bottom of his true soul he could not but have loathed. "It interests me no more than a squabble between black and red ants. . . . If you want the slaves to be free, let their masters go free first. . . . As for your precious proclamation . . . if I had it here— there's a fine north wind blowing, and I would give it to the first boy I met to fly at his kite's tail."

Norton took it all as part of his friend's freakish nature —freakish because, with the lack of balance common to an extraordinary mind, it sometimes did not know how to draw the line between logic that was sane and one that, like the faultless casuistry of some types of the deranged, belonged that side the moon. He accepted Ruskin as he found him, and put together in justification of the man the scraps of confidence his friend had both told and penned him.

Suddenly, from the storm head of religious doubt, Ruskin had sent out a revelatory flash. "I don't know in the least what might have been the end of it," he wrote, "if a little child (only thirteen last summer) hadn't put her fingers on the helm at the right time and chosen to make a pet of herself for me, and her mother to make a friend of herself." That had been after the cup of gall of *Unto this Last*.

There were many things, however, which Norton, for all his friend's confidences, did not know and could not have guessed. The shaken prophet had met Mrs. La Touche and her children after the dark purple orchis at Rheinfelden had wrought graver magic than Hermes' moly, for the inno-

cent flower, instead of rendering him insensitive, awakened
him to the spell of the enchantress he had so long ignored.
Again, his had been the reverse of Saint Ranier's conversion;
in lieu of turning, like the saint in Benozzo Gozzoli's fresco,
from his zithern playing and the dance of sweet maids,
instead of hearkening to a grave lady in purple summoning
him to the beatitudes of a nobler life, he bade her be still
and went on plucking the joyful strings. (Even in his
most evangelical days Ruskin had felt sorry for the eventually regenerate Ranier.)

Upon his return from Turin he visited the La Touches
in answer to an invitation from Mrs. La Touche that he
instruct her two daughters and her son in drawing. Ruskin
had never taught young children, but, the mother's letter
touching a vanity that made him feel his would be the key
opening virgin minds to the ideal of beauty, diffidently
acquiesced. It was a novel experience—in many ways.
He had always loved children, little girls better than boys,
who made him nervous with their wildness. He had a
thrill of emotion, therefore, undefinable to himself when,
while he was standing in the La Touche drawing-room, a
door opened and a pale-haired, serious child of nine entered,
studied him gravely out of large blue eyes, gave him her
hand, and stood shyly back. He did not know that those
clear blue eyes, while taking stock of him, had conveyed
their own impression to her mind, however influenced by
her mother's praise of the great man. Famous and learned
he might be, but from an imaginative girl's standards he
was not beautiful. In fact, Rosie thought the thin, tall,
pink-faced gentleman old and very ugly. She had expected,
if not the picturesqueness of a Mazzini or a Garibaldi, at
least the flowing patriarchality of a marble Zeus. However,
Ruskin's quick-flashing smile, as innocent as and far less self-
possessed than her own, won her to him.

Mrs. La Touche, a lady of considerable social aplomb,
deemed by her circle both fascinating and intellectual,

queened it over a home which she would have made the
élite of England with herself its Aspasia. At the time she
met Ruskin she had turned thirty-three and attained to her
fullest comeliness. Blood there was of the bluest in the
family, the La Touches having followed the banner of
William of Orange when the persecution of the escaped
Huguenots in Holland had proved beyond their saintly patience. Mr. La Touche himself never lost sight of his
inspiring beginnings, and clasped religion close — too close,
perhaps, for his brilliant wife's pleasure. A devout husband, after all, sheds but a dim ray, a mere taper glow, in
the flaring gas-light of the salon. Notwithstanding, Mrs.
La Touche was not discouraged. She received the Prince
of Wales, gave a déjeuner in his honor, and benignly invited
the villagers on the lawn to catch a glimpse of His Highness.
John James Ruskin was not averse to having his son travel
in high society — princes and the hostesses of princes for the
heir of the burgher wine merchant. Truly John James
had not done so badly in the world.

Of course both he and Mrs. Ruskin knew all that concerned their son's relations with the polite world. Each
time Mrs. La Touche's carriage drew up with its load of
children, their mother, — for she, too, was being instructed
in art, — and their governess, the old people were prompt
to greet them and lead them to John's study. After the
first few trials, however, lessons at Denmark Hill ceased.
The garden, the pictures on the walls, the curious collections
of minerals and crystals the big man kept in his cabinets like
a young boy — everything became too distracting to the
children, and the business of teaching was resumed in the
La Touche schoolroom.

A tender sympathy steadily grew between the master and
his youngest pupil. Something precociously understanding
in Rosie touched him as no woman's tact had done; before
long he found himself a child at the feet of the girl, seeking
advice and consolation which were given as unaffectedly as

he sought them. But Rosie, despite the maturity of her part, was still a child. To her the gentle, whimsical man whose happiness and sorrow she seemed so well to appreciate became something sweet and delicious, that gave pleasure. She called him "Crumpet" — later, when she learned to know him better, "Saint Crumpet." "Archegosaurus," too — but only when he seemed to be so old, and to know so much.

The master's visits grew frequent in the neighborhood of Green Street, the lady of the house always welcoming him as her particular guest. Rosie, quietly observant, thought her own thoughts and sometimes spoke them. She was a budding girl, nearing fourteen, when Mrs. La Touche, perhaps to sound her secret self as well as her daughter, asked her, during one of Ruskin's lengthy absences abroad: —

"Rosie, don't you wish Saint Crumpet would come home?" (So often, in innocent ears, a woman gives voice to her own longing.)

"Yes, indeed I do," said Rosie. "How tiresome of him!"

"Do you think he wants to see us at all?" (Out of the mouths of babes . . .)

"Well, perhaps he does. I think he wants to see me, Mamma."

"And doesn't he want to see me?"

"Well, you know — well, Mamma . . ." The girl grappled with truth. "I think he likes your letters quite as much as yourself, and you write so very often — and I can't write often. So he wants to see me."

A strange, puzzling, complicated tangle of emotions: on the one side a clever, socially ambitious woman married to a religious fanatic, seeking stimulation, sublimated or otherwise, in the intercourse of a celebrated man; between her and him, her daughter, roused prematurely to sentiments whose full import racked her young frame with womanly ills; on the other side a man approaching middle age, who saw the rivalry between mother and daughter and yet denied it was there, loved and did not understand his love: the three concealing their passions and rivalries from one another yet covertly making a clean breast of them to the least likely confidantes — Mrs. La Touche to Rosie and Ruskin, Ruskin to his father. The little dialogue between mother and daughter had run a course as circuitous as that of Midas's secret of the ass's ears. For no apparent reason Mrs. La Touche had reported it verbatim to Ruskin abroad; Ruskin, finding it too much to contain, had copied it out and sent it to his father; old John James read it to Margaret, who, wiser, held her peace.

Immediately upon John's setting out on his trip, little Rosie had fallen ill with severe headaches and other "languors" for which old Mr. Ruskin, with the forthrightness he prided himself upon, chided his son. "Rosie's illness has assuredly nothing to do with any regard she may have for me," John quickly exculpated himself. "She likes me to pet her, but is in no manner of trouble when I go away; her affection takes much more the form of a desire to please me and make me happy in any way she can. . . ."

Was he speaking truth, now, the son of the man who had taught him to speak it? And did he himself believe what he wrote? That Rosie's illness had nothing to do with her missing him he could not have known. Little cognizant of himself, he could not have seen into a delicate, sensitive, growing mind placed in a situation beyond its years to cope with. He was aware that Rosie cared for him enough to want to make him happy by being a good child, by loving the good and the beautiful, by patterning herself after the models he set up for her. Just so (had he had the knowledge of common humanity to understand) he would have seen any woman in love make herself the mirror of her love's desires. He should have seen it in Lizzie Rossetti, in Georgie Burne-Jones, who was even now learning to paint and doing the things her Ned loved. But he who knew to the least variation the veining of a bit of stone knew nothing of the emotions of a human heart, least of all of a child's heart passing through the storms of development. Even that he loved the child with a love he had not had for Euphemia, he did not know; though he carried a letter of Rosie's to her dearest Saint Crumpet folded between two thin gold plates against his heart. He could not hide from himself that often, when in London, he would go out of his way if only to pass that house near Green Street; but that his desire to be near her sprang from the same root as that which brings a lover to his lady, he would have denied. By some inner glimmer he was forced to envisage the unnaturalness of the relation. Since, under the cloud his doubt and the failure of his recent work had cast over him, it was the only thing that brought him light, he basked in it in a rapture of closed eyes.

Mrs. La Touche was too confident of her personal attractiveness to be other than amusedly piqued at Rosie's frank avowals. A mere child's infatuation with her master. Her son and her elder daughter were equally fond of him—at least, she liked to believe it. Rosie was simply a more difficult child, brighter than either of the others and perhaps not quite so healthy. In her quality of Lacerta, as one of her friends called her, she tried to have the wisdom of the serpent without its sting. Lizard-like, too, her tendency to sun herself in the more comforting hypothesis. Yes, Rosie was an ailing child. Those fainting spells and that dreaminess which made her seem only half herself. There was an unnatural depth in her eyes, with their heavily drooping lids. Her cheeks, when not vividly flushed, paled to dead white. Only the girl's lips, classically chiseled, bloomed full and turgid. An unusual child, and one who gave promise of rare budded beauty. Still, only a child.

Meanwhile Mrs. La Touche corresponded regularly with her children's tutor and had long, confidential talks with him whenever he visited her either in London or in Ireland. She knew of every fluctuation of his spirit — as who, once on terms of friendship with him, did not? He made no secret of himself to anyone. So, when Bishop Colenso's critical examinations of the Pentateuch began to appear in print, bringing to arms all religious England against such heretical questionings, Ruskin, struggling to painful certainties, could say, looking back upon his earlier stride, "I was then far beyond the point at which he is standing now." Mrs. La Touche listened with horror. A strict Evangelist like her husband, the letter of her faith ruled her acts. "Don't," she begged Ruskin on one of his Irish visits, — the very one, perhaps, during which Rosie came down to greet him in a tiny pink dressing gown that long flushed in his memory, — "don't make any public utterance of your views — promise — for ten years. . . ."

Ruskin gave his word. Nevertheless the crumbled creed could not be mended with a promise. An eternal questioning continued darkening, a gloomy wraith, the hours of his solitude, were it in his familiar Denmark Hill study or on the Alpine palisades, whither he journeyed back and forth in some obscure rite to shake it off. Not alone in his loneliness did it follow. At Miss Bell's school at Winnington, where amid the posies of gauzy white girls he sought distraction in country dances and cotillions, the shadow loomed in mockery of his play. With Ned and Georgie in Italy, where he terrified them with hazardous feats of roof climbing, it thrust its unwelcome face, and he fled, leaving his two young friends to resume alone the trip he had planned and financed for them. Never was a Hamlet pursued by a more relentless ghost.

In prostration of soul he would have withdrawn to the summit of Brezon, to wrestle once for all with his incubus, had not the Bonneville authorities, eyeing him and his guide climbing the steep with books and geological hammers, scented a gold mine, and refused to sell the lonely eyrie except at a price that even the open-handed foreigner deemed too high. The plan was abandoned in favor of a prospec-

tive retreat in England and the promise of a set of hangings
to be designed by Ned from Chaucer and embroidered by
Miss Bell's girls. Such slender threads helped to draw
him from the Haunter, though not so strongly as another,
less tangible, with which his little Rosie would have led
him from Bye-Path Meadow, the place of unbelief in her
own Pilgrim's Progress. But as for that strait old road,
"half Babel, quarter fiery furnace," he could not travel it
any more. "Meadow of some sort I must have," he complained pitifully, "though I go no further."

With hungry joy he garnered the gravely sweet words
of Rosie's mouth, dimly knowing that of their honey he was
storing up a bitter yield for future years. Sometimes it
frightened him, this concentration upon religion, in a blossoming girl. "How could one love you if you were a
pagan?" she asked him once. With the pain of his own
experience he would have eased her out of the mould into
which her parents were perforce thrusting her. Fools! As
if the fluid brightness of the stuff of life were precious only
when it came out in shapen—too often misshapen—lumps
of conformity! His father and mother had taken his young
spirit, cased it in their narrow Evangelicalism, and sat back,
complacently priding themselves on having produced a
righteous man. Little did they know the warped homun-
culus under their creation. He knew and he rebelled.
Theirs, like the hand of the potter, had left its stamp. It
was not too late for Rosie. She should not be warped.
Her straight young womanhood should rise up free as the
tree in the wood, the light of knowledge forming her evenly
on all sides, that not a blossom but would breathe of the
true health. She should be the divinely perfect case of
divinity; for that she must not be scorched with the breath
of fanaticism. In freedom she must grow whole and pure.
He was reckoning without the La Touches, however. What
was his desire against the constant pressure of their training?

At Miss Bell's school, to his wreath of admiring young

ROSE LA TOUCHE

FROM A PENCIL DRAWING BY JOHN RUSKIN

girls, he would speak of woman's function in the world, of how she should prepare herself early in life for the queen-dom of the earth, having before him, the while, the image of one sweet woman-to-be.   Out of his talks grew *Sesame and Lilies* and *Ethics of the Dust*.   "They cost me much thought and much strong emotion," he wrote of them years afterwards.   And indeed they must, these painstaking pillars of a temple which was never to house a goddess.

Little comfort came to him from the world.   His numer-ous charities only showed him the baser part of man; his written word had ceased to delight him.   Still seared in the mouth with the message he had for a blundering human-ity, he wrote another series of essays in which he expressed the needs of an economic society that took "dust for deity" and gathered it for treasure.   Froude, editor of *Frazer's Magazine*, offered him its pages.   The June number of 1862 contained the first essay of *Munera Pulveris;* two more appeared in the course of the year.   Again the public would not be warned by a prophet it refused to recognize. The magazine lost many of its subscribers, and the courageous Froude had to admit defeat by discontinuing the series.

When the news of his new fiasco reached him at Mornex, Ruskin paced the terrace in despairing rage.   What reason had he to live now?   The pen in his hand could never be turned to the feather with which to titillate the senses of a degraded society, nor could his voice, attuned to lofty music, take up the cacophany of the market place.   Better that his pen lie useless and his voice be dumb.   Years ago, when, ironically, only triumphs had been his, he could have borne the slight in the hope of soothing it in a world to come.   Now he had only blankness to look forward to.   A challenging blankness, however.   "It is a difficult thing," he confessed to his father from the depths of his disenchant-ments, "to live without hope of another world. . . . But by how far the more difficult, by so much it makes one bet-ter and stronger."

He had need of all his courage and strength.

Nine months of that dark year he spent in France and Switzerland, making short swallow visits to England, only to fly back more troubled than ever. Oh, for peace, peace in which to build again on the wreck of his work. *Stones of Venice*, the five volumes of *Modern Painters*, his art teachings — they were ruins in the convulsion of his spirit, waste shards in a waste place. All was to build anew, and he was old. Was he really only beginning to walk through the "Rue St. Thomas de l'Enfer" on the way to "das ewige Nein"? At times despair played on the low chords of his fancy the music that breeds madness.

Rosie was sixteen years old, no longer a child. He wore her favorite blue in his cravats ("Don't you know blue is the color you should wear?" she had observed, womanly coquettish at the age of nine), and wondered why she never wrote to him as openly as in those days: "Oh, St. Crumpet I think of you so much & of all your dearnesses to me. I wish so very much that you were happy — God can make you so. . . ."

God, God . . . the Name entered much more often in her conversation and writings.

XXII

"L'ENFANT TERRIBLE"

"You speak of not being able to hope enough for me," wrote
Swinburne in 1862, replying to a word of admonishment
from Ruskin. "Don't you think we had better leave hope
and faith to infants, adult or ungrown? You and I and
all men will probably do and endure what we are destined
for, as well as we can. . . . I don't want more praise and
success than I deserve, more suffering and failure than I
can avoid. . . . You compare my work to a temple where
the lizards have supplanted the gods. I prefer an indubitable and living lizard to a dead or doubtful god."

As he read the harsh yet dignified defiance, Ruskin must
have seen the dæmonic Algernon looking a stripling Lucifer.
And a Lucifer de Sade, Algernon did think himself. Ruskin need not suppose that because the admiring ladies at
Wallington treasured his sketches and made a godlet of
him that he, Algernon, would worship at his feet. He was
his equal, — "you and I and all men," — with his own
triumphs still to achieve. The living and indubitable lizards
of his creations were after all more precious, because his own,
than other men's dead gods. One could have heard the
falsetto shriek of challenge in the words.

Algernon was feeling unusually self-confident. What
with the learning he had gleaned at the inn of strange encounters under the ægis of his sapient guide, and what with
the encounters themselves, he felt a man in a man's world.
Browning he had met, and Froude, and Spencer, and Thackeray, and, best of all, the life-scarred man of action and

dark lore, Richard Burton, a lusty giant who found him not too callow for boon companionship. And an arduous companionship it was, which would have tried a more feckless constitution than Algernon's.

No greater contrast could have been imagined, even in the fiendish experimenting of an alchemist in human elements, than that which existed between Swinburne at twenty-five and Burton at forty. Milnes, finding it ready to hand, lost no time in seeing what fireworks might flare up. They were beyond his dreams in alternating brilliance and luridness. But it was Algernon alone who came out of them singed — and delighted. The urbane host beamed with the satisfaction of achievement whenever he observed the two together, the great bulk of the adventurer a roughhewn background for the delicate Algernon — one might have said some barbaric sculpture of an Oriental deity with its puny offspring, so wide the difference between them. The Oriental touch was not accidental. In Burton's own county the Romanies claimed him; in the bazaars of the east he passed for a Mussulman. Eight years before, he had made a pilgrimage to Mecca with the worshipers of Mohammed, none dreaming that the dark, craggy-browed stranger was not a devotee of Allah's prophet. The following year he explored Somaliland for the Indian Government, the first white man to set foot in Harrar and drink with the king. He came near dying of hunger and thirst in a four-months stay in the desert, and had a javelin thrust through his cheek that a savage had aimed at his skull.

With all his adventurousness, he was deeply a scholar. Learning a new language was for him a diversion from his life of action: when he was not engaged in discovering new lakes in the heart of Africa, he was sitting in his armchair grappling with words. Arabic, Hindustani, Persian — he knew them and their dialects as he knew English, and he was no mere surface student. The quaint and obsolete in words tempted him as survivals of civilizations no longer

there for him to explore, the floating jetsam of some literary Atlantis. He had never been a cloistered student —
rather, yes, at Trinity College, long enough to prove himself an untamed and untamable outsider. The inevitable
rustication had followed when he challenged a fellow student
to a duel for ridiculing his moustache, which even now hung,
an admiration to the eye, in a bifurcate droop along his
seamed cheeks. His latest exploit had been twofold: he
had made a fleeting visit to the Mormons in the United
States, out of which came his book, *The City of the Saints*,
full of praise for the polygamous latter-day religionists, and
he had married — a young girl from the very gates of a
Catholic college. The next adventure of his scholar-gypsy
life was to be his impending departure for Fernando Po as
consul.

The new friendship opened wide for Algernon the doors
of his mind's house, at least during the large hours when
the bowl went round spiced with romance and pornographic
anecdote. He beheld before him, in the powerful frame of
his friend, the heroic embodiment of what nature, in cruel
caprice, had left in him only as a sculptor's sketch — too
great for clay, too mean for man. But his spirit equaled
Burton's. Did the giant shake the rafters with the gross-
ness of his Rabelaisianisms? Swinburne showed him that
he, too, was past master in the art, of which Milnes and
Rossetti and Ned had many a hilarious specimen — especially Milnes, who encouraged with his tongue in his cheek.
Did Burton drink like a very Gargantua? Swinburne
showed him that he had as big a gullet if not so strong a
head. In his turn Burton admired his young friend's poems
and flattered him with a friendship few had enjoyed. Algernon's self-esteem grew apace. He fell in love.

Among the homes he frequented, the loadstone was that of
Dr. John Simon, whose wife was one of Ruskin's numerous
fair confidantes. From the moment Algernon had met their
adopted daughter, a vivacious young creature, dark-haired,

bright-eyed, though not strictly beautiful, he had bowed low
in the abasement of adoration.   Even her piano playing,
music which he could not abide at the hands of his sisters,
he listened to entranced, while poetical images vied for description of her charms.   He was badly smitten.   "Boo,"
the silly little nursery name by which her foster-parents
called Jane Faulkner, became for Algernon the quintessence
of euphony in the English language, and Boo herself the
paragon of womankind.   Jane, affected by the prophecies
she heard made on all sides of the young poet, flattered, too,
by the humility of his adoration, coquetted prettily with
him.   She read his manuscript verses, she sang to him, she
gave him roses—she turned his head.   One day, when she
had made herself irresistible, he flung himself upon his
knees at her feet, and, in the shrill, incoherent speech that
was his under excitement, declared his love.   The girl drew
back, frightened.   Far removed, this, from the polite
maundering of a Victorian lover.   The flushed face in its
halo of fire, the quivering boy's frame and his wild gesticu-
lations, were too much for her nerves.   Boo lifted a startled
brow askance and broke into hysterical laughter.   Lucifer
woke in Algernon.   As wildly as he had declared his passion, his wounded vanity spat forth the catalogue of invective he had gleaned from his murky readings.

He tore out of the house, another self.   Jane may not
have meant to be cruel, but with her laughter she had killed
whatever hope there had been of Swinburne's normal living.

"It will not grow again, this fruit of my heart," he wrote
prophetically, when, after months of futile raging, he found
the peace to solace himself in song.   In Northumberland,
where the low downs leaned to the sea, among the associations of his childhood, he plunged as in a bath of purification
to cleanse from him the insult of Jane's laughter, and in
the confidence of his mature power wrote the "Triumph of
Time."   It was a supreme gesture of resignation, noble because he still could see the worth of what had been denied,

though he knew it lost to him forever. The sea, however, symbol of life and death, love and hate, joy and pain — she still remained to him, and to her he went as to mother and mistress, crying for his soul to be set free of love's bondage, as she was free.

> O fair green-girdled mother of mine . . .
> Thy sweet hard kisses are strong like wine,
> Thy large embraces are keen like pain.

In the incestuous union he sought, if not healing, annihilation. But he could not yield up all without flinging in the face of the decorum that had rejected him the ashen vengeance of his dedication to evil.

> I would find a sin to do ere I die,
> Sure to dissolve and destroy me all through
> That would set you higher in heaven. . . .

Blindly he swore, —

> I shall never be friends again with roses,
> I shall loathe sweet tunes.

In reality it was the poison of his frustration still rankling within him, who would have saved himself through love, only to be cast back upon a fate ordained the hour of his conception.

Once scorned, Algernon did not renew his suit. However, when he would have wrung the exquisite of pleasure and pain from the experience, he induced images of himself and her bound breast to breast, as when

> Carrier came down to the Loire and slew . . .
> Bound and drowned, slaying two by two
> Maidens and young men, naked and wed.

He whipped up his manhood with the imagined sensuality of that death and that last uniting kiss after which

> The Loire would have driven us down to the sea. . . .

Dead sea fruits, that left the taste of their kernel of ashes.

He took his final leave of Jane in six resigned stanzas, solemn as a dirge, cadenced as a mournful sea.

> Let us go hence, my songs; she will not hear.
> Let us go hence together without fear;
> Keep silence now, for singing time is over
> And over all old things and all things dear.
> She loves not you nor me as all we love her.
> Yea, though we sang as angels in her ear,
> She would not hear.

In that leave-taking he said farewell to the sweet love that might have saved him. After it Dolores, monstrous flower of the Marquis's pleasure garden.

Monckton Milnes proved himself a blessing in many practical ways to those whom his fancy decided to adopt. He was no mean impresario for a poet to have. First of all, he introduced Algernon to Hutton, reasoning that a published piece, now and then, would prove useful advance publicity in the event of a volume. Accordingly, the guileless readers of the *Spectator* found themselves involved in long defenses of Mr. George Meredith's *Modern Love*, attacked by other reviewers tooth and claw; of Baudelaire's *Fleurs du Mal*, which several years before had created such a scandal in France that the poet's name could not be mentioned without personal reflection in polite society. Such unconventional fare was staple, however, to the poems that appeared at regular intervals. What, indeed, could the virtuous, nourished on the diluted honeydew of proper poetry, make of the pagan evil of the eternal vampire won by a throw of the die by Satan from God (a shocking sacrilege in itself), who, living,

> . . . loved the games men played with death,
> Where death must win;
> As though the slain man's blood and breath
> Revived Faustine, —

and who, dead, nourished the sexless root of sin and suffered the caresses of "curled obscene Small serpents with
soft stretching throats," until what time she rose again to
poison the world with her accursed beauty.

> You seem a thing that hinges hold.
> A love machine
> With clockwork joints of supple gold —
> No more, Faustine. . . .

This, after the connubial guidebooks of Patmore, with their
reverence of the Angel!

Had the readers of the *Spectator* had a peep into the
drawers of Swinburne's desk they might have seen much
more to horrify: manuscripts on two nonexistent French
decadent poets, Clouet and Cossu, whom Hutton, scenting
a hoax, had cut off from even the transient life of the review; scandalous translations from Villon, sensual lyrics,
sketches of a novel with the appalling name of *Lesbia
Brandon*, a play on Mary Stuart, and the beginning of an
unspeakable epic on flagellation. All these Swinburne had
written or was in the process of writing when he took up
quarters with Dante Gabriel Rossetti at the old Tudor
House in Cheyne Walk. *Atalanta*, on the crest of whose
white purity he was to be lifted to success, was not begun
until next year.

New experiences crowded, meantime, upon his limited
perceptions, sunning to distorted development what was
already pronounced in his nature, but leaving stunted the
rest of his psychic organization. In Paris, at the Louvre,
it was Hermaphroditus with its epicene grace and not Venus
that lifted him to sensual ecstasies. The four sonnets he
wrote upon it, while heralding the new poet whose art
scorned nothing human, stressed the peculiarity in his nature which found kinship with the perverse. As in his
æsthetic affinities, so in his life. Now he could be seen
companioned by the ephebic Simeon Solomon, himself like

an incarnation of his indeterminate, strangely wistful
creations.

Algernon brought him home to Cheyne Walk, introduced him to de Sade, read him his poems, praised and
flattered him.   At times they ran about naked through the
vast house, Algernon a slim pale satyr, Simeon a Phœbus,
Algernon insisted.   The distraught Rossetti fumed in his
studio, shouting to them to stop jumping about like wildcats.

In a manner, the unawakened Simeon became to the sen-
sually learned Algernon (learned with the deadlier knowledge of the mind) what he himself had once been to
Milnes — the virgin to be initiated into the seductions of the
senses.   It was a subtle ravishment, not the less a rape for
being mainly cerebral.   The young Hebrew's innocence
gave Algernon the illusion of potency; the shady nature of
their relations added the intoxicating poison of evil without
which no sex-expression would have satisfied.   Tales gained
currency of how, in the mysterious gloom of Tudor House,
antique cults were revived when the younger man donned
Grecian costume and, with wreath and lyre, sandals and
flowing drapery, flung the poet on his knees in worship.
Letters passed to and fro, Algernon's naughtily licentious.
Simeon read them and put them safely away, as he put
away "Erotion," written by Algernon to one of his drawings.
He went with the poet everywhere, met all his friends, but
never his family at East Dene.

Burning the candle at both ends hardly sufficed the hectic
sensualist Algernon had become.   As he fluttered from one
sensation to another, seeking an appeasement that never
came, he seemed like some creature compact of Greek fire
which, once possessed of an object, consumed it to the core.
The peril lay in that he fed chiefly on himself.

The Paris trip, with its new associations in Whistler,
Fantin-Latour, and Gautier, aggravated his weakness of
wanting to better people at their own game.   As usual he
drank with the thirstiest, and in the round of studio visits

extolled his propensities, boasted like a schoolboy, and strained his nerves to the danger point. The breakdown came. At the height of his excesses he was seized with an epileptic stroke and had to be rushed off to Cornwall, for a régime of walking, riding, and swimming, by his old master Jowett. It was a beautiful if ill-assorted relationship between Algernon and Jowett, who from the altitudes of Plato found himself many a time walking rugged earth, the guardian of a hilarious, staggering, semiconscious Bacchus assailing his ears with "bad songs, very bad songs."

The seizures which from now on followed in the wake of undue excitement were more terrifying for Algernon's friends to witness than of serious consequence to himself. By some mercy the unconsciousness acted as a sponge upon his spirit, wiping the slate clean—for newer beginnings. And he never failed to make them. Smilingly calm, he came out of each attack, a little apologetic for the embarrassment he had caused, and fuller of energy than ever. How he found time to write as much as he did, people often wondered. Perhaps his facility, at once his strength and his weakness, accounted for his mass of work. George Meredith, his housemate at Cheyne Walk, had a tale to tell of how Algernon had come to him at Copsham cottage, febrile with the discovery of Omar, of how he leapt like a flame and sang the new music with the voice of fire, vanishing as abruptly as he had appeared, to return shortly after with the first draft of "Laus Veneris" in the same dancing lambent measure, made his own by the Swinburnian magic.

For the magic he had mastered wholly, once he had broken free of the Pre-Raphaelite trammels. Fundamentally it was a simple magic, requiring but rhythm and the letters of the alphabet. The materials had been common to all; it remained for him to turn them to his uses. What was the secret he had acquired? The critics, when the ivory-colored quarto of 1865 brought them the virgin *Atalanta*, marveled, praised, but could not analyze, nor

were they the wiser of his craft when the candent volume
of the following year seared and blinded with its core of
fire.

Swinburne wrought essentially in music, playing upon
the alphabet as upon the keys of an instrument, reiterating,
combining in chords of vowels, insisting on a captivating
harmony to complete the patterns of his thought.   He was
so intoxicated by his own music that, like a mad Kreisler,
he lulled himself in his languorous phrases.   Once he found
the true notes of his song, he was to repeat them with little
variation throughout his life.   He was also a colorist,
master of a palette gorgeous with the hues of a torrid imagination; nothing in the universe but he must draw from it
splashes of imagery, often without sequence or coördination,
but always effectively.   The canvas of his fancies luxuriated
in tropical bloom — lush, fiery, monstrous, the coil of the
snake at one with the curl of the vine, a riot of passionate
vegetation, without plan or order, seething with the sap of
life and hiding death.

Poems and Ballads burst like a bombshell amid the pious
domesticity of England.   The Laureate, resigned to Omphale, had brought forth as his latest the idyll of Enoch
Arden, suggested to him by our friend Woolner.   Patmore
had followed up his angelic successes with other sanctioned
poems, under whose outward decency a generation of frustrate women could enjoy without sin the thrills of life.
Apart, Browning nursed the grief of his loss, but

> I was ever a fighter, so — one fight more
> The best and the last!

he proclaimed in the face of death, urging his courageous
optimism.   Admired by the very few, he wrote on because
only in writing did he live the true life, lover of life though
he was.   General misunderstanding affected him little
when within the circle of his midnight lamp he could resur-
rect the artists and philosophers and singers of the past, and

bring again before human sight the wrongs of dead days
for pity to assuage. The vellum-covered court record he
had picked up at a stall in Florence was even then slowly
transmuting itself under his hand to the very stuff of life,
ruthless, cruel, capable of all ill, yet, even at its worst,
often ennobled by a humanity akin to godhood. Two years
still were to pass before *The Ring and the Book* would see
the light and Pompilia's murder be avenged.

A., of the *Strayed Reveller*, had subsequently reissued his
poems under his own name. It was chiefly in the literary
circles of Oxford, however, that Matthew Arnold reigned
as the exponent of a new poetry embodying restraint of
form with loftiness of content. In spite of his prestige,
New Poems, then in preparation, was to mark almost the
last of his poetic output.

Christina Rossetti with *The Prince's Progress*, and William Morris with *The Life and Death of Jason*, launched
their barks anew that same year. Once more Christina was
welcomed, though not so enthusiastically as upon the advent
of *Goblin Market*, while Morris canceled in secure success the
neglect of his first, and perhaps his most impassioned, volume. Under the grass of Highgate cemetery, Dante Gabriel Rossetti's poems lay dead with the dead Lizzie.

A skillful campaign had been carried on for months before Swinburne's poems were allowed by his impresario to
shock Britannia out of her wits. Manuscript copies flew
from London to Fryston, Wallington, East Dene, even to
bourgeois Camberwell, to test how those whom Swinburne
counted his friends would receive his exotic nightingales.
Some counseled setting them loose to take their own chances
with the public; others would have their wings clipped, their
voices tempered to sensitive ears. Lady Trevelyan pleaded
with him not "to give people a handle" against him. Ned
Jones and Whistler were all for giving the poems to the
world; Meredith advised caution. Of all people, Burton
grew trepidant, fearful of their secret meanings, into whose

darkness he expected eyes used to noon to penetrate with his own nocturnal vision. Ruskin neither condemned nor praised, but brought in Turner and bemoaned the evil days fallen upon the world. "I should as soon think of finding fault with you as with a thundercloud or a nightshade blossom," he wrote Algernon. "All I can say for you or them is that God made you, and that you are very wonderful and beautiful. . . . There is assuredly something wrong with you. . . . So it was with Turner, so with Byron." "You have left the fearful and melancholy mystery untouched," he said to William Michael of his friendly brochure on *Poems and Ballads*, "the corruption which is peculiar to genius of modern days." Again, "I should no more think of advising him or criticizing him than of venturing to do it to Turner if he were alive again. . . . I'm *righter* than he is — so are the lambs and the swallows, but they're not his match."

Others, however, who had a vested right to censure, raised their shout against this "libidinous laureate of a pack of satyrs" who glorified in hendecasyllables of perfect delicacy all the bestial delights that "the subtleness of Greek depravity" had been able to contrive. Here was one,[1] at least, writing anonymously in the *Saturday Review*, who turned as expert an eye into the poet's vices as the wise Burton himself. Nor was he alone. Dallas of the *Times*, to whom the book had been sent for review, embarrassed out of all countenance by the handful of scarlet wickedness in that otherwise harmless bouquet, dashed off to Bertrand Payne of Moxon's and threatened, "Either you withdraw the book or I denounce it!"

Conservative publishers have always been known for peace-loving souls. Rather than have a suit upon his hands, Payne withdrew the offending volume, which was placed with the rest of Swinburne's copyrights with the flamboyant firm of Hotten.

[1] John Morley.

A *succès de scandale* staggered the never-steady Algernon under its flattering notoriety, and now no one was there to help him keep his balance. Lady Pauline had died shortly after the book's publication; Ruskin was traveling abroad and too much occupied with his own troubles; Rossetti had had enough of the fuss made over his little Northumbrian friend; and as for Meredith, he let it be known that in his opinion Swinburne had no "internal centre," so that he might just as well go through his bacchanalian measures with his vices and his roses.

Everywhere youth quoted, —

> We shift and bedeck and bedrape us,
> Thou art noble and nude and antique,

read with caught breath of the white wealth of a body made whiter by the flushes of amorous blows, thrilled at the excruciating canticle of Our Lady of Pain, but left the book uncorrupted because not understood. The newspaper wags, on the other hand, found rich material for parody in the kiss of her lips at whose touch men change

> The lilies and languors of virtue
> For the raptures and roses of vice.

They bloomed in strange gardens, those lilies and roses. The wicked, mad new poems were on every lip that dared utter them; that year Swinburne's character as the erotic poet of youth was fixed forever.

Nevertheless, among the amatory poems that so shocked the English-reading public of two hemispheres, much that was essentially Swinburne passed unobserved. His worship of greatness, in whose presence he was fervent with "all the sweet and sudden passion of youth," his recognition of his incapacity in the life of men, his yearning toward union with something vast and beautiful — all these, and his confession of frustration, his readers did not see, for they did not look beyond the sensual.

Swinburne, as some of his friends could not help observing with dismay, had failed to develop emotionally beyond adolescence; hence his delight in transmuted sensuality. Typical of the undeveloped, he refused to call it by its name, but needs must clothe its nakedness in figures as elaborate as ceremonial robes. Since, for all his going about with Monckton Milnes and the Solomons of his acquaintance, he lived more in his book-born dreams than in reality, he could not be satisfied with the experiences, so petty in comparison, which life provided. They were too bare, too much the stuff of prose. He must have loves more exotic, passions more devastating, women more human and more bestial. A tawdry actress becomes in his fancy a sleek black pantheress, a prostitute a Faustine, a Dolores a Madonna of Pain, bearing in her eternally renewed flesh the caresses of a thousand men, himself the last. He, the five-foot-four mannikin, became the dominating lover, capable of crushing in his arms the sweet flesh of the fairest women. But when he saw himself most truly, he was the white-breasted sea mew, a stranger to the abodes of men, exulting only in the freedom of the elemental waters, large and restless and eternal, and unchanged as on the first day of creation. Always he returned to the sea, his Mother and his Love.

XXIII

THE WORLDLY YEARS

PEOPLE passing by 16 Cheyne Walk, Chelsea, in the day-time, toward 1865, wondered what strange recluse lived in the immense old house, once the home of Princess Elizabeth, with its sombre windows and no sign of life. At night, when the five great bays awoke, and the sound of voices and laughter echoed through the hushed respectability of the Walk, when carriages drew up at the gate, letting out distinguished guests, they surmised some person of importance.

In the beginning of his tenancy, in the autumn of 1862, they had caught glimpses of him at times, walking solitary along the bordering garden path, a medium, slightly heavy figure, pale of face and gloomy-eyed, with a short, auburn-tinted beard. He wore a long, straight coat, buttoned at the chin, open at the front, with wide pockets in which his hands fumbled nervously. Those days other men were seen coming and going—a tall, bald, unobtrusive scholar; a queer, restless little fellow, immaculately dressed but for those times when he would be escorted home by nonde-script companions, his cravat and hat askew; and a handsome, English Apollo, tanned from the outdoors and talking always in a voice loud from full-expanded lungs. He came once a week at first, then at rarer intervals, and, in a year or so, ceased coming altogether. Somehow he seemed not to have belonged there, as if some pollard of the English countryside had been transplanted to a conservatory. Then there was the magnificent blonde woman, gorgeous in outlandish silks—too well kept to be the housekeeper, not quite lady enough to be anything higher.

It had been an uncommon household, that of Rossetti, William Michael, Swinburne, and Meredith, destined from the outset to short duration by the temperamental differences of the fellow tenants, whom even the largeness of the abode and the irregularity of their stay could not keep sufficiently isolated.

Always a hypochondriac, Gabriel came out of the ordeal of Lizzie's ambiguous death self-devouring with guilt. For many months he could not bear to be alone a moment. He stayed with his family a few weeks, then, while Tudor House was being made ready for him, at lodgings where William and Brown and others of his friends came to see him. At first, in the loneliness of his sudden freedom, he swung in reaction to the earliest ties, suggesting that his mother and sisters live with him. It was a momentary weakness, soon overcome. Fortunately, for he had strayed too far from Mrs. Rossetti's narrow morality to have made a common life anything but torturesome for her and difficult for himself. The bachelor ménage was therefore instituted, providing him with the society he required and the liberty of pursuing his work. Fanny — the Sumptuous, they dubbed her — furnished the lighter and indispensable side of his chaotically reorganized life.

The white sheep in that black fold, discounting William the candid lamb, was George Meredith. It may be that Algernon, who had known Meredith since Balliol, had suggested the co-tenancy; in 1862 he had held the editorship of *Once a Week* and had admitted therein a poem and a story by Algernon, who, that same year, had published his defense of Meredith's poems: a friendly exchange, what though the two men were personally as ill matched as a robin and a tropical cockatoo. Nor did Meredith sort better with Gabriel.

He had been only twenty-one when he married a widow of thirty. The difference in their years had meant little to the romantic boy against her being the sister of his dear

DANTE GABRIEL ROSSETTI

A PORTRAIT BY GEORGE FREDERICK WATTS

friend and the daughter of the famous Thomas Love Peacock: a hale eater, a refined drinker, and a power in literary
circles. It may have been the influence of the old epicure
which made the Merediths unite their efforts in the production of a cookbook. Meredith's first volume, the ill-
fated *Poems*, was entirely his own. "No sun warmed my
roof-tree," he said later of this marriage, and indeed no
sun could have ventured in an atmosphere so charged with
electricity, where husband and wife, both high-mettled,
caustic, and domineering, made of every difference the
occasion for a storm. As if they themselves did not provide
reason enough, poverty crooked his lean finger, and life and
death played gruesome pranks in a succession of short-lived
babies. Only Arthur liked life enough to cling to it.

As the years passed, brightened fitfully by the Aristo-
phanic humor of Peacock, the rift between the Merediths
widened, bringing havoc into the serenity of the *bon vivant*
whose house they shared for a time. It was a wearying
routine of violent quarrels, partings, and no less violent
reconciliations. Finally Mrs. Meredith eloped to Capri
with Henry Wallis (the "Chatterton" painter), leaving
Arthur with his father. They had been married nine years.
Her course, alas, was short and swift; within a year she
returned to England, a broken, half-crazed woman, friend-
less and outcast, to die. Meredith would not see her, nor
would he bring her their child, the only being she longed
for in the end.

William Rossetti said of him that he looked like the
statue of Emperor Hadrian. An accurate comparison: the
same perfect, unsympathetic beauty, fleshlike, but stony. A
little of that stoniness was in his heart. At Cheyne Walk
nobody knew anything of him but that he had won an en-
viable position in the literary world, and that he was a
widower with a child whom he kept in the country. By his
manners one might have thought him well born; by his
snobbery, shouted and grotesqued, one suspected. His al-

most psychopathic reticence on the subject of his origin gave grounds to fantastic legends which, far from discouraging, he abetted by an elaborate indifference. The author of a first novel which received the notice of George Eliot, and of *Richard Feverel*, whose praise had been splurged over three columns of the *Times*, could put to good use a little pleasant publicity. It limbered up failure and spurred on success — though his public career had been as auspicious as his private life had been unhappy, perhaps for the same cause. A man out of the common run must clear his own path, whether it lead to a dust heap or an oasis. Observers will watch and comment, praise or blame, urging toward the goal; step by step the yoked mate must go with him or be left behind, oftenest to perish.

In spite of his success, however, Meredith complained, with a grudging eye toward the royalties of poets and novelists he deemed beneath him. Little by little, like the myth he encouraged of his noble origins, he spread the rumor of unjust neglect, donning, when others were praised, a crown of thorns and a sackcloth of humiliation that became not at all his otherwise arrogant assurance. Such a man was hardly one to be long friendly with Algernon or to propitiate Gabriel. At the sight of the Rossetti breakfasts, six eggs and a round of ham consumed with no nicety of etiquette, Meredith turned queasily away. At Algernon's innate courtliness he took personal umbrage, though he tried to outdo it. The straw that broke the back of his pride was a pair of new boots which the Cheyne Walk fellow tenants, thinking him out of pocket, laid behind his door in place of the muddied ones he had left there. From that day he never came back — or was it because at about that time, while Gabriel was entertaining a number of patrons, Meredith saw fit, in a way he had, to ridicule him, half seriously, half in chaff — whereupon the tactless Gabriel turned upon him with "You are no gentleman"? A mortal sting, certainly, to the son and grandson of a tailor.

Meredith gone, Gabriel, tired of adjusting himself to the idiosyncrasies of his fellow boarders, decided to maintain the house alone. He was now earning upward of three thousand pounds a year, a handsome income even for one as loose of grasp as he. Therefore he approached his little Northumbrian friend, who had been unusually obstreperous, — he had taken to sliding down the banisters and landing with a thump, — and told him he needed the whole house for himself. The gentleman Algernon understood. Without a word he packed his belongings — books, snake-shaped candlesticks which he carried about with him like the most precious of talismans — and took quarters at Mount Street, not without regret for his little room facing the Thames where he had dreamed and realized his *Atalanta*.

Rossetti, again alone but for William Michael's regular and unexciting visits, resumed unrestrained the life into which he had plunged. After Lizzie's death he sought his pleasures where he could find them, alternately in vice and in spiritual elevation, loathing himself as he strove to drown those aspirations that made too inhuman a demand, and, in the midst of carnal delight, plagued with remorse. The Sumptuous and Beata Beatrix, angel of darkness and angel of light, walked with him between.

The intensification of his natural mysticism bridged easily, in the depth of his mourning, the division between earth and heaven. Literally with him, as with Dante, all that had been beautiful in his lady,

> Partendo se dalla nostra veduta
> Divenne spiritual bellezza grande,
> Che per lo cielo spande
> Luce d'Amor . . .

so that if in life the fervor of his love had cooled, in death it was as if until then he had not known the full meaning of love. In his sorrow he sought again the purest sources of his inspiration, to cleanse from him as in a lustral bath the

stains of living which would else have made him unworthy
to undertake his tribute to the dead.

During more than a year he had taken up neither brush
nor pen without laying it down with the heaviness of futility. Why paint when the flower of his life was cut down?
Why write when the corpses of his songs lay under the
Highgate sod? All reason for being seemed gone. But
with the gathering of his will a renewed power strengthened
his hand and sharpened the vision of his inward eyes. The
face of his wife, rendered clearer by the light of the divine,
glowed out of the darkness, commanding him to take his
brush and paint. And he painted her as he saw her, as
he had seen her many a time in life, the curve of her half-
closed lids spanning the trajectory of the human and divine.

"Beata Beatrix" he called her, for now that she was not
of the earth he could avow to himself and all men what she
had been to him. What mattered the earthly deception
that had kept her from his true sight? In death he knew
her for what she was, his soul's partner predestined since
the planets met in the fire of creation. "I loved her best!
I loved her best!" he had moaned before Swinburne, hardly
knowing what he confessed in the freshness of his grief.
Others may have lured him with the mystery of eyes that
had gazed on the Gulf; hers had seen God.

In the face of Beatrix, rapt in the trance of death, Lizzie's
face was caught, clear of all earthly taint, transfigured and
yet as real as when her parted lips had moved with words
for his mortal ears. Her head, shadowed by its hair as
by the wings of death, yearned upward on its throat, drinking flowerlike the light "of His countenance Who is blessed
throughout the ages." Palms open, her hands, empty of
earthly tasks, form a chalice for the dove's gift of the poppy
of death; when at last they hold it, they shall be clasped to
the final beatitude. No longer does she turn to the sunlight and shadow of the world beyond her balcony ledge;
the dial of her days has marked the hour when Love and he

who loved her shall be dim as figures of a dream before the true awakening, when they shall come to her clothed in their glory. Yes, she had seen God, and those eyes would no longer open to gladden the day.

In painting her, Gabriel drew from the many sketches he had made, drew also, perhaps unconsciously, from the little self-portrait she had painted years ago, when she would have attained to him by art. There was the same upward lift of the throat from the nunlike collar, the same shadowing of heavy hair, the same rapt expression but that in her painting of herself her eyes opened full to the sight of her lover.[1]

Had Gabriel been a Catholic and possessed no means of self-expression, he would have gone to the confessional. Having no faith, — he boasted of his unbelief in any established creed, — he made a confessional of his easel, poured out his whole soul in symbols, and imposed his own penance. "Beata Beatrix" was nothing other than a shrine erected in contrition to the memory of the love he had won and betrayed. The spiritual duty once accomplished, he threw himself deeper than ever into the delights of the body. Woman became to him a mystery and a cult, at once the Madonna and the Unmentionable Gulf which, by destroying, made him find himself. No longer is she herself alone, but, transformed by the workings of a formidable mysticism, she embodies the great Unity that holds in itself "the meaning of all things that are." Through her henceforth he would seek the revealing of the mystery.

With the coming of new acquaintances into his life, — for, after the initial seclusion, he swung to the extreme of worldliness, — the expression of his tastes increased. Whistler collected blue china and *lange Liszen* — "Long Elizas," the American called the slender damsels that adorned the length of the precious Nankin; Gabriel needs must have a collection to rival that of any curio lover in England. When

---

[1] No critic has ever commented upon this obvious influence.

not painting, he prowled about the shops, bargained with gusto, and usually returned to Cheyne Walk with a precious bundle under his Inverness. Tudor House little by little assumed the aspect of a museum under the management of an eccentric and untidy custodian.

In the sitting room, mirrors, of all shapes and varieties, reflected a bewildering assortment of chinoiseries, Dutch tiles, a stuffed and gilded sunfish, and cupboards full of rare English china. Thick curtains of seventeenth-century crewelwork bowered with stuffy fruit and flowers a massive four-poster; even in the bedroom the black oak mantelpiece held its store of vases and peacock feathers, bronze grotesques, and Venetian mirrors. The windows themselves, deeply recessed though they were, further concealed daylight with folds of heavy Genoese velvet. A gloomy picture, none knew by whom, caught and held the eye. On a sea raging with monsters, a woman drifts in a rudderless boat, its shrouds loose and flapping in the wind, while behind her the sky is alive with demons, pestilence, and conflagration. A pretty image to ponder on before sleep. No one knew why the fastidious artist kept it there, or why, towering above the Chinese grotesques on the mantel, the unbeliever had fixed a huge crucifix of ebony and ivory.

It was in the dining room, whose five enormous windows along the whole width of the house framed Chelsea Reach and its wooden bridge, that the visitors felt at ease. Here at least, despite the hothouse atmosphere, mingled a tang of the river, and into the quietism of an existence which its fitfully boisterous merrymaking only accentuated entered glimpses and sounds of harsh, yes, brutal, but healthy London life. Here too, Indian cabinets and carven couches contrasted with the comfortable red plush of neighboring luxury. Drawings and paintings by himself and others hung about the room, a mirror duplicating the motif of the Grail at Oxford, sketches of Christina, and two heads, twin male and female blooms, of Simeon Solomon's. He too

had fallen under the fascination of the young Jew's mystical
androgynes, creatures of some strangely luxurious heaven.

Once he gained back the power to work, the routine of
his studio life suffered no change from Lizzie's death. He
still rose at noon, later when the festivities kept him up till
morning, and, after taking a turn about his garden, painted
until the last streak of day.   Then supper, a walk along
the Thames with some old friend, and back to Cheyne Walk
for the intense night life.   The evenings William Michael
spent with him they talked or read from the treasures of
the studio bookcase, Gabriel with a nostalgic brooding. All
his friends sent him copies of their works, from Bell Scott to
Simeon Solomon, who had recently begun to write in a
peculiarly tenuous strain.   He alone was dumb, and yet he
knew that if only he wished it . . .

The admission of his potency, stemmed by that little
word "if," drove him to seek liberation in more desperate
living.   London's celebrated *bon vivants* now frequented
Tudor House, provided their tales could spice an evening
and they could listen as well as tell.   Those were the days
of Charles Augustus Howell the prodigious, and Sala, and
Sandys, raconteurs of Munchausen propensities and Casano-
van zest; of Whistler, whose wit added salt to the saltiest
till the sense was scarified.   Algernon and Morris and
Burne-Jones came, too, and Madox Brown, whom Gabriel
had induced to leave his rustic retirement and settle in
Fitzroy Square.

Ruskin alone of the old friends was conspicuously absent.
In fact, the open breach could not be concealed. No more
did the art critic praise Rossetti's paintings; he had grown
as far away from his favorite's work as Rossetti had himself
grown away from the early asceticisms that had delighted his
patron.   A frank sensuality now permeated his canvases,
and he had painted a nude half-figure!   "The change in
you may be right or towards right," Ruskin admitted, *but*,
"I am now wholly intolerant of what I once forgivingly

disliked." Of Venus Verticordia herself he would not deign to speak, condemning, instead, the meretricious screen of flowers that exposed her. "They are wonderful to me in their realism," he wrote to him after having seen it, "awful — I can use no other word — in their coarseness . . . showing certain conditions of non-sentiment which underlie all you are doing now. . . . I would give much," he said, regretfully, "to see you doing as you have done — and to be able to say what I once said." But he was nevermore to say it. He and Gabriel, both lost in the dark forest, struggled along opposite paths toward the clearing.

Charles Augustus Howell, however, kept them linked, as often, in a miniature, the arabesqued tail and horns of the devil bring together two saints in their golden lunettes. If ever Mephisto himself had walked the earth, — that is, the Mephisto of the romantic tradition, — he could not have chosen a more unscrupulous, conscienceless, debonair, dashing corporealness than Howell's. He was one of those men born figuratively with caul and tail, the good-luck cap prospering, till fate is bored, the mischievous proclivities of their not strictly human natures. William Michael, that finder of parallels, had immediately seen in the regally dashing boy who had come darkly into their midst, and as darkly vanished, a resemblance to Velasquez's Philip the Fourth, but for Howell's thick black hair.

Was he descended, bar sinister, from an English monarch, or, bar dexter, from Boabdil el Chico, as he would have one believe? And was his mother a renowned Portuguese beauty of title? His own physical attractiveness pointed in that direction. Had he really supported his family by diving for treasure on a sunken galleon? And had he trained horses for an Arabian sheikh, becoming a sheikh himself? Again his knowledge of diving and of horses lent him truth. In his young life — he was only twenty-five when he reappeared in London in 1864 — he had acquired an amazing number of hobbies and accumulated a knowledge of art and collecting that staggered many an expert. He could lead Whistler and Rossetti to veritable treasures in Wardour Street and obtain them for his friends at prices that delighted them and yet left liberal—they never knew how liberal—profits for himself. Swinburne was immediately attached to him: hadn't Howell confessed to having been instrumental in the attempt on Louis Napoleon's life, and hadn't he known Orsini?

Lord Houghton and Simeon Solomon were soon presented to the new-found wonder, and the dives of London became familiar with an odd quadrumvirate—for, with his caul and tail, the new Autolycus possessed also the sesame that threw wide the secretest dungeons. Algernon made a bosom friend of him, as much as could be made of a being so mercurial. "Je m'enfonce dans des systèmes qui mènent à tout," he wrote to him while preparing *Poems and Ballads*, "oui, chère fille, absolument à tout. O mon ami!" It was so much easier to express certain things in French. "Tout à toi," he ended familiarly, and sometimes signed himself Charles de Sade. In 1866, when the trepidant Payne hastily recalled the first edition of Algernon's poems, it was Howell who found him his new publisher, bolder, but less respectable, as were always the connections he made for his friends. From then on, for nearly ten years, he was unofficially Swinburne's man of business, a function he filled for Rossetti and Whistler, but briefly. Autolycus met his match.

There was no one he did not know. He introduced everybody to everyone else, clung to the fattest purses, and let go only when they were empty. He was so clever, however, that his victims enjoyed his rogueries. "What has the Owl done now?" opened hilarious table talk. And the Owl never failed. Wherever celebrities gathered he was sure to be seen, darting in their thickest with the broad red ribbon of a Portuguese order across his waistcoat, hand and eye alert for business. Many were his adventures, and

more the places he filled, but none so extraordinary as that
of dispenser of charities — for Ruskin!

The position was perhaps a little more involved: Howell
acted as Ruskin's secretary and literary assistant, agent and
entertainer, a part he could manage to perfection. Margaret Ruskin alone did not appreciate him. "How can you
two sit there and listen to such a pack of lies?" she exclaimed,
throwing down her netting, after some preposterous tale.
John smiled and soothed her, and Joan, his young cousin
who had come to stay with his mother in her widowhood,
widened her eyes with merriment.

Margaret Ruskin now more than ever lived for God and
her son. Denmark Hill none dared penetrate without the
approval of a probity grown rigid with observance. No
wonder John's friends, especially of Howell's kith, rarely
found welcome. To each new face that entered among the
Turners collected by her husband, that appeared at the
dinner table spread with the plenty of an honest merchant's
lifetime of toil, she turned piercingly questioning looks that
found out better than her son the worth of her guests. And
she did not hesitate to speak her mind. Right was on her
side, and her motherly protectiveness; for well she knew
that John in his trustfulness became a babe in the hands of
schemers — like that Howell person. His turning from
God was *their* doing, and she must watch over him more
than ever she had watched over his infant feet picking
their stumbling way over the patterned rugs. Now it was
the path of God she must keep clear for him.

As she held her place at the table among the unfamiliar
faces, — Howell brought along his following to the fountain of charities, — her erect old head uncovered for John's
sake despite her widowhood, and her brooch of diamond and
emerald, worn, too, for his sake, flashing endurance and hope
on the black of her mourning robe, she let no word escape
her of the conversation. "John, John Ruskin," she called
to him across the table, "What was that you said?" And

John Ruskin repeated dutifully for her enfeebled hearing. Later, from her place in the hearthside, she indulged in loud, sharp soliloquies and snapped like a taskmistress, "John Ruskin, you are talking great nonsense," at any dictum that did not suit her orthodoxy. John then with beautiful courtesy defended his views, as if his mother and Joan Agnew and Howell were a college of theologians. Margaret listened unmoved. An aiguille was she in her faith, upright, aloof, frozen, unassailable — except that the peak would have made an echo to his plea.

Before Howell had been long with Ruskin, the Rossetti circle knew his most intimate business. William Michael, quiet and long-eared, noted everything in his neat archives. "Howell says R's income is £22,000 a year out of which he only keeps £1500 for his own expenses. . . . He also maintains by an annual allowance the Father and Mother of his late wife! . . .

"Howell says that . . . at Ruskin's marriage £40,000 was settled on Mrs. Ruskin; and that as far as he can trace out in his accounts, this sum has remained with her. . . ."

"Howell says there appears a considerable prospect of Ruskin's marrying again shortly; he could not mention the lady's surname, but her Christian name is Rose. . . ."

Howell says . . . It became a byword, not always for truth. With smiling effrontery he would tell of how not a word of Ruskin's recent book — he would never mention it by title — had been written by the critic. "Every bit of it is mine. . . . He can't write any more. His mind . . ." One can see the long, expressive forefinger drawing circles in the air.

Gabriel would listen and laugh. He enjoyed seeing the rogue who made him somehow forget things that would be remembered.

There 's a Portuguese person called Howell
Who lays on his lies with a trowel . . .

he extemporized. But those lies helped to keep buried the discontent with himself and his work that would rise up to reproach him.

Since "Beata Beatrix" he had painted much and sold much at good prices, and for a time he thought he had found himself in his painting. There were "Belcolore" and "Lady Lilith," from the splendid fleshliness of Fanny; and "Monna Vanna" and "Il Ramoscello" and "Venus Verticordia" and "Joli Cœur," all luscious female figures with long lithe throats and searchless eyes whence his own unquiet spirit looked through. They were the symbols, drawn from the flesh and the souls of the women who now entered his life, whereby he would discover the Meaning—if any were. For him there had to be.

In the Chippendale bookcase of his studio the notebook of Blake furnished faint clues. And also the life of the mystic Alexander Gilchrist had left before he caught scarlet fever from his children and died. William had helped Mrs. Gilchrist with the sad task of publication, and he, Gabriel, had furnished some matter, here and there. But that had been in 1862, and Gabriel had gone far since then.

Blake's poems, often on his lips, quieted a restlessness in him. But they were only half answers to his seeking, as if the poet spoke in a hollow place and only the echo reached his ear. The awfulness and the mystery of the All were there; sometimes the Presence loomed, but human sight grew blind with the light of the advancing shadow. Blake too had been a seeker in the unknown, who through the human had reached for the divine.

> For Mercy has a human heart;
>   Pity, a human face;
> And Love, the human form divine . . .

Love, the human form divine. It was that divinity Gabriel would seek out in the heights and in the depths, and bring to earth what else would remain incommunicable but for the dim glimmerings of the mind. Less wise than Blake who warned, —

> Never seek to tell your love,
> Love that never told can be,
> For the gentle wind doth move
> Silently, invisibly . . .

he was impelled to cry out. For love in him was no gentle wind, but rather the fire-flaked hurricane in which he had painted the souls of Paolo and Francesca rushed in their Dantesque hell. He loved because he had to, because the fiery flakes pelted his soul, not because he chose to. Choice came in the use he would make of his experience. Again, he was hopelessly in the toils of an old love, and he must speak.

Meanwhile a new and dreaded spectre came nightly to perch at his bed's foot. Wide-eyed and pale, and like a self weary of sleep, it sat there holding Gabriel's eyes with its hollow orbs, questioning, taunting, until the day came and sleep had fled. How many things Insomnia made clear to him!

"Ah, you would have killed that love? You thought it dead?"

"I would have killed it, but it is not dead."

"Because she was another's?"

"Yes, my friend's."

"And yet your lives are never near?"

"Our thoughts are never far apart."

"And you have no hope?"

"It seems fainter now, and now more clear. . . ."

"No hope?"

"To-night Love claims his full control. My soul this hour has drawn her soul a little nearer yet."

"No hope?"

"If faith long bound may at length its hope beget, my soul that hour shall draw her soul forever nearer. . . ."

"If faith long bound . . ."

Ruthless, till morning, it held its inquisition until Gabriel had to confess to the reawakening of his passion with its urge to write and paint, to forge of his soul's and body's gold a crown for the beloved's hair and a glory for the world. However, it was only through his dead wife that that love could be hallowed.

He had the Morrises staying with him, and made a crayon of Janey as "La Donna della Finestra," the woman who, seeing Dante pass by bowed down with sorrow after the death of Beatrice, cast him so pitiful a look that all pity seemed gathered in her. As yet Gabriel did not dare merge her with his lost lady. Pity . . . pity . . . but one step more . . .

His ambition kindled, perhaps he might take up his pen again. Swinburne had gained fame — he had once been his pupil. Morris was about to publish *The Earthly Paradise*, verses of which, while Janey posed, he had composed at Tudor House and declaimed out of the back window, to the uneasiness of the neighbors, who wondered what new madman, roaring at emptiness, had come to live in that Colney Hatch. Morris, too, had been his disciple. All, all were doing the noble things of the earth; he alone had forced himself to dumbness. And yet, from underground, they might still live, his songs, for they had never died. He had buried them, the living with the dead. The living, whose appearance had been announced, long ago, in his volume of translations. . . .

XXIV

TRANSITION AND AN END

By 1870, nearly a quarter of a century since the group of young revolutionaries had taken England by the ears, the day of the Pre-Raphaelites had set, though its chief exponents were painting harder than ever. At the Plint sale, five years earlier, their works fetched low prices, and Gabriel, looking back at the old days over the blossoming exuberance of his present paintings, could speak with finality: "The epoch of Pre-Raphaelism was a short one, which is quite over, and its products will be exceptionally valuable one day, but not yet."

None the less the term continued to be used and abused. Hardly an exhibition, but the papers were full of references to the school. Pre-Raphaelitism? What was it now? The spirit that imbued with disturbing voluptuousness the Rossetti canvases, seen only by the favored at the homes of his patrons? If that were Pre-Raphaelitism, how did it agree with the prosy but decidedly pleasant productions of the Royal Academician Millais, which made William Michael deplore, "Millais, I fear, going off seriously"?

And what had Holman Hunt's geographically truthful, painfully accurate Biblical subjects, with their crowded stages and Oriental luxuriance — what had they in common either with Millais's pretty little girls in mobcaps, or Rossetti's women and flowers? And Edward Burne-Jones's painted poems, graced with chaste knights and ladies who resembled Gabriel's as the shadow resembles the body, — so long and thin and incorporeal they were, — what had these paintings, which began to stir the critics' gall some years since, of kinship with the rest?

For they, too, were Pre-Raphaelite. A light "that never was, on sea or land," or, indeed, on any canvas at the Academy, vibrated in them, blinding the Academicians to petulance. "Jones's picture . . . has been badly hung by men who could not understand the poetry of it," declared Madox Brown, grinding his private axe at the same time. "But he is all right for fame and fortune." Still, years had passed and neither fame nor fortune had befriended him, though Ruskin thrust his head out of the dark cloud that beset him to encourage as best he could. "Howell says," chronicled William, "that according to Mrs. Jones, Jones is (very needlessly) so down-hearted in consequence of the attacks and criticism . . . that he says it is just a toss-up whether or not he shall throw aside his brushes forever."

Howell was wrong. A formidable tenacity in the mild, consumptive youth compelled him to labor despite discouragement and ill health. Something different, new, completely his own, could not but strike even those who insisted on stressing his conscious, yes, feeble imitation of his master. There was, nevertheless, a pureness in his work beyond which Rossetti had not gone. By some whim of fashion it was fastened upon when success at last came to him, and Burne-Jones's painting was to stand to the rising generation as the true Pre-Raphaelite, with its poetic conceptions and vividness of presentment, realms removed from reality, as the Arthurian days he dwelt in were removed from the gas-burning, railroad-traveling era of Victoria.

The sunflower, celebrated by Rossetti in his Magdalen drawing and by Morris in the Oxford frescoes as well as in the "shop," in Jones attained to the apotheosis of an emblem, immediately adopted by the infant æsthetic movement. Henceforth Pre-Raphaelitism no longer implied sincerity and truth of portrayal of what the artist's eye perceived, but a certain flebile dreaminess, artificially induced, as a protest against reality. The reign of the sun-flower was at hand.

"Did you ever draw a sunflower?" Burne-Jones rhapso-dized. "It is a whole school of drawing. . . . Do you know what faces they have, how they peep and peer and look arch and winning, or bold and a little insolent at times? Have you ever noticed their back-hair, how beautifully curled it is?

"As to those sunflower worshipers, I do denounce them," he declared roundly. "I will not stand godfather to that feeble folly without crying out — Away with them, the feeblings."

Renounce them as he would, godfather nevertheless he had to stand, not only to the young group at Oxford, under whose towers the æsthetic movement was rising, and in London to the precious fops who, as they walked down Piccadilly, carried daintily a sunflower, "a poppy or a lily in their mediæval hand," but also as far away as New York, to fashionable young ladies who, driving through Central Park, sported a tall helianthus at their whip hand. Nor were the humorists of that reconstructed land unaware of the lightest ripples in the sea of art. Tongue in cheek, they pointed twofold barbs. "Cimabuella" Bayard Taylor named a product of the new Pre-Raffs, going on to describe her in the accents of Rossetti.

> Fair-tinted cheeks, clear eye-lids drawn
>   In crescent curves about the light
> Of eyes whose dim, uncertain dawn
>   Becomes not day; a forehead white
> Beneath long, yellow heaps of hair.
> She is so strange, she must be fair.

France, on the other side of the Channel, was too much occupied with the activities of her own to pay close heed to foreign movements. The year 1848, which had brought her another political revolution and England one in art, had borne, on the whole, short-lived fruits. Social unrest, impatient of restraint, seethed in the blood of the young French artists, manifesting itself not against the government,— though, indeed, even there they played no mean part,— but against the nearer tyranny of the Academy, whose shackle and vise were tradition and the "grand style." "Enough, enough of your eternal Greeks and Romans!" they protested. What were *they* doing in that *galère* of dead sculptures, when life and imagination lured them to adventure with Shakespeare and Goethe and Byron — most of all Byron!

And so Géricault and Delacroix set up their easels alike in the market place and in the lands of wonder, and the Romantic school for nearly four decades flourished, a long life for any movement. But by 1863 Delacroix was dead, barely outliving his time; already the sowing of his mature art had yielded a harvest of its own. Romanticism, freeing itself from the grand style to embrace life and imagination, clasped with them also the waif democracy in the person of Jean François Millet.

No scenes of large adventure for him, the peasant who had known what it was to rise when dawn hardly lined the east, whose nights, like those of bird and beast, began with the ringing of the Angelus. Enough for him the immensity of the furrowed fields waiting for the seed, bounded only by the empty granary and the sky — the good brown fields of fragrant earth where the Sower commanded the landscape and, with wide-armed motion, planted the future. Sufficient adventure was the ripening of the grain and at last the gleaning, with the final sheaf laid by before the vesper bell summoned home.

Realism, too, rounded its cycle. Peasant and workman succeeded king and hero; the thatched hut was found as beautiful as the classic ruin. Both were material for painting: it lay with the artist to make one as noble as the other. Matter agreed upon, it became a question of manner, and here France was not oblivious of what was being done about her. Those Pre-Raphaelite paintings that had been shown at the Paris Exhibition of 1855 — had they held the secret? Was it painting, that process of laying in a leaf, vein by vein? Certainly it made for perfection of detail. Was n't it told that an Oxford scientist used Millais's "Blind Girl" to illustrate grasses, birds, and moths? But was that painting? When the human eye looks on a landscape, does it see the pollen on the flower, or the harmony of sky and tree, flower and mead?

"The principal subject in a picture is the light," said Édouard Manet. In the dictum lay the first commandment of modern art. It was Claude Monet, however, with his sunset "Impressions," who, from the derision of those who saw the painting in the Salon of the Rejected, itself a mockery, gave the school a name. Many and varied the aims of the men who collected under the banner of Impressionism at the Café Guerbois in the Batignolles. Nearly all had been refused at the Salon, but their subversive band, rich in talent, was to lead the art of the world to a new freedom — and license. Renoir, Pissarro, Degas, Manet, Monet — these were the new lights on the other side of the Channel flashing across to the last glimmerings of a spent pharos.

Two men alone of the early Pre-Raphaelite band never abandoned the principles that had linked them. Indeed, with Holman Hunt those principles had not been disciplinary goads to keep him marching along the confined path. He had chosen the reasoned direction because it was the only one for him and the best for the expression of his individual talents: in that sense he had truly fathered the Pre-Raphaelite movement. Fortunately or not, once he had selected the way he followed it to the end, turning neither to the right nor to the left, unaffected alike by life about him and his own living of it. At the ripe age of thirty-eight, when his golden beard was fading, he married a Miss

Waugh, William Rossetti acting as best man for auld lang syne, and off he went again to the Holy Land.

He was never facile, and difficulties external and spiritual impeded his progress to a degree that made his religious mind settle upon the conviction that Satan was at war with him. "I have no more hesitation to admitting belief in a force of evil than I have in acknowledging belief in a power of good in life," he confessed, "and I believe that one or the other takes possession of each person, temporarily or permanently, as they are encouraged to take the mastery."

It was his life's struggle to keep Satan from taking the mastery. Year in, year out, the indefatigable brush labored on slow, conscientiously realized scenes swarming with figures, each finished as minutely as if painted under a magnifying glass. "The Miracle of the Sacred Fire" of his fully matured period dizzied with its crowded life — hundreds of individuals, each caught at the height of fanatical excitement, against balconies and porticoes whose devotional tapers needed no light for the fire of flaming eyes. An uneasy canvas, wherein, Byzantine fashion, he had put together a mosaic with human beings for pieces. What patience . . . what labor! But was it painting? Art? So, on a humbler scale, the prisoner carves his mounds of cherry stones, intricately, patiently, to the day of release when the hands ache for the consoling task. Each painting done, respite — and again the ache for the next. Holman Hunt remained the prisoner of his art.

Not once in his long life was he recognized by the powers of the Academy, nor did he seek their favors. He was content to toil in the knowledge that with each stroke of the brush he was celebrating the works of the Creator. He had his reward in peace with God when at last he died with the first decade of a new century, in a world that had seen great deaths and great births. Through them all he had gone, isolated in his ideal, the youth of 1848 grown old.

To Millais, life was an actuality to be lived and felt to

THE TRIUMPH OF THE INNOCENTS

BY W. HOLMAN HUNT

the utmost.   Dreams?   They were for the hours of sleep
— they had no place on canvas.   Far behind, the days when
he could poetize on the "Woodman's Daughter" and find
tragic beauty in "Ophelia."   Real life for him, and the
charm that lay in the simple story: "My First Sermon" —
his little daughter, muffled and bonneted, fallen asleep in
the pew; "The Widow's Mite," a lesson of a homelier sort,
in charity.   And portraits, portraits, portraits of the hour's
celebrities.   At off moments he would have recaptured the
old poetry, though he knew full well it had no business in
painting.   "The Eve of Saint Agnes."   It had been beloved of the old Pre-Raffs.   He would try it again!

Posing Euphemia as Madeline, he gave her a few un-
comfortable nights in the chill of an ancient castle, as he
painted her with the moonlight throwing "warm gules"
upon her breast and "rose-bloom" on her hands.   Effie bore
it all patiently for his great art's sake; it *had* to be done
in time for the exhibition.   A less impartial eye might have
told Millais that the full-blown Euphemia of the matter-
of-fact gaze would not have longed to dream the dream of
Madeline: that was not the way Effie went about getting
herself a husband.   He painted her, nevertheless — a
matronly figure in the centre of a dark room, the light from
the casement barring the floor and her plentiful under-
draperies.   "I cannot bear that woman with the gridiron!"
was all Grant, the President of the R. A., could say when
he saw it.   So much for poetry in painting!

In the London home Millais saw the best society, Effie
presiding in high-colored brocades to set off her obvious
handsomeness.   No spot had fallen upon her of the mud
that had spattered Ruskin after the annulment.   The marriage had not been consummated, that was all, and since
Ruskin had not defended the implication — well, let gossip
whisper as it would.   She was happily married, at any rate,
with a houseful of children and a husband who graced any
drawing-room.   With middle age, Millais had acquired an

imposing manliness. The lanky body of youth had filled
out as with the comforts of success; the lean cheeks gained
a healthy fullness, bronzed by the months in the outdoors
at the gentlemanly sport of hunting. Ah, what *did* Ruskin
say to this, he who preached against the killing of bird and
beast! But then, Ruskin was not really a man, and Effie's
husband was every inch masculine.

The doors of "all London" received husband and wife
with honor. In the beginning it had been embarrassing,
especially where Ruskin might have been found, but in
time things took care of themselves and the early scandal, at
least in polite society, was forgotten. With success came a
little touch of snobbery; arrogance and egotism had always
been Millais's: what he achieved was his own, arrived at
through his own efforts. And he was not free from jealousy.
Was there a new light on the horizon? He dashed out to
see it. People were talking of that American. He made it
his business to see Whistler's "arrangements." "It's damned
clever," he said, throwing them a look. "It's a damned
sight too clever." And off to the studio to show the world
what Millais could do.

Of the old friends only Hunt remained, who almost
threatened at the time of the exhibition of his Temple picture
to have a vogue as popular as himself. But Hunt couldn't
keep it up, and he could, by virtue of his quick, free technique
that saved hours of time, and the popular subjects that were
snapped up right off the easel. One can do much by painting down to people. "A physician sugars his pill and I must
do the same." Millais had no affinity with the closet
artist. Pageants, fires, or funerals, he witnessed them all,
from Wellington's burial, years ago, when even Gabriel,
that most unpolitical of men, had found enthusiasm to write
a poem, to Thackeray's on another wintry day, when the
crowd was so dense that the novelist's friends could not get
near the grave. There was always rich material to paint
from; the artist has only to select.

As he looked down from Theodore Martin's carriage, he could have chosen that crowd of women dressed in all colors, making the graveside a carnival scene with their scarlet and blue feathers. No, that required a Hogarthian brush, and he, goodness knows, preferred pleasant things for an agreeable public. "There was a great lack of 'high society,'" he communicated to Effie when he returned, subjectless, home to work on "what people liked."

Fitfully the olden fire lit up dead memories as the brush laid on its strong, skilled strokes alive with energy. What ease he had; it was almost like play for him! Quickly he came down to earth again. No more women with the gridiron for him, no Wardour Street mediævalism. He must go on portraying real men and women in the reality of life. Leave serious things to Hunt, who had a mind for them, the strange fellow, preaching even in his friendly encouragements. "In a few days we shall both be lying in our dark bed . . . and the growing soul of us will have no riches that we have not already laid up in heaven. . . ." No, no! He wanted his riches here and now.

Yet there had been something he had lost, a thing he beheld dimly at the bedside of Charlie Collins. Not long after those days at Worcester Park farm, when they were all Pre-Raphaelites, Charlie had laid aside his painting. The calf love that had then caused him such torment quieted, he married Dickens's daughter Kate, who had posed for Millais's "Black Brunswicker," and, with the help of Papa Dickens's magazine, saw himself in print. He did not write much, — light travel fiction, a supernatural story or two, for supernaturalism had spread over England like a plague, leaving no one untouched, — nothing that could have compared with Wilkie's haunted worlds. He and his muse, poor Charlie, had been of the earth, earthly. A regret for something missed, however, weighed him down, who else would have filled a modest vicarage, lived without wants, died without repining. But he "on honeydew had fed. . . ."

When Millais saw him that last time, it seemed to him he understood. On the deathbed, covering him like a shroud, lay the canvas he had painted long ago, unfinished. The eye, now closed, had seen at last: the hand was dead.

For him, Millais, however, the vision could wait. He had many more years in which to enjoy the fruits of the earth, falling even now, ripe to his mouth. Millais's luck? Perhaps, but with hard work behind it. The judges of the Paris International Exhibition of 1878 awarded him the Medaille d'Honneur; Oxford conferred upon him the distinction of D.C.L. Germany, not to appear laggard, honored him with the order Pour le Mérite, now not solely given for excellence in the art of killing, as Frederick the Great had intended. Her Majesty, too, was not unappreciative of worth. Thinking perhaps of the time when the dullness of the confinement chamber had been enlivened by the notorious "Carpenter's Shop," she approved the suggestion of Gladstone's government to grant Millais a baronetcy. The same year that saw his curly-headed blower of "Bubbles" decorating the advertisements of Messrs. Pears, to the horror of Marie Corelli, saw the artist knighted. Why not? He had none of the scruples of G. F. Watts, who had refused the honor. Here and now, the riches, here and now. There was always time for visions.

Good old Madox Brown would certainly not have rejected the fruits of Fortune if she had ever turned the cornucopia his way. Who knows, perhaps even had they come at the hands of the hated Academicians he might have modified his habitual oath to a thank-you. But he was never put to the test — not by them.

Emma and the children thrived under the livelihood he was able to make, Academy or no Academy; his "Work" was completed, and in 1865 he startled the art world with a novel undertaking, a one-man exhibition. London had long been accustomed to the showing of individual works, but not until Brown gathered together the mass of his pro-

WORK

BY FORD MADOX BROWN

duction in a gallery in Piccadilly had it been invited to see the spectacle of one man's artistic progress.

Occupying a whole wall, the Carlylean canvas delivered its message. At its centre the glorified navvy, noble as ⌐ Grecian athlete, wielded his spade in a gesture of dedication, for it was for the future he was building. About him his fellow laborers toiled or snatched a moment's ease, while at the outer circle society filed by in its ranks from wealth's idleness to the bootless yet sweet labor of the tattered zany, clutching to himself the basket of flowers and herbs that meant his day's keep. Animals and beggars, the pampered lap dog and the nondescript cur of the street Arab, the enforced idle deadening their hunger in sleep under the embankment, told their story before the saturnine leer of Carlyle. A sermon, yes, but one that society had never ceased deserving. Carlyle and his wife often stood before it through the month it was on exhibition, Jane a trifle dismayed by the expression of her prophet spouse.

For the first time in his life Brown enjoyed the exhilaration of success. The papers, impressed by the paintings, cartoons for stained glass, and designs for furniture (done for the Morris workshop), praised the versatility of the man and obtained him buyers. Years of comparative prosperity filled the house at Fitzroy Square with colorful gatherings where Joaquin Miller, the American poet, appeared in riding boots and a red cowboy shirt, a match for Howell's Portuguese decoration, and the Pre-Raphaelite ladies floated in their gowns of Morris blue dyed the right shade at the "works." There the blind boy Philip Marston, Nolly's friend, recited his lyrics, and Emma, the rough edges of her youth and country breeding clipped at last, sang to the pianoforte lines her husband had composed for her. Now Brown could set her up against the finest ladies of them all — no mean boast.

Nolly, through it all, walked apart, shut in a life they knew nothing of. He had always been a strange child, quiet, brooding, and full of a deep wisdom. Animals loved him, and he loved them with an almost Franciscan sympathy. At the parties he made his appearance among the guests, more often than not with his pet rat upon his shoulder, to the shrieking of the ladies. Then, without warning, he would go off on walks with Marston or alone, lured by the night haunters he met in lonely places, or watching, from London's bridges, the ghostly lights of the barges. His imagination reveled in gloom and mystery.

Madox Brown doted on this son of his, — his only son, — and was prouder of Nolly's paintings, rejected by the Academy, than of his daughter Cathy's, hung on the line. Nolly would be what he had failed to become, he humbly hoped. The greater power was surely housed in the vigorous youth, blessed with a double gift, like Rossetti. Proudly he showed his literary friends the scraps Nolly wrote, and turned from their faces to the wall the lad's paintings, glowing with promise. Yes, Nolly would be crowned with the laurels his father was now too old to strive for.

PART FOUR

". . . Is rounded with a sleep"

XXV

THE POET ROSSETTI

SOMETHING was assuredly wrong with Gabriel. The faithful William, arriving on his allotted evenings at Tudor House, found him gloomy and listless, his fine gray eyes ringed with insomnia, the bar between them deep as a wound. All night long Gabriel kept him up talking in the drawing-room until out of sheer exhaustion William fell asleep in his chair — to start up soon after when the morning light, forcing its shafts through the obscured windows, fell upon his brother, prone on the couch. His haggardness in the light, the lividness of his lids, told of another night without sleep. It was as if he feared to enter his bedroom, become a torture chamber. Perhaps it was not airy enough. The linden tree in the garden thrust its branches almost into the room, further muffled by the velvet draperies he would not take down at any cost. The branches of the linden were lopped off, the curtains drawn aside; but neither sleep nor light entered in. He complained of pains in his eyes. Imagination, William assured him. He had strained them too much when he had painted "The Beloved" for Mr. Rae; it had so many figures, such glowing colors. Did n't he remember in what a frenzy he had painted it? Yes, yes, but our father . . .

Despondently he would dwell on the old Professor's last years, recalling him as he had sat, with his peaked cap, and the candle held to his eyes, the book so close that a lock of his white hair curled over it — clutching, too, at that miraculous life that was dimming for him. Did n't William remember that their father had lived myopic and died nearly blind? He, Gabriel, was going blind like his father. How could he live then? What could he do? "You cannot dictate a picture," he despaired.

William had him examined by a specialist. There was nothing wrong with his eyes, but rest was prescribed. If he could be made to sleep he would not dwell so much upon himself.

The physical failing sharpened his inner vision, focusing its morbid light upon what had been wavering shapes in the thicket of his mind, and now gained force and body. No longer able to hide the guilt of his love from himself, he was haunted by Lizzie, who in his super-excited state appeared to him, closed and enigmatical as she had been in life, killing his soul with unspoken accusations. The circumstances of her death re-enacted themselves before him, hour by hour. The ride in the carriage to the Sablonière. Swinburne at the table rising with stiff courtesy to greet them. Lizzie feverishly excited, as she had often been those days. Then home again. Lizzie exhausted, undressing herself for bed — the last living glimpse he had of her till the nightmare of his return, her breathing struggling in the dark room with the rattle of death. Then the doctors, and their futile torturing of that poor, dying frame. And the phial beside her bed: *Laudanum: Poison* — empty. Had she killed herself, or had she, racked with pain, sought peace in sleep and found it in death? O God, would he ever know? She had always been jealous. What unbearable suspicions had strengthened her hand that night? She had borne pains of the body; what mental suffering had killed her? Oh, why had he ever gone to that accursed College? Yet if he had been guiltless that night, did that wipe out his guilt of the past? Guilt. Must a man be forever damned for the one sin? And how could he speak of sin, he who scoffed at religion? He found himself in the position of an unbeliever in an all-too-real hell.

Again he attended séances, as, half in fear, shortly after

Lizzie's death; and, possessed by her influence, he succumbed to drugs. He was deadly in earnest now. Those lips, too often silent in life, must speak in death. He must *know!* So cruel the persecution of his conscience, that he would willingly have been duped if only his searching were somehow answered. Skeptical William Bell Scott, invited to attend a private séance at Tudor House, insisted upon having a clear sight of the medium's feet before he would take his place at the table. It was Gabriel, not the medium, who indignantly objected.

Daniel Home, Mrs. Guppy, Mrs. Fawcett—all the fashionable ghost-summoners, he consulted; with no answer but the squirting of eau de Cologne and the playing of invisible guitars—ludicrous sport! Not there the knowledge he sought. But know he must before he could freely love again, that no prohibition from another world make that love a thing damned.

How he yearned for that perfect completion of his body's self through which his spirit could be reborn! It had never been his in his marriage to Lizzie. Fanny, the generous— not with her, either, had he found it. He kept her with him for her animal health alone. The models he chose now — Alexa Wilding, who stood to him for the Venus that lost him Ruskin; Miss Mackenzie; the Corsican girl, the sun-skinned gypsy, even the black child—all were there to give him, by their curative presence, joy of the pure, unblemished human body. "The Beloved," whose coronet of women dazzled amid jewels, colors, and flowers—what was it but his longing for beauty and the charm of spiritual woman-hood? Physical beauty alone no longer sufficed. If at this time he and One had been free to love, without the present, and no memories—But had he not foreseen, in unconscious clairvoyance, the wraith standing between?

Of her I thought who now is gone so far. . . .
Now when I passed your threshold and came in,
And glanced where you were sitting, and did see

Your tresses in these braids, and your hands thus, —
I knew that other figure, grieved and thin,
That seemed there, yea, that was there, could not be, —
Though like God's wrath it stood dividing us.[1]

The whole grim tragedy of his life had he foreknown in that bare little garret when he and William, mere boys, had whiled away the hours writing *bouts-rimés* sonnets. And would he seek to escape it now? That shadow, grieved and thin, *was* there, for all he wished it buried, walking before him on the goal to his desires. Some exorcism must be found to appease the dead. In the mist of the blank vigils he sought it, in the racked hours of daylight, in the studio, in lonely walks. He spent hours in the unkempt garden behind the house watching the beasts he kept there, bought at Jamrach's mart. Perhaps they held the key. Those kangaroos, mother and son — what human feud had rankled in them to make the son a murderer and then a suicide? Even the beasts knew love and hate; did they know sin? That poor peacock, once so proud of his plumage — what antipathy had he inspired in the deer to make her follow him, stamping out the tail feathers one by one? So creatures of another order stamp out the glories of their betters. And that Sunday, when the bells of Saint Luke's were ringing, what made the parrot say in a human voice: "You ought to be in church now"? Some power may have possessed itself of the bird to warn. Perhaps he ought to have been in church. . . . Too long had he been a heathen. So, out of incidents that would have made another smile, he wrested supernatural implications.

His friends began to be alarmed at these perversions of his mind. "There are traces of superstition noticeable in him, none of religion," remarked Allingham, who would have taken Gabriel from himself in the healthy spaciousness of the woods and the sea. But Gabriel had none of the

---

[1] "Some Scraps of Verse and Prose by Dante Gabriel Rossetti," edited by William Michael Rossetti: *Pall Mall Magazine*, December 1898.

Irishman's enthusiasm for nature. "Fancy carrying about grasses for hours and days from a field where Burns ploughed up a daisy!" he mocked at Allingham. "Good God, if I found the daisy itself there, I would sooner swallow it than be troubled to carry it twenty yards." The vacation was a failure, Allingham had to admit, disappointed that in Boswellian zeal he had nothing better to report than that Gabriel lounged rather than walked, humming "a *sotto-voce* note of defiance to the universe," to plump himself down shortly without warning and refuse to go a step farther. There, on his back, one knee raised and his hands behind his head, he shut the door to his world. "The simple, the natural are merely insipid in his mouth."

As Gabriel's morbid depression deepened, the doctors advised a complete change, suggesting a physical cure for a spiritual ill. Bell Scott thought of Penkill, Ayrshire, where his friend, Miss Boyd, would be glad to welcome Gabriel. A strange fellow, the drawing-master, a middling poet and less than middling painter, who lived openly with two women,—one his wife, one a dearer friend,—with no consciousness of wrongdoing in that most moral of eras. Dark and hairy, surly-faced but with kindly eyes, he was a mixture of extremes, helping a man and casting him down with the same act of his large, ringed hands. He suddenly lost his hair toward middle age, to the awe of Fanny. "O my, Mr. Scott is changed," she exclaimed to Gabriel. "He ain't got a hye-brow or a hye-lash—not a 'air on his 'ead!"

Before leaving for Ayrshire, Gabriel consulted with a lawyer about drawing up a deed of gift of all his property to William Michael. Death preyed constantly on his thoughts.

Penkill held much to interest him where Allingham's efforts had failed. First of all: Alice Boyd's castle, dark, mysterious, susurrous of legend with every breeze through the ivy; then Miss Boyd herself, with her quiet affection for Scott, and Miss Losh, her cousin, a lady of seventy whose

winter Gabriel unwittingly made to blossom. Indeed, the
old spinster was frankly taken with the wonderful sad
gentleman, no less poetic for being a trifle too plump. At
breakfast, whenever he made a mess of the table, she would
turn to Alice. "You see, dear, he's not like one of us. A
great man — can't attend to trifles." She would have done
anything to please him, but only one thing Gabriel accepted,
a loan which Scott never forgave him — unreasonably, for
he should have known that Gabriel could no more refuse
proffered money than he could refrain from leaving it in
the first curio shop he passed.

At first Ayrshire seemed beneficial to his health. His
sight improved so much that he took up his brushes after
months of neglect: a false hope that left him in more dismal
mind than before. "You cannot dictate a picture," he
reiterated. "Why should I live? Why should I live?"

"Live for your poetry," said Scott, meaning to cheer him.

How often had Gabriel thought the words in his mind,
when sick with dread of darkness he groped toward a way
out. Poetry? What poetry? Mournfully the question
had clanged in the hollowness of his despair. He had no
poetry to live for. One does not live for a corpse.

But when Scott uttered the command aloud, in his gruff
practicality, Gabriel, emboldened by the authority his own
thoughts had failed to give him, saw the way as a certainty.
Why not live for his poetry? Scott spoke of it as a fact,
that poetry which had long ceased to be. Nightly, now, by
the fire, both he and Miss Boyd recalled him to the past,
making him repeat the poems he remembered of the little
dead book. The rich Italian voice, that had for seven years
throbbed with no poems but other men's, haltingly sang his
own. Alas, he could remember so little! Swinburne was
summoned to help. Surely his phenomenal memory must
have stanzas, whole poems imprinted upon it. Gabriel
became obsessed with the desire to see them written out,
printed. Would they not have been published years ago,

before Swinburne's, before Morris's, if he had not destroyed
them in one impulsive action?   He wrote to his mother for
every scrap she could find.   There was so little!   Could he
not include his prose tale, "Hand and Soul," to fatten the
volume, he asked Scott.

"An exhibition of poverty not to be thought of!"

Suddenly Gabriel shocked his own ears by his utterance.
Why should he not reclaim the book buried with Lizzie?
How often had the thought been his!   At last it was ex-
pressed.

Expression was but the spur to action.   Had he not loved
Lizzie, he would not have made the sacrifice; would it be
less a sacrifice if he now took back a thing that served the
dead not at all but would give him a reason for living?   He
conceived of himself as wronged by the past act, wronged
by the tyranny of the dead.   He was alive, and living; he
must strive for the ambitions of the living: fame, love,
happiness.   Too long had the wraith stepped between.   Its
tyranny was over.

But was it over?   The prospective opening of Lizzie's
grave brought her materially before him.   Nightly she stood
at his bed's head, the whole thin body of her in a fold of
the curtain.   Her shadow followed his on moonlit walks;
that was the rustle of her ghostly garment behind those
shrubs; her face it was, peering in through the panes of his
closed room.   Did he bend to drink out of a woodside well?
The ripples spread to her waving hair; her eyes sank into
his; it was her cold mouth he touched.   By every tree he
passed a mournful form stood silent.   Ah, the hollow
faces burning white — himself, herself, the days that had
been, now joylessly relived.   Alas, the bitter banks of
Willow-Wood!   Better all life forget her than this, this
life in death.

Not alone in solitude did she haunt him.   One day, as
Scott and Gabriel were going an uphill way, they found a
chaffinch in their path.   It did not fly when Gabriel bent

down to it.   Not a feather stirred as he lifted it in his palm.
Quietly it lay there, looking at him out of its bright round
eye.

"What is the meaning of this?" he murmured, his hand
trembling.

"Put the pretty creature down," said Scott.   "Perhaps
a tame bird escaped from a cage——"

"Nonsense," Gabriel turned upon him fiercely.   "You're
always against me, Scott.   I can tell you what it is . . .
The spirit of my wife . . .   Her soul has taken this shape."

Scott knew better than to contradict him.   Silently they
walked home, where Miss Boyd greeted them with the news
that the heavy house-bell had been rung—by no one they
could see.   Gabriel knew the hand. . . .

Some time later they visited Lady's Glen, under the
guidance of their hostess, always proud to show the beauty
spots of Penkill.   Gabriel stood darkly on the edge of the
ravine, down which the stream plunged into a black pool:
the Devil's Punch Bowl, they called it.   Bending over the
margin of lichened rock, slippery as ice, one could see that
churning, hellish hole, so black it might have been fathoms
deep.   The smell of damp and decaying vegetation, the
forbidding darkness, made a setting perfect for some
Byronic crime.   Dizzily Gabriel stared at the waifs worried
in the whirlpool.   One step, and he too would be tossed
about with them.   Scott, sensing what was passing through
his mind, rushed to his side, trembling.   That daily talk
of suicide—One moment, and all would be past regret.
Suddenly Gabriel seized him by the hand without a word,
and the three walked away speechless at so near a glimpse
of death.

Miss Boyd was frankly relieved when the fearful guest
took his leave.   He had been too much even for her stout
nerves.   Was it still nerves that made her and Scott,
through the long nights that followed, listen tense to his dis-

embodied voice echoing, in the room he had occupied, the
cadences of his remembered verses?

Back in London, determined to recover his poems from
their resting-place, Gabriel gave himself again to his
painting—and the subconscious confession of his love.
His eyes, now that he wore glasses, troubled him little.   Or
was it that he had finally come to the desired aim and needed
no longer to pretend to himself?

> And now Love sang: but his was such a song
>   So meshed with half-remembrance hard to free
>   As souls disused in death's sterility
> May sing when the new birthday tarries long.

How long had his tarried because of his sense of duty!
Duty! He loathed the word.   Other men had been in like
predicaments and had walked cavalierly out of them.   But
now—now the tyranny of the dead *must* be at an end.   The
first link snapped when he had painted Janey as she was,
long and pale and sad, her gaze looking for something not
under the turreted roof of the little Red House.   Gabriel
knew, as she knew, what it was; though she, too, could never
see him without that other, standing between, out of the
grave. Janey seldom spoke. Silence was her proper language, and slow gestures of her long bloodless hands, accompanying the slowness of her eyes.   She had never been
strong: they said anæmia gave her face the pallor of those
flowers that bloom in sunless places, such flowers as cheer,
perhaps, the dim room of Hades. She was all that was
aloof and mysterious to Gabriel, whose imagination made of
the inarticulate a poem, and of sickness a spring of spiritual
life. A morbid revulsion, perhaps, from the Fannies and
Jennies.

How reconcile this old-new love with the dead? Pity,
the golden key, opens all ways. So Janey gazed down
upon him, "La Donna della Finestra." He did not dare

too soon to make the transition, not until he knew the old ghost could be appeased. As in occult lore,—and Gabriel was too much the romanticist to have no credence in mysteries,—he knew the dead may be propitiated, granted, in fact, another life, through assimilation with some living being. Wittingly or not, he performed the ritual. In May of 1869 he drew the head of Jane as Beatrice—the incarnation none but Elizabeth had ever taken. Janey, Lizzie, Beatrice: the merging was accomplished, releasing him at last. Was he not, in the body of another, worshiping the dead? Beatrice: to her second fleshly incarnation, he pledged his fidelity. To make the merging perfect in all ways, he had written Norton to return him Lizzie's feeble little "Clerk Saunders"; in exchange, he sent him a drawing of Janey. Completing the physical parallel, Janey left, shortly after, for Ems to regain her health.

Gabriel wrote feverishly in his recovered mastery, as if the "new birthday" had translated him at one bound to poetic adulthood. "I ought never to have been a painter, but a poet," he exulted; and with the help of his buried poems he would prove it to the world.

The little book was reclaimed five months after his soul had won to freedom. Mr. Bruce (Lord Aberdare) duly signed the order of exhumation; and steadied by its authority Howell, the only one who could have undertaken the task, led his confederates to Highgate. The hushed group huddled under a naked tree at the graveside while the diggers shoveled the earth by the light of a windy fire. In an undertone Howell gave the commands. A useless precaution— the dead cannot awaken after seven and a half years with grass for sleep covering. At length the spades struck wood, the dreadful sound startling the watchers. A groaning of rope, a hammering. It was a matter of minutes. By the weird flaming Lizzie's body was recognizable as hers by the sudden light of her hair; that had not died. A hand slipped quickly under the coffin-lid, closing over the book. After the first excitement it was discovered that a long strand of her hair had come away with it.

Gabriel had not been present. Awed and shaken, he was waiting at Howell's house, alone in a darkened room. Was he afraid — to face himself? In this, his most painful hour, William was not by to comfort. Some vague sense of delicacy had made Gabriel keep the deed secret till it was done, though he knew well his family had never shown any affection for Lizzie or for Lizzie's memory beyond what Christina had manifested in a decent mourning, dutifully but briefly worn. Freethinking William could not have had any religious scruples, but he might have objected on grounds harder still to overthrow. And Gabriel wanted above all things to have the manuscripts upon which his fame as a poet would rest. William would come round, if, indeed, he was not of the same mind as himself.

Dr. Llewellyn Williams, engaged by Howell, took charge of the recovered book. Its blue silk cover, stained and rotted by the humors of the grave, had served little to protect the pages, soaked through with mould and damp. A great hole perforated all the pages of "Jenny" which Gabriel had wanted most; in places the ink had been washed away. Dr. Williams in his laboratory further saturated the book with disinfectants, drying it carefully leaf by leaf.

"I got those papers to-day," Gabriel wrote Brown a week later. ". . . They are a sad wreck." Blind Gabriel, who could not see his own ruin!

"You have acted right on *both* occasions," Brother William reassured Gabriel's qualms now the deed had gone too far to be undone. No, Gabriel had not retracted the self-sacrifice, for had it not "taken actual effect in your being bereaved of due poetic fame these . . . years past?"

True; but what wind of words could dispel the cloud gathering, menacing, over Gabriel's spirit? Such deeds will bring their curse, he brooded, as he strove to blind his conscience in the refulgence of his first fire. Self-duped, he hymned:—

> This hour be her sweet body all my song. . .
> Her arms lie open, throbbing with their throng
> Of confluent pulses, bare and fair and strong.
> And her deep-freighted lips expect me now
> Amid the clustering hair that shrines her brow
> Five kisses broad, her neck ten kisses long. . .[1]

In the spring of 1870 Gabriel's book appeared under the simple title, *Poems*.

[1] This sonnet, "First Fire," written 1869–70, was never included in the "House of Life."

XXVI

RUSKIN'S ROSE

ONE afternoon in 1866 John Ruskin called at the door of No. 5 Cheyne Row with a gift of flowers for little Mrs. Carlyle, whose prophet was away delivering his rectorial address at Edinburgh; and, as he was himself about to conduct a party of friends — ladies — on a pleasure trip abroad, he knew the parting token would prove acceptable to Jane. There came no sound from the long, narrow garden back of the house where her generations of Neros endured their scratching, barking existences. He rang again. The servant shuffled to the door.

"Mrs. Carlyle is dead."

She had had a heart attack earlier that afternoon while out driving to give her latest dog its exercise. As it was frolicking in front of Victoria Gate, a passing carriage-wheel crushed its paw. Picking up the yelping, frightened beast, Jane got into the carriage and hurried the coachman home. She was sitting up when they returned to Cheyne Row, straight and still in her corner, her gloved hands composed, her bonnet fallen a little forward: she was dead.

Ruskin went away severely shocked. No more the bright little voice creaking like a household cricket's to the seer's ponderous silences. No more Neros pampered, no more finches rescued from the cat, no more excitement over the dumb beasts that gave her the illusion of motherhood. The ivy at the end of the garden might flourish and die, Carlyle, whose "light was gone out of his life" would see it no more. Who would pluck him sprays of lilac from the three bushes she had tended so carefully, or bring him the first-fruit of their solitary pear tree? No more would she sit under the small copper beech, away from the sun she had lately so seldom enjoyed in the long sieges of her illnesses. Jane Welsh Carlyle was gone, with her light joys and deep sorrows.

Once more death came close to Ruskin when Lady Pauline Trevelyan died during the trip abroad. When next it came how near might it strike! Margaret Ruskin was approaching ninety and he, protest though he would, still depended upon her as when he had lived upon her milk. It was spiritual sustenance he needed now to help him through the great decision of his life.

Rose La Touche, in the years that had passed, had grown into a beautiful young woman. She was just eighteen, her hair, light and fair as in childhood, bound up, and her tall, slim body perfect with balance. An excellent horsewoman, she rode in her elegant habit, captivating many a heart even less susceptible than her old teacher's. As Ruskin watched, reflecting upon his thin legs, good for nothing but climbing mountain passes, the early humiliations of the days his parents would have made a riding gentleman of him came to his mind. Here before him was a splendid creature, framed by nature to adorn whatever she undertook. If only she were not so devout! But who was he to pass judgment, he upon whom his Evangelical friends looked "with as much horror as one of the possessed Gennesaret pigs"? He knew only that he loved Rose, and that he could no longer bear to live without her.

He proposed to her after telling her the whole story of his marriage to Euphemia and the wretched years that followed, culminating in the suit for nullity. As wholly as only the truth-telling son of John James Ruskin could speak, he painted himself no better and no worse than he was — not a Saint Crumpet, yet far from the fiend gossip would have made of him.

Rose listened gravely and not unkindly, and, with dutiful submission, told her mother. What was she to do? She had always loved her old master, but this . . . this marriage. The La Touches learned of it with horror. It was a scandal, a breach of trust—he, a man of forty-seven, and their young daughter, sought after by eligible youths whose unspotted manhood they deemed not good enough for her! Mrs. La Touche took it extremely ill, and told Rosie what she thought Ruskin might have omitted. Then it had not been in her, the mature woman who was still years younger than he, that Ruskin had been interested! Her sympathy, her appreciation of his talents had been accepted simply for the sake of Rosie's raw charm — for how could the child compare with her?

Whatever Rosie's parents may have told her, and they told her a great deal, she would not give up Ruskin outright, but granted him three years' probation during which she would endeavor to know her heart and he cease his lapses into Bye-Path Meadow. He knew, did he not, that she could never marry "an unbeliever"?

Ruskin, happy that she had not definitely rejected him, hung upon her every word and act, as he gathered up his strength for the work he had to do. Waiting was no easy matter against rival suitors with, on their side, all that he could never hope to regain.

"Since Rosie sent me that last rose after refusing her other lover, I have felt so sure of her that everything else begins to be at peace with me," he confided to Margaret. Still her boy, as hopelessly in a muddle as ever in his affections! Would she live to see him through this, his gravest?

Rosie was not so easily gained. If she sent a rose one day, the next she wounded him by withdrawing from him the sight of her face. Between hope and despair he was kept wavering till he felt all balance had left him. But he could not blame the La Touches wholly for Rosie's behavior. She had never been like any of the other girls he had known,

and he recalled with pain the crises of illness she had suffered, as when, in secret guilt, he had sought to seem
blameless before his father. Those severe headaches that
dulled the clearness of her eyes; and then that dreadful
spell when the doctors thought her threatened with brain
fever . . . The child was overwrought, most cruelly, by
the religion which should have brought her calm.

What Ruskin in the blindness of his love failed to take
into account, and what her parents, engrossed in their own
problems, did not realize, was that Rosie's forced adolescence
had created an unnatural soil for the development of the
woman. Her unceasing activity in this thing and that, not
one pursued for any length of time before it was laid aside as
wearily futile, her insatiable craving for change no matter of
what and for what, furnished no reassuring symptoms. The
same instability that victimized her actions possessed her
moods. At times, as when she went out riding, one might
have thought her by her laughter a healthy young woman,
unconcerned with anything but the exhilaration of living;
but at home she became a morbid fanatic, moved almost to
hate of the man who loved her more than God. (How like
another, a woman of thirty-six whose passionate Italian
blood had been forced to run sterile, also for God's sake.
If the two had met, Ruskin's Rose, not yet too late to save,
and Christina Rossetti, the victim of her harsh sanctity,
would the young girl have rushed wide-armed toward love
at that example of holy life-in-death?)

"Howell says 'Ruskin's love affair is over.'" Thus William Michael, recording that prince of charlatans, not long
before the expiration of Ruskin's years of probation. What
had happened?

As time sped, the La Touches, fearing Rosie's love for
Ruskin, interposed stronger objections. She could not
marry a man so much older, so ill spoken of, an unbeliever
—worse, a renegade! She must not see him; she must not
even write to him. He had been a bad influence in her life

and she must try to forget him if she would save her soul.

"No, it was not so," she defended him. How had he been bad for her? "The letters Mr. Ruskin wrote me only helped me and did me no harm," she declared in her diary, —no harm, "whatever others may say." She dared not name those "others." Under the stress of her too great struggle, her health was breaking down. Ruskin was not allowed to see her.

She had not yet told him "No," and whenever he had managed to be with her alone, she had often been kind and tender, almost the little Rose of the letter he carried like a charm. He could not lose her now when he needed her, the anchor of his faith in life, since he had lost heaven. The La Touches doubled their rigorousness. Unbearable must his anguish have been when he, the soul of honesty, consented that Howell masquerade himself as a tramp to plead for him with Rosie in Ireland. Howell came back with bad news.

A period of darkness closed in upon Ruskin when work gave no forgetfulness, no, nor his well-earned honors, nor the praise of friends. What was it to him now that the chair of fine arts was offered to him at Oxford, where the wine merchant's son had been fagged by the young bucks? John Ruskin, Slade Professor of Art, the first to fill the chair.

"It would have given pleasure to my poor father, and therefore to me—once—" he wrote to Margaret from Hospenthal, "and perhaps may yet give some pleasure to—someone who has given me my worst pain." But how could he hope it! Still, she had not yet said "No."

The cruel uncertainty found strange alleviation by a transference of affection he unconsciously effected when, at the Academy in Venice, he discovered Carpaccio's Saint Ursula. She was very much like his Rose, that angelic girl whose counterpart—unless the artist had taken her from those pure regions where she dwelt—must have visited the earth how many centuries ago! Unlike Rosie, she could not be cruel, for, constant, as the artist had depicted her, she turned upon her lover the same look always, of pitying affection. His princess, he called her.

Queen of the Air came out at this time; and, as usual, he sent a copy to the master whom he visited regularly in the now lightless house. Changed were they both, the prophet and the disciple, and both grown weary. The "bottle of beautiful soda water," that the dyspeptic had been gladdened to enjoy, had lost its bubble. Ruskin could only repeat the strains of the fireside Jeremiah who, strangely for him who had known solely to complain, turned himself to comfort.

"Don't say most great thoughts are dressed *in shrouds*," Carlyle wrote to him in blue crayon with a failing hand that was soon to cease writing, the words amputated to the brutal shorthand that had always made Ruskin squirm. "Many, many are the Phœbus Apollo celestial arrows you still have to shoot into the foul Pythons, and poisonous abominable Megatheriums and Plesiosarians that go staggering about, large as cathedrals, in our sunk Epoch . . ." The hand might fail, the voice had lost none of its roar.

The Slade professorship, coming when it did, managed to keep Ruskin's mind occupied through the saddest years of his life. At first he lived in the capacious house of his friend Acland, Regius Professor of Medicine, where Dr. Pusey and Jowett and Liddell, Dean of Christ Church, — whose pretty daughters turned the head of a young mathematical don and charmed "Fessie Ruskin," — passed hours in urbane friendship spiced with discussion.

The undergraduates loved him. Besides lecturing in a way that held them fascinated and amused, he could entertain royally, especially in his rooms at Corpus, later, when he found the freedom of private quarters preferable to society. Favorite Turners, of course, hung on the walls, one beside the other in long rows; geological specimens sat in their cotton wool under glass — a miniature Denmark Hill in which he entertained his hosts of admirers. Not Pater, eloquent on the new Hellenism, in his apple-green silk tie and top hat, gathered about him such a following. The Professor, playful and childlike in intimacy, loaded his tables with sweets for which the privations of his childhood had given him an inordinate taste; and there, between reachings of his thin hand and the unconscious absorption of three or four pieces of cake in succession, he talked informally of the glory that was Turner.

The young men followed him in everything, not always to the comfort of their elders. There was a bad piece on the Hincksey Road, a disgrace to the community. Would it not be doing a noble work if he, Ruskin, and they, his fine, muscular youths, repaired that road? Certainly, sir. As once, at Saint Sixt, Ruskin had got on his knees with the paraphernalia of a charwoman, and scrubbed down a length of stone steps whose filth had offended his mother, so now he bought picks and spades, and with his body of undergraduates turned road-mender under the supervision of Downes, the Denmark Hill gardener. Classes were in confusion while the work progressed, students and dons standing gape-mouthed at the roadside. Jeers vied with cheers, till the noble mind sought redress from such scandal by a letter to that final vindicator, the press. British gentlemen doing navvies' work . . . shameful!

When finally the road was mended,—not too well, it had to be confessed,—naughty *Punch* celebrated the fytte in a mock-moral tirade. Surely, what Ruskin

> had writ in "The Stones of Venice"
> May be taught by the Stones of Hincksey, too.

In spite of such insubordination, the old-fashioned, pink-faced "Fessie" in his frock coat, velvet commoner's cap, and bright blue tie—worn for Rosie—won himself a popular place where so many were rivals. His lectures drew such crowds that they had often to be repeated for those who

had been turned away. Art began to flourish at Oxford —
Art, and Pater's æsthetic cult.

Rosie had become almost completely estranged. "Last
Friday about twelve o'clock at noon," he recorded, like
another Dante, "my mistress passed me and would not
speak." Cruel, to cause the strongest days of his life to
pass in pain — though not unserviceable pain, he hoped.
All was not yet lost. That she *would not* speak showed that
she was at least aware of this object to be scorned. Still
he sought light through black uncertainty.

Margaret Ruskin could give him no solace through his
trouble. Scarcely could he bear to forgive her, in moments .
of recrimination, for having made him effeminate and weak.
If she had not raised him in the shadow of her dominance,
how different might his life have been! But it was too late
for him, for her to learn wisdom. Did she learn it, perhaps, at last, when free from the taint of earth she joined
John James Ruskin in their not uncertain heaven, "to which
she did not aspire so high as to be with her husband, but
perhaps near enough to see him"?

The loss of her took away from Ruskin the power of
rest. Too late, too late, even her death. It had been
better if *he* had died, as he had been near doing not many
months before at Matlock, had not Cousin Joan, now Mrs.
Arthur Severn, come to nurse him back to health.

He could not bear to remain longer at Denmark Hill.
W. J. Linton, the artist, had a ramshackle house to sell amid
acres of woods and a setting of hills, and water — broad
navigable water, where sun and wind could play. Ruskin
bought it, to make up for the lost eyrie at Bonneville, and
Brantwood, Coniston, became his home whenever he was not
lecturing at Oxford or dispelling his bogeys in travel.

Peace, which he thought to have lost forever, seemed again
to befriend him, and he sank himself deep in work, keeping
in touch with his readers in a series of informal monthly
letters under the cryptic title of *Fors Clavigera*. Rosie,

too, smiled on him once more. Who knows but he might also recover the God he had lost? "In the morning in church at Toft beside Rose." He marked the red-letter day as a memory to be treasured. From church, the next step might be faith, faith gain him Rose, Rose win him heaven. Then for her, too, it might no longer be *Clouds and Light*,[1] but light alone.

Alas for hope! Even while he was building upon his gathering faith, the distracted girl was descending into a darkness he could never have conceived possible — not for her, his angel of light. Torn on the one hand by her love of him, on the other by the prohibitions of her mother, bewildered in the gloom of her religion, and despairing of his ever finding it sweeter to him than her bodily presence, Rosie lost her reason. All that Ruskin had "of preciousest" was now utterly gone — she, his dearest, in this most terrible way.

"I wanted my Rosie here," he moaned to gentle old Susie Beever, as if Rosie were already dead. "In heaven I mean to go to talk to Pythagoras and Socrates . . . What will gray eyes and red cheeks be good for there?"

He exhausted himself, brain and sinew, to forget the pain; and when, even then, he could not, he took the old remedy of distance. In the sacristan's cell of the little old church at Assisi, he found, where he would have shut himself from his torments, that he had only locked them in, the dread familiars of his nights and days. His strength failed; he felt aghast that his own mind was going. By the saving physic of nature, escape came to him in fever and delusion when, identifying himself with a tertiary friar in the cult of Saint Francis, he lived one with the brotherhood of meekness and love. The calm he found was real calm, and in that dreamland between death and life Rosie, for a time, drew away to the remoteness of another world.

---

[1] Title of a little volume of devotional prose and verse by Rose La Touche, published 1870.

When the Umbrian hills were putting on their autumn green, he was wakened with a shock to the news that Rosie was dying. Immediately he hurried back to England, and found that the La Touches had brought their daughter to London. She was indeed dying, if it needed physical dissolution to make that death complete. Again, after the sad time, he was permitted to see her, reposeful in a strange and noble serenity that knew more of heaven than of earth. So striking that unearthliness that a stranger, seeing her for the first time, said she looked like "a younger sister of Christ's."

Poor solace for Ruskin. How much rather would he have had her a robust, living girl who could have understood and returned his love. For brief moments the old Rosie flashed out of her eyes or in a tender word from that still so ruddy mouth. "She has come back to me," he rejoiced. "She can't get on without some of the love she used to have . . ." He took his pencil, one day, and made a drawing of her face; it was like the tracing of a funeral marble. With her fine hair combed in a coif close to the head wreathed in wild flowers, her pure features, her fallen lids, she seemed a mediæval Virgin heavy with the sorrows of Ophelia. But Rosie's was a sterner madness than Ophelia's had been.

She lingered on a few months longer, and died reproaching her lover with her last breath for loving her better than he loved God. How could he have lied—he, the son of Margaret and John James Ruskin? Ruthlessly in the face of anguish and death he spoke truth. You . . . you, better than God.

"A natural sorrow does not destroy strength but gives it —while an irregular, out of the way, avoidable sorrow kills —according to its weight," he had written when his father's death had left him unhappy but with strength to work. Rosie's deprived him of all power of hand and thought. It was as if that pearl for which he had fashioned the loveliest of settings had been lost in the depth of a well, his skill unneeded. The work behind him, more than ever vain, taunted his fifty-five wasted years. He had none to give urge to the future; and he still had long to live.

Like Rossetti, but spurred by yearning rather than remorse, he attended spiritualist groups, half fearing what he might discover. If he could not have Rose on earth, perhaps there might be another life—who knows? Quite different, now that he knew her dead, his reception of Susie Beever's consolation. Not Pythagoras, not Socrates, but Rosie. At a séance he was convinced that her spirit had been shown by the medium. She smiled, serene and kind, the lovely Saint Ursula whose photograph he carried against his heart with Rosie's first letter. Rosie, Saint Ursula . . . Who still lived? Who had died? The two became so indissolubly linked that in the nearness of Carpaccio's saint he found the happiness that he had known, so briefly, with Rose.

Eight months he kept his unhinged mind occupied in work that never seemed to end, as he made one study after the other of his "dear little princess." He could hardly tear himself away. "Last night St. Ursula sent me her dianthus 'out of her bedroom window with her love,'" he wrote earnestly in one issue of *Fors*. Saint Ursula, Rose — she had sent him her flowering plant as a love token from the world beyond, and he was happy in this augury of a future life.

XXVII

VICTORIAN WOMEN

> Her heart sat silent through the noise
> And concourse of the street.
> There was no hurry in her hands,
> No hurry in her feet.

THE little sister of Upper Albany Street could not have described her life better had she herself been the unhappy princess. Ten years ago, five years ago, one year ago — even then he had arrived in time. But now, too late for love, too late for joy, —

> There was no bliss drew nigh to her
> That she might run to greet.

But, as in all sublimation of actual experience, Christina dramatized only part of her situation — the poetically useful. Too late, too late . . . the refrain of the princess's mourners did not ring strictly true in her case, at least not after her singing-bird heart had found its nest. Nevertheless, too late, too late, she sang. "A princess king-descended, decked with jewels, gilded, drest," she had to think of her lineage and of herself before she could surrender to the love that came wooing. The cognizance of her intellectual superiority over the women about her — always, of course, with the exception of her mother and Maria — kept her on a throne. There was her poetic gift, at last recognized, and her devotion to God: one set apart by such signal attributes could not, and would not, take her obscure place in the ranks of wives and breeders, what though, in moments of drooping

under the weight of her crown, she would rather have been
"a peasant with her baby at her breast." Sweetly painful
moments, which princesses have no right to indulge in.

Through the years of Gabriel's long engagement, Christina, her desire for the world still unassuaged, looked yearn-
ingly toward Blackfriars. When Lizzie took her place
there as its rightful mistress and with health miraculously
reëstablished, Christina knew she could hope no more.
Her hands folded in resignation, she turned away her face,
and, as years ago after Collinson had been renounced, she
transformed the world she could not have to a thing of
loathing. So a nun of the Dark Ages would have made
the bleakness of her cell more bearable. By day the world
wooed her, soft, exceeding fair, bringing before her eyes
ripe fruits, sweet flowers, —

> But through the night a beast she grins at me,
> A very monster void of love and prayer.

By day a lie; by night, more horrible in her true form, —

> With pushing horns and clawed and clutching hands.

No, Christina had seen enough of the horror to loathe it,
and therefore she resolutely turned her back upon it. Let
it be for those deluded ones who did not know: her mission
henceforth to cure the halt and maimed of the world's
ravages. On Highgate Hill, at St. Mary Magdalene's,
she put on the dress of the associates — black with hanging
sleeves, and a lace-edged muslin cap with a veil. "Quite
becoming to her," appraised Mrs. Bell Scott, visiting her
the summer Gabriel and Lizzie were spending their tardy
honeymoon in Paris. Was it missionary work she was
doing, the pure Christina, or was it that she purged her own
passionate heart by the example of the world's castaways?
And was it of one of these she wrote, or of herself?

> A silly sheep benighted from the fold,
> A sluggard with a thorn-choked garden plot.

Proud of her mind's queenship, she bowed the lowliest of the low—in sin. After all, what difference between her in her own "thorn-choked plot" and those benighted sheep in their cheerless fold on Highgate Hill? An accident, and her place might have been interchanged with theirs. As it was, she must have been culpable in the sight of Heaven to feel the rod upon her unchastened flesh. God does not punish without reason.

For years, before Cayley came significantly into her life, she had grieved over "one buried yet not dead," whose memory she nursed in her bosom and hid in her heart. "None know the choice I made . . . I make it still," she boasted, though her heart withered and the time grew old in which she grieved. But even after "a birthday" made that heart burgeon in an unawaited spring, she still kept within her a room "whereinto no one enters Save I myself alone." But now she no more bowed her head before *his* face or bent her knee there. She watched with clear eyes, and thought of "how it will be in Paradise, when we're together." Still the old love, though she had given the fullness of it to another.

Was that blind buzzard Cayley so blind that he could not see, even to read the red-hot avowals of her writing? Or did he fail to waken her as one less worthy had once wakened her, for disillusion? "The heart knoweth its own bitterness." Christina knew hers. In the swift pulses of her blood more passion flowed than a thousand Cayleys could have allayed had they had it in them to understand what passion meant in that tight-laced breast swathed in its black associate's robe. "To give, to give . . . I long to pour myself, my soul," she cried, self-tortured. "I long for one to stir my deep—for one to search and sift myself, to take myself!" Collinson had failed, and Cayley—what sort of match was he for her exigence? Where was he, where were they, who could have brought measure for measure?

How should I spend my heart on you,
My heart that so outweighs you all? —

Your vessels are by much too strait:
Were I to pour, you could not hold . . .

Had there been one like Gabriel, magnificent for good
and ill — in such brother pulses, but not of a brother, could
she have found the rhythms to her own.   Then, who knows,
perhaps neither God nor heaven could have availed to keep
back the rush of their meeting ecstasies.   But it was not to
be.   His lot to carry on his shoulders the weight and the
memory of a cold bride, hers to embrace a vast heaven for
lack of a bud, one small twig, of the earthly garden from
which she was shut out.   Aloof and sterile, the fountain
surging under its frozen seal — was it Christina Algernon
depicted, with the weird penetration of the perverse, in his
own *Lesbia Brandon?*

Few incidents occurred in her external life to keep her
from living so intensely within herself in her half-tomb,
half-cloister.   Twice William, always the dutiful son and
brother, took his mother and Christina abroad, first to
Rouen and Normandy, and then to North Italy.   The
Italian blood in her responded to the land that was more
nearly hers than England had ever been.   "Wherefore
art thou strange and not my mother?" she asked in Swinburnian worship.   "Would that I might call thy sons 'My
brother.'"   First shoot of a transplanted tree, she expanded in the sun that should have blessed the rich life
never to be hers.   Yet Italy alone, or one of her generation
of males, would not have made it possible.   Like Gabriel
she was the child of another Italy and of another day, when
he would have drunk deep of the bitter savors of art and
life, dying either murdered in an intrigue, or on the field,
kissing the cross at last; when she, splendid in the luxuries
mind and body craved, had lived a sinner and died a saint.
"You sinned with me a pleasant sin: Repent with me, for

I repent." In her actual living only the repentance was real. And — "Woe's me the lore I must unlearn!" That, too — too real; and the lore, flesh of her flesh, never to be unlearnt.

Lizzie dead, there came a closer approach between her and her brother. She was often to be seen in the Tudor House garden, walking delighted among its uncouth armadillos, raccoons, peacocks, deer — even a white Brahmin bull, a veritable fiend who refused to accept all proffers of friendship. The young Oxford don, Mr. Dodgson, caught her several times with his formidable camera; and she obligingly "sat to the sun" for him with Maria and her mother, and also with Gabriel. Perhaps, sensing a timid soul in Dodgson, she chatted of how she and William Michael had discovered the furry wombat at the zoo, of how they had introduced the delightful creature to Gabriel, and of how he had made of it a pet and a fad — yes, the little round wombat that slept all day long in the epergne on the dining-room table and ate expensive cigars that the careless Gabriel, no smoker himself, left lying about. She may have thought of the wombat and of the Tudor House visits when she chuckled over the misadventures of a certain sleepy dormouse in a presentation copy of Lewis Carroll's fairy tale of Alice.

What did Christina think of the Sumptuous in her white silk gowns, eating strawberries on the lawn and feeding the "chickings" — Fanny's plural for chicken? Did she envy, condemn, — or, in the little upper bedroom at home, weep and understand, with a prayer for that brother soul that was so like her own?

She saw much of Gabriel's friends in the intervals of her devotions and seclusion; went to Penkill with the Scotts; visited Alexander Gilchrist's widow in her country home at Brookbank, and talked and read Whitman. Little did she or anyone else suspect the tempest of love that was being stirred by that wind from the West!

One June day in 1869 Anne Gilchrist was visiting the

Browns when Ford put into her hands William Michael's selection of Walt Whitman's poems, recently come off the press. "It holds me entirely spellbound," she wrote William effusively, "and I go through it again and again."

Except for a few solid defenders things had gone hard for Whitman in England. Paragraphs appeared everywhere against the shameless poet who, meanwhile, was living in penury. Anne, filled with mad zeal, wrote William a long letter defending the bard—a sound, courageous estimate, rich in Anne's common sense which yet had no power over her actions. William, seeing in it a neat piece of publicity, made Anne work it up into an article and sent it off to America where it appeared in the *Boston Radical*. Anne glowed in new Godiva-like fame. "For she stripped the veil from woman's body for a good cause and I from a woman's soul for a great cause," she said. For two years she read the poems, word for word, even those that had made two continents lift hands in horror; until there was not a verse she did not know by heart to repeat nightly on her widowed bed. "If a thing a word stands for exists by divine appointment," she urged roundly against Whitman's detractors, "that word need never be ashamed of itself."

She did not stop with the writing of her defense. One day, in September 1871, the graybeard bard must have felt he held a firebrand in his hand when he read the letter sent him by the woman of forty-three. "To the last my soul dwelt apart and unmated, and his soul dwelt apart and unmated," she wrote of herself and Alexander turned to clay; but when she had read a few hours in Whitman's book, "it was the divine soul embracing mine." A daring letter and abandoned, without a shred of veil to cover the nakedness of Godiva's body and soul.

Whitman, perplexed, did not know what to do. He had long been in love hopelessly with a married lady, and here was another giving herself to him. A second letter, franker still, arrived a month later. "I am yet young enough to bear thee children, my darling, if God would bless me." A predicament for a poet. The letter certainly required an answer. He wrote, cautious and circumspect, pleading business and no time, crossing out the words, writing them over in the attempt to choose the right expression, as if he were answering in kind a literary composition. "I too send you my love . . . My book is my best letter, my response, my truest explanation of all." Explanation of all? Poor Walt, when he could understand nothing of it himself.

Year in, year out, Anne's letters flew, flame-birds across the ocean. "You might not be able to give me your great love yet . . . but I can wait." Whitman's responses came short and businesslike. They were getting too numerous, those flaming coveys, for him to manage. He struck on a plan of sending her newspapers to let her know how he was, for the war had left the hospital assistant an invalid. A word underscored on the address meant he was better; none, this his health was failing: a nineteenth-century Abelard and Héloïse correspondence, the woman ardent, the man fordone.

Anne wrote of going to America, of playing the piano to him, and, if he wanted quiet, of doing needlework for him. "I could be very happy so." The suggestion of her coming to him in person frightened him. He wrote one cold, brief note and maintained a ten-month silence. Anne was not to be put off. "Shall you never find it in your heart to say a kind word to me again?" she pleaded. The cavalier in him melted; the correspondence was resumed. Three years after this last epistle he received Anne's picture and a letter informing him that she was sailing for America with all but one of her children. (Percy had married.) "Oh may I be full of sweet comfort for my Beloved's Soul and Body through life, through and after death."

Alas, here also "too late for love, too late for joy." She was now forty-eight years old, though still fresh and de-

sirable, and the bard anxious only for stockinged comfort
in his emotional life. Anne dwelt three sober years in
America, whither she had transported her furniture and
pianoforte, and then went back home to grandmotherly
peace. In the epistles she sent Whitman, no more rapture,
no more allusion to bearing sweet comfort. Both soul and
body were tired and spent. Nothing to do but warm the
hands in the last feeble glow and then to sleep.

Victorian women, soul-awakened — "whose heart was
breaking for a little love" — how far they traveled to attain
it! From the first conscious escape of L.E.L.[1] who sang
before her song-time and died, her youth scarcely begun,
self-slain or murdered in a far strange land, what did their
protest avail? In that world suddenly come of age,
shadowed by phantasms of dead pasts, whirling in the
abysms of space and time, between the infinitely great and
the infinitely small and all still in darkness, what chance
had they, these women, all too suddenly awakened? A
few only found the light. Most stopped at the halfway
station of renunciation. It had been so with Ruskin's Rose;
so it was with Christina.

With her, however, renunciation came of inner as of
outer compulsion. Life was too imperfect, man too puny.
To the physical lover she was required to give nothing but
the alms of herself, such alms as society would not have
deemed too great or too small — just adequate, when she
would have given all "for a little love" — moments when
she would gladly have surrendered the crown of her superiority, become a woman and suffered love "to fill her girth."
But Cayley saw no farther than the set, calm face, little
guessing that, as under the hieroglyphics of his recondite
scripts lay marvelous meaning, even there, within those eyes
that gazed so composedly into his, were hidden arcana un-
dreamed of in his learning. He had not the simple lore
to discover them. Sometimes, in 1864, however, he saw

[1] Lætitia Elizabeth Landon.

sufficiently to make him propose. He had little to live on, his money swallowed up in that ill-fated advertising venture, his writings bringing him only enough to fill his modest needs—if the sale of *Psyche's Interludes* could be said to have brought him anything. He had no post like his brother Arthur, and his newspaper connections could not be counted upon as a source of income. To Christina, economic objections were insignificant. She had not been raised in such luxury that her life with him need have changed. Confronted with the necessity for decision, however, she hesitated. There was her mother whom she would have had to leave, and her brothers. She would no longer belong to herself. Did she love so deeply as to override all these sacrifices?

"Addio, diletto amico." She had bade him and love go, even as she had avowed to herself that she loved again. "Farewell, dear friend; love is not for me whose heart was slain by another, dearly beloved." She made her confessions in that closer yet not so familiar language which relieved her like intimacies spoken by one other than herself, whom she could judge and advise. No one saw her write, no one knew in what secret drawer she hid her self-communings. Gabriel perhaps would have understood, but to him she was powerless to speak. "Please, if any of my beggaries bore you, reject them with scorn"—and it had been of written, less personal, things she had consulted him.

Though she did love deeply, was that other love altogether rooted out of her heart? She knew it was not. How often, when she thought of the new, she caught herself confounding it with the old, until the two stood a unity that she hastened to shut out of her mind, dazzled with constancy. No, she could not accept Cayley in fairness to herself and to him. Nor could she reject him on the grounds of poverty, even if William Michael had not offered to make room for him, too, in the house he was supporting. Ah, there was Cayley's religion! Although he had been brought

up a Church of England man, he did not practise. Inquiry
and a dash of free thought ruined him for salvation. "No,
Charles, I cannot." She rejected him as she had rejected
the other, the two loves now balanced equally in the common relinquishment.

But Christina would not let this, her second crime against
life, prey upon her conscience. She had not injured, but had
suffered injury, she justified herself; which, ultimately, in
the two-edged way of Fors, proved too true.

> I took my heart in my hand,
> (O my love, O my love),
> I said: Let me fall or stand,
> Let me live or die,
> But this once hear me speak. . . .
>
> You took my heart in your hand
> With a friendly smile,
> With a critical eye you scanned
> Then set it down. . . .
>
> As you set it down it broke —
> Broke, but I did not wince. . . .
>
> I take my heart in my hand,
> O my God, O my God,
> My broken heart in my hand:
> Thou hast seen, judge Thou. . . .
>
> This contemned of a man,
> This marred one heedless day,
> This heart take Thou to scan. . . .
>
> All that I have I bring,
> All that I am I give,
> Smile Thou and I shall sing,
> But shall not question much.

"Twice," she called it, significantly.
Meanwhile within herself she had to face the truth. A

strange thing had happened. In her hunger for the life she denied herself as too imperfect for her desires, she had set her affection upon the impractical scholar, choosing him as the eidolon upon whom to spend her worship. "I loved you more than thou didst love me . . . I loved you first," the while "one buried yet not dead" took the image now of Collinson, now of Cayley. Collinson was far and out of reach. "Star Sirius and the Pole Star dwell afar, Beyond the drawings each of other's strength." More intimately she evoked in Italian the happy home wherein her beloved talks and laughs, the blissful woman who, sitting beside him, rejoices him with words and deeds, the happy garden where she herself had walked, thinking, thinking of him, but holding her peace. Was it Collinson or Cayley of whom she wrote? Surely of the married Collinson, for no blissful woman rejoiced Cayley where he lived, unless it were his mother or one of his sisters. Christina disclosed a little more. O happy day when she would revisit the place where she had thought of him! If he should be there, if he should greet her with his smile, then every bird would burst into song, each rose flush in its beauty. God grant them for eternity that day, and heaven for that earthly garden.[1] Again, Collinson or Cayley? Those Italian love poems were addressed to Cayley: the yearning often was for Collinson. As time passed, the nearsighted Cayley, clothed in the attributes Christina gave him, felt convinced of his own worth and succeeded in convincing her. She loved him then as an equal. But by that time the weeds of her renunciation shrouded her completely from mundane joys. Too late again; too late. Henceforth, Cayley's soul became her only concern — that after death, in that life in which she so firmly believed, they might be reunited. The passion notes of her poetry deepened, reverberant of the music played; during the remainder of her life religion alone inspired her.

[1] Paraphrased by the author, from the original.

She made an effort to give Gabriel a little happiness before she bade farewell. Would he consent to have some of "dear Lizzie's" poems come out in a volume of hers? She wrote to him from Hastings, Lizzie's place of anguish, where now she too was seeking to fight an old weakness of her lungs. Gabriel sent her those poor, mournful little poems which she, in the generosity of her mastery, deemed "full of beauty." "But how painful," she exclaimed, before the evidence of another woman's bared, embittered soul. They would have been as cankered weeds in the garden of her verse. "I think with you," she said at last, relieved, "that between your volume and mine, their due post of honor is yours." They appeared in neither.

Gradually her brown hair showed threads of white. She became an elderly woman, a sort of younger sister of her mother's. After William married Lucy Brown and Maria crossed the convent threshold, she settled down to a hushed old age, afflicted with disease, sustained with prayer. William Michael took a separate home for his wife, who was now entirely unattuned to her former preceptresses. Christina with her mother and her two aunts, Charlotte and Eliza, removed to 30 Torrington Square, near Cayley at South Crescent. She was no longer beautiful. A painful affliction altered the color of her skin and made her eyes, always large and prominent, seem to start from their sockets. Her figure shrank so that she looked small under her bonnet and shawl. Now and then, people, curious to meet the poet, gained admittance into that convent whose walls glowed incongruously with Gabriel's paintings, and where all but old age had died. Christina received them in her black taffeta, a cap set back on her head and half-covering her hair parted in the middle and sleeked down thinly to a knot at the nape of the neck. Her eyes poised quickly upon the face of the visitor and then as quickly withdrew, bearing to the mind their shrewd appraisals. A bow of lavender ribbon held the narrow frill at her throat; no other ornament but a long gold watch-guard, falling along her flattened, scarcely heaving bosom to her lap where the uneasy hands twisted and turned it in the lulls of speech.

Sometimes Swinburne came, a chastened Swinburne like a moulted flamingo. And Bell Scott, and the Browns, and Shields, the artist. And of course Cayley, with books and manuscripts and queer little gifts of sea mice preserved in alcohol, or some innocent oddity for them both to smile at in a now gray love that held nought else of delight.

Life passed her by, but death made often the swift swoops that warn that all is here for but a little space. She saw with no deep sorrow friends and nearer ones go. It was the way of all flesh, and after death is life. Collinson's death was not unnoticed, though she breathed no word of it to that mother who had long ago forbidden her to talk of him.

He died as obscurely as he had lived. In Christina's path, however, he had been the thorn unmarked by most, but by her gathered to the drawing of her blood. The scars had blanched, unseen of others; for her they bled fresh to the end, the mystic stigmata of the early, self-inflicted sorrow. Long ago she had forgiven him whatever there had been for her, the doer, to forgive—perhaps the sovereign fault that he, the clod, had not known how to sparkle even in the glory of Gabriel's light. It was some faint nimbus she would have placed round the head of one now truly dead, when, at the Reverend Horder's request for a contribution to include in a book of religious poems, she swept her own aside and offered Collinson's "on the sorrowful mysteries," long forgotten in the *Germ*.

XXVIII

FALLEN ANGELS

ALGERNON's diabolics reached such excess after the scandalous triumph of *Poems and Ballads* that his friends put their heads together in alarm to see what they could do *"with* and *for"* him. He had turned thirty, an age at which even a poet may learn discretion, though to feed some childish vanity he had it rumored by and large that he was four years younger, and still he behaved with the wildness of immaturity. "A manchild with an ungrown God's desire," he wrote of himself when he could look back more calmly upon his youthful fever. In the meantime he continued sleepless of soul "as wind or wave or fire," conceding that he had overstepped the godlike desire only when nature demonstrated too painfully the very human weakness of the man.

The world and his new group of acquaintances encouraged his darker leanings. A firm of London tailors, seizing upon his notoriety, published a picture of the long-haired poet as a model for their full-dress suits. Algernon blossomed out longer of hair, daintier of clothes. G. F. Watts invited him to sit for his portrait, mane and all. Requests for autographs, invitations to the salons of lion hunters, poured in. He did the gentlemanly thing until, unfortunately, the bowls were passed round. Nor was pungency lacking in anonymous letters reviling him for the immorality of his poems — one irate gentleman from Dublin threatening to waylay him, slip his head into a bag, and do to him what he had seen his gamekeeper do to cats. Algernon, incensed but immensely flattered, retailed the anonymous threats with zest. Not even de Sade had had such things written to him, certainly not at his age. He peacocked about, stiffer of carriage, louder of voice, more arrogant face to face with fellow poets, to whom he granted not a cubit of poetic stature above his own.

Indeed, his arbiter Milnes had to reprove him on the occasion of his meeting with Tennyson, for inexcusable rudeness. What did Algernon mean by snubbing the Laureate, and withdrawing into an adjoining room to carry on some Corybantic soliloquy, sounds of which came, tantalizing but meaningless, to polite ears? Algernon would not deign to bow down before reproof. Overbold in the confidence success had given, he went his chosen way. Ladies and youths literally knelt at his feet, listening for hours to declamations in Greek they could not understand, and following with rapt eyes the maze of ceremonial dance he did in a clearing out of which the salon plush had been removed for the occasion. At Balliol, the place of his defeat, his inflammatory volume lighted many a mischief among the undergraduates, for whom he became a torch and a burning. Little gray Oxford burst into flamboyant bloom as young Pater and his circle espoused the pagan freedom of the *Ballads*. In a word, Algernon was made and unmade.

Gentle Jowett of the golden voice exercised it upon him in all its persuasiveness; but the ears were filled with the siren songs of pleasure and flattery. One note alone could penetrate, the trumpet peal of freedom from the mouth of one who could bend the hedonist's mind to subservience.

A few years previously, Algernon had been diverted from danger by the simple expedient of having his passion of hero worship wakened by a timely introduction to Landor, then living in Florence in an atmosphere of mouldy volumes and worthless art which he deemed superb. Before the poet patriarch, Algernon — fallen on both knees and gestic-

ular with emotion—loosed the floodgates of his adoration.
Alas—Landor, though magnificent as a Zeus in white hair
and beard, had not escaped the frailties of humankind, and
in his deafness grasped nothing of the vehement worship
but the suspicion that he was at the mercy of an escaped
lunatic, whom he conducted, gently but firmly, to the door.
Swinburne, more coherent in writing than in speech where
he would protest his love, sent the poet a letter of explanation.   A second, and this time highly satisfactory interview,
took place—wherein Algernon read to his newest divinity
the dedication in Greek with which he offered him the virgin
Atalanta, and whence he issued the richer by a Correggio,
which Landor had taken down from its nail on the wall and
forced upon him.   The aged poet did not live to read *Atalanta*, and the Correggio proved spurious; but the resulting
beneficial effects were genuine enough in Algernon, who
always worked the better for emulous inspiration.

Some such effect Jowett sought when he arranged to have
Algernon meet his old-time hero, Mazzini.   The scene
was set.   Karl Blind, a friend of the patriot's, was admitted
into the conspiracy, and one evening at his house a tamed
Algernon walked worshipfully before the presence.   The
rite of prostration and the kissing of the hero's hand duly
performed by Algernon, Mazzini, seizing the moment, pronounced in solemn adjuration, "No more of this love-frenzy,
my son.   You must dedicate your glorious powers to the
Republic."   Algernon rose like one healed before the miraculous saint.   The Republic!   Liberty!   He had ever
wished to raise his voice in the cause of the Republic.   As
a boy, years ago, had he not written odes to Mazzini?
Liberty had been his goddess.   The worship of her was
in the blood of the Swinburnes.   Had not his grandfather
nearly lost his head for the liberation of France?   And his
ancestors—had they not laid down their lives for Mary
Stuart?   The incongruity of his fealties mattered not to
Algernon.   Then and there he curled himself at Mazzini's

feet and shrilled in his most eldritch tones that astounding pæan, *A Song of Italy.*

Mazzini, O our prophet, O our priest . . .

It was as much as the dazed patriot could do to distinguish his name among the hail of syllables that "lapidated"[1] him, so he gave the poet an Angora kitten and sent him home. He knew, however, and Jowett knew, that the conversion Algernon loudly claimed had been effected over his writings — not over his ways: that had been too much to demand. If he did at last feel the "winds round him shake and shiver the rose-red and the blood-red leaf," and could say of delight that its germ grew never grain; if he did ultimately bind for sandals on his feet knowledge and patience, were it but as metaphors; if "actual earth's equalities" rather than strengthless dreams were henceforth to inspire him; if all these things came to pass, it was enough of a triumph. The flame of the "dæmonic youth" could at least be made to light a darkness instead of spending itself in vain.

So Algernon metaphorically renounced Dolores's wreath of thorny roses and put on the red cap of liberty. In actual life Dolores possessed him, liberty cap and all. Yet it was a very real passion that turned his rhythms from the celebration of bitter delights and the wise flesh of women to the higher joys of the spirit made free. With the same fervor that he had brought to his youthful depravities, he paid tribute to the deity who was to bring forth the World Revolution. Reborn, Dolores became Mater Dolorosa; liberty, freed of her chains, Mater Triumphalis. When and where the unchaining was to take place, Algernon knew but vaguely. Perhaps in Italy, in the struggle of the Risorgimento, when again the power of the Church would be brought low and "les boyaux du dernier prêtre" throttle the last tyrant; perhaps in America, which had won a physical struggle and now, at the clarion of Whitman, would rise

---

[1] One of his Latinisms that used to amuse the Carlyles.

spiritually liberated. He worshiped liberty in all her ages and all her incarnations; shrined her in the world and in the soul of man. She was Hertha, God. He worked himself into a frenzy, whirling dervish-like till "actual earth's equalities," men and the universe, confounded themselves into one dizziness, and that dizziness the ecstasy of Freedom. It was all real, very real, to Algernon — the worship, the self-abnegation, and the passion; for did it not all happen in the one reality he knew — his own, self-fertilizing mind? The world and what took place there were the dream.

The readers felt the transference of poetic lust in the *Songs before Sunrise*. The same magic music — richer, if possible, in unimaginable effects from the orchestra of the alphabet; the same adornment of Swinburnian metaphor; the same ecstasy pitched excruciatingly high till sense reeled and sound alone intoxicated. Freedom had become his divine Woman, a marmoreal Titaness at whose chained feet he shouted his exhortations. The parodist put pen to paper, and in the *St. James Gazette* Algernon is made to chant a mock-pæan to her: —

> Set on her motherly knee,
> Her nursing arms around me,
> I will cling about her neck as a child clings,
> Re-wounding with my kiss
> Each scarce-healed cicatrice,
> Doing to her divers and disgusting things,
> Whilst in her ears my chaunt
> Re-risen and reboant
> Sounds as one sounds, who, being senseless, sings.

Long past the time when ridicule could have harmed, Algernon, crowned with the red dignity of his revolutionary cardinalate, pursued his defiance of respectability. Most of the friends of the old days he abandoned or saw but rarely. Monckton Milnes had exercised too much guidance to please him; sequestered Gabriel took little pleasure in friendship;

Ned Jones had a family and an assured career—and other interests; Morris had not the time.   Only Howell, Solomon, and his Jewish friends remained—and Burton, returned from Fernando Po.

Those were exciting nights at Bartolini's in Leicester Square, where the Cannibal Club held its dinners.   Full-panoplied in wickedness, Algernon shone, reciting preposterous hymns he had composed as a member of the Anthropological Society, to which, through friend Burton, he had been admitted, and drinking till he sank unconscious, deathly pale in the red gowns he affected.   Those were the times when he pinned a label with his name and address on the collar of his coat, directing the cabman to drop him off at home.   He felt bold and assertive among those men of action, for whom all time was as a day and whose toys were the bones of extinct ages; and he thrilled primitively when a huge platter was placed upon the table, containing a smoking mass modeled to a Negro's head devouring a human rump.   He delighted in this cultured cannibalism, as he enjoyed visiting certain establishments where dormant lust could be roused at sight and sound of pain.[1]

Gabriel, watching from a distance this woeful self-squandering, shook his head, as Jowett never ceased to do, wondering how he could set him right.   Algernon's fits recurred with greater frequency; it was obvious he was walking willfully to destruction.   If he could be made to interest himself in pleasures of healthy men . . .   He had responded to Lizzie's helplessness; he had loved with a man's love, once. He might be moved again.   To that end Gabriel enlisted the help of London's current sensation, Adah Isaacs Menken.

Nobody knew with certainty any of her history, but rumor

---

[1] It was not till 1885 when, through W. T. Stead (who was rewarded with three months' penal servitude for his pains), an investigation was carried on, that the practices of sadism and flagellation were made public and scandal roused all England with the publication in the *Pall Mall Gazette* (July 6, 7, 8, 10, 1885) of a series of articles under the heading *Maiden Tribute of Modern Babylon.*

excelled with the clangor of a thousand hypotheses. She was born in New Orleans, of mixed blood, with a strain of Semitic and Spanish that lent a dreaminess to her eyes and accounted for the quest of romance that sent her from the stool of a schoolmistress to the back of a prancing steed at Astley's theatre. She had talents of sorts, knew a number of languages, did a little modeling, painted, danced, and wrote verses that were found acceptable by American journals. Her special faculty, however, lay in her ability to acquire husbands, legal and sanctioned; so that had her name been sounded in its accreted fullness it would have out-reverberated the titles of a princess of the blood. She clung only to Isaacs Menken, the first perhaps for sentimental reasons, and bore the patronymic of the quiet Jewish musician through peripeties that would have scandalized the very cherubim. She had danced in ballets, acted in third-rate stock companies, done anything open to a comely wench, till one day a well-disposed gentleman of discrimination, noting how villainously she mouthed her lines but how superbly she demeaned her luscious body, gave her words of advice that led her on to fame. She recited little behind the footlights, but let her body speak for her. The furore of her amazonian feats in *Mazeppa* brought Albany's male population crowding to the theatres; while the more puritan of their wives vented their spleen at home upon the hussy who flung stays and crinoline to the winds and showed herself as good as naked, my dear. She was supposed to be a page, was she! No mere boy-actor would have packed the house, however thrilling his feats.

The production came to Astley's, in 1864, where success was even greater for the full-curved hero strapped to a wild horse and looking magnificent. Everyone went to see Mazeppa in his (her) flesh-colored tights. Gallants waited with posies at the stage door; gifts and proposals were proffered — and accepted. She became the darling of the gay monde. Soon, however, she returned to New York, to acquire her last husband; and three years later found her again in London, the friend of Dickens and of Rossetti. She had a flair for celebrity, but so far none of her conquests had been truly great. Heenan, the pugilist, had been a nine days' wonder during that famous prize fight; he proved less interesting as a husband. Orpheus C. Kerr, who came after, had enjoyed a certain reputation as a humorist. But Dickens and Rossetti — and now, Swinburne!

Even before Rossetti had brought the bountiful lady to Algernon's bedchamber, she had been known to him through Thomson, his secretary. Algernon had not been curious. Adah knew how to be persistent, however. Algernon was the bard of the moment; she had poetic ambitions; he could help her lick into shape that uncouth little bear of a volume she was dedicating to Dickens. Algernon obligingly read the proofs and offered suggestions — generous services for one whose eyes and ears must have been rudely assailed by Adah's preposterous efforts. But did he love the "Ancient Dame," as naughty Ned called the buxom lady of thirty-two? Howell, the gazeteer, helped spread the ticklish gossip.

Yes, Rossetti had made a wager with "Dolores" Adah, for her to spend a night successfully with the poet. And, well — honester than her sort, she had returned Rossetti his money the next day. Really! Not even the glamorous Mazeppa, in her fascinating ambiguity!

Sometimes the story had a different ending. In the light of the Great James Street dawn, where Algernon now lived, with the cobra candlesticks shining on the mantel and Mazzini's Angora cat stretching herself in a patch of sun, Algernon awoke and found himself companioned. Dolores? Faustine? Mazeppa? Who was she? He recognized her as Adah when she began to talk to him of poetry. "Darling," he said, "a woman who has such beautiful legs need not discuss poetry."

A perky, dainty Algernon allowed himself to be photo-
graphed with her as, hardly a few months later, did a beam-
ing fat old lecher in France, raising a nation to laughter.
The Swinburne family was horrified. Algernon with that
woman! Better that he associate with the Solomons and
the Howells than find his manhood there!

> Combien de temps, dis, la belle,
> Dis, veux-tu m'être fidèle? —
> Pour une nuit, pour un jour,
> Mon amour,

he wrote in her album, borrowing from his unpublished
Lesbia Brandon. What implication did the verses have?
"How long, fair one, say, how long shalt thou be true?"
To what strange love, if any? Again, a cerebral stimula-
tion, probably, had been all even Mazeppa had availed to
arouse.

All Paris next year was scandalized by her doings with
the suddenly rejuvenated Dumas. And was it true, as it
was whispered, that La Menken was going to appear in a
ballet with Swinburne as Cupid?

Paris had not much time to speculate. In August of that
year she lay dying in a wretched lodging-house garret on
Rue de Bondy. Men still gathered nightly as usual at the
stage door of the Porte St. Martin across the street; but no
one had gifts for her, none thought of her, La Menken, up
there, within sound of their laughter. Already forgotten!
"Lo, this is she that was the world's delight!"[1] Dolores,
Infelicia . . . They buried her in a corner of the little
Jewish cemetery of Montparnasse, and on her grave they
wrote the two words she had chosen for her epitaph, "Thou
knowest," from Swinburne's *Ilicet*. God knew she had been
fair and frail, that she had drunk of life with her whole
being, and paid.

It was with emotion recollected, but not in tranquillity,

---

[1] Inscribed by Swinburne in *Infelicia*, her volume of verse.

that Swinburne wrote "The End of a Month,"[1] when he, the light, white sea mew, took leave of his sleek black pantheress, at that place of all beginnings and ends, the sea.

> So once with fiery breath and flying
>   Your winged heart touched mine and went
> And the swift spirits kissed, and sighing
>   Sundered and smiled and were content. . . .
>
> But this one broken foam-white feather
>   I throw you off the hither wing
> Splashed stiff with sea-surf and salt weather,
>   This song for sleep to learn and sing.

So, to his soul, her "savage stamp and savor" hung; so the "print and perfume of old passion" — with more potency in reminiscence than the actual pantheress had been able to arouse. He had not changed with the years.

> There is nothing nor shall be
> So sweet, so wicked, but my verse
> Can dream of worse . . .

he had boasted, in youth — offering at the same time a startling insight into his essential deficiency. Man, woman, life, experience: they were and remained blank shadows to the creations of his imagination.

The June issue of the fleeting periodical that had published Swinburne's poem had a long review by him of Simeon Solomon's *A Vision of Love Revealed in Sleep*. They were still fast friends, how fast the Swinburnes dared not surmise — nor Jowett, who observed under lifted brows the change that like a spreading vapor was clouding the fair spirit of Oxford. One thing the idyllic affection of an Arnold and a Clough seeking, scholar-gypsy like, "a fugitive and gracious light, shy to illumine"; quite another the cult that set the

---

[1] From the *Dark Blue* for April 1871, where it appeared, subsequent quotations are drawn. The title was altered to "At a Month's End" in *Poems and Ballads*, sec. series.

undergraduates burning incense and hanging their walls
with reproductions of Simeon Solomon.[1] The Slade Professor of Art also noticed the change with misgiving and
cast a slanting eye in the direction of Walter Pater. Art,
æsthetics — the cult held almost as many sects as religion;
and none would be shown the way to the right.

Simeon Solomon, through Pater, who had taken him into
his fold, was a well-known figure in the Oxford of those days
— a small, graceful man, odd in his ways and fond of the
company of adolescents. He had gone far in fame since
the day Thackeray had praised his "Moses." For nearly
ten years he was almost as popular as Millais and coveted
by the magazines for the black and white drawings that
people wanted without understanding their attraction. In
the college rooms the thin, blue-bound volume of *A Vision
of Love* passed from hand to hand, as one voice and then
another took up that disturbing allegory and quavered at
passages too dreamily pitched for speech. A new realm between glamour and sleep opened for them where Love, a
youth like themselves, but beautiful as no mortal could ever
be, walked, a Christ and Eros, the stations of his passion.
None could say he understood, not even in the sanctum of
Pater, where the rose-jar, filled with petals preserved in a
scented death, cast just the nebula for the dream. The
same hybrid mysticism spoke in the words as looked out of
his paintings. Hellenic purity? Oriental sensuality? The
frontispiece gave no key. "Until the day break, and the
shadows flee away . . ." Were those two faces, one
crowned with stars, one in a halo of light, night and day?
Allegorical representation alone could not compel to that
uneasy yearning, the yearning of those eyes and lips, communicated so powerfully through the paper. What did they
really convey, those two heads, repeated again and again
with slight variation under other names — windblown of

[1] His Solomons were among the treasures the prisoner Wilde regretted
losing.

hair in the illustration of Algernon's poem, sensual in "Solomon and the Shulamite," indeterminate in "Christ and
Mary Magdalen"?   Those spent pupils had wearied of
all lusts; the thick, curved mouths, paired as a rose with its
reflection, had known all satiety — and yet they yearned.
Were they souls in quest of bodies, or weariness of the flesh
made spirit?   What land was their true land?   What epoch
had given them birth?   Whether in black and white or in
the colors he borrowed from faint flowers and twilights to
garment them, always they peered out of their realm, dead
but for the live desire.   Even his portrait of Walter Pater,
despite the clear intellect of brow and eyes, had about the
winged nostrils, the sullen lower lip, the hunger and satiety
of exotic tastes.   A fallen angel, Simeon cast about men
and things the glare of his sulphuric glory.

As once, in the beginning of things, Lucifer fell from too
much pride, Simeon, at the height of his creative power,
walked already on the downward path.   The flattery of his
friendships and the adulation of youth, also the influence of
Algernon who needed a companion for those adventures that
abstracted him periodically from the world, all combined
with an inherent weakness of will, incapacitated him for distinguishing between the pleasures that society tolerated and
those that were taboo.   A scandal more than usually hectic
brought him to a prison cell on conviction of pederasty.   His
mind weakened.   Those of his friends who still had some
hope of reclaiming him paid for his cure in a private asylum,
from which he was dismissed to practise his art.

Unfortunately, public obloquy had wrought more than
the well-meaning could have imagined.   He found *himself*,
the self that under the veil of spirituality hid a dominant
lust; and he made his choice — cheerfully, it might almost
seem, from the manner in which he threw himself into the
thick of the underworld that henceforth became his own.
Drink, through Swinburne acknowledged the tribute to the
Muses, brought him the exhilaration his work no longer

provided, though he still drew his vague, lost angels, portraits of himself, on the tables of gin shops, selling them for
whatever he could get.   Murray Marks, the art dealer,
found him in the Brompton Road diligently working as
a pavement artist.   For old times' sake he took him home,
cleansed him of the accumulated dirt of gutter and lock-up,
and gave him an allowance to start him afresh.   Simeon took
the money and returned to the sewer he seemed so much to
enjoy.   It was all hopeless; he was no longer of the world.
Society refrained from speaking of the drunkard Jew who
had become a Catholic and used the stews as the pulpits
for the words of Christ; his former friends said his name
with a shrug; all mention of the artist was obliterated from
the records of the Pre-Raphaelites, who had welcomed him
in the days of his triumph.

Whitechapel and Houndsditch claimed him now, and
thieves were his companions.   One day he was surprised in
the house of a friend who had helped him, in the act of
stealing his silver.   Again, he was seen selling matches in
the streets.   Far away, the little gray Oxford of Pater, and
the rose-scented room, and the slim, beautiful youths.
But he did not complain.   Couldn't they see he was happy
where he was?   That he found all he wanted there — drink
and drugs and friends?   Why didn't the old ghosts let him
alone?   He could get along his own way.   *They* had not
forsaken him, his onetime friends; it was he who had turned
his back on them and on their safe little lives.   And with
the freedom of a Villon he amused chance gatherings with
obscene little anecdotes of Swinburne, mimicking his ways
and speech, and then suddenly breaking into verses of
"Erotion" and the "Song of Songs" and the Catholic ritual.
"You must all become Catholics and be saved," he exhorted,
drawing illustrations from the Talmud; all the time he was
blissfully drunk.

"This is thy hour, O soul," he quoted from Whitman to
one who came to him toward the end of his life.

"Thee freely emerging, silent gazing, pondering the themes thou
   lovest best;
Night, Sleep, Death and the Stars . . .

"Ah, that is finer than anything I have done," murmured an
echo of his old self. "Night, Sleep, Death and the Stars.
They are the themes I love best."

The dome of heaven, star-sprent, whence he had derived
his dark divinity, the hollow of earthly sleep and death to
which he plunged: Lucifer ran the circle of his fate.

Many years after he had really died, the police concerned
themselves briefly with the death of a tattered old derelict
found lying in an alley near Holborn.

There, but for the mercy of God, had lain Algernon
Charles Swinburne.

XXIX

THE FLESHLY SCHOOL

For nearly two thousand years a seed of Laurium had been buried, withholding its kernel of life till the appointed time. In 1859 a friendship sprang up between two youths in Glasgow, bearing in itself the germ of Dante Gabriel Rossetti's destruction.

In the free-thought atmosphere of the Scottish metropolis, Buchanan, a newspaper proprietor, lost his money in a hazardous venture and left his son, Robert, to shift for himself. At nineteen Robert possessed his own notions of his power with the pen. He and David Gray, a pupil teacher in the normal schools, used to read aloud every leisure hour the verses they should excel when they launched upon their respective careers. Even then each was sure he had in his waistcoat pocket enough to set not only the Luggie but the Thames on fire. Robert, of course, was thought to have the Muses upon his side. Through his intellectual father and the hosts of liberals who used to shout their disbelief in God he had developed that breadth of thought so necessary to a literary gentleman. David, on the other hand, sprung in a hand-loom weaver's cottage, felt the divinity of the "call."

The friends parted. Early in the spring of 1860 Robert, armed with an introduction to Lewes, left Glasgow for London. It was not so easy to propitiate the great ones of the magazines, but after a visit at the Priory, North Bank, where Lewes showed himself most kind, — and the Sybil deigned only to intimate she could not be disturbed, —

Buchanan obtained enough connections to keep him with at least a garret roof over his head in Stamford Street, Black-friars.

Like most romantic youths come to seek their fortune in London, he wandered up and he wandered down the long bleak streets on foggy nights when the lamps glowed dim and red and the bells boomed thick with omen, thinking of Chatterton whom the city had slain. He had lived in a Broad Street attic, not far different from his own; he had walked those self-same, pitiless streets until at last, starving and unhoping of soul, he had torn up whatever scrap he had remaining, and taken the arsenic he had had money to buy — not enough to keep him alive, but sufficient for death. There was something soothingly melancholy about such nocturnal reflections. He, too, was a Chatterton, in a way; but he meant to conquer, in London's and in God's despite.

In some such mood he wandered into one of London's parks one winter's night and sat down on a bench beside a man, poorly clad and huddled in newspapers. A familiar stoop made Buchanan look more closely in the gloom. A cry of recognition, quickly echoed: it was David Gray.

He too had traveled the road to the big town to seek his fortune, but, less well-recommended than Buchanan, he had found nothing but coldness. The little money he had started out with, had long given out; he had sold or pawned whatever he could. Now, without food or lodgings, he had come, the way of the hopeless, to the park bench; the next step would have been the river bank; after that — God knows. Buchanan took him home with him and put him to bed on the rickety old sofa. David looked worn and ill, with feverishly bright eyes and a racking cough that would not let him sleep. "It is nothing, nothing," he would say. "Only a cold."

It was the cough of consumption, as the physician made only too plain — consumption that left no hope of recovery.

The truth had to be told him; he was so young, so full of dreams that in spite of youth could never be realized. He did not want to die. Desperately he fastened on every meagre hope, and, writing, writing, writing, struggled to finish at least one work to win for him but a leaf of the poets' wreath and make him of their company. Buchanan wrote in his behalf to Monckton Milnes and Dobell, who helped the youth with money and had him admitted to a sanitarium. There was nothing David would not do or endure to gain him time, just enough time to prove his promise. He traveled back and forth, from London to the provinces, to the weaver's cottage in Scotland beside his beloved Luggie, the old brook that rippled fresh and young as ever, while he was wasting away. At last he finished his poem about it. Buchanan gave it with the rest of David's verses to Dobell, who put it into the printer's hands.

Long, long — how long the time seemed to David, who had so little left, before he could see the book in print! Weeks, months; still he lingered, and still the day lagged. Then one morning, the following December, he received a specimen page of *The Luggie*. With tears in his eyes he read over the verses, in print like those of the noblest poets; he corrected the printer's errors; and, sighing, laid the page by. Next day, at the age of twenty-four, he died.

> 'T was not a life,
> 'T was but a piece of childhood thrown away.

He had chosen the epitaph himself, from one of England's great poets.

The death of his friend intensified in Buchanan a sense of divine injustice that had been but too well fed by his atheist father. He himself believed, but what God he could not then have defined: the Jehovah of the Jews, Zeus, Allah, Thor? Or, nearer his concept of Godhood, the Primal Mystery, the Infinite, the Life in Life? "Oh, Thou art beautiful," he could exclaim at the mystery of sky and hill in the stillness of Loch Coruisk, apostrophizing God. "Oh, Thou art pitiless," he accused in the presence of poverty and death in the city streets, "where blood runs like wine, and foul spirits sit and rule." If God were as good as He is beautiful, he could not bear to look upon such pain, as he could not permit the priest to use Him as a hangman's cord. Could God be judged, how many tongues would lash against the angels of hunger and distortion and decay He sends to haunt the streets. "Who shall judge Thee upon Thy judgment day?" Christ, the "Man Divine," he admired but did not worship. The sacrifice of a powerless Father, he had suffered — uselessly. The world was still as unregenerate as it had ever been and would ever be.

Yet between the writing of literary reviews, — wherein he abused high and low in revenge for David's snatched laurels and his own, tardy to win, — he produced ballads of Christ and Judas, grim, powerful imaginings, which, had he stopped with them, had brought him to the high place. Seeing the distance great and the way crowded with men of nobler stride, he preferred to climb upon their shoulders when he could not crawl between their feet, crying aloud his resentment before their calm dignity. He published his books and they were well received, even by those whom in his office of critic he had maligned. He published, too, a memorial to David Gray, sole star of his murky heaven, that his waning name might be kept alive at least a little longer. That boyhood friendship assumed the holiness of a religion, one that could be believed in; for had David not suffered martyrdom before his eyes — the sacrifice of a world as powerless as Christ's Father? Certainly, as indifferent.

For years the pale face haunted him, and the great thoughtful eyes, too soon averted from life, yet so unschooled to look upon "the dark and fatal leap." "Like a child that in the night-time cries for light, I cry," David had moaned. What Christian martyr had won to sainthood by deeper anguish than the knowledge that earthly winter would yield for him no more to earthly spring? "Hew Atlas for my monument; upraise A pyramid for my tomb," despaired the youth's ambition, his life's progression so early come to nought. It was that cry Buchanan would have answered, in his own way.

Up in "the old ghostly bankrupt garret" of Stamford Street he set up a shrine of David's mementoes; he wrote poems to him; he recalled the old days so full of dreams. David became whatever had been selfless, pure and beautiful in his life. Suddenly, upon this shrine a stone was cast, when Algernon Swinburne — no respecter, at best, of others' susceptibilities — made a contemptuous reference to the dead poet. Buchanan, vicious in his own attacks, could not forgive the slight to his friend He lay in wait, and at the height of Swinburne's fame, fell upon him with a scourging in verse. The anonymity he affected availed him nothing, for William Michael, discovering him, returned the insult in ill-advised loyalty. "The advent of a new great poet is sure to cause a commotion . . . and it would be hard were it otherwise . . . when the advent of even so poor and pretentious a poetaster as Robert Buchanan stirs storms in teapots."

Injudicious words for the usually level-headed William, even if, when comparing Swinburne's poetry with Buchanan's uneven muse, they were not undeserved. If criticism's standard is high, none but the greatest may be accoladed *poet*, but woe to the man who dares add *aster* to the title of one of the singing tribe! That man, were he a thousand times less rancorous than Buchanan, would bide his enemy for life. Too soon did William prove it. Anything of his that came into print was sure to receive the wry compliments of Buchanan, anonymously or otherwise. The harshest greeted his edition of Shelley, when Buchanan used all the resources of his caustic and eminently readable style to damn a work, inoffensive at best. Buchanan was obviously on the warpath, looking only for the object on whom to spend his grievance.

Matters had reached this pass when Gabriel's *Poems* appeared, heralded by loud and unstinted flourishes from all such friends as could make themselves heard — not without invitation, it must be confessed. But Gabriel, who had never withheld his generosity, saw no harm in receiving now that his turn had come. Moreover, he was suffering from scruples of conscience at his robbing of the dead. Acutely sensitive to criticism, he could not bear the thought of being held up to censure. A morbid strain in him kept him from willfully causing pain, knowing how little he himself could bear it. In the case of his art, his reluctance to place it at the mercy of the public critic had worked toward his gain: perhaps if the mouthpieces of the press could be prompted by the right persons . . . He did not know himself why he feared; but fear he did, else he would not have been at such pains to ease the reception of his book.

"Swinburne's article will be in the May *Fortnightly*, one by Skelton in May *Frazer*, and Top (I trust) in May *Academy* . . ." he informed William. "So Buchanan may, let us hope, be caught just in the act." Buchanan! Did Gabriel then fear *him*? Even without the feud between William and the critic, it was a reasonable fear. Not for nothing had Buchanan won his reputation of authors' Attila: the higher the man, the severer his scourging — a compensation for his secretly admitted mediocrity. And from the ire of the mediocre, the Lord God deliver us!

Gabriel swept to unexampled glory. Within a few months of the book's publication, not only his friends but all England acclaimed him poet. The first edition went quickly as if the world could not snatch too eagerly at what death had kept from it so long. Printing followed printing, each edition bought up as fast as Disraeli's latest political romance. It was an interesting phenomenon for a book of transcendental verse, above the comprehension of even the intelligent reader, to run a race for popularity with *Lothair* — and win.

Gabriel was reassured. Certainly it was no sin he had committed, or success had not come so gloriously. All the literary magazines rang with his praises. Months passed, and not a word from Buchanan. The beast had been cowed by the too great light. The old year passed, the new was half over, with Gabriel enjoying at Kelmscott such content-ment as he had never known, and still no drop of venom to embitter his cup. He was settling down to the full en-joyment of his celebrity, when an ominous rumor rumbled overhead. "I see by advertisements," he wrote to Bell Scott, "I figure as the first figure in a series . . . under the title of 'The Fleshly School of Poetry' in the *Contemporary Review* for October, but I have n't seen it yet." He had not seen it, but he was alarmed to the extent of writing care-lessly — he, the impeccable stylist.

Buchanan? No. The article bore the signature of Thomas Maitland.

Who was he, this Thomas Maitland, who wielded a pen more scurrilous even than Buchanan's, and who, with pious morality, smirched a poet to save poetry that needed no saving? The attack was too grossly abusive to be unprej-udiced; it shrieked its protest too loud for impersonal criticism. What had Rossetti done to Thomas Maitland to have him vent his animus under the banner of morality? And since when had art needed morals to clothe it?

Maitland began by introducing "Mr. Rossetti" as a mem-ber of the Pre-Raphaelite School who seemed "to have many points in common" with Simeon Solomon — a knowing choice to score his condemnation. Then, touching upon and dismissing Swinburne's poetry as the vaporings of a boy who screams "I *will* be naughty," he swung into a moral tirade against Gabriel's, the work of a mature man who should have known better than to "wheel his nuptial couch into the streets." Out of their proper place in the "House of Life" sequence, the fourteen painfully concrete lines of "Nuptial Sleep" struck hard against prudery ever easy to scathe. It is said that Tennyson, being shown them thus barely, like some licentious square cut out of a solemn Dance of Death, pronounced them the "filthiest" he had ever read. Yet what was there about them, subtly elaborated with the skill the artist employed in the fancywork of his paintings, to offend more than nature offended?

> At length their long kiss severed with sweet smart:
>   And as the last slow sudden drops are shed
>   From sparkling eaves when all the storm has fled,
> So singly flagged the pulses of each heart.
>
> Their bosoms sundered, with the opening start
>   Of married flowers to either side outspread
>   From the knit stem; yet still their mouths, burnt red,
> Fawned on each other as they lay apart.
>
> Sleep sank them lower than the tide of dreams,
>   And their dreams watched them sink, and slid away;
> Slowly their souls swam up again, through gleams
>   Of watered light and dull, drowned waifs of day;
> Till from some wonder of new woods and streams
>   He woke, and wondered more; for there she lay.

The mediævalist brought into his pagan sensations the overscrupulous examination of detail that nature, and, better than nature, the Victorian mind, preferred to leave in a haze. Detail he then transmuted to allied imaginings, enriching the sensation till every depth and color and feeling of the present emotion were heightened to the ecstasy beyond which words cannot reach. Flesh made spirit, spirit made flesh; love and the loved one, God and the universe, mingled in a oneness that made man divine and brought the angels down. As in "Nuptial Sleep,"[1] so in all the sonnets

---

[1] This sonnet was excluded by Rossetti, and later by William Michael, from subsequent editions of the "House of Life" sequence.

that treated of love. What did Maitland make of them?

"Here is a full-grown man, presumably intelligent and cultivated, putting on record . . . the most secret mysteries of sexual connection, and that with so sickening a desire to reproduce the sensual mood, so careful a choice of epithet to convey mere animal sensations, that we merely shudder at the shameless nakedness." (Read and judge, Posterity: which brings the blush, the poet's treatment of a "shameful" thing, or the shame of the moralist?)

Little did Thomas Maitland find to leave uncensored. Nothing spontaneous could he discern in the volume, nothing original. "We cannot forbear expressing our wonder . . . of the kind of women whom it seems the unhappy lot of these gentlemen to encounter. . . . Females who bite, scratch, scream, bubble, munch, sweat, writhe, twist, wiggle, foam, and in a general way slaver over their lovers." (This of "The Blessed Damozel" and "Sister Helen," and the two women of the "House of Life.")

"Whether he is writing of . . . the Virgin herself, or of Lilith . . . or of Dante, or of Jenny the street-walker, he is fleshly all over, from the roots of his hair to the tip of his toes. . . . In petticoats or pantaloons, in modern times or in the Middle Ages, he is just Mr. Rossetti, a fleshly person, with nothing particular to tell us or teach us." Down, down, in the slough of abuse and ridicule, the unknown Maitland cast the poet in his ferocity of attack. What axe had he to grind? Did its edge peep out in the comparison between Rossetti's "Jenny" and the work of another? "It is a production that bears signs of having been suggested by Mr. Buchanan's quasi-lyrical poems, which it copies in the style of title, and particularly by 'Artist and Model.'" And was it malice or ignorance, that covert charge of plagiarism of a poem that had been written when Buchanan, a boy of twelve, knew no life and no world out of a Glasgow school?

A hate-bearing man had seen at once that the attack concealed motives that should have no place in criticism. But

Gabriel, incapable of bearing rancor, brooded long over the stranger who pinned him naked before the public, and flayed and ripped him open, till no shred of self remained to make him recognizable as Rossetti. That baited mass, that was not he, but the pitiful torn flesh of one that had suffered for him. It was not he, as those writings the Accuser fouled were not his: the spirit he had made flesh in those hands had become corruption. Who was he, what was he, this Curse that had been sent, none knew from what hell, to tear him from peace, as he himself had torn Lizzie from that sleep that should know no violence?

It was the violation of that sleep that now kept him in nightlong agony—that, and the persecution of the Accuser. Gabriel saw his hand in everything; everywhere heard his mocking laugh and the words of obloquy. He, Gabriel, had forfeited his right in society; he was being hounded out of it; Maitland had been only the first to show his fangs. But who was he, this stranger? Where could he be met face to face? How could Gabriel make him understand how wrong had been his scorn? William, scouting to find the man for him, had no success. Swinburne could not ferret him out. In the face of failure, Gabriel became suspicious; and, his suspicions magnified by the drugs he took to bring him sleep, he looked for the enemy in everyone. All his friends but Howell, who could bear much where much was to be gained, he alienated one by one. Strangers he would not meet. Slowly, relentlessly, the poison was eating into his being.

A wild unbalance upset his nature, now setting the once domineering master mind fawning on pity, now, for no reason apparent to sanity, throwing it into storms of rage devastating more of himself than of the objects of his fury.

One day Bell Scott, having invited some friends to dinner, was waiting with them in the drawing-room until all should be assembled, when a violent peal of the doorbell and a tremendous knocking made them stare at one another in alarm. A noise of one coming up the stairs at breakneck speed, and Gabriel burst in, crying wildly, "Robert Buchanan! Robert Buchanan!" Nothing but the name, roared and shouted as if he would have had it penetrate the deepest cave of hell. Long after they had gathered from him that Robert Buchanan in pseudonymous concealment was the true author of the attack, he still shouted "Robert Buchanan!" — making their ears shudder with the thunder of his agony.

It had been Robert Buchanan. Jealous of another's success, when his, as he thought, superior achievements failed of due recognition, he had put his "drop of gall into the sea of *eau sucrée*," settling in that one revenge a number of ancient scores. William Michael and Swinburne had offended him; they had spoken slightingly of the one beautiful thing in his life; therefore he had struck where it had wounded deepest. An eye for an eye — that law, at least, of Jehovah's code, he accepted. What matter if the victim were innocent? The Man Divine had been innocent.

One thing Buchanan could not satisfactorily explain: the signature of Thomas Maitland. Why a cowardly mask, if he were performing an honorable work, even a work of vengeance? Perhaps, like most whose pleasure is to abuse, he flinched from personal martyrdom and therefore put up a substitute target. Worse, he turned suspicion elsewhere in that reference to himself, so naturally, so openly, introduced that none but another Buchanan would have detected foul play. A covert fighter, he would kill and remain immune.

But that was not to be. Gabriel, in whatever calm he could muster, answered with a counter-article, as dignified as he himself was shaken. It was wholly ineffectual. Swinburne defended both himself and his friend in "Under the Microscope." Buchanan, now brought to the open, amplified his attack and sent it broadcast in pamphlet form. He wrote an answer to Swinburne, — lower, more offensive

in tone, — and called it "The Monkey and the Microscope."
In turn Swinburne, in whom the lapse of three years since
the original offense had brought no cooling of the head,
published a letter, "The Devil's Due," in the *Examiner*,
and signed it Thomas Maitland. At this the critic raised
a hue and cry and — brought a suit for libel against innocent
William Minto and his scapegoat periodical. Hot, polem-
ical days charged with green lightnings — ending, when the
storm broke, in a scurry for shelter in the house of Law.
It was a feud to madness, ending at last too late.

In the sudden table-turning, Buchanan was ostracized from
society. George Lewes, once so kind, scarcely greeted him
when they met. Friends no longer trusted him, not knowing when he might turn against them. A pariah, he dared
not put his name for years to the works he published, to
spare them the dishonor of it — all because in his youth he
had loved nobly and selflessly.

Poor accursed one; even his good turned to evil in his
hands.

XXX

THE CRITIC AND THE BUTTERFLY

In May 1877 a new interest drew the polite world to Bond Street upon the opening of the Grosvenor Gallery. Excitement was expected, for everyone knew Sir Coutts Lindsay, the wealthy banker and amateur in the arts, had had the gallery built at his expense that those rejected of the Academy might find a place wherein to exhibit. Not that Royal Academicians were barred. Far from it. Millais contributed, and when he, the Academy darling, led the way, others followed. Holman Hunt sent in his work, and Burne-Jones. Rossetti, always isolated and further repelled from public appearance by Buchanan's attack, refused to show anything. Madox Brown followed suit, not from any reluctance to exhibit but because, singed by the Academicians as he had been, he feared a trick in this new gallery as in everything not tried and tested by his skepticism.

The opening was superb. The rooms, decorated to set off the canvases in an innovation that was to influence future exhibitions, glowed with the prevailing Pre-Raphaelite colors. To be Pre-Raphaelite was now to be æsthetic, and what art-for-art's-sake young blade preferred Philistinism to the suavely decadent cult that marked one of the elect? "Greenery-yallery, Grosvenor Gallery" æsthetes were in the making. Chief among the exhibitors, and conspicuous in his top hat, monocle, and tall, gold-headed cane, strutted James Abbott McNeill Whistler on varnishing day. He had no less than seven canvases, all too original to be classed with any school at that first exhibition. No wonder, since the Academy, after repeated quarrels, had ultimately shut its doors to him — and an artist must show his work if he would keep a charming White House to shelter its "Mrs. Whistler" and its Japanese bric-a-brac.

London had not been kind to him; not alone because of the enmity of its art clique, but not less for the concerted activity of the critics to abuse work they could not grasp. It must be said, however, he did little to bring it to the comprehension of a stolid clan, appreciative only of the subject picture, whether in Frith's sporting pageants or in the pseudo-Grecian, architecturally bedizened exoticism of Alma-Tadema of the golden stairs. Both, though so far apart in race and art, were comprehensibly British. Whistler's queernesses, with their Japanese details and telling no story, were beyond their ken. Surely out of pure malice he went out of his way to make confusion worse confounded by the oddest titles a madman's mind could invent. Nocturnes, arrangements in this and that color, symphonies . . . When they, poor souls, in obvious puzzlement, said ridiculous things in the columns they had to fill, he came back at them with a sting they had come to dread.

The Butterfly, he signed himself in a lepidopterous evolution of his initials, suggested by Rossetti; but no butterfly had ever possessed such a sting as curled impudently from its tail. If his fiendish "Ha! Ha!" imitated by Irving in his Mephistopheles made his enemies blench, the sight of the Butterfly, pointing its forked end in malicious whimsy, brought terror to the hearts of its recipients. Sooner would they have suffered the bite of the tarantula, which, at least, they might attempt to crush. This creature had wings as well as a tail.

Of "Symphony in White No. III," an incautious gentleman of the clan had demurred at the "White." "One lady has a yellowish dress . . . and a bit of blue ribbon, and the other has a red fan, and there are flowers and green leaves." . . . "*Bon Dieu!*" the Butterfly stung. "Did this wise person expect white hair and chalked faces? . . . And does he then believe . . . that a Symphony in F contains no other note but *F. F. F.?* . . . Fool!" Then there had been that portrait of his mother, a sweet old lady sitting, in the peace of folded hands, against a background of wall paper and Japanese curtain. He had called it an "Arrangement in Grey and Black." "That's what it is," he insisted. "To me it is interesting as a picture of my mother; but what can the public care about the identity of the portrait?" The Academy, antagonized by such lack of sentiment, would have had nothing of it had it not been for Sir William Boxall's threat to resign unless they hung it. But this last affront to British sensibility had effectively shut the Academy to him.

It was Frederick Leyland, the shipowner for whom he had lately decorated the "Peacock Room," who suggested to him the title of Nocturnes for his paintings of night scenes—a stroke of genius on the part of the "Liverpool Medicis," whose incessant practising of scales at the piano had at last given the artist more than a headache. Unfortunately, it was to turn the critics still more against him. An unpleasant rumor went round that Whistler had the diabolic faculty of driving people mad. When Jekyll, the artist who had designed Leyland's dining room and hung it in antique Spanish leather, came back and saw what Whistler had done to it with peacock decorations and gold, he hurried home and locked himself in his chamber. Later, when the door was broken in, they found him sitting in the middle of the floor he had gilded in mockery of the Whistler style —hopelessly mad. The critics had no wish to be driven to a like extremity, so they warded off the evil by corporate and consistent abuse.

For all their campaigning, the devil persisted in his crimes, and at the virgin Grosvenor Gallery again upreared his head, more brazen than ever. Here the venerable Carlyle was made to appear as an "Arrangement in Brown," a disguise even Teufelsdröckh had not thought of; Irving, in the trappings of Philip II as "Arrangement in Black No. III"; and here were also more of those exasperating Nocturnes — four of them, in blue and silver, blue and gold, black and gold, purporting otherwise to be moonlight impressions of the riverside.

Now until that time no artist but Turner (who, after all, was mad) had thought of portraying the Thames except by daylight, when every familiar object could be painted in for the dullest to recognize. What was the critics' consternation when they were confronted by stretches of confined luminosity cut through by rearing black forms, the skeleton of Battersea Bridge, beneath which the river heaved tremulous with moonlight and the far-off wharves blinked sleepy eyes of light; by sky and water hushed in the river mist, and in the distance the gay lights of Cremorne beckoning across the river to the city of chimneys and warehouses hanging in the heavens in spectral peace. They were more than puzzled; they were shocked.

Suddenly, from the thick of their incoherent parleyings, a voice broke out in no uncertain terms of condemnation. It came not from one of them — they knew too well the Whistler sting to declare themselves individually — but from none other than the High Priest of Art himself. *Fors Clavigera* for July 1877 was explicit. "I have seen and heard much of cockney impudence before now; but never expected to hear a coxcomb ask two hundred guineas for flinging a pot of paint in the public's face." This from John Ruskin, the lifelong champion of an artist as rudely maltreated by his generation! This bourgeois haggling at price from the man who had paid a thousand pounds per inch for a Meissonier! What ailed John Ruskin to make him so forget his mission and side with them whose snouts he had always soundly trounced?

As a matter of fact, since the death of Rose La Touche he had not been the same. Fors, that power that had smiled so benignantly upon his undertakings, had fickly turned away, letting whatever he touched crumble in his hands. That love which could find no outlet he had sublimated to a practical well-doing in the utopian St. George's Guild; but where he would have had humanity show itself at its ideal he found selfishness, weakness, and failure. His writing wearied him. When he returned from Venice that June, his mind exhausted by the emotions fruitlessly spent on his "little princess" in her painted room, he was incapable of sound judgment. Empty in body and brain, he still would fulfill his duty toward his readers; so that where, in health, he would have tempered his criticism by sober reflection, he now vented at white heat the irritation his spirit and flesh too frequently caused him. He was wholly intolerant of what he once condoned; worse, in his pettishness he shut his eyes against what he himself had condemned a blind world for not seeing in Turner.

Meanwhile Whistler, who had hoped the exhibition would prove profitable, found his canvases hanging unsold and himself spoken of as a charlatan. When, next year, his pictures were again avoided by his purchasers, he blamed "savage Ruskin" and decided to bring his grievance before the courts of justice. Accordingly he accused Ruskin of libel with the consequent result of depriving him, the artist, of his legitimate livelihood, and sued for a thousand pounds' damages. A lively contest this, between the Critic and the Butterfly, and all London stood agog with anticipation. Ruskin, the boar, would know well how to use his tusk; the Butterfly how to elude and at the same time where to sting to the quick.

The middle of November of the following year the case was brought before Baron Huddleston and a jury especially empaneled. But Ruskin did not appear. The merciless taxing of his mental faculties, whereby he would have chastised his body, had brought its revenge; the brilliant mind had broken down. Two whole months he had lain in con-

tinual delirium, himself translated to that misty region
where Rose and Saint Ursula, at last attainable, came gentle
and kind, offering the solace they had not given in the
mortal world. A period of slow convalescence, restoring
the wanderer to life, brought a changed man. That taste
of "Nebuchadnezzar's bitter grass" worked its spell as subtly
as Proserpine's pomegranate seeds; henceforth he was to
be of two divided worlds.

Though he had recovered from the attack of "brain
fever" by the time the case came to trial, he was forbidden
to excite himself; and the hearing proceeded with the at-
torney-general and Mr. Bowen to defend Ruskin, against
Mr. Sergeant Parry and Mr. Petheram for Whistler.

"Who stole the tarts?" If the learned court had been
called to unravel the Wonderland imbroglio, it could not
have struck upon anything more fantastic. A pretty kettle
of fish, this — to settle whether Mr. Whistler was asking
two hundred guineas for a work of art, or for a pot of paint
flung in the face of the public, that sacred body of which
they were part. Since Mr. Ruskin, for once on their side,
had brought up that pot of paint, there could be no doubt
that it had been flung; each individual cheek flushed its indignation under the insulting spots. The jury sat listening
to the witnesses on both sides. Good heavens, as if there
could be any other side when Mr. Ruskin said a thing was
so. Nevertheless, as the case proceeded and Mr. Whistler
was called upon to speak, the lines of solemnity loosened
about the juridical mouths; smiles actually creased those
respectable faces; guffaws burst out, bringing down the
gavel. Here was indeed a merry jester with his trim,
wiry little figure and that single tuft of white on his head,
a dropped feather of his fool's crest. He had surely missed
his vocation splashing paints on stretched cloth, when he
could have held all London in an uproar!

The offending canvas was brought before the court.
Now, honorable gentlemen, it is for you to decide whether

"Nocturne in Black and Gold," otherwise the "Falling Rocket," is a work of art, or whether it is what Mr. Ruskin claims, the honorable gentlemen having lived, of course, amid art from the cradle, and quite capable intellectually of distinguishing between the philosophical A and Not A of æsthetics. All they could see was a dark ground with indistinct smudges splashed with light—the falling rocket, probably. They looked their bewilderment. *That*, a painting valued at two hundred pounds, when they could get— and did get—for their drawing-rooms whole pageants in full light, every hair on the figures' heads as real as your own, for twenty?

"How long did it take Mr. Whistler to paint that Nocturne?"

"Two days," Mr. Whistler informed them.

"The labor of two days, then," scoffed the opposing counsel, "is that for which you ask two hundred guineas?"

"No," Whistler retorted, chin high. "I ask it for the knowledge of a lifetime." This time he did not jest, the mountebank. The smiles on the faces of the jury composed themselves, as the public broke into applause. The court rapped for order.

One by one the witnesses gave evidence. Burne-Jones, speaking for Ruskin, thought Mr. Whistler's Nocturne "a work of art, but a very incomplete one . . . in color beautiful,"—beautiful color, that queer darkness?—"but deficient in form, and form is as essential as color." The painting lacked complete finish. And what might complete finish be? Tom Taylor, art critic of the *Times*, also on Ruskin's side, would show them, and he presented before the jury a picture by Titian. The good gentlemen, inattentive when the amusing jester was not on the floor, handed the "complete finish" Titian round, yawning. "Oh, come, come," said one, impatiently pushing it aside, "we've had enough of these Whistlers," and the rest declined to inspect it further. A matter of no consequence, after all; they

were the good British public, and their judgment came to
them by a transference of that divine right their succession
of Majesties had enjoyed.

William Michael Rossetti and Albert Moore spoke for
Whistler, both declaring roundly the Nocturnes were true
works of art, against Frith's equally round "No, they are
not!" A vain task, theirs, of making a jury, divinely inspired, see the difference between eccentricity and originality. William Michael shrugged his philosophic shrug, relieved when at length his part in the affair was over. It
had been no easy matter for him to appear on the side opposite his brother's early patron, Lizzie's benefactor, the
man who had done sundry things to help him, too. But
his convictions were his convictions; no one could buy them
with money or sentiment.

Under his quiet melancholy he concealed a nature as complex as Gabriel's or Christina's except that the resulting
struggles sprang from without rather than from within himself. A liberal with the straitness of a tory, a cautious Bohemian and a reckless bourgeois, agnostic to bigotry intellectually though most prudent in practice, he tried hard to
follow upon his brother's footsteps the while in reality he
trod the well-marked way of the safer travelers. He kept
the illusion, however. Did Gabriel write poetry? Why,
he could write, too; and proved it with the occasional production of a leaden sonnet. Did Gabriel attend séances?
He, the skeptic, frequented the mediums. Did Gabriel
keep a stuffed sunfish in his drawing-room? William
bought one, too, had it gilded, and hung it up on the wall
of his parlor. Did Gabriel collect "pots," spending as
much as a hundred pounds for a single piece? William
needs must buy some of Henry Taylor's blue china for
two pounds twelve shillings — the same thrill, at a modest
investment. Long ago Ruskin had accused him of aping
his brother, of stuffing his head with Gabriel's art crotchets,
and William had taken it amiss. He was not expressing

any of Gabriel's crotchets before Justice Huddleston, surely, when he defended against the Philistines, with Ruskin mistakenly at their head, art as great in its way as Whitman's poetry in another.

For old times' sake Ned Burne-Jones could not help feeling embarrassed at what seemed a breach of friendship on William Michael's part. But then, William was a recognized critic, and he was acting in a professional capacity. No one guessed Ned's own extreme nervousness as he gave his evidence — little enough for the many benefactions he had received from his Dear, the man who in those first hard years — when in sickness and discouragement he, Jones, had almost abandoned painting forever — had subsidized the rogue Howell to live near him and keep him in spirits if not in health. He knew now, though he did not then, with whose money Howell had bought every little scrap he painted and in whom were incorporated the numerous dealers who so suddenly manifested an interest in the artist Burne-Jones.

His testimony, Frith's, and Taylor's, together with the prestige of the ailing High Priest, bore weight with the jurors, who nevertheless had been too gayly entertained by the waggish American to bring in an ungracious verdict. With the customary British sense of equity derived rather from Solomon than from the Romans, they awarded Whistler damages to the amount of one farthing! So at one farthing's weight the scale of justice tipped on the side of an artist's reputation!

Alas, the moral victory of the Butterfly was worth that and no more, one little farthing punched through and worn as a watch charm when the artist's pockets could not boast its mate. *Punch*, of course, had his little acid commentary, sparing of none. So, the augustness of the Law had been called upon to vindicate the artist! Here was matter for history. Sambourne, the caricaturist, seized the moment of culmination when Baron Huddleston in full majesty is awarding the indigestible triumph to Whistler, a cocky little bird, under the mournful eyes of old pelican Ruskin denuding his breast to no purpose in the wilderness of art.

Punishment — or justice — was meted alike to Boar and Butterfly: they had to sustain the costs. Ruskin's partisans rushed at once to his rescue, and their subscription more than amply covered the amount which, after all, the wine merchant's heir could have met without undue lightening of his purse. Nobody offered to send round a list for the penniless artist. Had it been sent, who knows whether there would have been friends enough among the unstung to prevent a generous gesture from becoming an insult? As it was, all the precious "blue," the Japanese embroideries, rugs, furnishings, and knickknacks of the White House had to be sold to meet the exorbitant tax. Buyers avoided his paintings, for had they not been pronounced excommunicate by the Art Pontiff? The Butterfly in time found himself as impoverished as the cricket of the fable; and the frost was setting in.

Defiantly he twiddled his watch charm under the very noses of his enemies and sent out a flying squib in *Art and Art Critics* to put them once for all in their places. The pamphlet only swelled the ranks against him. Living in London became impossible, at least for the present. Happily he still had his skill as an etcher, and there was Howell, his man of business. One London firm had confidence enough to give him a commission, and, after the Chelsea house was dismantled, Whistler removed to Venice. Busier than ever, he puffed and blew in a fever of enthusiasm, scattering the fine grains of copper dust from the plates that were to be his artistic reassertion. Scenes of Venice's water and sunlight were re-created with a new brilliance under his hand, wide horizons captured in the small dimensions of the plate. No more the detail of the Thames set of his youth. Now a few delicate strokes, like the suggestions of a poet's metaphors, sufficed to fling wide the gates of vision. The same luminosity as in the Nocturnes vibrated, but in full daylight, in the vistas enfolded by the minute magic casement. The Butterfly, out of his White House chrysalis, had grown new wings.

Again in London, the petty enmities re-awoke. If he had grown new wings he had also developed a longer and more poignant sting, which he showed rampant before provocation offered. The critics had not learned their lesson, meanly paid for though it had been by that little farthing. Wise collectors, however, who needed no sanction to strengthen confidence in their taste, bought, and bought generously. Moreover, Howell knew where to find the best markets, with a thought to his own pockets. The merchants, and gradually the aristocracy, sent their wives again to be painted by Whistler. Another house was set up and decorated with loftier flights of fans, screens, and other *japonaiseries;* the same gay round of American luncheons returned, presided over by Maud — "Mrs. Whistler" by the engraving on her dainty visiting cards, though without benefit of clergy.

Howell flitted in and out of his four-wheelers stacked with the day's haul. He was a wonder as a salesman, even if the profits had to be reckoned with discounts of prints pulled without authority — sometimes of graver spoliations. Whistler loved to tell the story of how one day Howell showed Rossetti a copy of one of his water colors — the combined labor, it was later learned, of Howell and his friend Rosa Corder, who had been carrying on a thriving business for some time with these fake Rossettis. It was so good a copy that it fooled Rossetti, who, on discovering the dupe, frothed at the mouth and was speechless with rage. But Whistler could laugh at himself, too. Some prints of his had unaccountably disappeared, and when he spoke to Howell about them the wily Portuguese turned upon him a face of innocence. "Nobody could have taken them but me," he said piously, "and that, you know, is impossible."

Who could be long angry with the rogue? He was as charming as he was wicked, and he had been made on unstinted lines. The "Gil Blas Robinson Crusoe hero," the "creature of top-boots and plumes," had to take his England as he found it and make of his epoch what he could. Respectability would have none of a man without a pedigree as well authenticated as a race horse's; he therefore took respectability by the nose and led it his own dubious road. Judges and pawnbrokers, prophets and gutter hounds, artists and thieves, he shifted from one milieu to another, equally at home in all, with that glib tongue of his as ready in dialects as in scandals. He had set himself up in a house in Fulham with the two hundred pounds furnished by Ruskin to keep Ned in "health and spirits," for while still acting as secretary to the critic who "could not give him a character and could not let the fellow starve," he had married his cousin Kate, somehow curiously involved with dead royalty, who brought him as a portion odds and ends of Stuart relics.

The ménage had no equal. In spite of Kitty Howell's wifely supremacy, the house was overrun by women whose business nobody knew, though they were unanimous in a barnyard admiration of their strutting lord. A child whom they tended in common — as, oddly, her *maternity* could not be discovered — throve as best she could in an atmosphere halfway between a marauder's den and an art museum. A foreign old gentleman sat always in a conspicuous place, saying never a word, but fixing Howell with his eyes. "Count Brugiani," they called him; and legend had it — not gossip, where Howell was concerned — legend had it that he once owned a magnificent villa in Naples till Howell had lost it for him. Now, homeless and disgraced, he shadowed his destroyer, a pathetic and ineffectual Nemesis.

Howell lived openly by his wits, and those who had no scruples welcomed the fellow ever ready for no matter what enterprise. A connoisseur among connoisseurs, the rarities he brought home from heaven knows what unfathomed caves made Rossetti's eyes goggle and his fingers itch. But he, every man's match, found the Owl too clever. There was that exquisite Nankin dish inaugurated by Howell with a dinner party and carried away by Rossetti in the folds of his Inverness. "Come to my house," he invited the guests, "and see a bit of ware superior to Howell's." But the Owl had discovered the ruse, and when the triumphant Rossetti went to the cupboard to fetch the Nankin, behold the platter transformed to cheap pottery. "Confound it, see what the spirits have done!" he cried.

Howell's private little devils could accomplish greater mystification by the help of his daring imagination. He could palm off drawings as Michael Angelo originals, fooling even the pawnbrokers; and with a deft touch turn all to the gold he was forever in need of. He had some black ware which he had picked up like many another curiosity. Paddon, the diamond merchant, catching sight of it among some precious pieces, asked with the glint of a collector what it was. "Oh, those are some black pots Emperor So-and-So [he baulked at no name] brought out in mourning for his wife. Precious, very precious." Of course Paddon bought, and paid well, only to find in an Oxford Street shop a few days later shelves full of the bereaved emperor's memorial ware—of domestic manufacture.

Labor lost for anyone to seek redress against Howell. As he charmed women, so was he able to win over the very judges on the bench—soft-hearted gentlemen, amenable to sentiment, as Gilbert and Sullivan had shown in their *Trial by Jury*. A nine days' wonder was the case of the forty pots, for instance. Nobody knew the basis for the litigation: impossible ever to learn anything definite of Howell's shady tergiversations. It was understood, however, that he had in his keeping forty unusually valuable pots, which someone, for some reason, claimed, but which the Owl would not surrender. The court demanded to be shown the exhibit. The day of the trial a line of four-wheelers, beginning at the door of the palace of justice, serpentined between rows of gapers the length of many streets. There was nothing in each but a precious pot, in solitary grandeur, swathed round with wadding like the cushions about some portly dowager. The court, awed no less than the street urchins by the procession of four-wheelers, — forty of them, by every count, — and moved, moreover, by the rascal's claim, awarded him damages (none could say for what) and even complimented him. The case won, the Owl proceeded homeward at the head of the extraordinary defile.

Like everything else, however, the pots remained not long in his keeping. His was the halfway station; possessions or friendships, it mattered not which — all went the golden way. Not that he wanted money for its own sake. A hazardous card player, he lost it as quickly as he made it, enjoying the fever of the quest and the intoxicating triumph involved in the achievement, however tortuous the means. Nevertheless, when his pockets were empty, he stopped at nothing. The little business of producing fake Rossettis was but one way of making money: at need there were others, many others.

In October 1879 Algernon wrote a letter to his friend Gosse, full of bitter complaints against early associates. Solomon was making him ridiculous by obscene slander. Now "another, who is . . . a thing unmentionable alike by men and women and equally abhorrent to either — nay, to the very beasts, [is] raising money by the sale of my letters to him in past years. . . ."

It was true. Arrived at a pecuniary *impasse*, Howell was hawking the letters about — some two dozen of them, containing "much foolish burlesque and now regrettable

nonsense." *Now* regrettable? Was Algernon ashamed —
Algernon of the splendid wings that had hovered incontam-
inate, as he thought, over the dungheaps of life for the
rare flowers they bore? He that had plucked and dallied
with those flowers, was he tender of his reputation now that
a few dead petals of them were strewn about the decay from
which they sprang? Startling, his condemnation of the
boon companion of those nights and days when shame alone
was shameful, of the *chère fille*,[1] the *mon ami!* Surely
Howell had not transformed himself all at once to the
thing abhorrent: for the virtuous of society he had always
been so. It was Algernon who had changed, and changed
how deeply few yet knew.

No open break ever occurred between Rossetti and his
man of business, even after the little affair of the spurious
copies had lent weight to the fanatical animosities of the solicitor Watts, a new friend of Gabriel's. Whenever the
proper little lawyer strutted into the hodgepodge of the
greenroom at Tudor House and saw Howell occupying
the place of honor beside the sofa where Gabriel sprawled,
his head low on the cushion, his feet thrown over the back, he
bowed, glared at the intruder (anyone else became an intruder whenever Watts took possession of a man), and,
when no move was made to leave him alone with the host,
he spun on his despotic little heel and left. Howell's sen-
sibilities were of the toughest. Merely turning again to
Gabriel he resumed his preposterous chatter, coaxing an
echo of the old hearty laughter, now, alas, so infrequent.
Gabriel listened to the endless gossip, shifting his position,
contemplating his hands soft and small as a woman's, and,
when the tales became exciting, clicking the long nails of
his thumb and middle fingers in an accompaniment as of
crackling warmth. Howell brought life home to him and
he was grateful. What if, in exchange, Howell duped and

---

[1] See letters to Howell, in *The Letters of Algernon Charles Swinburne,*
edited by E. Gosse.

stole, and made *him* matter for sport at other men's tables?
That was the man, and that was life — from which he had
withdrawn to the apparently less hurtful realities of chloral.

Howell did not fail to justify his suspicions. At Whistler's, at the odd places he frequented, he shocked the gatherings with choicest anecdote. Once Rossetti was painting
from Mrs. Morris, while she embroidered a curtain he had
designed for her bedroom. When it was finished Howell
was commissioned to hang it up between the beds; it missed
the floor by a foot. "Some night Topsy might crawl
under." "He wouldn't dare," roared Rossetti. "He
wouldn't dare!"

Yet even this wandering bark had its fixed star in Rosa
Corder, whose lustre was enhanced, in Howell's eyes, by
the fact that for a brief season both Rossetti and Whistler
had crossed her orbit. She had posed to Rossetti for her
magnificent hair which fell to her feet. Whistler had painted
her portrait, the only known thing for which Howell had
paid, though only seventy of the hundred pounds of the commission. She was not beautiful in a romantic or Pre-
Raphaelite way. Tall, svelte, athletic, she rode race horses
as skillfully as she painted them, and she cared for them
herself. Like Rosa Bonheur, she was thoroughly emanci-
pated, but valued her feminine charms too highly to make
herself the sort of half-abbé, half-woman, that the older
painter had finally become. In Southampton Row, Rosa
Corder had her rooms where she painted and entertained, not
bothering to explain her well-manned celibacy, nor prefixing
her name with the title of propriety like many another in
artistic circles. She was Miss Rosa Corder, painter of race
horses, and incidentally, copyist; and that was that.

Perhaps she, too, loved the Portuguese and looked on the
tempests of his career never shaken, guiding with her fixed
ray the shattered bark to haven at last. Be that as it may,
it was to her rooms at Southampton Row that Howell was
taken one night to die, after he had been picked up in the

gutter outside a Chelsea dive, his throat cut from ear to ear and a ten-shilling piece between his set teeth.

When Howell's blue china, Stuart relics, Whistlers, Rossettis, and Burne-Joneses were sold at Christie's, they fetched nearly five thousand pounds, which were to have gone to, among others, Rosa Frances Corder, spinster, mentioned in his will. None knew what became of the money or of the trunkful of letters good for blackmail which Howell left as a dower to his daughter.

XXXI

NEBUCHADNEZZAR'S BITTER GRASS

BROWNING had just published his *Fifine at the Fair*, and, for old friendship's sake as well as to prove to Gabriel of how little account were the snarls of envious critics, he sent a complimentary copy to Tudor House. Little did he guess how his courtesy would be interpreted.

Buchanan's attack had wounded deeper than anyone, the victim included, had at first suspected. Morbidly sensitive and therefore readily vulnerable, it was Gabriel's brain that received the knife edge, sooner than his heart. Wounds of the heart, figurative wounds, may hold the blades and shed a crimson light of transfigured pain, as instance the daggers the mystic church sees flowering from the breasts of Mary and Her Son. Wounds of the brain, when not instantly fatal, kill with a languishing, inveterate death.

Gabriel had never been linked to the real with a strong chain. None but the supremest artists, the Dantes and the Shakespeares, ever are. However far and many the regions they roam, the tough guiding thread of sanity brings them back to reality. In Dante Gabriel Rossetti the connection between the real and the dream, both intensely lived and sounded the while he was immersed in them, was nevertheless worn so frail that a word, a breath of suggestion, could snap it and lose him in the shadowy gulf between. He had withdrawn consciously from that word or suggestion. But he was not to escape. Even as he could not keep his paintings from the public, jealously though he guarded them from the vulgarization of exhibitions, or his mystically nurtured poems, born of life and death, from the irreverent handling of the paid critic, he could not protect his essential self from the buffets of the world.

As a sturdy and strong-limbed little lad he had loved to twist himself into a cripple to rouse the pity of the passer-by —a childish prank, but also a withdrawal of the true self for a motive beyond the child's understanding. As the boy Gabriel hid himself in a pretended infirmity, the man withdrew in an imagination of himself. Often had his intimate friends marked the melancholy he would have masked in robustiousness. When alone, and apparently unobserved, he sank into a gloom out of which it seemed impossible to draw him. A hand on the latch, and the disguise again was on. As with himself, so with those who played their part in his life. When first he had been brought face to face with Elizabeth Siddal, he had been struck not so much by her as by the imagined ideal she incarnated—a dangerous transfiguration, but one without which she had remained an obscure milliner's assistant in the gas-lit murk of Cranbourne Alley. Her, Gabriel could never have loved; the incarnation of Beatrice in her and in the Other enslaved him forever.

The transformation, and finally the merging of his love's identities, had worked themselves out in dark but definite ways.[1] First the portrait of the new-old love as she was, then as the Lady of Pity, finally as Beatrice herself, the one for whom, alive and dead, none but Elizabeth till then had sat. But scruples troubled the artist mind. With the sundering of fidelities by death, he is free to love; but his lady is not. There's a bride's ring on her finger; her husband is his friend. In his imagination she becomes La Pia.

[1] Never before has this striking psychological process been indicated. The dates of the works bear me out: Portrait of Mrs. Morris, in 1868; then the crayon of "La Donna della Finestra," later that same year, followed by a sketch for "Dante's Dream" (finished with Mrs. Morris as Beatrice in 1870). At that time, too, were made the crayon sketches for "La Pia." In 1871 "Water Willow" was executed at Kelmscott from Mrs. Morris, as well as a crayon of "Proserpine" finished in oil in 1874.

Me
Siena, me Maremma, made, unmade.
· He knoweth this thing in his heart — even he
With whose fair jewel I was ringed and wed.[1]

His friend knew — even he. . . . Meanwhile Gabriel por-
trayed her under the sycamore, the tree of mourning.
Kelmscott became the imaginary Maremma where, with
long throat bowed sorrowfully and fingers intertwined about
that jewel that holds her bound in faith, Janey Morris, La
Pia, gazes outward toward the farness of things that were
and shall be, while the book of hours lies weighted with a
cross and the dial marks irrevocable time. Against the
sky, in the one patch of bright air, the doves coo with swell-
ing throats, and spread their wings all amorous; her gaze is
turned away, waiting, waiting, tragic and submissive. What
was she, what were they all, but will-less patterns in the unalterable design?

He drew her, too, as Pandora, the bringer of gifts, her
eyes burning with her seeking, her lips full, passionate,
Asiatic in their sensuality. It was the mouth of all satieties,
and there, as in the other portrayals of Janey Morris, Gabriel betrayed himself. In all his canvases, now, the moody,
far-eyed, longing face looked out. She was the Beatrice in
"Dante's Dream," the phantom of "Water Willow." She
was at last Proserpine, yearning earthward from the sunless
depths — the symbolic Hades to which, making her his
equal in guilt, he had consigned her.

Side by side Beata Beatrix and Proserpine stood on his
easels at Kelmscott. Vague qualms troubled him at the
juxtaposition, and he took refuge in bravado. "I have been
doing a replica here [of 'Beata Beatrix'] — a beastly job,
but lucre was the lure." Fear slinks behind the callousness.
That painting of Lizzie, feature for feature as he had known
her, that raising of her from the dead as in some intolerable

---

[1] D. G. Rossetti's translation.

PROSERPINE

BY DANTE GABRIEL ROSSETTI

thaumaturgy, unnerved him. The publication of the poems, news of which reached him daily in press clippings and the letters of friends, the tress of hair that had come twined round the book like some keepsake from the dead, brought her too corporeally before him. That had been in September of 1871. The following month Buchanan's attack had come, as an avenging bolt for the violated grave. So Gabriel interpreted it. The superstitions which in his worldly life took the place of religion gave him no rest. He was a doomed man.

How deceptive the peace of that first summer in Kelmscott Manor, after Morris had gone on his Icelandic voyage and left him home with Janey and her two little daughters! How mysterious those walks at dusk, when he would leave the painting room and wander with his incarnate dream! Sometimes Janey remained behind. Then it was a double delight to lose himself in the twilit solitude and grope homeward toward candlelight and the ever-waiting dream. By day he painted, never wearying of reduplicating Janey's face and hair and throat, or tracing what he saw of her in the faces of her children. He, the hater of domesticity—"I loathe and despise family life!"—he, the impatient with children, was tenderness itself with Janey's: he even talked of adopting little May.

Friends remembered him, those days, at the evening parties at Brown's, where Bell Scott sported his newest wig and Nolly Brown walked unconsciously among the celebrities, holding a secret all his own. Gabriel, "too stout for elegance," Edmund Gosse thought, "squatted" on a hassock at the feet of Mrs. Morris, "dressed in an unfashionable gown of ivory velvet," as she drooped in her great length of body on the painting throne. Still, like his own Chiaro, Gabriel grew faint in the presence of stately persons.

A wholly different man the Cheyne Walk recluse of a year later. The change had been obvious enough, even at Kelmscott, in the sickly intentness with which he listened to the weird snoring of young owls in the oak-beamed attics, as if in the sound he were seeking a message meant for his ears alone. The peculiarity grew upon him. As he increased the doses of chloral his senses, always acute, were painfully sharpened. In the voices of passing fishermen he heard insults to himself and he would turn in a rage upon them. Vainly Morris expostulated with him that it had been only a trick of the imagination. Gabriel refused to be pacified. Those fishermen had been posted to deride him. They were the hirelings of a clique of which Buchanan was a member, plotting to drive him out of society. He knew it; none could tell him otherwise.

Back in Cheyne Walk the delusions persisted. A thrush near by was singing its note. Gabriel stopped his work, his face suddenly darkening as he turned fiercely upon William. "You hear!" he shouted. "You hear!" William assured him he could hear nothing but the thrush in its customary song. No, it was not so simple, Gabriel insisted. That thrush was calling him an unbearable name. He had been trained to ejaculate it over and over to drive him mad. "Listen! There! You hear! You hear!" The thrush, too, had part in the conspiracy to punish him for having permitted that dreadful deed. The curse—the plot— Lizzie—Buchanan: all knotted themselves inextricably to nest in his sick mind. Physically, too, he weakened. For some years he had been under regular treatment "for a complaint which required surgical care from time to time," William ambiguously explained.

The growing paranoia boded ill; but it was only when *Fifine* was brought to Gabriel that his friends knew beyond a doubt that they were dealing with an insane man. He had opened the book, turned the pages, and looked into it moodily. All of a sudden he blackened to the fury they had learned to dread, and fixing upon some verses toward the close, he shouted that they had been obviously meant as an attack upon him. Browning was the leader of the conspiracy, he declared, pitching the book away from him.

William, realizing that his brother could not be allowed to continue in his delusions, induced him to accompany him for a short stay at Roehampton. Sinisterly docile, Gabriel acquiesced; and that Saturday, when William could be spared at the Excise Office, they arrived at Dr. Hake's.

No sooner had Gabriel laid his head upon the pillow, that night, than he heard a voice calling out a gross, shameful name. Not only at Kelmscott, not only at Cheyne Walk — here, even here, they sought him out for their vengeance! Once, twice, in the silence, the obloquy was flung at him. He was not deluded, in spite of what everyone said to quiet him. It was true, too true, this persecution by enemies who would not let him be for the crime he had committed!

During the night William Michael, listening at Gabriel's door, heard no disquieting noise. Sunday dawned peacefully. Several times Dr. Hake went up to his patient's room and reported him sleeping quietly. All through the morning he lay in a calm he had not known for years. William and Brown were congratulating themselves upon what appeared to be a turn for the better when, toward four in the afternoon, Dr. Hake burst in upon them, looking ominously grave. Gabriel was in a state of coma.

Immediately Brown dashed off to Savile Row for Dr. Marshall, who had been in regular attendance; and when they were alone Dr. Hake drew William aside and showed him a small bottle. "*Laudanum: Poison*" he read, as on another phial he had seen, long ago. The doctor had discovered it in a drawer at Gabriel's bedside. It was Lizzie's drug, the smell of which had clung about her like the essence of death. Where had he obtained it? They never learned. Who knows — perhaps it was some of Lizzie's own, kept by the conscience-burdened man for what he thought the moment of final choice.

On his arrival Dr. Marshall prescribed strong coffee, the

antidote, those days, for the drug whose secrets were still to be learned. It had no immediate effect. All through Sunday evening and night the men watched at the bedside for the least flutter of returning consciousness. Monday, and still that sleep, heavy as death. In the course of the day at last he awoke.

Mrs. Rossetti and Christina were never told of Gabriel's attempt to do away with himself by the same drug that had killed Lizzie. They learned only that he had passed a dangerous crisis in an illness that defied diagnosis. Too well the careful William knew in what horror that devout household held those who doomed themselves by self-slaughter to eternal damnation. To the end of their days the knowledge was kept from bringing the beloved son and brother even in momentary alliance with Byron's Dr. John Polidori, Mrs. Rossetti's brother, who had taken his life by a subtle poison of his own brewing. Oddly enough, the portrait of the talented, unhappy youth always hung in the Rossetti drawing-rooms, from Albany Street to Torrington Square; it was among the last things Christina looked upon before she died.

Certainly Gabriel came rightly by his morbid strain, so subtly—and at what cost to him—spiritualized in his creations. There dawned the day when the power to sublimate weakened; and then . . .

Meanwhile Gabriel rapidly recovered from the laudanum poisoning, and for a time, it seemed, from his painful delusions. After a few weeks spent with good old Brown, and a short vacation in Scotland, he was strong enough to finish the "beastly job" for Graham. What fortitude it required none can imagine. Happily the Pandoras, Proserpines, and pitiful ladies outnumbered that one Beatrice, and with their united strength dispelled her deadly influence. When they did not avail, there was still Fanny in the flesh, coarse, healthy, and undisturbed by such a thing as the spirit. And there was alcohol.

Indeed, Fanny, chloral, and alcohol became indissoluble adjuncts to the life at Tudor House after the Kelmscott tenancy had been given up and the Morris friendship irreparably broken — on the surface, upon the dissolution of the Pre-Raphaelite firm.   It was as good a pretext as any. "He is the only man I have known who beats every other man at his own game," Gabriel had said of Morris.   In his work, perhaps; but in life?

Those who met the brawny, smocked artisan found something excessive in his ceaseless activity.   At home, where he hung the precious dining-room carpet on the wall and walked on drugget, he sat at the head of the table, uncouth as a servant in his master's place, his hands still stained from the dye-vats, his wild shock of hair, graying now, as unkempt as ever.   The still beautiful eyes sparkled in the energy of his speech; in repose they were sad.   For him rest was torment; then those hurts he could but hint of in the "word spinning" that was his relaxation became too poignant.

> I have beheld him tremble oft enough
> At things he could not choose but trust to me,

the book, *his* book, speaks for him.   Alone, uncomprehended because there was no human being who could understand, disillusioned in love and friendship, he did what as a child he had done, and armored his heart as he had armored his body.   But he could not long ensteel his love of love.   For that living heart there was no impenetrable armor.   He did the next best thing.   Like Ruskin, lacking One, he gave himself to humanity, which, however, myriadhearted as myriad-headed, can inflict a thousand times more pain than any individual.

Years later his erstwhile friends, a little ashamed, would catch sight of him among the red flags, singing revolutionary songs louder than any.   They would listen to his plea for free speech in the public streets, and stand aside as he passed with a paper-selling brigade, offering Socialist propaganda amid jeers and insult.   They saw the derided Capitalist-Socialist as a pallbearer with Stead and Cunninghame Graham at the burial of Alfred Linnell, killed by police violence at the demonstration in Trafalgar Square against the hanging of the Chicago anarchists who had been found guilty of inciting the Haymarket riots in that city.   "Bloody Sunday," that 13th of November won for name.   Humanity, complex monster, self-murdering and self-engendering for the everlastingness of its dreadful strife; on the one side, the forces of established order; on the other, the oppressed, burying their dead—to this side Morris gave himself. "There was to me something awful . . . in such a tremendous mass of people, organized, unhelped, and so harmless and good-tempered."   The builder of the Pre-Raphaelite refuge found sympathy in the mass; the lover of beauty a greater, pitiful love in a martyred brother laid to rest in the gloom of a wintry dusk, to the words of the funeral service read haltingly by lantern light.

His talents, too, he brought to the altar of his humanistic ideal.   Abandoning for the time his tales and the all too personal poems of frustrate loves and lives, he wrote a merry farce for the proletariat, *The Tables Turned, or Nupkins Awakened*, which he and his daughter May and other fervid amateurs enacted in the Hall of the Socialist League, Farrington Road, before a crowd of stamping, vociferous, enthusiastic sympathizers.   One Bernard Shaw, critic and Socialist, declared he had never before seen such a successful first night.

Red flags, the mass, martyrs, theatricals—how much of the great heart did they fill?   Not so much, perhaps, as the lavender he dabbed from Janey's flask on his big bandanna handkerchief, breathing in the swiftly lost sweetness with all the hunger of his being.   Not so much as the quiet joy of watching, in the secret morning when all were asleep, the flowerlike patterns unfold themselves on the tapestry he was weaving on his bedroom loom. Not so much as a smile from Janey's Proserpine mouth. But they helped him to live.

Gabriel had no embracing love for humanity—no interest in it, in fact, outside whatever needy representatives of it entered the circle of his existence. In the large, humanity was too vast for him to care for. Like the sun, he accepted it on the evidence of his senses, but took to himself only that portion of it which came through his studio windows and lighted his labor. Therein lay his strength and his weakness. With greater human sympathy he might have overcome himself and gained a world: he was to lose the whole world and, after teetering on the ledge between hell and heaven, gain his soul.

Once the great fire was spent, he painted and painted, more out of dread of poverty than inspiration—reproducing the lush single figures the dealers demanded, in hues that grew from rich to violent in the iridescence of decay. He shut himself in from the world, admitting only a few, accredited new friends, besides good old Brown. Feeling too keenly the "fleshly" brand, he wrote little until Walter Theodore Watts came into his life with all his gypsy foibles and literary lore, and, with the prophetic assurance of Romany, bade him write. The suggestion strengthening the pent urge from within, Gabriel wrote; and a new *Poems and Ballads* eventually saw the light.

Dark myths, meanwhile, circulated in the outer world concerning the strange man who lived with a she-devil and fed on drugs, whom decent society had abandoned to his recondite lusts—a ghoul, a fiend. Buchanan's asp, far from having died a death, its purpose once accomplished, had engendered a brood which, incestuously fecund as is all evil, had spread through literary circles till there was no journal but some critic nursed one at his bosom. The Enemy . . . Everywhere the wretched man saw the glint of its lidless eyes, in every sound heart its hiss, until all senses were dulled in the unholy mercy of chloral and brandy.

The house decayed with its master. Tough wild ivy, never cut, fastened upon the crumbling brick walls and stretched its ropes over the windows—a needless emphasis: they never opened to the winds of heaven. Beyond the rusty gate railings, the flags of the court, the recesses of the porch steps, sheltered clusters of weeds, seldom trod by the feet of visitors, hardly ever by the master of the house, whose sole exercise—a halting, lonely walk—was taken round and round the garden path. The prisoner had no wish to go beyond his yard. Untended, the lime trees sprawled. The lawn, neglected by the indifferent servants, spurted into ugly tufts and sank upon itself to die. No more peahens, whose broods had caused the delight of many a long day; no more wombats and raccoons. The menagerie had long been abandoned, the beasts dying of neglect or "lost" by the housekeepers. Only tramp sparrows and now and then a linnet flitted among the leaves of this forsaken garden in the heart of London.

No escape for the inmate save to the pastures of Nebuchadnezzar. Strange how through love of women both Ruskin and Rossetti lost the sovereignty of their intellects! He who had scaled the mountain summits fell by the stab of a rose; that other, who had drunk of the cup of dreams, came to find the illimitable thirst quenchable by the wine-red drug love had taught him. "Eleven years I have waited," wrote one, looking back upon the plighting day that had become sacred. "How wonderful the slow sadness . . ." while in the ghostly prison house the other entertained delusion and remorse.

Time brought to each its solace: to Ruskin a calm, slow dying, warmed by the memories of a lost childhood, the last and only gleanings[1] of four years of repeated wanderings in the bitter fields. Then no more of writing, no more of

[1] *Præterita*, Ruskin's charming fragment of autobiography.

life; but only a quiet-breathing dream, whose light, whether of Saint Ursula's smile or Rose's, flitted on the peaceful countenance, to fade again in a kinder forgetfulness. Sometimes in momentary awakening, he retired to his bedroom and sat before the worktable spread with papers. From one thing to another he went, hoping to arrest the wandering mind through some of its olden activities. Unsteadily it hovered, here, there . . . His eyes closed, the once so active hands folded in mute despair, and he sank back into the dream. When, with the setting of the century, he left the world, two tokens from those who loved him rounded the tale of his life: a wreath of olive, and a cross — of red roses.

Rossetti's end, like his life, came with no calm. Time's solace was a merciful cutting short of an existence which, with the years, deepened in hopelessness and moral anguish. The old days of friends and aspirations, as effectively shut out by the rusty gate of Tudor House as by the slab of the tomb, gave place to a hell peopled with phantoms vainly exorcised by the presence of Fanny. He had painted her once, at the height of her beauty, as a sort of barbaric Gudrun, laden with silks and pearls and golden links and her own burnished hair, offering with the seductiveness of a sinful saint a loving cup — the draught of forgetfulness for him, that the other might be forever obliterated from his soul. She came to him now, when the watchful eyes of William could not see, bearing in one hand the brandy bottle and in the other the apple of temptation. Though she had lost her beauty, her animal ascendency over him she had not lost, weakened as he was by the drug without which he could not bear to live. He was worse than dead, however, as even those who still loved him admitted by their despairing silences. What thoughts passed through the mind of the tall, pale visitor with the walk of a queen, who entered unannounced the gloomy mausoleum, and left with hurried step and head sunk low? The silent Janey never told. Perhaps she spoke most out of the regretful gaze of Pluto's queen, whose light was all behind her.

Young, devoted friends, unaffected by the onus cast upon his name, aspiring poets who worshiped the tragic figure as they would have an exiled king, lightened Gabriel's last days. There was blind Philip Marston, the friend of poor Nolly, who had revealed the secret of his genius in a novel of weirdly mature passion, only to die at the age of nineteen; and Dr. Hake's son, and Hall Caine, a promising journalist from the Isle of Man who had endeared himself to the poet by the lecture he, a youngster of twenty-five, had delivered in defense of the writings of a man he had heard mentioned, in far-off Ballaugh, as a robber of graves.

It was Hall Caine who, in a sanguine effort to bring the poet to health, proposed a trip to the Vale of St. John. Gabriel agreed to go with him, but Fanny must come, too. No persuasion, cajoling, or well-meant trickery could make him alter his mind, sometimes, as in this instance, roused to its old masterfulness. And Fanny went, full of singular eagerness—for what could the cockney have hoped to find for her amusement among the lonely hills of the lake country, in the dying of the year? She had her own little plan. Far from the watchfulness of William, with only the inexperienced Hall Caine to deal with, she thought her way clear to bend the poor sick mind of Gabriel toward making out a will in her favor. Brandy she had brought with her, and the drug, and her old fascination. Besotting and threatening him by turns, she would have accomplished her purpose had not Caine rushed the poet back to London, a dying man.

And now an extraordinary thing happened. Gabriel, the brother of Maria who had died in the conviction of everlasting life, the son of a quasi-saint, fell prey to terror of the death he knew, with the knowledge of the dying, to be so near. More and more he spoke of those who had gone, and often, in the studio full of the pictured phantoms of his past, he fell into heartbreaking depression, out of which, as at the toll of the neighboring church bells, he started with a shiver that betrayed all too clearly the trend of his musings. Once, when Caine was with him, he opened a drawer of the bookcase, and from under the accumulation of papers and books, took out a long tress of coppery red hair, still undimmed. Did he know where it came from? Who did not know? Soon he too would be going where she had preceded him: to everlasting life? to eternal nothingness? Ah, to know — only to know!

One day he awoke from a drugged stupor with the demand for a priest to give him absolution. It was the last thing his friends had expected, and at first they thought his mind was wandering. Gabriel repeated his request, leaving no doubt that he was fully conscious. "But you're no papist," protested Scott, with more logic than sympathy. "You've always been an agnostic." "I don't care about that," said the sick man, oddly. "I can make nothing of Christianity . . . I only want a confessor to give me absolution for my sins."

Sins? What sins? Those of omission of love and understanding that had fed on his brain till nothing remained of the old, bright intellect? Or those others, like that pride of creation which had made him rob death, all combining to precipitate a man of the enlightened nineteenth century down to the dreadest hell the Dark Ages had been able to imagine — a hell so real, however, that not all the panaceas of science succeeded in robbing it of its horrors? "I believe in a future life," cried the desperate man. How could he not believe, he who had passed through incredible torment? Had he not heard and seen those who had died long years ago? Now he must have absolution for his sins, that in the future life he might face the living dead behind the invulnerable shield his hell on earth had forged for him.

For the last time he left Cheyne Walk in January 1882, looking back as Eurydice looked back upon the earth she was nevermore to see. The studio and its record of his

days, the dark, haunted bedroom with its little table holding the shrouded light and the phial of chloral, the garden,
taken from him, and dug up by the builders for the foundation of another house,—symbolic of the world's flux,—
the little room where Swinburne had written his *Atalanta*,
so long ago—everything, men and memories, would be his
no more.

He left with Caine for Birchington, Kent, in a last attempt to prolong a life all knew to be doomed. The one-
story bungalow, placed at his disposal by John Seddon the
architect, stood apart from the village, between the church
and the hill of sea filling the wide horizon. Not a tree in
that barren land, no green living thing to break the
monotony of desolate waters and unseen cliffs known to be
there for the churning of the waves. Here came Gabriel
for peace, but carrying with him all his obsessions, no less
harrowing for the knowledge that Buchanan, the old Enemy,
had publicly recanted in a dedication in his novel, *God and
the Man.*

> I would have snatched a bay-leaf from thy brow
>   Wronging the chaplet on an honored head;
> In peace and charity I bring thee now
>   A lily-flower instead.
>
> Pure as thy purpose, blameless as thy song,
>   Sweet as thy spirit may this offering be. . .[1]

Aye, but too late, too late! The bay-leaf chaplet had long
been flung away from a head too heavy with anguished
delusions; the lily-flower had no spell to cheer the spirit
cankered by remorse.

Every morning of that promised spring, Caine took his
charge for a short walk while strength lasted. Leaning on
a stick, and with his arm on his young friend's, Gabriel

---

[1] "If for the word 'charity' 'penitence' were substituted, the dedication
would be all that could be desired." — The *Gentleman's Magazine* for
January 1882.

walked heavily from the bungalow to the path leading to the little Gothic church, all gray and green with age, and round by the churchyard, so still it seemed one could at last find sleep there without drugs. But Gabriel grew so weak that he had to take to his bed — not before he had finished a replica of Proserpine, his dark goddess yearning out to him from the land of shadow. Soon the midnight of her hair would cover him, those eyes sear earthly memory from his gaze, those long, thin hands, so white their touch must be cold as snow, cool forever the fever of that brow. Incense, and ivy, and forgetfulness. But where now was Beatrice? Still, still in his dreams, the shadow grieved and thin, coming between him and peace!

William sent for his mother and sister to come to Birchington, and, at the sight of the two women murmuring prayer beside the bed of sickness, Gabriel knew all hope was gone. Easter morning the bell of the church summoned to the service. Christina and her mother left with the rest — there had seemed to be a change for the better in the patient. Noon came, warm with the breath of spring, and twilight, closing gently on the empty sea. Some days before a stranded ship anchored a mile offshore had caught fire, and Gabriel had sat up to look at the blaze, a large, burning sun in the night's horizon. All the crew had been saved, he was told, but they had left in the flaming pyre the body of a sailor who had died in the night. Through the dark hours he and Caine had watched in silence. Was one of them thinking of Carlyle's words likening a man of genius to "a burning ship set on fire for the glorification of the spectators on the land"?

Gabriel's own pyre had reached sea level; that Easter night its oblivion covered him.

Those who had been at the bungalow toward the end had marked nothing unusual; in fact, they thought him sleeping quietly. Suddenly a cry brought them to his room. Gabriel was dead.

Far away from all of his blood they laid him to rest, in the hushed little cemetery under the shadow of the church, there where no sound would reach his last natural sleep but the boom of the sea. None had spoken of burying him at Highgate beside his wife. Knowing, perhaps, what a power for good and evil she had been in that storm-tossed life, they would have freed him in death from the cruel obsession.

No friends of the early days stood at the graveside; only his family, and Theodore Watts, and Marston the poet, his sightless eyes filled with tears for the monarch who had departed.

XXXII

"POOR SPLENDID WINGS . . ."

WALTER THEODORE WATTS, or, as he later styled himself
for reasons of literary convenience, Theodore Watts-
Dunton,[1] was an unknown suburban lawyer when he came
to London. A widely read man, especially in the obscure
fields of Zenoni mysticism, he had always had a devouring
desire for literary fame. It was said that in his youth he
had prepared a book of poems which, when about to be
turned over to the publishers, had unaccountably disappeared
—a tragedy in the life of the would-be man of letters,
always referred to with moist eyes and a lump in the throat
so pathetic that, little by little, it came to be believed that
the lost book covered an agreeable pretense to excuse his
long laboring and little fruit. However, he could still
write a sonnet on occasion, especially upon some notable
death; so that "And Watts wrote a sonnet" as surely sounded
the obituary as the tolling bell.

In his home provinces at St. Ives, he had had his first
experience at hero-worship—in him no ecstatic abasement,
as with Swinburne, but rather a projection of his ego to the
stature of his giants — dogging the steps of *Lavengro's*
author, and himself spreading the pleasant fiction that he
too came of gypsy stock. His swarthy skin and shaggy hair,
his long walrus moustache and the beady brightness of his
eyes, might have led one to believe him; his expert talk
of Romany *chies* and Romany *chals*, *trushuls* and *dukkeri-*

---

[1] "Theodore! What's Dunton?" was the card, signed with the
Butterfly, that Whistler sent him upon learning of the change.

pens, left little doubt. But then, Watts was an expert at so many things! He could talk of the mysteries of Isis as if they were the fireside tales of his grandmother, discuss books with the bibliophile, and teach prosody to the Laureate himself. In justice to him, he knew whereof he spoke. Had he been able to follow his own precepts he might have been a poet among poets — but then nature would have had to change her mould.

By dint of his conversational powers and an ingratiating way, — those who loved him not called it "fawning," — he easily made friends; it was to be remarked, however, that he chose them always from among the "arrived." With the others, he adopted that conventional civility that said louder than words, "Thank you, indeed, but let me see no more of you." So far the polestar of his friendships had been Rossetti, of whom he had been worshipful and a little jealous, not so much of him or of his achievements, as of that kingly charm which, when his "summer friends" had flown, had built about him a court of youthful spirits who claimed as sole guerdon the leave to carry on *his* school, *his* tradition. It was something to have that power, and Watts sedulously cultivated it. Then Rossetti had gone; and Watts wrote a sonnet — nay, several — to evidence the strength of their love.

But even before Gabriel's death, Watts had soldered another friendship — as valuable, if not more valuable, despite the unpropitiousness of its beginnings. Since the red-letter year of 1866, he had yearned with great yearning toward Swinburne. His poems shocked him; his fame roused in him the barnacle instinct to fasten upon the winging craft and sail onward to triumph. As a critic of no mean pen, he could have approached Swinburne. He preferred, however, the surer way of professional introduction. Through Madox Brown he had learned in what a hopeless muddle were the poet's financial arrangements, and in what need he stood of a legal adviser. Armed with a letter, therefore, he presented himself one day at Number Three Great James Street. The respectable gentleman gained easy access into Swinburne's parlor, where many a queer individual, but seldom a one like him, was known to enter. Was the poet at home? Ah, yes, the gentleman was to wait. Letter in hand, the gentleman entered, surveying the furnishings of the lodging house, a mean dwelling for a nobleman's son. Those candlesticks, the books, the mosaic-top table, were surely his. As Watts waited, he became aware of a peculiar chanting and stamping in the adjoining room. Discreetly he let the moments pass. The poet was dressing, perhaps; he might be having some other visitor. As the time dragged, and still no sign of that door's opening, Watts knocked above the continued chanting and then turned the knob, ever so gently. What was his astonishment upon beholding a naked mænad—faun?—he could not say —dancing with lifted knee and ceremonial gestures before a pier glass, and meeting the green scintillations of eyes ablaze under a flaming aureole. He had no time to recover himself; before he knew it, he was outside the street door, the naked creature close upon his hurrying little heels.

Not long after, he obtained the desired introduction at a moment when Algernon was free of his Dionysiac frenzy, and, to Lady Jane's relief, he became her son's adviser. How much the Swinburne of the seventies needed someone to take care of him his parents only knew. Periodically Dr. Bird was commissioned to hunt him throughout London, in dives the good man had not known existed, and, after sobering the prodigal and making him presentable, brought him reformed and docile to the new Swinburne place at Holmwood. Algernon possessed a cat's power of recovery. A month or two of rest, during which he shone in filial virtues, and he was ready for the world again. None seeing his courtliness and the sweet amenity of his behavior at home

would have thought him the same *visionnaire malade*[1]
who, with his "perverse and magic" enthusiasms, had
troubled Maupassant at Étretat; or the drunken gnome
who had knocked down the hats of his fellow members at the
Arts Club and hopped upon them in shrieking glee—no,
nor the sadist, bent over obscene illustrations by Simeon
Solomon, adding new horrors to his epic of flagellation.

London intoxicated him more than brandy. Associations
of earlier days and comradeships of which he had not then
been ashamed worked in his blood and he lost hold of himself. His work showed fatigue: the second series of *Poems
and Ballads,* though kindled at the same fire, did not burn,
in spite of superior technical excellence and purity of conception. The splendid bonfire was of the past—now, only
the smouldering.

Yet he was still young; though at times, to see him dragging himself along after some extraordinary debauch, he
might have been mistaken for an old man. The red flame
of his hair mingled with ashes; ashes also smothered his
spirit. What remained after the drunken nights and intolerable pleasures? Only a weariness, and worse: the
irrefutable certainty that he was cut off from common manhood by laws over which he had, and could have, no control.
Then what to do but question his place in the scheme of
things? Fame, spiced with notoriety, had had a heady
savor in the beginning; now it palled. Again, it had to be
admitted that the first success had not been repeated, and he
relished the *outré*. Ennui, the morass which a Baudelaire
could make to bloom with his *fleurs du mal,* sucked from
Algernon the strength of conception. He could only repeat
himself, again, again, to a hypnosis that the inevitable bottle
alone dispelled. Days passed without sight of him at the
familiar haunts; and Dr. Bird, ever on the trail, would end

---

[1] "Ils avaient [Swinburne and Powell] une manière de voir et de
comprendre qui me les montrait comme deux visionnaires malades, ivres de
poèsie perverse et magique." — Maupassant.

by finding him sitting before the fire in Great James Street, the empty flasks beside him, the aureole ragged, and the poor body weak from lack of food. Another stay at Holmwood, the return to London; and, once more, the repetition.

In 1877 Holmwood was visited for the last time when the Admiral was buried; then a wild course for Algernon in London, and a series of violent breakdowns. Hardly two years later, Swinburne lay on the point of death in the lodging-house rooms. Lady Jane, advised of his state, urged him to come home and rest. Did he not see he was dying? But Algernon would hear of no more curative vacations. He had chosen his milieu, and he would stay in it. It was then that Lady Jane thought of the plump little solicitor who had a will of iron under his cherubic exterior; and one day a cab stopped at the door of the lodging house. The officious Watts trotted up the stairs into the parlor — and a few minutes later the poet was abducted, like any weak damsel, and carried away to the lawyer's own rooms. "From that moment," Watts would say, complacently self-flattering, "his connection with Bohemian London ceased entirely."

Poor splendid wings, so frayed and soiled and torn!

Little remained of the young, fiery Swinburne. An archangel, in human frailty, had trailed his splendor through mire and abominable stews, marking his downward path in tufts of torn plumage — divinity thrown away!

Watts rescued a man suddenly grown old; it is the penalty of all wanderers out of their spheres.

Number Two, the Pines. Here, in the plushy respectability of Putney, London, another Swinburne came into being. Was it some awful enchantment on the part of the gypsy student of occult lore that transformed an untamed spirit to a ventriloquist's dummy that spoke with the breath of the manipulator? Then indeed Watts wielded a dangerous magic, however beneficent it appeared on the surface. He had taken a corpse and revitalized it, but what had happened to its animating core?

A comfortable little villa, the Pines, chosen by Watts for his poet charge — and paid for by Lady Jane, though of course Swinburne was kept ignorant of the arrangement, for whereas he accepted Watts's hospitality as a paying guest, and obeyed him with the courtesy he owed his host, as fellow tenant he might have exercised a will of his own, and a defiant will it could be, Watts had been told. Not far from the railway station and affording pleasant walks, it was the ideal situation for a solicitor with literary ambitions and a regenerated bard. A fine garden lay in the back; its hedge, well tended, promised to grow to a good, thick wall, lending Watts further security in the effectual possession of his poet. The interior deviated in no way from the decorative scheme of the surrounding houses. Solid comfort, said the chairs and the tables and the bedsteads. It was as if Morris's firm had never existed; indeed, as if Morris himself had never been known of Swinburne. After Rossetti's death a gaunt, draped marble female that had stood in a corner of the Tudor House garden occupied the middle of the Pines grass patch. A great number of Rossetti's crayons and water colors descended to Watts; and so art entered Putney — keeping, however, its respectful distance among the accumulations of half a century of prudent living.

At first old friends were forbidden to see Algernon. They might rouse wicked urges, stir the tamed bird to leave his perch. Watts would not even allow him to talk of them. "Bad, dear friend, very bad, and after all, as my guest . . ." Yes, yes. The fluttering of clipped wings ceased and the nostalgic cheeping gave way to silence — but not to oblivion. In the writings of those thirty years of captivity, now and then the old song broke out, trilling of the great, lost freedom. But he was soon recalled to the prettiness of the perch and the beautiful security, my friend, the beautiful security.

As the taming was accomplished, the ban on friends was lifted, provided, of course, the poet's "hours" were undisturbed and Watts could be present at the interviews. Useless caution. Swinburne had ceased to think or speak for himself. What wonder? Everything financial and material was regulated by "dear Walter." His books, to the selection and rejection of their contents, Walter arranged. The joint of mutton was carved for him; the bottle of Bass's ale (No more wine!) dispensed. And there were other delicate services. That the sea gull might not pine for lack of his salt air, Swinburne was provided with Samphire soap, which the advertisements said smelled of the sea and which came with a quotation from *King Lear:* —

> Halfway down
> Hangs one that gathers samphire . . .

What captive could fail to respond in the midst of such loving luxury? And so old friends who ventured within the Putney cage were astonished at the utterances of the voice they knew. "Watts and I are both deeply shocked at the audacious indecency of the opening lines of Warton's *Ode to Spring*. How can anyone have the effrontery to put a volume containing a picture so improper into female hands?" *Watts and I* — there was the key to the preposterous enigma.

Wherever literary men and artists gathered, Watts strutted about boasting, in his self-effacing way, of the captive he had at home. None knew what were the financial understandings at the suburban villa. Watts, like a good solicitor, never told. In such matters it is best to let public opinion have its way, since in the possible good and bad it is always simple to steer the ship the way of one's advantage. Watts gained much in the esteem of the world. He had saved Swinburne from ignominious death, — had he not?

—and with his tender care enabled England to pride herself on a new and better, because regenerated, poet. Swinburne's old friends chafed. Better had the poet died in the defiance of an unbroken spirit, than lived on, the submissive ward of a whiskered wet nurse. Watts the parasite, they grumbled; Watts the leech who battened on the blood of greatness.

The would-be author was forever writing. No matter when a visitor called, he was eternally rummaging among a mass of material that could not long bode interruption. A novel, yes, a most unusual novel,[1] excerpts of which he read in unctuous orotundity; and, of course, his work for the *important* magazines. They kept him very busy, the magazines. At regular intervals his inevitable four-page review appeared in the *Athenæum* or the *Nineteenth Century*. Patiently might the reader plough through paragraph on paragraph upon Zoroaster's type of art, "apparent pictures of unapparent realities," as opposed to Goethe's "simple representation," to arrive at the occasion for the essay. Fortunate was the writer who received a two-line mention of his book in Watts's mass of "first principles." "My method of reviewing," Watts would justify himself over the roast leg of mutton, "though it is well understood by the more famous men, does not seem to please and to satisfy the less distinguished ones." "The hated of New Grub Street," he referred to himself.

Certainly there was no love lost between him and the younger writers. It was well for Mr. Watts to be favored by the "distinguished," who had nothing to gain or lose by his erudite maunderings. They, the young ones, had their reputation to win, and a little word in appreciation of their work would have edified them infinitely more than Mr. Watts's display of learning. A good thing, his essay on poetry and the "renascence of wonder"; a much better thing had he taken the trouble to find a little of that wonder in

[1] *Aylwin*, which eventually saw the light and some success in 1898.

the creations of his juniors. They dubbed him the "Ogre of the *Athenæum*," and made no bones about airing their grievances. They knew him and his jealous impotence. Let one of them bring out a new book, and Watts would instantly pounce upon it and tear it to shreds—in overlarded prose. *Fee-fi-fo-fum*—they feared and hated him.

Yet what a modest gentleman he was in the bosom of famous intimates. "A more obscure literary man than I now am," he prefixed his opinions, and then waved a deprecating hand at Swinburne's quick defense: "The first critic of his time, perhaps the largest-minded and surest-sighted of any age." It was no small advantage to have a captive bard so quick to learn new tunes.

Swinburne's output from the Pines crowded the market. Old and new, his poetry and prose came out in neat volumes through the agency of Watts, and returned substantial royalties. The year after the hegira no less than four works appeared: the *Study of Shakespeare*, which inflamed Furnivall's head to indecency with the exchange of compliments in a puerile calling of names, Piggsbrook for the bard, Brotheldyke for the scholar; *Songs of the Springtides* and *Studies in Song;* and *Heptalogia,* begun at Oxford. Something extraneous crept into this last, published anonymously. Whereas the parodies of Rossetti, Patmore, Tennyson, and the Brownings contained only well-meant and brilliant roguery, especially the one on Robert Browning, of which he said he could imitate his discords with impunity since Browning could not revenge himself by parodying his harmonies, the burlesque on Owen Meredith (the second Lord Lytton) was too brutal for play. Swinburne—or for that matter, any other artist possessing his conception of the requirements of poetry—could have had no great respect for the cleverly assimilated hodgepodge of Owen Meredith's style. Yet here was more than literary antipathy. A personal grudge, perhaps? Well—Meredith had once snubbed Watts, and Watts could never forgive an insult.

He himself had only a plodding humor at his command and the tortiveness of his style, both feeble weapons as compared with the rapier wit at his call.

It came to be suspected that besides a pet poet Watts kept a convenient cat's-paw for his private animosities. Not otherwise could have been explained the later Swinburnian attack against old Jimmy, for whose "White Girl" he had composed the exquisite tribute of "Before the Mirror," or his vicious cutting-up of Walt Whitman, subject of his earliest adorations. Pernicious indeed the Putney influence that could make Swinburne transform the Titan Muse of the American poet to the "drunken apple-woman indecently sprawling in the slush and garbage of the gutter amid the rotten refuse of her overturned fruit stall"!

The two poetic volumes of 1880 came as an anticlimax to the second series of *Poems and Ballads* and failed to hold their own against Rossetti's *Ballads and Sonnets* and the Laureate's renewed spring. *Mary Stuart*, the following year, showed sparks of the olden passion, and the *Tristram of Lyonesse* would have re-established him in the high place had not the mentor persuaded him to smother the incandescent passages in a bulk of "proper" lyrics. Then in 1883 a puzzling psychological phenomenon manifested itself in the pretty trifles of *A Century of Roundels*. "It is too much to expect that all schools of poetry are to be forever subordinate to the one . . . whose scope of sight is bounded by the nursery walls," he had written long ago in defense of *Modern Love*,[1] continuing, with the well-known Swinburnian egregiousness: "that all Muses are to bow down before her who babbles, with lips yet warm from their pristine pap, after the dangling delights of a child's coral; and jingles with flaccid fingers one knows not whether a jester or a baby's bells." What had happened? The bard of the "raptures and roses" had himself taken up the infant's bells, to jingle

[1] In a letter to the Editor of the *Spectator*, June 7, 1862.

Love hails it, day and night
The sweetest thing that may be
Yet cannot praise aright
A baby,

with other hardly precious nonsense in the same strain.
Dolores's votary had turned devotee of a cult that threw him
into raptures before the "darling dimples" of many an
astonished nursemaid's "little duck," and weighed down
the postman with gifts of baby photographs, draped and
undraped, from doting mothers. How trace the origin of
this anomalous worship? Walter Watts had a baby nephew.

Swinburne dedicated the roundels to Christina Rossetti.
Did he himself think them the appropriate tribute to one
as sterile in life as his own Lesbia, or did the preceptor again
prompt? How much nearer the gift would have been a
garland of his own flammiferous flowers, to her whose garden, like Sappho's, had borne few blooms,[1] but all of them
roses?

The homage stirred but vaguely the now hushed drama
of Christina's life. Day followed day, in prayerful duty
toward God and the old women in her keep, which left only
time for her writing, grown pronouncedly religious. The
Society for Promoting Christian Knowledge enlisted her
services, and she wrote for them devotional manuals interspersed with verse, symbolic interpretations, strange ad-
mixtures of mysticism and the quaint bestiaries and herbals
that formed the reading of mediæval nuns. Her poetry
took on the simplicity of "the little flowers," with an echo
of the Franciscan note sounded centuries ago by Jacopone
da Todi. She found her way, no less certainly than Gabriel
had found his, to her true home.

The close of 1883 snapped the last link that still held her
to the world. The morning of her birthday she appeared
pale and tight-lipped in William's office at Somerset House;

[1] Discounting the great bulk of devotional poems.

with hardly a quaver of the voice, "Charles Cayley — Charles is dead," she told him. Alone, she went to buy a wreath at Covent Garden; and with her own hands laid it on the sheet with the other tributes. There lay the corpse of the life she had not lived, a sorrowful spectacle, though she could still say, "They shall perish, but Thou remainest." "How easy the words are to utter and how difficult their meaning to attain," she confessed in a last pathetic moment of human weakness.

Thenceforward, more deeply after the death of her mother, she lived in the hope of life everlasting, where all she held dear awaited her. In a drawer of her writing table she buried yet another thing — *Il Rosseggiar dell'Oriente*,[1] whose wonderful daybreak would be hers in heaven. This was the woman whom the roundels were to have delighted. And to the writing of such "pap" had fallen the original for the fleshly poet "Bunthorne" who, for two and a half years, — since April 1881, — had been entertaining the audiences first at the Opera Comique and then at the Savoy Theatre in London.

Did the chubby little gadabout ever take his ward to see a performance of *Patience*, and did he, with deprecating podgy digits, wave aside, in company, the theory that the twenty-six-year-old Oscar Wilde was the inspiration for "Bunthorne"?

Certainly the self-styled Professor of Æsthetics and Critic of Art, newly down from Oxford with a fanfare conducted by his journalist brother Willie Wilde, did his best to carry off the dubious laurels. A product of Pater, the French *décadents*, and "sage green" æstheticism, he had launched at his expense his initiatory volume of verse, — all cream color and gold and wide margins, — and disposed of four editions in as many weeks, thanks to the reputation he had gained by his radiant good humor and cultivated

---

[1] Her Italian poems, which William found after her death in the drawer where she had left them.

eccentricities. A gracious flatterer, he knew how to oil the vehicles that would carry him farthest; attended first nights, made serviceable contacts, affected knee-breeches and silken hose, and got himself talked about at the fashionable tea tables. He became a celebrity; but he was only a follower. The *Athenæum* said of his volume: "From other gospels it differs in coming after, instead of before, the cult it seeks to establish." *Punch* put it still more explicitly: "Mr. Wilde is . . . Swinburne and Water."

Watts's poet, therefore, was unquestionably preëminent, though now, alas, by virtue of the past. Year in, year out, with hardly a lapse, dramas, lyrics, ballads, criticisms, came pouring from the tamed pen. But no more the ecstatic hymns to Freedom. Odes to Landor, to Mazzini, to Hugo, yes — long-winded and elaborate: the thrill was gone. What need had the caged bird for song that would have come back to him as a reproach? Better silence.

He came to look like a moulted bird, the fringe of hair about the enormous cranium faded and thin, the beautiful eyes sharp and quick-darting to make up for his increasing deafness. Courteous he remained to the last — never voicing regret for the lost glorious, if dangerous, youth stifled by the plush of Putney. But once, as at the brushing of memorial wings against the panes, he confessed his heart's sadness to the sea mew, of all living things his kin: —

> When I had wings, my brother,
>   Such wings were mine as thine:
> Such life my heart remembers
> In all as wild Septembers
> As this when life seems other
>   Though sweet, than once was mine;
> When I had wings, my brother,
>   Such wings were mine as thine.

Years, years — still many years before he left the cage. Then, Watts-Dunton wrote a sonnet.

XXXIII

CLOSE

CONTRARY to tradition, the great Millais held a review of his life's work in his fifty-seventh year at Sir Coutts Lindsay's elegant gallery. As a rule, the Royal Academy considered it its prerogative to collect a painter's works after his death and display them on its walls as a final tribute. It had done it for its famous deceased, and, strangely, for Dante Gabriel Rossetti, who during his life had been worse than ignored by the august body. Impetuous, turbulent, unjust, but ever-faithful Brown had sensed treason from the outset; indeed, more than one voice had been raised against the disorderly hanging of the pictures, with no purpose, it seemed, but "to burke rather than promote" the dead man's reputation. Indignant protests reached Leighton, President, and the harm was remedied, but none of Gabriel's remaining friends ever forgave the Academy its final insult.

Millais's exhibition at the Grosvenor Gallery brought together his complete works, from the Pre-Raphaelite "Isabella" to the "Ruling Passion" of 1885. Two years before, something analogous had been done at Burlington House — where his "Idyll" hung side by side with a painting of his early years. Morris, seeing the two together, mourned. "A sorry sight indeed; the record of a ruined reputation, of a wasted life, of a genius bought and sold and thrown away." Millais never learned the verdict; but somehow that same something which had spoken to Morris was not silent to him. Meeting Stephens at the gallery, entranced before the early canvases, he greeted him with moist eyes. "Really, I did not paint so badly in those days, old man," he said, huskily, and turned away. Brought face to face with himself, he became uneasy. What a comfort, had he been able to outstare those ghosts, and say: "I have gone far, since then; I have fulfilled myself." He could only haunt the gallery after everyone had gone, and hold reckoning. So Noel Paton found him, standing for a long time sadly before the works of his youth, till he fled from their accusation, and, stopping at the first tobacconist's, bought himself the biggest cigar he could find.

During his last years he returned to the earlier fount of his inspiration; somehow the water no longer ran clear. As President of the Academy after Leighton, he showed himself considerate of the new members. If one grumbled at the hanging of his picture, — youth is always exacting, — "Take one of my places," he said, his voice a mere whisper through illness; and he meant it.

"The Last Trek" was to have been his next work, but death forbade. In the painters' corner of St. Paul's Cathedral, near the "Sir Sloshua" he had once despised, among Opie and Fuseli and Boehm, with earls and marquesses as his pallbearers, he came to his final abiding-place. Holman Hunt alone of the Pre-Raphaelites stood at the coffin-head — the only one who had kept the faith; so he who had wandered farthest and he who had not strayed rounded the circle of that early truth, "perfect, great or small."[1]

What of the others? Woolner had attained "academic opulence" with sculptures that had in no sense ever been Pre-Raphaelite. In his later years, when his hated rival Marochetti had returned to Italy and other competitors had left the field clear, he failed to assert himself. The colossal statues of trowsered patriots which he sent to embellish Australian cities had nothing but size to dignify them among their ilk; his portraits, though faithful, were soulless. As a friend of the great, with whose wives he carried on extensive

---

[1] From William Michael's explanatory sonnet on the cover of the *Germ*.

correspondence, he furnished the Laureate with themes when inspiration failed, and discovered a new formation of the human ear for Darwin, who suggested that the peculiarity of the tip be called *Angulus Woolnerianus.* He carried on further researches for him on human blushes,[1] after Darwin begged him to find out "how far down the body the blush extends" in young and inexperienced girls; for Moreau claimed "a celebrated French painter once saw a new model blush all over her body." Finding sculpture, but for the public monuments, a thankless drudgery, Woolner turned in the end to the buying and selling of pictures, and left a considerable estate.

Good old Madox Brown at sixty lived to enact that sundering from the near and dear foreshadowed in "The Last of England," when, his Nolly dead, and his daughters in hearths of their own, he left London and carried away his ailing Emma to Manchester, which had offered him, at a pittance a lesser artist would have scorned, a commission to execute the series of historical frescoes in the Town Hall. He died as he had lived, working without hope of reward, but for the approbation of his honest mind.

And what of those who remained? William Michael Rossetti and Frederic Stephens continued faithful to their commemorative mission of glossing the Pre-Raphaelite gospel. Newer schools did away with the old, and they lived to see their holy temple thrown down and irreverent youths dancing over its ruins. But there were still its flowers, culled and treasured by William, surviving all the rest as sexton and grave-digger. The symbol of spades, fallen to him as a child, ruled over his life. Beloved brother, mother, wife, sisters, friends of the dear past gone, Christina in an anguish of mind he had thought unworthy of a merciful God, he comforted his hoary years digging and delving and setting up memorial stones, until he too lay down among them.

[1] In 1871.

Many years ago, the silent Janey had had a dream. It seemed to her that she found herself alone in the market place of a town unknown to her, when a coach drew up and stopped before her. A flight of rickety steps was let down from within, and out tottered a feeble old woman with white hair — a little old woman, who had been young with her in a world all bright and beautiful. Sorrowfully they took each other by the hand and kissed in solemn greeting, and Janey spoke.

"They are all gone, dear friend."

And they mourned together.

BIBLIOGRAPHY

ABBOTT, EVELYN, AND LEWIS CAMPBELL, *Life and Letters of Benjamin Jowett.* London, 1897.

ACLAND, H. W., AND J. RUSKIN, *The Oxford Museum.* London, 1893.

AGRESTI, ALBERTO, *I Prerafaellisti.* Societa Nazionale, Italy, 1908.

ALLINGHAM, WILLIAM, *A Diary.* Edited by H. Allingham and D. Radford. London, 1907.

———*Day and Night Songs.* London, 1855.

ARMSTRONG, WALTER, *Sir John Everett Millais; His Life and Work.* London, 1885.

ARNOLD, MATTHEW, *Poetical Works.* New York, 1897.

Art Journal, Vols. 1–7. London, 1856–1861.

Athenæum, Review of *Heptalogia,* March 12, 1881.

———Obituary of James Collinson, April 9, 1881.

ATKINSON, J. B., *Overbeck.* London, 1882.

BALDRY, ALFRED L., *Sir J. E. Millais; His Art and Influence.* London, 1899.

BATE, PERCY, *The English Pre-Raphaelite Painters.* London, 1901.

BAUM, PAULL F., *Dante Gabriel Rossetti. An Analytical List of Manuscripts in the Duke University Library, with Hitherto Unpublished Verse and Prose.* Durham, N. C., 1931.

———*The House of Life.* Harvard University Press, 1928.

BAYNE, THOMAS, "The Poetry of D. G. Rossetti," in *Frazer's Magazine,* March 1882.

BEERBOHM, MAX, *And Even Now.* London, 1920.

——*Rossetti and His Circle* (Caricatures). London, 1922.

BELL, MACKENZIE, *Christina Rossetti.* London, 1898.

BELL, MALCOLM, *Edward Burne-Jones; a Record and Review.* London, 1893.

BENSON, A. C., *Alfred Tennyson.* New York, 1904.

——*Edward Fitzgerald.* London, 1905.

——*Rossetti.* London, 1904.

BENSON, E. F., *As We Were; a Victorian Peep Show.* London, 1930.

BICKLEY, FRANCIS, *The Pre-Raphaelite Comedy.* London, 1932.

BREME, IGNATIA, *Christina Rossetti und der Einfluss der Bibel auf ihre Dichtung.* Münster, 1907.

BROWN, OLIVER MADOX, *The Dwale Bluth, Hebditch's Legacy, and Other Literary Remains.* 2 vols. Ed. by W. M. Rossetti and F. Hueffer. London, 1876.

BROWNING, ROBERT, *Complete Poetic and Dramatic Works.* Cambridge Edition. 18 vols. Boston and New York, 1895.

BUCHANAN, ROBERT, *David Gray and Other Essays, Chiefly on Poetry.* London, 1868.

——"The Fleshly School of Poetry," in *Contemporary Review,* October 1871. In pamphlet form (Strahan and Co.), 1872.

——*Poetical Works.* 3 vols. Boston, 1873.

BURNE-JONES, LADY G., *Memorials of Edward Burne-Jones.* 2 vols. London, 1904.

CAINE, T. HALL, *Recollections of Dante Gabriel Rossetti.* London, 1882.

——Later edition, *My Story,* 1908.

CARLYLE, THOMAS, *Collected Works.* 34 vols. London, 1870–1882.

——*New Letters and Memorials of Jane Welsh Carlyle.*

Ed. by Thomas and A. Carlyle. London and New York, 1903.

———*Reminiscences.* Ed. by J. A. Froude. New York, 1881.

CARR, J. COMYNS, *Coasting Bohemia.* London, 1914.

CARY, ELIZABETH L., *The Rossettis, Dante Gabriel and Christina.* New York, 1900.

———*William Morris: Poet, Craftsman, Socialist.* New York, 1902.

CAZAMIAN, MADELINE, "Christina Rossetti," in *Revue de Paris.* August, 1911.

CHAMPNEYS, B., *Memoirs and Correspondence of Coventry Patmore.* 2 vols. London, 1900.

CHEW, SAMUEL C., *Swinburne.* Boston, 1929.

CHURCH, R. W., *The Oxford Movement.* London, 1909.

COLLINGWOOD, W. G., *Life and Work of John Ruskin.* 2 vols. Boston and New York, 1893.

COMPTON-RICKETT, A., *William Morris, a Study in Personality.* London, 1913.

COOK, E. T., *Life of John Ruskin.* 2 vols. London, 1911.

Daily News, for account of E. E. Rossetti's death. London, February 1862. (In the newspaper account her name appears as "Eliza Eleanor Rosetti.")

DANEL, JOSEPH, *Les idées économiques et sociales de Ruskin.* Paris, 1912.

DANTE, *Vita Nuova, con le illustrazioni di D. G. Rossetti.* With introduction by Alberto Agresti. Torino, Roma, 1902.

Dark Blue, June 1871.

DE REUL, PAUL, *L'Œuvre de Swinburne.* Brussels, 1922.

DOUGHTY, OSWALD, Ed., *The Letters of Dante Gabriel Rossetti to His Publisher, F. S. Ellis.* London, 1928.

DOUGLAS, JAMES, *Theodore Watts-Dunton; Poet, Novelist, Critic.* London, 1904.

DRINKWATER, JOHN, *William Morris; a Critical Study.* London, 1912.

DUCKWORTH, F. R. G., *Browning; Background and Conflict.* New York, 1931.

DUNN, HENRY T., *Recollections of Dante Gabriel Rossetti and His Circle.* (Cheyne Walk Life.) Edited and annotated by Gale Pedrick. London, 1904.

EARLAND, ADA, *Ruskin and His Circle.* London, 1910.

Edinburgh Review, for a review of Rossetti's poems. April 1882.

FISH, ARTHUR, *John Everett Millais.* New York, 1923.

FORD, FORD MADOX, *Ancient Lights and Certain New Reflections.* London, 1911.

——— "Christina Rossetti," in *Fortnightly Review,* Vol. 95, 1911.

——— *Ford Madox Brown, a Record of His Life and Works.* London, 1896.

——— *The Pre-Raphaelite Brotherhood; a Critical Monograph.* London, 1907.

FORD, JULIA ELLSWORTH, *Simeon Solomon: an Appreciation.* New York, 1908.

Freeman's Journal, for obituary of Mrs. La Touche and note on Rose, November 27, 1906.

FRITH, W. P., *My Autobiography and Reminiscences.* 2 vols. New York, 1888.

FRITZSCHE, DR. GUSTAV, *William Morris Sozialismus und anarchistischer Kommunismus.* Leipzig, 1927.

FROUDE, J. A., *Thomas Carlyle: a History of His Life in London.* 2 vols. New York, 1904.

GARNETT, RICHARD, *Christina Rossetti.* London, 1908–1909.

Gentleman's Magazine, for Sylvanus Urban's remarks on Buchanan's dedication to Rossetti. January 1882.

Germ, reprinted (facsimile) by Thomas Mosher, in Portland, Maine, 1898.

GILCHRIST, ALEXANDER, *Life of William Blake, "Pictor Ignotus."* 2 vols. London, 1863.

GILCHRIST, H. H., *Anne Gilchrist, Her Life and Writings. With a Prefatory Notice by William Michael Rossetti.* New York, 1887.

GONCOURT, E., *Journal des Goncourts. Mémoires de la vie littéraire. 1851–1895.* 9 vols. Paris.

GOSSE, EDMUND, *The Life of Algernon Charles Swinburne.* New York, 1917.

——*Portraits and Sketches.* London, 1913.

GOSSE, EDMUND, AND THOMAS J. WISE, editors, *The Letters of Algernon Charles Swinburne.* 2 vols. London, 1919.

HAKE, THOMAS GORDON, *Memoirs of Eighty Years.* London, 1892.

HAKE, THOMAS, AND A. COMPTON-RICKETT, *The Letters of A. C. Swinburne, with Some Personal Recollections.* London, 1918.

——*Life and Letters of Theodore Watts-Dunton,* London, 1916.

HARNED, THOMAS B., Ed., *The Letters of Anne Gilchrist and Walt Whitman.* New York, 1918.

HARPER, G. McL., *William Wordsworth.* 2 vols. New York, 1916.

HENDERSON, W. DRAYTON, *Swinburne and Landor.* London, 1918.

Heptalogia: the Seven Against Sense (Swinburne's parodies, issued anonymously), London, 1880.

HILL, G. BIRKBECK, Ed., *Letters of Dante Gabriel Rossetti to William Allingham. 1854–1870.* New York, 1897.

HOBSON, J. A., *John Ruskin, Social Reformer.* Boston, 1898.

HOWITT, MARY, *An Autobiography.* Edited by Margaret Howitt. Boston, 1889.

HUE, A., "Ruskin et la femme," in *Le Correspondant.* Vol. 204, pp. 762–778.

HUEFFER, FRANCIS, *Half a Century of Music in England.* London, 1889.

HUNT, WILLIAM HOLMAN, *Pre-Raphaelitism and the Pre-Raphaelite Brotherhood.* 2 vols. London, 1905.

INGRAM, JOHN H., *Oliver Madox Brown.* London, 1883.

JAY, HARRIET, *Robert Buchanan.* London, 1903.

KENYON, SIR F. G., *Letters of E. B. Browning.* 2 vols. New York and London, 1897.

KERNAHAN, COULSON, *In Good Company.* London, 1917.

—— *Swinburne as I Knew Him; with Some Unpublished Letters.* London, 1919.

—— "Watts-Dunton as 'the Ogre of the Athenæum,'" in the *National Review.* Vol. 67. London, 1916.

KITCHIN, GEORGE, *A Survey of Burlesque and Parody in English.* Edinburgh and London, 1931.

KITCHIN, G. WILLIAM, D.D., *Ruskin in Oxford, and Other Studies.* London, 1904.

KING, BOLTON, *A History of Italian Unity.* 2 vols. London, 1912.

—— *Life of Mazzini.* London, 1911.

KNIGHT, JOSEPH, *Life of Dante Gabriel Rossetti.* London, 1887.

LAFOURCADE, GEORGES, *La Jeunesse de Swinburne, 1837–1867.* 2 vols. Les Belles Lettres. Oxford Union Press, 1928.

LA SIZERANNE, R. DE, *Ruskin et la religion de la beauté.* Paris, 1898.

LAYARD, GEORGE S., *Tennyson and His Pre-Raphaelite Illustrators.* London, 1894.

LE GALLIENNE, RICHARD, *Loves of the Poets.* New York, 1911.

LÉGER, AUGUSTIN, "Le poète de l'amour, Coventry Patmore," in *Le Correspondant.* Vol. 203. Pp. 287–306.

LEGOUIS, EMILE H., *La Jeunesse de William Wordsworth.* Paris, 1896.

————*William Wordsworth and Annette Vallon.* London, 1922.

LEITH, MARY C. J., *The Boyhood of A. C. Swinburne.* London, 1917.

London Times, for comments on the Pre-Raphaelites, May 5, 1856.

LUCAS, E. V., *At "The Pines."* Privately printed, London, 1916.

MACKAIL, J. W., *Life of William Morris.* 2 vols. London, 1899.

————*Swinburne, a Lecture.* Clarendon Press, 1909.

MALLOCK, W. H., *The New Republic, or Culture, Faith and Philosophy in an English Country House.* New York, 1878.

MANSON, J. B., Ed., *Frederic George Stephens and His Pre-Raphaelite Brothers.* London, 1920.

MARILLIER, H. C., *Dante Gabriel Rossetti; an Illustrated Memorial of His Art and Life.* 2 vols. London, 1899.

MATHER, J. MARSHALL, *John Ruskin, His Life and Teaching.* London, 1897.

MAURICE, FREDERICK, *Life of F. D. Maurice, Chiefly Told in His Own Letters.* 2 vols. New York, 1884.

MAURICE, F. D., *Administrative Reform and Its Connexion with Working Men's Colleges: an Address.* Cambridge, 1855.

————*Plan of a Female College for the Help of the Rich and the Poor: Lecture Delivered at the Working Men's College.* Cambridge, 1855.

MÉGROZ, R. L., *Dante Gabriel Rossetti: Painter Poet of Heaven in Earth.* London, 1928.

MENPES, MORTIMER, *Whistler as I Knew Him.* New York, 1904.

MEYNELL, MRS. A., *John Ruskin.* Edinburgh, 1900.

MILLAIS, JOHN GUILLE, *The Life and Letters of Sir John Everett Millais, P.R.A., by His Son.* 2 vols. London, 1899.

MONCKTON MILNES, RICHARD (LORD HOUGHTON), *Life, Letters and Literary Remains of John Keats.* New York, 1848. (This is the book the first edition of which inspired the youthful Pre-Raphaelites, but which was qualified by the grim Carlyle as "fricassee of dead dog.")

———*Palm Leaves.* (A book of poems.) London, 1844.

MORRIS, WILLIAM, *Art and Socialism.* Lecture. London, 1884.

———*Chants for Socialists.* London, 1885.

———*Collected Works of William Morris,* with introductions by his daughter, May Morris. 24 vols. London, 1910–1914.

NEWMAN, JOHN HENRY, *Apologia pro vita sua.* London, 1864.

New Review, for "Letters of John Ruskin to His Secretary," March 1892.

NICOLSON, HAROLD, *Swinburne.* London, New York, 1926.

NOBLE, J. ASHCROFT, "A Pre-Raphaelite Magazine," in *Frazer's Magazine,* May 1882. Pp. 568–580.

NORTON, CHARLES E., Ed., *Letters of John Ruskin to Charles Eliot Norton.* 2 vols. Boston, 1904.

Notes and Queries, for reminiscences of Kelmscott days by Mr. Hake. June 7, 1902.

OLLARD, S. L., *A Short History of the Oxford Movement.* London, 1915.

Oxford and Cambridge Magazine, London (Bell and Daldy, publishers). Twelve numbers, the first of which was issued January 1856.

Pall Mall Gazette, "Maiden Tribute of Modern Babylon." (An investigation relative to the prostitution of young girls.) July 6–8, 10, 1885.

PATMORE, COVENTRY, *The Angel in the House; the Espousals.* Boston, 1856.

PENNELL, JOSEPH AND E. R., *The Life of J. A. M. Whistler.* Philadelphia, 1908.

————*The Whistler Journal.* Edited by J. and E. R. Pennell, Philadelphia, 1921.

PÖLNITZ, W. F. VON, "Friedrich Overbeck; ein Lebenslauf im Dienste der christlichen Kunst," in *Gelbe Heft.* IV Jahrgang, pp. 407–438.

POUGIN, ARTHUR, *Verdi.* Paris, 1886.

PRAZ, MARIO, *La carne, la morte e il diavolo nella letteratura romantica.* Milano, 1930.

————"Swinburne," in *Cultura.* Vol. I, pp. 536–553.

————"Trilogia di Maria Stuarda," in *Cultura.* February 15, 1921.

PURVES, JOHN, "Letters to Miss Alice Boyd by D. G. Rossetti," in *Fortnightly Review,* May 1, 1928.

REID, T. W., *Life, Letters, and Friendships of Richard Monckton Milnes, first Lord Houghton.* 2 vols. London, 1890.

ROSENBLATT, LOUISE, *L'idée de l'art pour l'art dans la littérature anglaise pendant la periode victorienne.* Paris, 1931.

ROSSETTI, CHRISTINA, *Called to be Saints.* 1902.

————*Face of the Deep.* 1911.

————*Time Flies.* 1895. Published by the Society for Promoting Christian Knowledge. (These are all reprints.)

————*The Family Letters of Christina Georgina Rossetti, with Some Supplementary Letters,* ed. by W. M. Rossetti. London, 1908.

————*The Poetical Works of Christina Georgina Rossetti, with Memoir and Notes by W. M. Rossetti.* London and New York, 1914. (First edition, 1904.)

ROSSETTI, DANTE GABRIEL, *Collected Works.* Edited with

preface and notes by W. M. Rossetti. 2 vols. London, 1890.

——"The Stealthy School of Criticism," in the *Athenæum*, December 16, 1871.

ROSSETTI, MARIA F., *A Shadow of Dante.* London, 1871.

ROSSETTI, WILLIAM M., *Gabriele Rossetti* [the poet's father]; *a Versified Autobiography. Translated and Supplemented by W. M. R.* New York and London, 1902.

——*Pre-Raphaelite Diaries and Letters, 1835–1853.* London, 1900.

——"Portraits of Dante Gabriel Rossetti," in *Magazine of Art*, Vol 12. (In installments, pp. 21, 57, 138.)

——"Dante Gabriel Rossetti and Elizabeth Siddal," in *Burlington Magazine*, Vol. I, 1903, pp. 273–295.

——*Dante Gabriel Rossetti: His Family Letters, with a Memoir.* 2 vols. Boston, 1895.

——*Rossetti Papers: 1862–1870.* New York, 1903.

——*Ruskin: Rossetti: Pre-Raphaelitism.* New York, 1899.

——*Some Reminiscences.* 2 vols. New York, 1906.

——"Some Scraps of Verse and Prose by Dante Gabriel Rossetti," in *Pall Mall Magazine*, December 1898.

——*Swinburne's "Poems and Ballads"; a Criticism.* London, 1866.

ROTHENSTEIN, WILLIAM, *Men and Memories.* 2 vols. London and New York, 1931–1932.

RUSKIN, JOHN, *Complete Works.* (Ed. de luxe.) New York, 1894.

——*Præterita.* Twenty-eight parts, 1885–1889. (George Allen, publisher.)

SANDARS, MARY F., *The Life of Christina Rossetti.* London, 1930.

Saturday Review, for adverse criticism of Swinburne's *Poems and Ballads.* August 4, 1866.

SCHÜCKING, LEVIN L., "Rossettis Persönlichkeit," in *Englische Studien*, Band 51, 1917–1918, pp. 189–225.

SCOTT, W. BELL, *Autobiographical Notes*, ed. by W. Minto. 2 vols. London, 1892.

———*Poems*. London, 1875.

SHARP, WILLIAM, *Dante Gabriel Rossetti; a Record and a Study*. London, 1882.

SPIELMANN, M. H., *John Ruskin; a Sketch of His Life, His Work, etc., with Personal Reminiscences*. Philadelphia, 1900.

STEPHENS, F. G., *Dante Gabriel Rossetti*. London, 1899.

———*Grosvenor Gallery: Exhibition of the Works of Sir John Everett Millais, with Notes by F. G. Stephens*. London, 1886.

STUART, DOROTHY M., *Christina Rossetti*. London, 1930.

SWINBURNE, A. C., *A Pilgrimage of Pleasure; Essays and Studies*. Boston, 1913.

———*Complete Works*. Bonchurch edition, 20 vols. 1925–1927.

———*Mr. Whistler's Lecture on Art*. Boston, 1913.

———"The New Terror," in *Fortnightly Review*, December 1892.

———*The Queen Mother; Rosamond*. London, 1860.

———*Under the Microscope*. London, 1872.

SYMONS, ARTHUR, *Dramatis Personæ*. Indianapolis, 1923.

TAYLOR, SIR HENRY, *Philip van Artevelde: a Dramatic Romance*. (Second edition.) London, 1834.

THOMAS, EDWARD, *A. C. Swinburne, a Critical Study*. London, 1912.

THOMAS, ELEONOR W., *Christina Georgina Rossetti*. (Columbia University Press.) New York, 1931.

THORNBURY, WALTER, *Life of J. M. W. Turner; Founded on Letters and Papers, etc.* 2 vols. London, 1862.

TOLLEMACHE, L. A., *Benjamin Jowett*. London, 1895.

TYNAN, KATHERINE, "Christina Rossetti," in the *Bookman*, February 1895.

———*Twenty-five Years' Reminiscences.* London, 1913.

———*Undergraduate Papers*, for Swinburne's contributions, December 1857–March 1858.

WATTS-DUNTON, CLARA, *The Home Life of Swinburne.* London, 1922.

WATTS-DUNTON, THEODORE, *Aylwin, a Novel.* London and New York, 1898.

———"Christina Rossetti's New Poem," in the *Athenæum*, 1896.

———*Old Familiar Faces.* London, 1916.

———*Poetry and the Renascence of Wonder.* London, 1916.

———"Reminiscences of Christina Rossetti," in the *Nineteenth Century*, 1895.

———"The Truth about Rossetti," in the *Nineteenth Century*, March 1883.

WAUGH, EVELYN, *Rossetti, His Life and Work.* (An attack, prejudiced and unsympathetic.) London, 1928.

WELBY, T. EARLE, *A Study of Swinburne.* New York, 1926.

———*The Victorian Romantics.* London, 1929.

WILLIAMS-ELLIS, MABEL, *The Tragedy of John Ruskin.* London, 1928.

WILLIAMSON, DR. G. C., *Murray Marks and His Friends.* London, 1909.

WISE, THOMAS, *A Bibliography of the Writings in Prose and Verse of A. C. Swinburne.* 2 vols. (Privately printed, 1919–1920.)

WOOD, ESTHER, *Dante Rossetti and the Pre-Raphaelite Movement.* New York, 1894.

WOOLNER, AMY, *Thomas Woolner, R. A., Sculptor and Poet; His Life in Letters.* London, 1917.

WOOLNER, THOMAS, *My Beautiful Lady.* London (3rd ed.), 1866.

INDEX